THE DEVELOPMENT OF THE MIND

Psychoanalytic Papers on Clinical and
Theoretical Problems

THE DEVELOPMENT
OF THE MIND

*Psychoanalytic Papers on Clinical
and Theoretical Problems*

JEANNE LAMPL-DE GROOT, M.D.

Foreword by ANNA FREUD

INTERNATIONAL UNIVERSITIES PRESS, INC.

Contents

Foreword

The author of this book belongs to a small but prominent group of psychoanalysts who served their apprenticeship in Vienna in the twenties of the century and who are now, one after the other, approaching, celebrating, or looking back on their 70th birthday.

The members of this group were fortunate in their professional career in several respects. They entered the analytic field late enough to be spared many of the setbacks, hardships, and attacks by a hostile world to which the pioneering generation had been subjected. They were early enough, on the other hand, to be taught by the originator of psychoanalysis himself, and to develop their ideas in lively interchange with him. They entered the Vienna Society when scientific life there was at its height. And, when this Society broke up, they dispersed all over the world, to become the mainstay of analytic branches elsewhere, valued teachers in new analytic Institutes, editors of or contributors to analytic journals, and guiding figures in the International Psycho-Analytical Association.

Jeanne Lampl-de Groot is conducting her life as an analyst in conformity with this exacting tradition. In practical terms this implies that she does a great deal of hard work with minimal interruptions; that she carries out as many analytic treatments herself as she supervises therapy done by others; that by means of training analyses, seminar and lecture work, she cooperates in producing succeeding generations of well-informed and capable representatives and teachers of psychoanalysis. It implies above all that she extracts from her activities the insights needed to break new ground and increase the volume of psychoanalytic knowledge, a task to which she brings considerable acumen, conscientiousness, prudence, and complete scientific integrity. That her interest embraces a wide range of psychoanalytic problems and that, with her, theoretical deduction never appears divorced from clinical experience, is borne out by the scope, the quality, and the variety of papers presented in this book.

ANNA FREUD

London, March, 1965

Introduction

In this volume have been assembled most of my contributions to psychoanalysis written between 1927 and 1964. Many of them appear here in English for the first time and several chapters have never been published before. They are presented in chronological order and almost entirely in the original form. Though at the present time I probably would formulate some of the phenomena and ideas put forward in the earlier papers in a slightly different way, I preferred to present the original text because I feel that in this way a certain development of my understanding of human mental processes comes to the fore more naturally.

Like every psychoanalyst I am greatly indebted to Sigmund Freud, and I always tried to start my contributions from observations and from the body of theoretical concepts he presented to the world. I was encouraged by Freud to enlarge and to modify some of his hypotheses and conceptualizations whenever newly gained material made it necessary. As psychoanalytic theory is still a growing body of science, there will have to be more extensions and modifications in the future. The essential discoveries, however, we owe to Freud. His basic finding of the existence of an unconscious part of the mind, not only in a descriptive sense but as a system separated from the conscious part by mental forces (countercathexis), stimulated my therapeutic endeavors. It became fascinating to try to find regularities and irregularities in the dynamic course of a psychoanalytic treatment, to become aware of its possibilities and limitations, and to struggle with the many difficulties involved in the treatment of mentally disturbed patients.

Freud's discovery of the importance of the early developmental stages in the infantile instinctual life stimulated me to study the negative oedipal situation and the preoedipal phase first in little girls and later on in little boys as well.

Freud's refined description of the structured mind, the mutual inter-play of forces at work in the id, the ego, and the superego influenced by environmental factors and the relations to the parents, enabled me to go further into the substructures of ego organization, into the different origins of the superego proper and the ego ideal, and into their in-fluence on each other. Furthermore, I became interested in a variety of factors responsible for a harmonious ("normal") as well as for a patho-logical outcome of the processes of mental growth. I tried, too, to high-light some of the special events leading to the different forms of mental illness.

More and more it became clear that a study of the genesis (develop-ment) of the interplay of forces (dynamics) working between the vari-ous (structured) parts of the mind, including the quantitative (eco-nomic) viewpoint, is indispensable for a better understanding of men-tal processes.

A great number of other psychoanalysts, friends and colleagues, have influenced and stimulated me as well. I am greatly indebted to them in-deed. I cannot name all of them; the list would be too long. I want, however, to thank Anna Freud warmly for her willingness to write a few lines to accompany this publication.

February, 1965

THE DEVELOPMENT OF THE MIND

Psychoanalytic Papers on Clinical and
Theoretical Problems

CHAPTER 1

The Evolution of the Oedipus Complex in Women

(1927)

One of the earliest discoveries of psychoanalysis was the existence of the oedipus complex. Freud found the libidinal relations to the parents to be the center and the acme of the development of infantile sexuality and soon recognized in them the nucleus of the neuroses. Many years of psychoanalytic work greatly enriched his knowledge of the developmental processes in this period of childhood; it gradually became clear to him that in both sexes there are a positive and a negative oedipus complex and that at this time the libido finds a physical outlet in the practice of masturbation. Hence the oedipus complex makes its appearance only when the phallic phase of libido development is reached and when the tide of infantile sexuality recedes, that complex must pass in order to make way for the period of latency, during which the instinctual tendencies are inhibited in their aim. Nevertheless, in spite of the many observations and studies by Freud and other authors, it is remarkable how many obscure problems have for years remained unsolved (Abraham, 1920; Alexander, 1923; H. Deutsch, 1925; Horney, 1923, 1926; Van Ophuijsen, 1918).

It seemed that one very important factor was the connection between the oedipus and the castration complexes, and there were many points

---

See Chapters 7, 14, and 26 for further considerations of the topics discussed here.

about this which were obscure. Moreover, understanding of the processes in male children had been carried much further than with the analogous processes in females. Freud ascribed the difficulties in elucidating the early infantile love relations to the difficulty of getting at the material relating to them: he thought that this was due to the profound repression to which these impulses are subjected. The greater difficulty of understanding these particular mental processes in little girls may arise, on the one hand, from the fact that they are in themselves more complicated than the analogous processes in boys and, on the other hand, from the greater intensity with which the libido is repressed in women. Horney thinks that another reason is that, so far, analytical observations have been made principally by men.

In 1924 and 1925 Freud published two works which threw much light on the origin of the oedipus complex and its connection with the castration complex. The first of these, "The Dissolution of the Oedipus Complex" (1924b), shows what happens to that complex in little boys. It is true that several years previously, in "From the History of an Infantile Neurosis" (1918), and again in 1923 in "A Seventeenth-Century Demonological Neurosis" (1923a), its fate in certain individual cases had been described. But in "The Dissolution of the Oedipus Complex" we have the general application and the theoretical appreciation of this discovery and also the further conclusions to be deduced from it. The conclusion arrived at in this paper is as follows: the oedipus complex in male children receives its death blow from the castration complex, that is to say, in both the positive and the negative oedipal attitudes the boy has to fear castration by his father, whose strength is superior to his own. In the first, castration is the punishment for the inadmissible incest wish and, in the second, it is the necessary condition of the boy's adopting the feminine role in relation to his father. Thus, in order to escape castration and to retain his genital he must renounce his love relations with both parents. We see the peculiarly important part which this organ plays in boys and the enormous psychic significance it acquires in their mental life. Furthermore, analytic experience has shown how extraordinarily difficult it is for a child to give up the possession of the mother, who has been his love object ever since he was capable of object love. This reflection leads us to wonder whether the victory of

4

the castration complex over the oedipus complex, together with the narcissistic interest in the highly prized organ, may not also be due to still another factor, namely, the tenacity of this first love relation. The following train of thought may also have some significance: if the boy gives up the ownership of his penis, it means that the possession of the mother (or mother substitute) becomes forever impossible to him. If, however, forced by the superior power of that far stronger rival, his father, he renounces the fulfillment of his desire, the way remains open to him at some later period to fight his father more successfully and to return to his first love object, or, more correctly, to her substitute. It does not seem impossible that this knowledge of a future opportunity to fulfill his wish (a knowledge probably phylogenetically acquired and, of course, unconscious) may be a contributing motive in the boy's temporary renunciation of the prohibited love craving. This would also explain why before, or just at the beginning of, the latency period a little boy longs so intensely to be "big" and "grown-up."

In this work, then, Freud in large part explains the connection between the oedipus and the castration complexes in little boys, but he does not tell us much that is new about the same process in little girls. However, his paper, "Some Psychical Consequences of the Anatomical Distinction between the Sexes" (1925), does throw more light on the fate of the early infantile love impulses of the little girl. Freud holds that in girls the oedipus complex (he is speaking of the attitude which for the girl is positive: love for the father and rivalry with the mother) is a secondary formation, first introduced by the castration complex; that is to say, it arises after the little girl has become aware of the difference between the sexes and has accepted the fact of her own castration. This theory throws a new light on many hitherto obscure problems. With this assumption Freud explains many later developmental characteristics, various differences in the further vicissitudes of the oedipus complex in girls and in boys and in the superego formation in the two sexes, and so forth.

Nevertheless, even after the discovery of this connection, several problems remain unsolved. Freud mentions that when the castration complex has become operative in the girl, that is, when she has accepted her lack of a penis and therefore become a victim of penis envy, "a loosening of the girl's relation with her mother as a love-object" (p. 254) begins to take place. He thinks that one possible reason for this may be the fact that the girl ultimately holds her mother responsible for her own lack of a penis and he further cites a historical factor in the case, namely, that often jealousy is conceived later on against a second child who is more beloved by the mother. But, Freud says, "The situation as a whole is not very clear" (p. 254). According to him, another remarkable effect of penis envy is the girl's struggle against masturbation, a struggle which is more intense than that of the boy and which, in general, makes itself felt at a later age. Freud's view is that the reason why the little girl revolts so strongly against phallic masturbation is the blow dealt to her narcissism in connection with her penis envy: she suspects that in this matter it is useless to compete with the boy and therefore it is best not to enter into rivalry with him. This statement gives rise to the involuntary thought: Why should the little girl who never possessed a penis, and therefore never knew its value from her own experience, regard it as so precious? Why has the little girl's discovery of this lack in herself such far-reaching mental consequences? And, above all, why should it begin to produce a mental effect at a particular moment when it is probable that the physical difference between herself and little boys has been perceived countless times previously without any reaction? Probably the little girl produces pleasurable physical sensations in the clitoris in the same way and presumably with the same degree of intensity as the boy does in the penis, and perhaps she feels them in the vagina too. On this latter point I received a communication from Josine Müller of the German Psychoanalytic Society; I have also been told of it by an acquaintance, the mother of two little girls. Why, then, should the little girl have this mental reaction to the discovery that her own member is smaller than the boy's or is lacking altogether? I should like to present the following considerations, which have been suggested to me by experiences in my analytic practice, in the hope that they will bring us a little nearer to answering these questions.

I think that several points will be clearer to us if we consider the previous history of the castration complex or penis envy in little girls, but before doing so it is advisable to re-examine the analogous process in boys. As soon as the little boy is capable of an object relation, he takes as his first love object the mother who feeds and tends him. As he passes through the pregenital phases of libidinal development, he retains the same object. When he reaches the phallic stage, he adopts the typical oedipal attitude, i.e., he loves his mother and desires to possess her and to get rid of his rival, the father. Throughout this development his love object remains the same. An alteration in his love attitude, an alteration characteristic of his sex, occurs at the moment when he accepts the possibility of castration as a punishment threatened by his powerful father for these libidinal desires of his. It is not impossible, indeed it is very probable, that even before the boy reaches the phallic stage and adopts the oedipal attitude which coincides with it, he has perceived the difference between the sexes by observing either a sister or a girl playmate, but we assume that he attributed little significance to this perception. If, however, such a perception occurs when he is already in the oedipal situation and is experiencing castration anxiety, we know how great an impact this may have on his mind. The child's first reaction is an endeavor to deny the actuality of castration and to hold very tenaciously to his first love object. After violent inward struggles, however, the little boy makes a virtue of necessity; he renounces his love object in order to retain his penis. Possibly he thus ensures for himself the chance of a renewed and more successful battle with his father at some later date—a possibility which I suggested earlier in this paper. As we know, when the young man reaches maturity, he does succeed in wresting the victory from his father, normally with a mother substitute.

But what happens in the little girl? She, too, takes as her first love object the mother who feeds and tends her. She, too, retains the same love object as she passes through the pregenital phases of libidinal evolution. She, too, enters the phallic stage of libido development. Moreover, the little girl has a body organ analogous to the little boy's penis, namely, the clitoris, which gives her pleasurable feelings in masturbation. Physically she behaves exactly like the little boy. We may suppose that in the psychic realm too children of both sexes develop in a similar manner up to this point; that is to say, girls and boys both enter into an oedipal situation when they reach the phallic stage. However, for the girl it is a negative situation—she wants to conquer the mother for herself and to get rid of the father. Up to this point, too, a chance observation by the little girl of the difference between the sexes may have been without significance; now, however, a perception of this sort is fraught with serious consequences for her. It strikes her that the boy's genital is larger, stronger, and more visible than her own, and that he can use it actively in urinating, a process which for the child has a sexual significance. When she makes this comparison, the little girl must feel her own organ to be inferior. She imagines that hers was once like the boy's and that it has been taken from her as a punishment for her prohibited love cravings toward the mother. At first the little girl tries, as does the boy, to deny the fact of castration or to comfort herself with the idea that she will still grow a genital. The acceptance of castration has for her the same consequences as for the boy: not only does her narcissism suffer a blow on account of her physical inferiority, but she is forced to renounce the fulfillment of her first love longings. It is at this point that the difference in the psychic development of the two sexes sets in in connection with the perception of the anatomical difference between male and female. To the boy castration is only a threat, which can be escaped by a suitable modification of behavior. To the girl it is an accomplished fact, which is irrevocable, but the recognition of which compels her finally to renounce her first love object and to taste to the full the bitterness of its loss. Normally, the female child is bound at some time to come to this recognition: she is thereby forced to abandon completely her negative oedipal attitude, and with it the masturbation which is its accompaniment. The object-libidinal relation to the mother is transformed into an identification with her; the father is chosen as a love object; the enemy becomes the beloved. Now there also arises, in place of the wish for a penis, the desire for a child. A child of her own acquires for the girl a narcissistic value similar to that which the penis possesses for the boy; for only a woman, and never a man, can have children.

The little girl, then, has now adopted the positive oedipal attitude, with the very far-reaching afterresults with which we are so familiar. Freud has explained more than once that there is no motive for the shattering of the positive oedipus complex in the girl such as we have in the threat of castration in the case of the boy. Therefore the female oedipus complex vanishes gradually, is largely incorporated in the

normal development of the woman, and explains many of the differences between the mental lives of women and men.

We may now sum up by saying that the little girl's castration complex
(or her discovery of the anatomical difference between the sexes) which,
according to Freud, ushers in and renders possible her normal, positive
oedipal attitude, has its psychic correlative just like that of the boy,
and it is only this correlative which lends it its enormous significance
for the mental evolution of the female child. In the first years of her development as an individual (leaving out of consideration the phylogenetic influences which, of course, are undeniable) the little girl behaves exactly like a boy, not only in the matter of masturbation but in
other aspects of her mental life: in her love aim and object choice she is
actually a little man. When she has discovered and fully accepted the
fact that castration has taken place, the little girl is forced once and for
all to renounce her mother as love object and therewith to give up the
active, conquering tendency of her love aim as well as the practice of
clitoral masturbation. Perhaps here we also have the explanation of a
fact with which we have long been familiar, namely, that the woman
who is wholly feminine does not know object love in the true sense of
the word—she can only "let herself be loved." Thus it is to the mental
accompaniments of phallic masturbation that we must ascribe the fact
that the little girl normally represses this practice much more energetically than the boy and has a far more intense struggle. For she has to
forget with it the first love-disappointment, the pain of the first loss of a
love object.

We know how often this repression of the little girl's negative oedipal
attitude is wholly or partly unsuccessful. For the female as well as for
the male child it is very hard to give up the first love object: in many
cases the little girl clings to it for an abnormally long time. She tries to
deny the punishment (castration) which would inevitably convince her
of the forbidden nature of her desire. She firmly refuses to give up her
masculine position. If later her love longing is disappointed a second
time, this time in relation to the father who does not give way to her
passive wooing of his love, she often tries to return to her former situation and to resume a masculine attitude. In extreme cases this leads to
the manifest homosexuality of which Freud gives so excellent and clear

an account in "The Psychogenesis of a Case of Homosexuality in a Woman" (1920b). The patient about whom Freud tells us in this work made a faint effort, on entering puberty, to adopt a feminine love attitude but later in the period of puberty she behaved toward an older woman whom she loved exactly like a young man in love. At the same time she was a pronounced feminist, denying the difference between men and women; thus she had gone right back to the first, negative phase of the oedipus complex.

There is another process which is perhaps commoner. The girl does not entirely deny the fact of castration but seeks overcompensation for her body inferiority on some plane other than the sexual (in her work, her profession). However, in so doing she represses sexual desire altogether, that is, she remains sexually unmoved. It is as if she wished to say: "I may not and cannot love my mother, and so I must give up any further attempt to love at all." Her belief in her possession of a penis has thus been shifted to the intellectual sphere; there she can be masculine and compete with men.

We may observe as a third possible outcome that a woman may form relationships with a man yet remain inwardly attached to the first object of her love, her mother. She is obliged to be frigid in coitus because she does not really desire the father or his substitute, but the mother. Now these considerations place in a somewhat different light the fantasies of prostitution so common among women. According to this view, they are an act of revenge not so much against the father as against the mother. The fact that prostitutes are so often manifest or disguised homosexuals might be explained in an analogous fashion: the prostitute turns to the man out of revenge against the mother, but she is not motivated by a wish for passive feminine surrender; rather she displays masculine activity: she captures the man on the street, castrates him by taking his money, and thus makes herself the masculine and him the feminine partner in the sexual act.

I think that in considering these disturbances in the woman's development to complete femininity we must keep two possibilities in view. Either the little girl has never been able wholly to give up her longing to possess her mother and thus has formed only a weak attachment to her father, or she has made an energetic attempt to substitute her father for her mother as love object but, after suffering a fresh disappointment at his hands, has returned to her first position.

In the paper "Some Psychical Consequences of the Anatomical Distinction between the Sexes" (1925), Freud draws attention to the fact that jealousy plays a far greater part in the mental life of women than in that of men. He thinks that the reason for this is that in women jealousy is reinforced by the deflected penis envy. Perhaps one might add that a woman's jealousy is stronger than a man's because she can never succeed in securing her first love object, while the man, when he grows up, can do so.

In another paragraph (1925, p. 254) Freud traces the fantasy of "a child is being beaten" ultimately to the masturbation of the little girl during the phallic phase. The child who is beaten or caressed is at bottom the clitoris (i.e., the penis); the being beaten is on the one hand the punishment for the forbidden genital relation and on the other a regressive substitute for it. But in this phase the punishment for prohibited libidinal relations is precisely castration. Thus the formula "a child is being beaten" means "a child is being castrated." In the fantasies in which the child being beaten is a stranger, the idea of its being castrated is intelligible at first glance. It means: "No one else shall have what I have not got." Now we know that in the fantasies of puberty, which are often greatly metamorphosed and condensed, the child beaten by the father always represents the girl herself as well. Thus she is constantly subjecting herself to castration, for this is the necessary condition for being loved by the father; she is making a fresh effort to get clear of her old love relations and to reconcile herself to her womanhood. In spite of the many punishments, pains, and tortures which the hero has to undergo, "the fantasies always end happily" (see A. Freud, 1922), i.e., after the sacrifices have been made, the passive, feminine love is allowed to be victorious. Sometimes this immolation permits the return to masturbation, the first forbidden love tendency having been duly expiated. Often, however, masturbation remains none the less prohibited, or it becomes unconscious and is practiced in some disguised form, sometimes accompanied by a deep sense of guilt. It seems as if the repeated submission to the punishment of castration signifies not only the expiation due to the feelings of guilt but also a form of wooing the father, whereby the subject also experiences masochistic pleasure.

To sum up what I have said above: in little boys who develop normally, the positive oedipal attitude is by far the more prevalent because, by adopting it, the child, through his temporary renunciation of the mother object, can retain his genital and perhaps thereby ensure for himself the possibility of winning later in life a mother substitute; if he adopted the negative attitude, it would mean that he must renounce both from the outset. Little girls, however, normally pass through both situations in the oedipus complex: first the negative, which occurs under precisely the same conditions as in boys, but which they are finally compelled to abandon when they discover and accept the fact of their castration. Then the girl's attitude changes: she identifies herself with the lost love object and puts in its place her former rival, the father, thus passing into the positive oedipal situation. Thus in female children the castration complex deals a deathblow to the negative oedipal attitude and ushers in the positive oedipus complex.

This view confirms Freud's hypothesis that the (positive) oedipus complex in women is made possible and ushered in by the castration complex. But, in contradistinction to Freud, we are assuming that the castration complex in female children is a secondary formation and that its precursor is the negative oedipal situation; further, that it is only from the latter that the castration complex derives its greater psychic significance, and it is probably this negative attitude which enables us to explain in greater detail many peculiarities subsequently met with in the mental life of women.

I am afraid there will be objections that this hypothesis looks like speculation and lacks an empirical basis. I must reply that this objection may be just in regard to part of what I have said, but that nevertheless the whole argument is built on a foundation of practical experience, although unfortunately this is still meager. I shall now give a short account of the material which has led me to my conclusions:

Some time ago I was treating a young girl who had been sent to me by a male colleague. He had analyzed her for some years, but there were certain difficulties connected with the transference which resisted solution. This girl had suffered from a rather severe hysterical neurosis. Her analysis had already been carried a good way. The normal, positive oedipus complex, her rivalry with her sister, and her envy of her younger brother's penis had been dealt with thoroughly, and the patient had understood and accepted them. Many of her symptoms had disappeared, but to her great regret she remained unfit for work. When she came to me, the unresolved, ambivalent transference to the male analyst was playing a principal part in the situation. It was difficult to determine which was the stronger, her passionate love or her no less passionate hate. I knew this patient personally before she came to me for treatment and the analysis began with a strong positive transference to me. Her attitude was rather like that of a child who goes to his mother for protection. But after a short time a profound change began to take place. The patient's behavior became first rebellious and hostile and soon, behind this attitude, there was revealed a deep-seated and wholly active tendency to woo my love. She behaved just like a young man in love, displaying, for instance, violent jealousy of a young man whom she suspected of being her rival in real life. One day she came to analysis with the idea that she would like to read all Freud's writings and become an analyst herself. The obvious interpretation which we tried first, namely, that she wanted to identify herself with me, proved inadequate. A series of dreams showed an unmistakable desire to get rid of my own analyst, to "castrate" him and take his place, so as to be able to analyze (possess) me.

In this connection the patient remembered various situations in her childhood when her parents quarreled and she assumed a defensive and protective attitude toward her mother, and also times when they displayed mutual affection and she detested her father and wished to have her mother to herself. The analysis had long ago revealed both a strong positive attachment to the father and the experience which put an end to it. As a child the patient slept in a room next to her parents and was in the habit of calling them at night when she had to urinate; of course the intention was to disturb them. At first she generally demanded that her mother come, but later on, she demanded her father.

She said that when she was five years old, this happened once more and her father came to her and quite unexpectedly boxed her ears. From that moment the child resolved to hate him. The patient produced yet another recollection: when she was four years old she dreamed that she was

13

lying in bed with her mother beside her and that she had a sense of supreme bliss. In her dream her mother said: "That is right, that is how it ought to be." The patient awoke and found that she had passed urine in bed; she was greatly disappointed and felt very unhappy.

She had various recollections of the time when she still slept in her parents' room. She said that she often used to awake in the night and sit up in bed. These recollections are a fairly certain indication that she observed her parents' coitus. The dream she had as a child may very well have been dreamed after such an observation. It clearly represented coitus with her mother, accompanied by a sense of bliss. Even in later life urethral erotism played a particularly important part in this patient. Her disappointment on awakening showed that she was already conscious of her inability to possess her mother: she had long ago discovered the male genital in her younger brother. The bed wetting can be construed as either a substitute for or a continuation of masturbation; the dream shows how intense must have been her emotional relation to her mother at that time. Hence it is clear that the patient, after her disappointment with her father (the box on the ears), tried to return to the earlier object, whom she had loved at the time of the dream, i.e., her mother. When she grew up she made a similar attempt. After an unsuccessful love affair with a younger brother of her father, she had, for a short time, a homosexual relation. This situation was repeated in her analysis when she came from the male analyst to me.

This patient stated that she had had a special form of the beating fantasy when she was from eight to ten years old. She described it as "the hospital fantasy." The gist of it was as follows. A large number of patients went to a hospital to get well, but they had to endure the most frightful pains and tortures. One of the most frequent practices was that they were flayed alive. The patient had a feeling of shuddering pleasure when she imagined their painful, bleeding wounds. Her associations brought recollections of how her younger brother sometimes pushed back the foreskin of his penis, whereupon she saw something red, which she thought of as a wound. The method of cure in her fantasy was therefore obviously a representation of castration. She identified herself on one occasion with the patients, who at the end always got well and left the hospital with great gratitude, but generally she had a different role. She was the protecting, compassionate Christ, who flew over the beds in the ward in order to bring relief and comfort to the sick people. In this fantasy, which reveals its sexual-symbolic character in the detail of *flying*, the patient is the man who alone possesses his mother (for Christ was born without a father), but who finally, to atone for the guilt and to be able to reach God the Father, offered the sacrifice of crucifixion (castration). After we broke off the analysis, which the patient gave up in a state of negative transference, a reaction to the disappointment of her love, she tried to translate this fantasy into reality by deciding to become a nurse. After a year, however, she abandoned this new profession for her earlier one, which was more masculine in character and much more suited to her temperament. Gradually her feelings of hate toward me also disappeared.

I had a second patient in whom I discovered similar processes with regard to the transference. In the first two months of treatment this patient produced very strong resistances. She acted the part of a naughty, defiant child and would utter nothing but monotonous complaints to the effect that she was forsaken and that her husband treated her badly. After we had succeeded in discovering that her resistance arose from feelings of hatred toward me, due to envy and jealousy, the full, positive, feminine oedipal attitude gradually developed in her—there entered into it both love for the father and the wish for a child. Soon, too, penis envy began to show itself. She produced a recollection from her fifth or sixth year. She said that she had once put on her elder brother's clothes and displayed herself proudly to all and sundry. Besides this she had made repeated efforts to urinate like a boy. At a later period she always felt that she was very stupid and inferior and thought that the other members of her family treated her as if this were the case. During puberty she conceived a remarkably strong aversion to every sort of sexual interest. She would listen to none of the mysterious conversations in which her girl friends engaged. She was interested only in intellectual subjects, literature, etc. When she married she was frigid. During her analysis she experienced a desire to have some profession; to her, this stood for being male. But her feelings of inferiority forbade any real attempt to achieve this ambition. Up to this point the analysis had made splendid progress. The patient had one peculiarity: she remembered very little, instead she acted out a good deal. Envy and jealousy and the desire to do away with the mother were repeated in the most diverse guises in the transference. After this position had been worked through, a new resistance presented itself; we discovered behind it deep homosexual desires related to me. The patient now began to woo my love in a thoroughly masculine manner. The occasions of these declarations of love, during which in her dreams and fantasies she always pictured herself with a male genital, invariably coincided with some active behavior in real life. They alternated, however, with periods in which her behavior was wholly passive. At such times the patient was once more incapable of anything; she failed at everything, suffered from her inferiority, and was tortured by feelings of guilt. The meaning of this was that every time she conquered the mother, she was impelled to castrate herself in order to get free from her sense of guilt. Her attitude toward masturbation was also noteworthy. Before analysis she had never consciously practised this habit; during the period when she was being treated she began clitoral masturbation. At first this masturbation was accompanied by a strong sense of guilt; later, at times when her love wishes toward her father were most vehemently manifested, the feelings of guilt abated. They were succeeded by the fear that the masturbation might do her some physical harm: "weaken her genitals." At the stage when she was in love with me, the sense of guilt reappeared and she gave up masturbating because this fear became a certainty in her mind. This "weakening" of the genital organs signified castration. Thus the patient constantly oscillated between homosexual and heterosexual love. She had a tendency to regress to her first love relation—with the mother—and at this stage tried to deny the fact of castration. To make up, however, she had to refrain from masturbation and sexual gratification of any kind. She could not derive satisfaction from her husband, because she herself really wanted to be a man in order to be able to possess the mother.

Thus in both of the cases which I have discussed it was plain that behind the woman's positive oedipal attitude there lay a negative attitude, with the mother as love object, which revealed itself later in the analysis and therefore had been experienced at an earlier stage of development. Whether this evolution is typical cannot, of course, be asserted with any

certainty from the observation of two cases. I should be inclined to believe that in other female patients the oedipus complex has had a similar previous history, but I have not been able to gather enough material from their analyses to establish this beyond question. The phase
of the negative oedipal attitude, lying, as it does, so far back in the patient's mental history, cannot be reached until the analysis has made
very considerable progress. Perhaps it is very hard to bring this period
to light with a male analyst for it is difficult for a female patient to enter rivalry with the father analyst; possibly treatment under these conditions cannot get beyond the analysis of the positive oedipal attitude.
The homosexual tendency, which can hardly be missed in any analysis,
may then merely give the impression of a later reaction to the disappointment experienced at the father's hands. In the cases described
above, however, it was clearly a regression to an earlier phase—a circumstance which may help us to understand better the enormous psychic
significance that the lack of a penis has in the erotic life of women. I do
not know whether in the future it will turn out that my exposition in
this paper explains the development of only these two patients of mine.
I think it is not impossible that it may be found to have a more general
significance. Only the gathering of further material will enable us to decide this question.

This Chapter also appeared in *The Psychoanalytic Reader*, edited by
Robert Fliess (1948). His editorial comments follow (pp. 207-208):

In his paper "On Female Sexuality" Freud has expressed agreement with the essentials of this contribution, published first in
1927. "Here," he comments, "the complete identity of the preoedipal phase in the boy and the girl is recognized, the sexual (phallic)
activity in the little girl's attitude towards the mother is stated and
proven by observation. The turning-away from the mother is traced
back to the influence of the child's acknowledgment of castration,
which forces it to abandon the sexual object, and often at the same
time the practice of masturbation. The whole development is epit-
omized in the formula, that the little girl has to pass through a
phase of the 'negative' oedipus complex before arriving at the
positive one ..."
One inadequacy is found by Freud in Dr. Lampl's report: the

17

author has failed to describe the hostility which accompanies the girl's turning-away from the mother.

Dr. Lampl, upon editorial request, has put the following note at our disposal:

"In the nineteen years since the appearance of my paper, the observations recorded in it have been fully confirmed by many colleagues as well as by myself. Their full significance, however, was brought out through Freud's magnificent formulation of the pre-oedipal mother-attachment. The negative oedipal attitude, described by me, is the terminal phase in the female child's early attachment to her mother; it introduces the oedipal father-attachment. The latter is indeed made possible only through the little girl's becoming inimical towards her mother, in other words, through the hostility, referred to by Freud in his criticism of my paper.

"In the meantime reference has also been made occasionally to the significance for the development of the boy of this preoedipal attachment to the mother, in particular to the conditioning of his passive feminine attitude (homosexuality) by it. I hope to describe the influence of this early object-relation upon the ego development of both sexes in the near future."

Amsterdam, Holland [1947]   J. L. de G.

CHAPTER 2

Problems of Femininity

(1933)

Though I started this paper from observations on female patients, some of which I had already presented in Chapter 1, I gradually came to some hypothetical ideas. Many people may call them no more than mere speculations and reject them completely. Perhaps this paper is partly a youthful sin; perhaps I should have changed more than only a few of the formulations. Be that as it may, I have decided to publish it with only slight differences in wording because I myself cannot reject it altogether, though I am quite aware of its speculative side and am prepared to abandon it whenever different and better hypotheses are presented.

I

Implicit in Freud's doctrine of bisexuality is the warning against too schematic an apposition of femininity in woman and masculinity in man. It is well recognized that no man exists whose masculine traits are not accompanied by more or less obviously feminine characteristics, and that likewise there are no women who fail to show masculine tendencies. Physical examination of the male reveals female residuals, while the female body shows vestigial male characteristics. Psychological investigations demonstrate bisexual elements even more strikingly; these are not only present, but are of important functional significance. Analytic experience reveals many feminine characteristics that man must confront in the course of his psychic development, and many

19

masculine traits complicating or disturbing the development of femininity. This psychic struggle takes place in the development of every man and woman, whereas the presence of physical rudiments of the opposite sex has little recognizable effect except in rare cases of hermaphroditism where the reproductive function is impaired.

Demonstration of the processes and forces which affect the differentiation of the sexes in their embryonic development admittedly belongs to the field of biology. Freud pointed out many years ago that the discovery of the organic basis of psychic forces is also one of the tasks of biology. At present, Bernfeld and Feitelberg are attempting experiments from which they hope to be able to deduce a physico-biological concept of psychic energy and of the drive theory as well. For the present, however, psychology must satisfy itself with hypotheses concerning the correspondences and differences in physical and psychic development. Nevertheless, we should guard against overlooking those psychological differences in men and women which are caused by a different physical setup (Anlage), and against underestimating the possibility of similar development of both sexes during a given period.

Although the child is provided at birth with masculine or feminine genitals, it is only after the passage of years, in puberty, that the ultimate physical development and functioning are attained. The final psychic forms of masculinity and femininity are achieved even later, after the completion of physical maturity. We know, however, that the instinctual life has had a flourishing development much earlier and that the patterns attained then serve as models for the reactions at puberty. Infantile sexuality shows all the psychic characteristics to be found in the later love life. The child falls in love, desires the exclusive possession of the love object, defends this object with the same jealousy, hate, and revenge manifestations found among adults. The child has fantasies, sexual wishes, and aims similar to those of adults. Infantile sexuality is, however, doomed to frustration from the beginning, since the genital apparatus cannot yet perform its ultimate functions. The incestuous love object must be abandoned. Masturbation, the form of physical discharge of sexual tension, which is appropriate to the infantile period, has to be replaced by an adult love life. All these characteristics appear in children of both sexes. Even the first love object, the nurturing mother, is the same for both. This correspondence persists until that period of infantile sexuality when the oedipus complex is in the process of formation. At this time a difference manifests itself, not only in respect to the drive itself, but in respect to the object choice as well, thus preparing for later adolescent processes. If a normal development ensues at this time, a satisfactory final pattern is laid for the love life of maturity in respect to body function and object choice. The youth is then capable of securing a wife whom he can love and fertilize in a completely masculine fashion; the girl becomes capable of motherhood and yields herself in a feminine manner to the man from whom she can receive a child.

II

Before discussing this development it seems imperative to attempt a more exact description of the concepts of "masculinity" and "femininity." The words "masculine" and "feminine" are not scientifically precise concepts, but have been borrowed from colloquial speech. When Freud uses the word "masculine," it seems clear that he does not mean to designate a quality or a characteristic of behavior which belongs exclusively to men. In Freud's later works masculinity is more and more definitely made analogous to activity, while femininity and passivity appear to be identical. If one accepts this designation, one must next consider the meaning of "activity" and "passivity." The concepts of activity and passivity are borrowed from the sexual behavior of men and animals. One calls active the individual who approaches his sexual object and conquers it. The partner who submits to the approach and yields is passive. The first procedure is generally attributed to man, while woman usually plays the latter role. This general rule may have caused the apposition masculine-active, feminine-passive, as found in current speech. However, since Freud's doctrine recognizes that men and women each have active and passive drive impulses, it immediately becomes obvious that, in the analytic sense, the concepts of masculinity and femininity have no exclusive reference to either sex. Correspondingly, one may not impute to either of the concepts an appreciative or depreciative evaluation. The terms

21

merely describe forms of expression or directions of the libido. In his article on "Female Sexuality" (1931b) Freud speaks of libidinal strivings with active and passive goals.

Active and passive behaviors occur outside the love life as well. In the above-mentioned article (1931b, p. 236) Freud says, "It can easily be observed that in every field of mental experience, not merely that of sexuality, when a child receives a passive impression it has a tendency to produce an active reaction."

In the newborn, all libido is originally lodged in the person; this is the condition known as primary narcissism (Freud, 1914). If a person loves an object actively, he cathects that object with libido. This cathexis occurs at the expense of the amount of narcissistic energy, an impoverishment of this source ensues, and this condition can be endured by the person only when a sufficient narcissistic supply is available or when there is compensation for this loss through love received from objects. Frustrations induce the person to withdraw object love into the self, thus reinforcing narcissistic cathexis (secondary narcissism). A certain amount of narcissism is indispensable for enabling the person to cathect an object representation actively. An impairment of his narcissism leads him to strive for object love by surrendering to the object libido strivings with a passive aim, therefore serving the restoration of narcissistic cathexis. This demand to be loved, calculated to increase narcissism, at the same time creates a particularly strong dependence upon the object. An intense anxiety occurs at the prospect of a possible loss of love, since every disappointment constitutes a narcissistic insult.

On the other hand, someone who has achieved real object love suffers, if disappointed or disillusioned, an actual object loss. If development has been normal, the person knows how to help himself by withdrawing his libido into his self (as already mentioned above) preparatory to making a new love attempt with another object. This mechanism, which permits him to recover his narcissism intact, makes him less dependent upon his former love object than in the case of the person whose love has been passive (Freud, 1931a). In summary, an adequate amount of narcissism enables the person to accomplish object love, whereas an insufficient supply of self-love or narcissistic injury incapacitates the person for cathecting an object. If narcissism is severely depleted, the person attempts to restore it by permitting himself to be loved. Activity, then, in contrast to passivity, denotes object cathexis. A person loves his object with his "masculinity," and permits himself to be loved with his "femininity."

III

We now turn to two questions:

(1) How do we meet with the active and passive strivings alongside each other in a particular person?

(2) How can we explain the differences and the similarities in the love lives of the two sexes?

As usual, we shall look into pathology to learn more about these matters.

An especially impressive instance of the apposition of actively and passively directed libido strivings came to my attention during the analysis of a strongly impulsive young man. At first sight it was completely impossible to understand how this exceptionally virile, masculine-looking young man had been severely paralyzed in his love life and his work, and how he had attained such marked feminine behavior. During a lengthy analysis it was discovered that as a small boy, feeling himself unloved by his parents, he had reacted to each disappointment in love with intense rage and spitefulness. The governess, whom he soon attempted to love in place of his mother, punished him for these attacks with physical blows, which he regarded as monstrously degrading. This new insult, this new lack of love, increased his need to be loved and caused him to become a "good little boy" for the sake of inducing love. When he assumed his obedient attitude, he did not immediately abandon his aggressive behavior; he did so only later, in response to violent reactions to castration threats from his governess and father regarding his masturbatory activities. These threats were vivified during sexual play instigated by an older brother, who recounted the most creepy tales of castration until finally the patient was convinced that he would lose his penis in any case and consequently might as well forfeit it. A surrender of the active role in his love life accompanied his renunciation of his penis. This sacrifice created an acute

23

need to be loved, which the boy sought by becoming completely good and obedient. At the same time his aggression was turned inward and procured for him masochistic pleasure, shown in many diversified fantasies, and he became inhibited, shy, and incapacitated in his studies.

Summarizing, we might say, (1) disappointment in love and narcissistic insults diminished the patient's ability to play the active role in his love life and established a preference for passively directed libido strivings; (2) actual paralysis of activity occurred only when the boy, under the pressure of extremely vivid castration threats, saw the necessity for renouncing his penis; (3) the increase in passivity was accompanied by a turning inward of his aggressiveness, which became fixated in later life (masochism).

From this extreme case we turn now to the state of affairs in normal development. Every child suffers frustration in love and narcissistic insults, and every child becomes aware of sex differences. Anxiety concerning the genital is, therefore, never completely lacking. It is inevitable too, that a certain portion of the aggressive tendency should be turned inward. Nevertheless, the vigorous little boy who undergoes what is called normal development manages to surmount these difficulties. He becomes a man, capable of playing the active role in love life, having such a large store of libido that he is in a position to cathect his actual love object. From this store of narcissistic libido in the self surge the forces peculiar to man, making it possible for him to fulfill his potentialities for marriage and reproduction. His aggressive tendencies find an outlet partly in the "sadism" necessary for approaching the love object and partly in the sublimated form necessary to the rest of his lifework, his profession, social interests and relationships. The passive strivings which the small boy does not lack are subordinated to the active tendency. Only in pathological cases is this subordination not achieved; in such cases the narcissistic insults produce an excessive effect, notably where there is immoderate castration anxiety.

The situation is different in the case of the woman. Achievement of adequate femininity requires a preference for passivity. The aggressive tendency finds an outlet in that form of aggression which is directed inward (masochism). Some of the most important processes

24

in the sexual life of women, defloration and giving birth, are quite normally accompanied by the pleasure of pain (H. Deutsch, 1930). The passive, "feminine" woman exhibits few aggressive tendencies toward love partners or in other spheres of life. Karen Horney assumes that the aggressive tendency is a priori stronger in the man, that the libido in the case of the woman gives preference to passive goals from the beginning, and that this is a simple biological law which one can never explain psychologically. It is obvious that differences in physical make-up and in biological functions must necessarily be accompanied by different psychic expressions. However, one may be too easily satisfied by such an assumption and fail to pursue psychological investigation as far as possible. The psychoanalytic libido (drive) theory, though based upon biological factors, is aware of the fact that in psychological manifestations there is only *one* "libido" whose direction and aim can be changed, but which is essentially the same in men and in women. Therefore we have to pursue its vicissitudes in males and in females with psychological means. Moreover, no theory of phylogenetic inheritance relieves us of the necessity of investigating the time and occasion in the life of the person when the functioning of given tendencies becomes observable.

Besides these theoretical considerations, there is a whole series of empirical observations which require study. Analysis of adults as well as observations on little girls demonstrate that the female is not a passive yielding being who permits herself to be loved from the beginning, but that she reveals active as well as passive tendencies often not unlike those of the boy, even quantitatively. The little girl, like the boy, courts with actively directed love, as long as the mother is still the love object. It is necessary, then, to explain how it happens that the little girl, in the course of normal development, renounces her activity. Of course, the little girl, like the boy, knows of passive modes of satisfaction, and with disappointments she longs to be loved, as do boys. The length of the period in which the little girl displays activity varies in each individual. In one little girl an actively directed relation to the mother was predominant until her fifth year. Not until the sixth year did this situation change and the oedipal situation become perceptible. The father relation up to that time had been exactly the same as that to any other member of the family circle. It was often friendly, often distant, according to the little one's disposition. The passionate love attachment, with all the accompanying feelings of demand for exclusiveness, jealousy, envy, hate when disappointed, were retained for the mother, and secondarily for a nurse who often took the mother's place. One may assume with confidence that the turning to the father, and the accompanying preference for the passively directed libidinal drives, occurs in many little girls at an earlier age, about five, four, or perhaps even three.

The duration of the preoedipal mother attachment is of the greatest significance for the later events in the life of the child. In all cases, however, the mother is the first object which the child cathects and this must leave traces in later life. What is the cause of this turning and of the preference for passively directed drives? We repeat that for the achievement of object cathexis (which occurs by means of active tendencies) the person requires a certain amount of free libido at his disposal, a superabundance of narcissism; and the person who is subjected to narcissistic wounds attempts to salve them by adopting passive behavior in the hope of inducing love. The little child suffers from disappointments in love and narcissistic blows even more than the adult; and there is a further difference—the little child is doomed not to succeed with his incestuous love objects. The child—both male and female—also suffers continuously from the stigma of being small, of being regarded by adults as not complete, as inadequate, even as an object of ridicule. Karen Horney describes the anxiety of the boy that his member may be too small or that the mother will laugh at him or ridicule him. The little girl fears that her vagina may be too small for her father's organ and has exactly the same feeling of insufficiency, of inferiority to her mother, and of anxiety lest she be ridiculed and set aside as wanting. Moreover, this experience of not being sufficient for father has an earlier pattern in not having been adequate for mother, the first love object, by whom the child was also frustrated. In my paper, "The Evolution of the Oedipus Complex in Women" (Chapter 1) I expressed the belief that the inevitability of this frustration is recognized as a corollary of the discovery of the anatomical sex differences. Freud confirms this opinion in his paper on "Female Sexuality"

(1931b) and shows that the little girl always holds her mother responsible for her lack of a penis and that this is the most important motive of resentment toward her.

At this point the development of the girl begins to diverge from that of the boy in normal cases, and it is here that the psychological differences between the sexes have a definite beginning. As long as the children of both sexes have the same love object—the mother—the possibility of satisfying passive as well as active libidinal strivings exists to the same extent (in the oral, anal, and phallic phases), and both sexes are subject to the same disappointments in love and the same narcissistic blows. A certain fundamental identity in the development of boy and girl is present even if there should be a difference in the quantitative relationship between activity and passivity in the two cases. Not until the fact of anatomical differences in sex begins to play a role in the psyche does this fundamental difference in development begin to occur. If the little girl discovers that the boy has something which she lacks, that the little boy can accomplish deeds of which she is not capable (exhibitionism, visible masturbation, urination, etc.), if the little girl comes to the conclusion that such an organ is really indispensable to the possession of the mother, she experiences, in addition to the narcissistic insults common to children of both sexes, still another blow, namely, a feeling of inferiority concerning her genitals. The absence of a penis cannot be regarded as a matter of secondary and trifling significance for the little girl, as Karen Horney does. Careful and complete analyses of women provide daily evidence of the significance of the phenomenon. Any simple observation of little girls leaves no ambiguity concerning the girl's wish for a penis, her feeling of being harmed not only by grownups but also by her brother or playmates, and her difficulty in reconciling herself to this status. A little girl, well informed about all sexual processes and already aware of the gratification she could derive from the clitoris or the vaginal entrance, who, moreover, knew that she was capable of motherhood which would be denied to the boy, nevertheless insisted with astonishing stubbornness, "But I want a little tassel right now." For the girl the possibility of bearing a child in the dim future furnishes cold comfort—she wishes to have what the boy has, and the discovery that the boy's organ is so much

27

bigger, so much more tangible and more obviously capable of performance than her own, regularly arouses a feeling of envy and deprivation.

To be sure, in the analysis of feminine men one frequently finds
the wish to bear a child. Karen Horney regards birth envy among
men as analogous to the penis envy of the woman. Birth envy is part of
an attempt to rival the mother in the passive object relation to the
father. In contrast to the little girl, however, who suffers from the
deprivation of something possessed at that very moment by her brother, the boy's envy of the sister is an envy of something obtainable by her
only in the remote future and therefore an envy of much less intensity.
The question, much discussed recently, whether the little girl masturbates on the clitoris, or the vulva, or the entrance of the vagina, has
little to do with the fact of penis envy, however important it may be
theoretically. Without a doubt the little girl is capable of masturbatory
satisfaction; whether more or less than the boy, one cannot decide. But
no matter from what source the girl succeeds in obtaining satisfaction,
the wish for a penis is actively present and has far-reaching consequences for further development. Freud (1925) demonstrated that the
castration complex in the little girl appears before the oedipus complex
and that the discovery that she lacks a penis leads her to adopt a passive love orientation to the father. In my above-mentioned work
(Chapter 1), I was able to demonstrate an actively directed object love
for the mother present in the girl before the appearance of the castration complex, and this was confirmed by Freud. It is possible now to
understand these processes in more detail. The severe narcissistic insults
which the little girl feels because of her genital inferiority, and the
coincidental appearance of resentment toward her mother, who is made
responsible for this inferiority, are the cause of the girl's surrender of
active love and acceptance of the passive role. She must permit herself
to be loved in order to augment her injured self-love. She gradually
begins to turn her passively directed love wishes from her mother to
her father. This complete change of object is accomplished with the
aid of increased enmity toward the mother; hatred and rage complete
the process of turning away from the first love object. Then, simultaneously with the paralyzing of the little girl's activity, aggression is
inhibited as well and that part of her aggression which may not be

turned outward is directed inward and expresses itself in a variety of masochistic fantasies and modes of behavior which are normal for women. Should, however, the little boy give such preference to passively directed libido, this process would take place only as the result of excessive castration anxiety and his development would not continue normally.

IV

A few theoretical questions present themselves: (1) Why does the individual require such a high degree of narcissistic cathexis? (2) How is one to explain the fact that the individual's attempt to restore his injured narcissism is accompanied by turning aggression toward his own person? (3) What is the relationship of actively and passively directed libidinal strivings to the active and passive reactions outside the sphere of sexuality? (4) What does psychoanalytic theory contribute toward the explanation of the biological fact that male sexual life is accomplished with the help of actively directed libidinal strivings while the woman utilizes libidinal strivings with a passive aim?

According to Freud's first views, in the very beginning of psychic existence there is an interaction of two different types of drive impulse—self-preservation and libidinal object love. It was discovered, however, that self-preservation is accomplished with the aid of a certain amount of libidinal cathexis, and the dualism between self-preservation and libidinal object love was redefined as one of libidinal drives (ego and object) and other ego drives, which at the time were not defined more specifically. Further observations then revealed the existence of destructive drive impulses, striving in a direction opposed to the libido, which were evident in sadism. Biological considerations led Freud to the concepts of life and death impulses (drives) which reveal themselves in the biophysiological processes of the organism from the beginning of life and later also manifest themselves in psychic reactions, becoming perceptible as outwardly directed object libido and aggression (1920a, 1923b).

The theory of instinctual drives attempts to indicate the relationship between psychological and biological events. Such an attempt seems necessary since the sources of the impulses functioning in the psyche are somatic. What are the biological functions of the life and death instincts? The general aim of an instinctual drive is, according to Freud, the reinstatement of an earlier condition. The death instinct tends to reduce the organic to the inorganic. When it is successful, the unity of the living being is assailed, there is disintegration, and death. The life instinct (drive) (Eros) works in the opposite direction—its function is to increase the stability of life by aggregating unities (cells). In this manner, the life instinct (drive) also strives for a restitution of a previous condition, inasmuch as the origin of life is conceived as a dispersion of lifeless substances into numerous particles. The conception, however, remains for the present an unprovable speculation. On the other hand, the aggregating tendency of the life instinct in its effort to preserve individual life, and thus the life of the species, is unmistakable. The acme of its potency is reached during the fusion of the germinal cells, which are laden with incomparable vital energy, when a new unity is formed and the problem of race preservation is solved. The death instinct present in the individual cells of the organism must be neutralized by the life instinct in order that the individual life may be maintained. Freud conceives of these processes as being analogous to the physiological processes of anabolism and catabolism.

As long as the individual is at one with his environment, as in the case of the foetus in utero, the contest between life and death instinctual drives occurs exclusively within the organism. Birth creates a change in the situation. As soon as the child is delivered, new problems must be met. It is now surrounded by a number of dangers, of which the most threatening is the cessation of the previously continuous source of nourishment. It is remarkable that the process of birth, which initiates the independent life of the person, is in the biological sense a victory of the death instinct: birth causes the disruption of the mother-child unity and threatens the child daily with vital dangers. It is patent that the life instinct is responsible for overcoming these dangers. The combining tendency of Eros causes the child to seek union with the mother. At first, physical union with the mother's breast is the only objective. The life instinct cathects this indispensable object with its energy and there arises a libidinal object relationship, at first, however, in the service of self-preservation. But it is necessary for the child that the mother, too, form an object relationship with the child, providing it with care as well as with nourishment. In the case of such animals as are born dependent upon care, the mother instinct is found to ensure food until such time as the offspring can provide for itself. In the case of man, mother love has become a form of libido development which persists throughout life.

The cathexis of the mother object with libido occasions changes in the relationship between the life and death instincts. By diverting portions of the death instinct (tendencies to destruction, aggression, and overpowering of objects) to the outside world (Freud, 1923b), the internal equilibrium of instincts may be restored. In addition, the life instinct forces the death instinct into service during the conquest of the needed object, at which time an extremely intense union with the object is produced. Moreover, the mechanism of turning drive components outward for the purpose of self-preservation also occurs in the service of Eros. In this process portions of the two kinds of drives merge and interrelate.

The newborn child has other tasks to perform besides that of defense against the danger of death. On entrance into the world he becomes subject to the greatest variety of stimuli, arising in part internally from his own organism, since, on separation from the mother, tensions of needs, hunger, etc., arise, and in part from stimuli and impressions which penetrate through the sense organs from the outside world. The death instinct, which seeks reduction of tension, must master these stimuli if possible (Fechner's principle of constancy).

The organism deals with these stimuli in a way which is actually in opposition to the unifying tendency of Eros and in harmony with the separating tendency of the death instinct. This process may be observed most clearly in the mastery of stimuli from the outside world when this is accomplished by direct motor flight. This method, however, while often useful in later life, is of no value to the helpless infant. He must manage by means of another mechanism. He is separated from the stimuli of the outside world by a layer of the nervous apparatus organized in such a way that the stimuli are prevented from penetrating into the rest of it. This structured layer is rendered permeable to

31

stimuli, however, only when cathected with energy which has been mobile (Freud, 1920a).

How is the mastery of inner tension accomplished? Apparently the organism attempts to meet this situation in a manner similar to that used against external stimuli. Motor flight and stimuli defense are, however, of no avail. A psychic mechanism similar to flight is nevertheless used, since the person attempts to ward off the disturbing inner stimuli by means of repression (or other psychic defense mechanisms). This psychic process also occurs by means of cathexis, consequently by means of binding mobile energy. Cathexis is necessary to prevent penetration of internal stimuli (the claims of the drives) into consciousness. Freud, in *The Ego and the Id* (1923b), regards the energy utilized in cathexis as desexualized Eros, or energy originating from the life instinct. This explanation sounds plausible, at least in regard to the energy used in cathecting the protective barrier against outer stimuli, since the energy used in this manner is unifying and binding, several cells being combined into a single structure entrusted with a definite function. If we accept this hypothesis, we discern in the process of mastering stimuli an instance of the death instinct making use of a part of its antagonist, Eros, for its own purposes. Incidentally, this process is doubtless chronologically the earlier one, since the task of mastering stimuli occurs at the moment of entrance into the outside world, while the necessity of establishing a libidinal object relation for the purpose of satisfying hunger and other needs arises later. It seems that the two instinctual drives, usually in conflict with one another, may unite in the battle against their common enemy, the outside world. In the beginning the infant is threatened only with physical dangers from without. It seeks to protect itself on the one hand by separating itself from these stimuli by means of the protective nerve layer and on the other hand by binding itself libidinally to the object which is necessary for its preservation. However, in the course of the first years of life physical dependence on the mother becomes transformed into psychic dependence. The long-continued bodily helplessness appears to have necessitated a libidinal object cathexis. The intensity of psychic fixation to the object, as well as its frequent persistence beyond the time when the individual is physically independent, is unmistakable. This depend-

32

ence upon objects complicates human relationships enormously and may create a great variety of ties and fusions of the instinctual drives.

Psychic development proceeds not only by the addition of new psychic content to object relationships, but also by a modification of the stability principle. Although the tendency to reduce tensions remains through the whole life, the person soon discovers certain tensions which, in themselves, may give him the gratification of organ pleasure. An explanation of this phenomenon presents us with great difficulty, since we have assumed to date that pleasure ensues from the reduction of tension and not as a result of tension. The nature of instinctual tensions is an extremely elusive problem, and quantitative instances seem to play a role in the production of pleasure and pain, as well as rhythm and the intensity of excitement within a given time unit. Perhaps the relationship between the two types of instinctual drives is also of decisive significance.

The child's first pleasurable sensations arise through the excitation of erotogenic zones during the process of taking nourishment and of being cared for by the mother. This naturally increases the intensity of the mother tie. The constancy principle becomes modified by the pleasure-pain principle. At this time defense is directed only against pain-bringing tensions. Pleasure-bringing stimuli are not only tolerated but sought. The pleasure-pain principle, then, sometimes supersedes the constancy principle in the service of the sexual (life) instincts, necessitating a new and even more complicated interrelation of the two types of instinctual drives. Gradually pleasure and pain sensations extend to pure psychic object relationships. The mere presence of the object or slight contacts, which are not necessarily accompanied by stimulation of the erogenous zones, may produce pleasure. The absence of the mother, withdrawal of love, or any other type of disappointment occasion pain. Thus the object is not only a source of pleasure but also a possible source of pain and disappointment, a part of the inimical outside world against which the child must protect himself. He attempts to master these unpleasant psychic experiences in a manner similar to the one employed in dealing with disturbing body stimuli—by flight from or rejection of the object, or by turning aggression outward in an attempt to destroy the object. Libido withdrawn from the object is reinvested in

33

the self in an attempt to render it more resistant to further pain and so creates secondary narcissism.

Freud in *The Ego and the Id* (1923b) regards these different processes as the dynamic forces which produce the various organizations in the psyche. The original inner struggle between Eros and the death instinct takes place in the id. The need to distinguish itself from the outside world (Freud, 1920a) causes the id to surround itself with a layer which will take over the business of intercourse with the outside world. This differentiation within the personality makes it possible to describe the above processes topographically. The ego is at first a body ego, concerning itself with perceptions and the mastery of external stimuli. As soon as the ego has achieved a certain independence from the id, it also receives stimuli from within, from the id. The ego is the agent for the object relationships of the id; however, if libido is withdrawn from objects, it is utilized to cathect the ego.[1] Thus secondary narcissism is a cathexis of the ego. Withdrawal of libido from the object frees the originally bound aggression. This freed aggression, tending to destroy the object, gradually comes to serve the feelings of hate and revenge. Naturally the defense mechanisms of flight from and destruction of the object appear only incompletely in the case of the small child, who is so extremely dependent upon the object and must make every effort to retain it. He becomes, therefore, inevitably involved in an ambivalence conflict, with both libidinal and aggressive tendencies directed toward one and the same object. We have seen that certain libidinal strivings which have been withdrawn from the object and which cannot be directed outward, turn themselves secondarily back again to the individual's own person. This is also true of the aggression freed in the process of withdrawal. It appears, then, that the union which the two kinds of instinctual drives form in the battle against the outside world can be dissolved. A new battle between the life and death instincts within the self ensues as a result of redirecting libido and aggression toward the self, and during this process dissociation or defusion of the drives occurs. The contest between secondary narcissism and self-destruction parallels the original battle between the

---

[1] We now would say "the self."

life and death instincts in the id. Since the processes by which both kinds of drive are directed toward objects and withdrawn again into the ego are repeated innumerable times with varying intensity and always with different degrees of fusion and defusion, it is obvious that these events gradually become extremely complicated. Changes in the cathexis of objects affect the general internal drive economy and changes in internal equilibrium have a corresponding effect upon object relationships. Indeed, since there is such an interlacing of relationships, and since it is impossible to determine the intensity of excitation and the relationship of fusion and defusion, there is at present little prospect of observing the exact manner in which this equilibrium is maintained in any individual case.

It becomes evident, however, from the previous discussion, that the ego requires a definite level of libido cathexis, a certain quantity of narcissism, for the purpose of neutralizing self-destructive tendencies. The relationships in the ego are comparable to the biological processes in the id, where sufficient energy of the life instinct must be present in order to neutralize the death instinct present in the cells. The danger of self-mutilation or self-destruction is incurred if there is an insufficient amount of narcissistic ego cathexis, or an unusual amount of destructive excitation directed toward the ego. In pathological cases self-damage may very often occur under the influence of the superego. The superego is a further differentiation of the psyche, a substructure of the ego, which arises from the necessity to renounce object relations at the time when the oedipus complex is pressing for a solution. The superego represents an introjection of the parental imagos into the ego which perhaps occurs because the alternative of complete emancipation from the object is still impossible for the dependent child. To repeat, the return of libido to the ego on surrender of an object is accomplished by desexualization of the libido, dissociation of the two kinds of drives, and direction of aggression inward. If the ego does not succeed in restoring the instinctual equilibrium, the superego may avail itself of the inwardly directed aggression to threaten the ego, in which case a masochistic relationship to the superego results. Further details of superego formation will be considered later.

The second question will now be examined: Why is the attempt to restore wounded narcissism accompanied by the turning of aggression against the self? Raising the level of the narcissistic cathexis is accomplished by withdrawal of object libido into the ego. The desexualization of this libido causes dissociation (defusion) of the two kinds of drive whereby destructive tendencies are freed which cannot be directed outward and must therefore be turned inward. The dependence of the child on the object prevents complete emancipation, and therefore the object is maintained by means of a preference for a passive love orientation, which strengthens the narcissism and enhances mastery of the increased tendency to self-destruction. The child must abandon active object relationships more and more, since these would further impoverish the narcissistic cathexis, a state of affairs which cannot be tolerated because a rich supply of narcissism is required for neutralizing the self-destructive tendencies present.

This leads us to the problem of libido with active and passive aims. As we have seen, a person may be driven to withdraw object cathexes that had previously been actively directed if his internal equilibrium is threatened by disappointment in love or by other severe narcissistic injuries. This withdrawal may also occur if the destructive excitations are prevented from being directed outward by an especially rigid upbringing, so that a turning inward occurs to such an extreme degree that drive equilibrium is threatened. Dependence upon the object and the necessity for increasing narcissism cause an increase in the passively directed libido strivings. When, as often occurs, withdrawal of love and suppression of aggression occur together, the conversion of activity to passivity is increased. In the case of the patient mentioned above, this is obviously what happened. But how can we understand the fact that in females passivity in love life is the normal outcome of development?

The problems of active and passive goals are ultimately biological ones. The procedure by which the ego seeks to keep narcissism on a definite level for the purpose of neutralizing self-destructive tendencies is analogous to the biological events in the cells where the life instinct seeks to bind the death instinct. It may be possible to find parallel processes in the establishment of passive goals by the libido. We have already noted that passivity in sexual life is one aspect of a general passivity of behavior toward the outside world. This consideration leads us to the third question.

It was suggested at the beginning of this paper that the concepts of "activity" and "passivity" were derived from the different types of behavior of man and woman in love life. In general, the former wishes to seize his love object and conquer it, while the latter surrenders herself to the object. The reaction to the outside world, outside the sphere of sexuality, is a similar one. The person may simply permit stimuli and impressions from the outside world to be borne in upon him, in which case he behaves passively, or he may react actively to the outside world in attempting to seize and master it. It is obvious that in passive behavior inner reactions are always present. The terms "active" and "passive" merely describe the observed behavior toward the outside world and toward the love object. The phenomena of activity and passivity do not appear until the person comes to see himself in relation to an outside world. As long as the child is still one with his environment, such a distinction is impossible. At first, then, the two types of drives follow exclusively their inner biological tasks. The striving and the goal of the drives coincide. Only after birth, when the person can be differentiated from the outside world, is it meaningful to make a distinction between striving and goal. The striving of the instinct always remains the same. The death instinct strives to shatter unity and to decrease tension, while the libido is binding and unifying. In so far as the drive is a force, there is always an element of activity (Freud, 1915). The drives seek differently directed goals only after the outside world enters as a factor compelling the person to send out portions of drive energies as well as to produce inner reactive instinctual processes.

Observing the reactions of the newborn child, we find that his first relationships to the outside world, from which he receives impressions and stimuli, are unquestionably of a passive nature. He reacts to these impressions and stimuli in accordance with the constancy principle; he attempts a defense against them. There are two methods of defense. The first is actual physical flight or, where this is impossible, an inner process, the formation of a protective nervous layer, comes into existence. This inner process is accomplished at the behest of the death in-

stinct with the help of energy from the life instinct. The reaction to
the outside world remains a purely passive one. The second procedure
for mastering stimuli is the seizing of the outer world to serve the
person's own purposes. This process occurs in the service of Eros
which is striving for union with the outside world, aided by aggressive
energy. The inner processes are accompanied by sending out portions
of drive energies, resulting in active behavior toward the outside world.
Every person makes use of both mechanisms and a passively received
impression often calls forth active behavior. Nevertheless, the relationship between active and passive reactions varies greatly in each person.
Even in infancy the passive flight mechanism takes precedence in one
case, while the active, seizing mechanism predominates in another case.
The explanation of this fact, in which disposition, the original peculiarities of the drives, plays a role, is not easy. It seems evident, however,
that the preference for active behavior is dependent upon the capacity
to turn instinctual energy outward, and the problem, in the last
analysis, consists of the dynamic relations between Eros and aggression.

The stimuli which the newborn child does not need to dispose of,
since they are pleasurable, are those which rise through the excitation
of erotogenic zones. A modification of the constancy principle by the
pleasure principle takes place under the influence of these experiences. Inasmuch as the pleasure principle ultimately requires diminution of tension, it may be said to serve the death instinct. However, it
also accommodates itself to the demands of Eros, since it not only
tolerates libidinal tensions but in some circumstances even aspires to
them. Extraordinarily little is known about the nature of feelings and
emotions, but perhaps one may risk the suspicion that pleasure and
pain feelings correspond to quantitative tension units or intensities
of Eros energy. The first sexual feelings of pleasure which are con-
veyed to the child from the outside world (the mother) are received
by the child purely passively, as are all stimuli at first. The child's reactions are, however, different from those toward unpleasant stimuli.
The mechanism of stimuli protection is utilized only in relation to the
latter, whereas the pleasant excitations are taken up and the child
seeks to bring about their repetition, in cathecting the object with
libido. This mother tie now no longer serves exclusively for the satis-

faction of tension needs, such as hunger. It also provides the child with new sexual tensions perceived by the child's ego, which differentiates and conveys them to the id. The mother has thus become a valuable love object. The mode of satisfaction continues to be passive, since sexual tensions are received quite accidentally in relation to the acts of taking nourishment and being cared for. Even here, however, passive experience releases an active reaction, the object is cathected with libido, Eros conquers it with the help of aggressive tendencies. The first signs of activity then introduce the consideration of goal. These processes appear very clearly in the first object relation of the infant to the mother's breast. The pleasure feelings originating in the act of nursing lead to active sucking and biting. Both types of drive are to be seen functioning in this oral object relation; taking the object to one's self represents intense union and at the same time annihilation of the object.

For the sake of completeness we must state that pleasurable organ excitations may also be aroused from parts of the person's own body. At first these are perceived as if they emanated from objects in the outside world. The development of body feelings permits the child to make the distinction between autoerotic satisfactions and those dependent upon the mother; the child becomes aware that the bodily sensations are always present, while the mother often disappears.

In summary: The first sexual satisfactions provided by the mother are of a passive nature, but they release an active reaction which leads to an object cathexis. The first object relation has an active goal. The passive experiences are repeated, however, and since they are pleasurable are desired again. The once-established object relation is utilized for passively experienced satisfactions, and thus a passive goal is set up. The libido strives again toward the object, but demands from it passive modes of satisfaction (to be loved, as well as to be looked at, to be touched, to be beaten, and the like). In the service of the death instinct the stability principle seeks flight from external stimuli, while Eros, which aspires to a union with the surroundings for self-preservation and later for preservation of the species, encourages active reactions to these passive experiences. The sex instincts, originating in Eros, follow this example, preferring actively directed erotic object cathexis, but passive experiences are again aspired to, in so far as they are pleasurable, that is, in so far as they are of a sexual nature or are connected with direct or sublimated sexual strivings. From now on, libido strivings with active goals, as well as those with passive goals, often occur together.

What determines the relationship of these strivings to each other? Both seek sexual satisfaction and therefore oppose the tendency of the death instinct. The libido strivings with an active goal, however, confer libido upon objects, while aggressive energy is turned outward in an effort to master the objects. When a passive goal is instituted, libidinal tension is taken back into the ego, and now Eros and aggression oppose each other within the person. The preference for active object cathexes or for passive goals is a matter dependent upon the relative strength of Eros vis-à-vis aggression, above all upon the capacity of Eros to expel destructive excitations from within. We have already seen that situations in the outside world may influence the relation between activity and passivity. Of course, there is one relation between the two which is present ipso facto, namely, the quantitative dynamic relation existing between libido and aggression. This is, to be sure, modifiable by external circumstances, but only within limits which vary for each person.

We now turn to the fourth question, that of the preference of the biological sex functions for activity in males and passivity in females. The greatest increase of sexual excitation is present in the act of reproduction, in which the unifying tendency of Eros culminates. In the case of the male, following this increase in tension, there is a release of it in the sex act, when the germinal cells laden with enormous vital energy are emitted. These are introduced into the woman, in whom there is a heightening of vital energy after the fusion of a spermatozoon with an ovum. The sex function of the man, subserving Eros and the preservation of the race, consists of bestowing some vital energy on an object. For the conquering of the object, aggression is utilized by Eros for its own purposes, and when the task is completed, Eros again abandons the temporarily associated instinct. (In the case of certain lower animals the victory of the death instinct is complete, since the male dies after sexual union [Freud, 1923b]). The function

40

assigned to the woman by Eros consists of the reception of vital energy which has been introduced for the purpose of producing a new living being, in the service of race preservation. The psychic processes in love life partly reflect the biological ones, since the man loves actively and the woman lets herself be loved. The battle between Eros and the death instinct in relation to the sexual function, serving race preservation, is apportioned to two beings. In men it is turned to the outside world and manifests itself in relation to the partner. In women it is internal and proceeds in the newly created life. The process of giving birth implies a temporary loss of vital energy, which is regained by loving the newborn.

It is clear that biological processes determine the relationship between Eros and aggression in the two sexes, perhaps by obscure physical and chemical processes within the sex organs. These processes reach their peak during sexual maturity and create the final shapes of masculinity and femininity. However, they have been in preparation from the beginning of life. Analytic observations reveal clearly the significance of bisexuality for the development of psychic life and the developmental complications during the preparatory phases.

V

Subordination of active to passive libidinal strivings, however, is seldom complete in women, and it behooves us to consider the fate of these various active strivings. Their metamorphosis is so varied, complicated, and intricately structured that I must confine myself at present to only a few considerations.

The purely feminine love orientation of the woman to the man leaves no place for activity. Feminine love is passive, a narcissistic process; the purely feminine woman does not love, she lets herself be loved. When a woman does accomplish active object love, however, as in her relation to her child, she does so with actively directed libidinal components (Freud, 1914). It is well known that many women also retain some of this activity in their relations to men and love them with real object love, that is, with "masculinity."[2] Just as the little girl

---

[2] That is, impulses with active aims.

satisfies her activity in her play with dolls, so the woman utilizes part of her "masculinity" in nourishing and caring for her child and later in educating it. It is quite understandable that the narcissistic satisfaction which motherhood offers woman may so increase her self-love that she has sufficient active strivings for object cathexis. After all, the child satisfies the early infantile desire for a penis which was transformed into a wish for a child during the oedipal stage. This process is especially perceptible in the study of the psychic life of young girls and childless women who have chosen professions having to do with children (teachers, pedagogues, etc.). The children whom they teach are substitutes for their own children and at the same time satisfy their "masculinity" wishes. Their work requires activity. Feminine, narcissistic women are usually poor mothers. Children are a burden to them. On the other hand, there are very maternal women who are so devoted to their children that they are sometimes disturbed in their feminine sensations, have a poor relationship to their husbands, and suffer from frigidity or other disturbances. Normal development would consist of the attainment of a balance between passivity and activity in which a woman who is feminine in her sexual life develops a strong maternal feeling for her children. The role of the man in the act of reproduction is completed with conception. The woman's role, however, does not cease with the passively experienced impregnation; the woman must nourish the child, first inside her body, later outside, and then guard it, care for it, and train it. For this purpose she must establish an object relationship by means of active libido.

However, this use of active strivings is possible only in adult life. What does the little girl do, since she can find no place for activity in the oedipal orientation to her father? She renounces her active wishes with great difficulty, tries to deny the absence of a penis, and attempts to insist upon her masculinity. After a disappointment from the father she often returns to her old mother tie, using the original activity in homosexual strivings. Often some of her dependence upon her mother remains beside the father relation, in which case a continuous oscillation between the two may be observed. Further analytic research will throw light upon these extremely complicated relationships.

VI

It is necessary to turn our attention to a process inaugurated at the time of the latency period when the child has given up the oedipal orientation to the parents, having repressed libidinal and aggressive strivings and replaced them by aim-inhibited, tender feelings. The original parent relationship disappears, although not completely, being moved away and incorporated in the psyche by a process known as introjection. The part of the ego thus modified becomes the superego. The introjection or the incorporation of an object is an oral process; it is therefore the first form of object relationship. The unpleasure of hunger and other dangers causes the infant to desire possession of the satisfaction-producing object, the mother. The aggression against the object called forth by Eros is accompanied by libidinal object cathexis in order to protect the object representation from destruction, while the passively experienced libidinal satisfactions which the infant is proffered simultaneously with feeding and bodily care serve to strengthen his narcissism and bind the aggression against his own person. The incorporation of the object representation during the formation of the superego represents a psychic possession of the object and must be accomplished by the same energies employed in the oral phase to conquer the mother's breast, namely aggression. Libido strivings which are actively directed and which accompany aggression secure the intrapsychic existence of the object representations. Passive libido components are not involved in the process of introjection.

Let us now see how this process takes place in the two sexes. The little boy who has, let us assume, developed in a masculine manner, and who has therefore subordinated his passivity to his masculinity, forms a simple oedipus complex; he loves the mother and wishes to remove the father as a rival. He fears punishment (castration) by this powerful rival, so that narcissistic interest in retaining his organ forces him to renounce his oedipal desires. Desexualization of his sexual wishes and defusion of the drives takes place. The aggression which, as mentioned above, has gradually stepped into the service of the hostile feelings, is utilized to introject the hated paternal object representation, while the active libido strivings toward the father, since he is also loved and admired, assure the further existence of the father imago

43

in the superego. The actual father relationship becomes characterized by tolerated tenderness. The love of the mother also becomes desexualized. However, since the mother is no rival, but only a love object (the hatred arising out of the preoedipal phase can be transferred in the oedipal situation to hatred of the father), there is no occasion to destroy, to introject her image. She remains the tenderly loved object in the outside world while only the father image is concerned with the formation of the superego. The gross sexual desires undergo repression. The more completely the introjective process succeeds, the stronger, more energic, and active will the paternal superego be. Therefore such an individual would presumably be capable, in his mature years, of rendering important social and cultural contributions.

A complication occurs, however, if strong femininity has developed in the boy. A double oedipus complex ensues. In addition to loving the mother, in which case he regards the father as a rival, he permits himself to be loved passively by the father, in which case the mother becomes a competitor. Passive love for the father presupposes a renunciation of the penis, so that the boy must also renounce the negative oedipus complex, because his narcissism requires the preservation of the genital. In such a case introjection of both mother and father images must take place since both are to be disposed of as rivals. The superego will then show traits of both parents and correspondingly will be less uniform and less stable. In the case of my already mentioned effeminate patient, it was clear that his superego represented at times the demands of the father and at other times those of the mother. It is no wonder that such a discordant superego would exert an inhibiting and dissipating influence upon the adult man's accomplishments.

In so far as the different instinctual drives have not been repressed, in the boy, what has happened to them? The aggression directed against the two partly hated objects is responsible for the destructive introjection, while the libido accompanying the aggressive tendencies is concerned with the preservation of the object representations in the superego. The passively directed libido components play no role in the mechanism of superego formation. Their sexual aim is abandoned, but the real objects are retained, although tenderness replaces sexual interest. Great dependence upon the object persists, since the intensity of the desexualized relationship is still very strong. The aggression which has been turned inward, fixated by portions of repressed libido, gives rise to secondary masochism, which may lead to conscious or unconscious masochistic fantasies and behavior. It is precisely in such feminine personalities that the fear of loss of love plays an important role and brings about an extreme dependence upon the object. This condition makes the emancipation from the parents in later years difficult and threatens the achievement of independence.

What happens in the process of superego formation in the case of the little girl? The essential similarity of her first preoedipal period of development to that of the boy allows the assumption of a certain parallelism in the formation of the superego precursors. However, her oedipus complex, which is directly responsible for the formation of the superego, differs greatly from that of the boy. The positive oedipal situation, in which the girl loves her father passively and hates her mother as a rival, occurs only when the negative oedipus complex (love for the mother and hatred toward the father as a rival) is given up. This renunciation takes place by virtue of hostility toward the mother, and by an increase of passivity and strong repression of masculinity. Let us assume for a moment that this process in the little girl was completely successful and that all sexual strivings had been directed into paths of femininity, or that she was originally endowed with merely passive strivings. Experience proves that the girl, too, must give up the oedipus complex. Her motives for doing so are different from those of the boy, whose main narcissistic motive is the preservation of the penis. However, fear of losing love and other possible dangers from the outside as well as from inner drive constellations prevail upon the little girl to renounce her sexual oedipal wishes, and she gradually converts her feelings into tender, aim-inhibited ones. Secondary masochism, which had already arisen in the process of subordinating her activity to passivity, is now increased by the repressed portions of libido which ally themselves with the aggressive tendencies directed against her own person. Accordingly there arises a passive, tender object dependence with strong masochistic fantasies which may be either conscious or unconscious. Since we have assumed that in this case activity is lacking altogether, the process is herewith finished. In

45

the case of a theoretically purely feminine, completely passive woman, superego formation does not occur.

However, this course of events practically never occurs in real life. There are no people without a bisexual Anlage, a fact which is of much greater significance to women than to men, because subordination of active libido to passively directed tendencies never completely succeeds. Even where complete femininity in love life is achieved, more or less vigorous active tendencies are demonstrable. We have already seen that maternity requires the use of active tendencies. It becomes clear, then, that the little girl, in giving up the oedipus complex, also forms a superego. The girl, like the boy, utilizes activity, that is, her "masculinity," to accomplish this process. This may be the reason why the female's superego resembles more closely that of a feminine man than that of a markedly masculine man. The little girl also has a double oedipus complex to overcome. She introjects both parental object images, and the superego receives a double character, rendering it less powerful, unified, and imperative. These peculiarities are also favored by the circumstance that the little girl only gradually renounces her oedipal wishes and achieves superego formation slowly and less completely than the boy. It is no wonder that the superego of the woman usually allows her less significant social and cultural achievements than the man. On the other hand, it is not surprising that the complexity of the early instinctual development of the little girl and the formation of her feminine oedipus complex cause the later development of the woman, as well as her superego formation, to show the greatest variations and differences of character. I shall attempt to describe some of the varieties in subsequent chapters.

CHAPTER 3

Review of "Fear of Castration in Women," by Sandor Rado

(1934)

Rado's work is worth our attention for three reasons: (1) it is a contribution to the developmental history of women; (2) it proposes a new theory of anxiety; and (3) it tries to establish a new general theory of the neuroses.

It seems to be difficult to do justice to a work which touches upon such comprehensive problems. However, we may find relief in the facts first, that, Rado presents his theories of anxiety and neuroses in connection with his conception of the little girl's development, and second, that a single vicissitude of the instinctual drives, namely masochism, is considered to be the cornerstone of all three hypotheses. Psychoanalysis has never underestimated the significance of masochism in human psychic life. Freud pointed out repeatedly that masochism has a particular relation to feminity, and therefore plays an important role in female development as well as in those phenomena in male mental life which are based on passive-feminine tendencies. Furthermore, we must pay due attention to masochism because it may reveal itself in a perversion and in a general kind of behavior in life which Freud called

Rado's essay was first published in *Psychoanalytic Quarterly*, 2:425-475, 1933. This work was subsequently published in German as *Die Kastrationsangst des Weibes* (Vienna: Internationaler Psychoanalytischer Verlag, 1934). Though the original review was based on the German edition, the quotations are taken from the English 1933 edition.

moral masochism. Analytic therapy convinces us time and again of the intensity of masochistic drive processes and of the difficulty of influencing them. We certainly have to give Rado credit for having drawn attention to these phenomena once again. Many of his delineations of female neuroses (phobia and anxiety hysteria), of character peculiarities of women, of expressions of the masculinity complex are very impressive, colorful, and stimulating. The simplicity of his theory of anxiety is highly attractive. However, if we consider the complexity of mental events, the many and various factors causing inner and outer conflicts, we feel somewhat surprised at an attempt to hold one single process, the ego's struggle against masochism, responsible for all these phenomena.

We shall follow Rado's statements in detail. To begin with, we shall examine his theory of the development of the little girl toward femininity. The title of the work does not seem to be very appropriate since Rado confirms Freud's finding that women cannot experience real castration anxiety, being already "castrated" and therefore not exposed to the danger of castration. Thus, the female's anxieties, though sometimes resembling the male's castration fear in some way or other, should be termed differently. This, however, is of only secondary importance.

In Rado's Introduction to his work, he confirms Freud's discovery that penis envy is in the center of the feminine castration complex. Further on Rado looks for an explanation of the female's anxieties about being damaged, which according to clinical experience, are connected with the castration complex but which cannot be understood through the existence of penis envy. In the first chapter Rado tries to solve this problem in the following way: he suggests that the little girl, after having discovered that other human beings possess a penis of which she is envious, "hallucinates" this organ as being part of her own body and genital. This hallucinated organ is called an "illusory penis" by Rado. He assumes this hallucination will be soon corrected. However, this done, the illusory penis is set up anew on another part of the body. The female's "castration anxiety" therefore should be a fear of losing this "illusory penis" or its "symbolic substitute." Here the first objection arises. Psychoanalysis has good reasons to assume that the infant hallucinates satisfaction whenever he is exposed to need tensions. However, a little child of three to six years old is not likely to hallucinate a body organ, even if he has first dreamed of having it. Furthermore, observations on little girls contradict this. Rado states explicitly that he himself has not made any observations in this connection. It is true that a little girl can produce a strong wish for a penis. She may imagine and play that she possesses a male organ. In later years fantasies of having a penis can be uncovered and brought to consciousness during the analysis of dreams and, for instance, neurotic symptoms of hysterical patients. However, we do not encounter Rado's construction of a "hallucinatory illusory penis." Freud's discovery that little girls may produce a strong wish for a penis, which incidentally may be retained in the unconscious for any length of time, seems to explain the observed facts sufficiently.

In the second chapter, Rado looks for a solution of the economic problem of these processes. He believes that his hypothesis of the "illusory penis" describes them, to be sure, but that it does not explain their dynamics. At this point Rado turns to his theory of "trauma." He says: " . . . the anatomical experience was for these girls [who later on are "plagued . . . by castration fantasies"] a psychic trauma. On perceiving the penis they lost self-esteem, suffered a severe emotional upset—and the sanguinary fantasies of castration appeared as a consequence of this narcissistic shock" (pp. 432-433). He continues: "The little girl suddenly catches sight of a penis. She is startled and fascinated. . . . From her emotional chaos emerges the strident desire: 'I want it!' which is followed immediately in fantasy by, 'I have it'. Then comes the humiliating reflection, 'But I haven't';—this knowledge produces severe psychic pain, and terminates in something like a paralyis of feeling" (p. 433).

And still further: "The narcissistic shock at once inhibits the girl's actively directed desire for gratification, which up to this time was discharged in masturbation. But the intense mental pain which she experienced excited her sexually and supplied her with a 'substitutive gratification'. This emotional experience teaches her that she may obtain a new pleasure in place of the one that was destroyed by the traumatic event—passive pleasure in pain" (pp. 433-434).

49

According to Rado, we must assume that a traumatic experience produces a shock which causes a sudden renunciation of actively directed masturbation and the replacement of a libidinal satisfaction by a masochistic one.

During the discussion of Rado's work in the Vienna Psychoanalytic Society, one of the discussants drew attention to the fact that a trauma theory can be controlled. Though the author, in his Introduction, promises to prove his statements with observational experiences, he now admits the lack of material gained in observations of children. His theory was developed from a combination of watching children's reactions to "innocuous experiences that astonish children or bring them disillusion," impressions gained from them "through empathy," and conclusions drawn from analyses of adults (p. 433). Therefore the author could not produce direct proof of his trauma theory. The Viennese child analysts, in the just mentioned discussion, declared that neither of them had at any time observed the course of development described by Rado. Moreover, analyses of women reveal different outcomes. Reactions of little girls on the observation of the anatomical sex difference vary. However, it very often occurs that a little girl does not give up masturbation after she has discovered the existence of the male organ. In those cases she continues to masturbate with strong opposition, rage, and tenacity; she clings to actively directed desires and their satisfaction; she may hold to the fantasy that a penis will grow on her sometime or other. Only very gradually will she finally give up this position. A variety of factors is responsible for this: for instance, a strong demand from outside, an ever-increasing disappointment in the mother, an inner dissatisfaction with her "inferior" genital, perhaps a fear of the intensity of her own rage and hate, and maybe also other still unknown factors. But time and again it has been confirmed that little girls usually have to go through a long and difficult struggle before they are able to part from their active position and to adopt finally their passive role.

Sometimes, in normal cases, the development toward femininity will run a much easier course. However, in just such cases as described by Rado, in which hysterical symptoms, severe anxieties, and masculine character deformities occur, the active sexual strivings are only abandoned after a long and hard struggle, and one does not observe an "erotogenic masochism" becoming operative as a surrogate for masturbatory libidinal pleasure. It may happen in some little girls that masochism plays an important role in fantasies or in a neurosis. We have already given Rado credit for having described this process in various neurotic disorders in a beautiful way. The origin of these masochistic fantasies and behavior was recorded by Freud some time ago and has been presented by Helene Deutsch in many convincing observations. A little girl with a strong wish for a penis produces intense aggressive impulses, strong feelings of hate and rage, which reach a peak when she can no longer deny her own "inferior" organ and therefore has to give up her activity. If she has finally accepted her passive feminine role, she cannot get rid of her aggression in the outer world and has to turn it toward her own person. The turning inward of aggression coincides approximately with another process, namely the structuration of a part of the mind into ego and superego, with the consequence that the superego incorporates the aggression. A sadistic superego evolves and the ego becomes masochistically shaped.

Rado does not mention these processes, which are of paramount importance in understanding neurotic disorders. This secondary masochism is based on the original erotogenic form of masochism, the latter possibly providing the personality with its masochistic attitude. That is all we can say about erotogenic masochism in this connection.

The core of Rado's train of thought is the following idea: If drive satisfaction is interrupted, masochistic pleasure gain immediately comes to the fore as a substitute. The same process is the base of his theory of anxiety and of his theory of neurosis as well. One gains the impression that the theory of anxiety was the first to be developed and only later on transferred to the neuroses of women. However, Rado promised to study the latter in observations, with which unfortunately we are not presented.

As we have to discard the author's theory of masochistic deformation of the genital drive as the immediate consequence of the upsetting discovery of a penis, we cannot at the same time accept his concept of an "illusory penis" as a reaction formation against the shock, as a "phallic complementation" in the service of the defense against masochism. In the last decade we have learned a good deal about a little girl's early develop-ment. The study of the preoedipal phase has revealed an intense and rich mother relationship long before the little girl enters the oedipal situation. In connection with man's bisexual disposition, drives with passive as well as with active aims come to the fore during the preoedipal phase (the oral, anal, and phallic stages of development). In the phallic period of the preoedipal phase, penis envy and a wish for a penis are of great significance and especially strong in little girls with a clear bisexual disposition (masculinity). The little girl's wish for a penis is a "pri-mary" one, stimulated by active drive tendencies. It exists long before she turns toward the father in passive surrender, and even earlier than masochism is found to play a role in her fantasy life or in a neurosis. It goes without saying that in later times (in latency and adolescence) the original wish for a penis can be reawakened, especially in those girls who have suffered severe disappointments from the father, spoil-ing her female role and throwing her back into the earlier active posi-tion. The power of these secondary reactive processes should not be underestimated. However, they are built upon the earlier preoedipal experiences and draw their force from them.

Rado does not mention Freud's latest findings, laid down in his paper "Female Sexuality" (1931b), which appeared two years before Rado's work. Where Rado considers recent literature, he refers only to details and presents them in a distorted manner. I cite Rado (p. 460): "I do not share the view of those writers that *the little girl at first feels as a boy does*, directing her 'phallic' genital impulses to her mother, and passing through a 'negative oedipus complex' in a *genital* sense be-fore she begins her female genital career" (italics added). Indeed, one could stress the improbability of a little boy's feeling himself to be a girl from the very start as well. Children of both sexes develop im-pulses with active as well as with passive aims directed to the mother in analogous ways though with individually different intensities. The sex difference is originally unknown to boys and girls. Therefore those desires do not include a wish to belong to the other sex. Children of both sexes desire to be loved by the mother and to love and to possess her. When Rado relates a dream in which a woman dreams of having sexual intercourse with her mother, he is quite right in his assertion that the dream represents a wish of a later period. In *this shape* a desire to possess the mother can only come into existence after the person has learned about the nature of sexual intercourse. The desire itself stems from earlier times and is shaped in accordance with the infantile psychic representations present in infants of both sexes. Little boys and little girls have no knowledge of the existence of a vagina, and their fantasies of possessing the mother are born out of their fantasies about the adults' being together. These fantasies may vary, for instance, from mutual masturbation or mutual urinating to fantasies of urinating into the mouth or the anus, to other bodily contacts, to sadistic scenes, etc. In any case, observation has taught us that the little girl's wish for a penis and her demand that the mother must present her with it have already entered into her desires and ideas in the preoedipal phase. The same is valid for her aggression, hate, and rage, which are reactions to her final disappointment. In his dream example Rado does not present us with historical data about the woman's childhood. His attempt to use this material to prove his theories of femininity, of masochistic deformation of the genital drive, and of the "illusory penis" is therefore not convincing. His explanation of the dream is based upon these theories and thus cannot be used to prove them.

There seems to be a similar misunderstanding in Rado's rejection of Freud's term "phallic phase" (p. 434). This term does *not* apply to the idea of a little girl's already differentiating between male and female. On the contrary, it means that both boys and girls do *not* have any knowledge of the female organ and that their sexual activites take place almost exclusively on the phallic organs, penis and clitoris (sometimes labia and vulva). Rado's suggestion that the term "phallic phase" be replaced by "amorphous genital phase of the ego" (p. 434) seems to be superfluous and confusing.

One more point about Rado's conception of femininity should be considered. According to him, a pathological, masochistically deformed femininity develops if the discovery of the penis takes place in a period of masturbation and thus has a traumatic result. Normal femininity should emerge whenever the discovery of the penis coincides with a period of "genital latency." The simplicity of this theory is tempting.

However, the complexity of the preoedipal mother attachment reveals to us how manifold are the fixation points of the drives in this period, causing a variety of starting points for neurotic reactions. Furthermore, we know that a seemingly uneventful experience in infancy can give rise to a traumatic reaction in later periods. The little girl's discovery of a penis may be without consequence at the time, whereas later on many disturbances may develop as an afterreaction without the girl's having had the opportunity of observing the male organ again. The moment of penis observation does not seem to be decisive.

We now turn our attention to Rado's theory of anxiety in the fourth chapter. The author attempts to fill a gap in Freud's theory of anxiety. In his first theory, Freud assumed that anxiety emerges from the suppression of a libidinal impulse the energy of which is discharged in anxiety. The later hypothesis reads that this kind of discharge may take place in a traumatic situation (as a breaking of the stimulus barrier), that, however, later on anxiety is used as a signal for the ego in order to take action upon a danger situation. In this case it is no longer of importance where the energy for the signal comes from. Rado, however, prefers to hold to the first theory and believes that anxiety is exclusively derived from masochistic instinctual drives. He argues in the following way: The ego itself is not the place where anxiety originates. Even language assigns the active role to anxiety and the passive one to the ego, because we say "we are beset, attacked, overcome, overwhelmed, or shaken by ... anxiety" (p. 454). Here Rado neglects the fact that we often say "I am anxious." Furthermore, the author says that anxiety produces a constriction of breathing followed by a remedial acceleration of the heart (p. 455). Many physiologists, however, have observed that anxiety may equally frequently give rise to acceleration of breathing without "remedial" action of the heart. Rado's idea that the nucleus of the experience of anxiety is a paralysis caused by masochism (p. 455) is in contradiction to the opinion of physiologists as well as of psychologists. In the beginning anxiety does not have a paralyzing effect, it first leads to a mobilization of energies (see Freud, 1926). The latter promotes activity aiming at an attempt to fly in order to escape a danger situation. Masochism is not involved in this process. In cases of "anxiety paralysis" a second danger is added to the original one. It may be that here Rado's train of thought becomes valuable. This second danger could be a masochistic one. In a footnote in *Inhibitions, Symptoms and Anxiety* (1926, p. 168), which Rado uses without citing it, Freud writes:

> It may quite often happen that although a danger-situation is correctly estimated in itself, a certain amount of instinctual anxiety is added to the realistic anxiety. In that case the instinctual demand before whose satisfaction the ego recoils is a masochistic one: the instinct of destruction directed against the subject himself. Perhaps an addition of this kind explains cases in which reactions of anxiety are exaggerated, inexpedient, or paralysing. Phobias of heights (windows, towers, precipices and so on) may have some such origin. Their hidden feminine significance is closely connected with masochism.

These sentences comprise the essence of the psychic processes involved. It is the *additional* masochism which has a paralyzing effect in anxiety states. The hypothesis that anxiety (and signal anxiety) is masochism cannot be affirmed. Another of Rado's ideas, that anxiety in the so-called "actual neuroses" should be masochism because every suppression of genital excitation, each "Inhibition of a pleasure-giving activity is always reacted to by an unleashing of masochism" (p. 456), runs parallel to his theory of the traumatic shock-producing effect of the penis observation in little girls. Both hypotheses must be rejected in regard to the psychic events as observed. A similar motive is made use of in Rado's bioanalytic speculation on the phylogenesis of signal anxiety. According to him, an injury of a primitive creature "restricts the animal's freedom of motion, lessens or frustrates his pleasure-giving acts, and thus compels the pleasure function to turn to pain-pleasure. In other words, the wound is elaborated masochistically by the ego" (p. 457). One of the participants in the above-mentioned discussion in Vienna suggested that if every restriction of freedom of action caused masochistic self-damaging reactions in living beings, the living world would have been reduced to an inorganic world millions of years ago.

We now come to Rado's theory of neuroses. We have already mentioned Freud's view that masochism plays a role in height phobias.

However, this form of masochism is the secondary one, the result of inwardly turned destructive tendencies, playing a role in various neuroses. It can finally become dangerous and has to be warded off. However, the original danger situation, which may raise anxiety, defensive processes, and sometimes a neurotic disposition, is a real one (see Freud, 1933). One of the earliest real dangers is the danger of losing the love object (or its love). This danger continues to exist in females. In analytic treatment we invariably discover at the bottom of the so-called "castration anxieties" in women just this fear of losing love. In later life this fear may be colored and reshaped in (unconscious) fantasies in which the wish for a penis and its derivatives may in fact play a role. Similar fantasies may enter into hysterical conversion symptoms as well. Rado's descriptions of female neuroses and character deformations under the influence of the masculinity complex are interesting. However, in tracing back every symptom and every character formation to the sole influence of the masochistic deformation of the genital drive and the reactive "illusory penis," he is simplifying and distorting the observed material.

In the section on "The Choice of the Lesser Evil," Rado elaborates on physical as well as psychic self-damage, which he attributes solely to masochistic action. However, he forgets about self-destruction. Masochism is destruction bound by libido. In actual self-injuries a defusion of libido and destruction has occurred prior to the deed, and this Rado does not mention. Masochism indeed plays an important role in male neuroses and in passive-feminine tendencies in men. However, observations do *not* permit us to accept Rado's two final theses, that (1) "the danger from the masochistic genital instinct . . . determine[s] the pathogenicity of the oedipus conflicts and hence ... health or neurosis" (p. 473), and (2) "the basic phenomenon of a neurosis is the deformation of the ego-inherent genital impulse into ego-adverse genital masochism" (p. 475).

Neuroses are not the outcome of a struggle between a reduced personality and a single drive impulse. I cite the last sentences of Freud's "Libidinal Types":

It is a familiar fact that the aetiological preconditions of neurosis are not yet known. The precipitating causes of it are frustrations and internal conflicts: conflicts between the three major psychical agencies, conflicts arising within the libidinal economy in consequence of our bisexual disposition and conflicts between the erotic and the aggressive instinctual components. It is the endeavour of the psychology of the neuroses to discover what makes these processes, which belong to the normal course of mental life, become pathogenic [1931a, p. 220].

Rado's simplified theory neglects all of these inner conflicts as well as the significance of the frustrations the helpless and dependent little child suffers from the environment.

In *Inhibitions, Symptoms and Anxiety* (1926, pp. 152-153), Freud says:

It is to be feared that our need to find a single, tangible 'ultimate cause' of neurotic illness will remain unsatisfied. The ideal solution, which medical men no doubt still yearn for, would be to discover some bacillus which could be isolated and bred in a pure culture and which, when injected into anyone, would invariably produce the same illness; or, to put it rather less extravagantly, to demonstrate the existence of certain chemical substances the administration of which would bring about or cure particular neuroses. But the probability of a solution of this kind seems slight. Psycho-analysis leads to less simple and satisfactory conclusions.

Apparently, Rado's hypotheses do not provide us with the desired solution either.

CHAPTER 4

Inhibition and Narcissism

(1936)

The starting point of this paper is the investigation of a mental process which, though well known, is of general importance and perhaps occurs regularly. I would formulate this psychic process as follows:

A number of mental processes with different and sometimes opposite goals can run a course that finally leads to identical results. This means that they bring about similar conditions in ego organization. We can study these processes by examining the genesis of neurotic inhibitions, which represent restrictions of ego functions. We may then discover that in one patient a certain inhibition is the result of special instinctual processes, whereas in a second patient it is caused by just the opposite course of the drives involved. I will give some illustrations, but before doing so, I want to state explicitly that the similar outcomes in ego organization are reached in the most different ways. I will not go into these intermediate events for the time being.

THE CONNECTION BETWEEN NEUROTIC WORK INHIBITIONS AND MASTURBATION[1]

Psychoanalysis showed very early that work and learning inhibitions often originate in masturbatory processes. If a patient masturbates ex-

---

[1] I presented a paper on this theme at the Thirteenth Congress of the International Psycho-Analytical Association, Lucerne, August 31, 1934.

cessively, the phenomenon is not so difficult to explain: most of his psychic energy is being used for masturbatory satisfaction and there is not enough left for other activities. His work inhibition, a curtailment of ego achievements, is a direct consequence of the masturbatory activity. An additional factor can be derived from the accompanying guilt feelings, which demand self-punishment in the shape of inhibition of functioning. It is basically masturbation, with its accompanying psychic phenomena, which causes the neurotic inhibitions.

The analyses of adolescents and adults demonstrate that excessive masturbatory activity has a previous history in infantile masturbation, which was usually very intense as well. In the struggle against it the little child had achieved no success, or only a partial or temporary one. The excessive masturbation of adolescents is usually a direct continuation or a repetition of a childhood period in which drive tensions found discharge in masturbatory activities.

In these cases the analyst is satisfied if the analysis succeeds in freeing the patient of his excessive masturbation with the accompanying guilt feelings, thus providing him with the necessary forces and energy to remove his work inhibition. As such cases are well known to every analyst, a more detailed description of the processes is superfluous.

However, I want to single out another group of patients suffering from work inhibitions who do not masturbate at all. These patients usually report that they cannot remember having masturbated at any period of life, or, if they did so, it was merely occasionally and of very short duration. However, a prolonged analysis reveals, with great regularity in my experience, a quite different picture. It gradually becomes clear that in early childhood these patients went through a period of intense masturbatory activity that was suppressed and completely abandoned, usually after a long and hard struggle. Such struggles occur within the personality between ego and id. In the first-mentioned patients, who have continued masturbation either without or with short interruptions, the id has gained victory. In the last-mentioned cases the ego has proved to be the stronger. However, it had to pay for its triumph with the same curtailment that brought about its defeat in the first-mentioned group of patients. In both groups the ego has become inhibited in its functions.

59

Case 1

The significance of this connection strongly impressed me in the analysis of an intelligent young girl suffering from a work inhibition. The patient could not remember having masturbated at any time in her life. The analysis revealed that as a little girl she had gone through a period of intense, passionate masturbation that lasted until her seventh year. This period came to an end with a complete suppression of masturbatory activities, accomplished without any help or interference from the environment. The little girl took great pride in this achievement. However, in later years the proud satisfaction was nullified by a tormenting work inhibition. A long and laborious analysis brought little relief until the moment when the patient became able to resume masturbating. This occurred only after certain connections, of which I will speak later, had been uncovered in the treatment. From this moment on, a significant release of energy and fading away of her inhibition occurred. I will report later on the causes of the rigorous suppression of the masturbation in childhood. I now want to summarize a tentative conclusion:

Disturbances of ego functions (for instance, work inhibitions) can be the result of an unsuccessful struggle against masturbation as well as of its successful suppression. In other words, the struggle between ego and id for masturbatory discharge of libidinal tensions may cause identical outcomes in ego organization whether the ego was victorious or was defeated. This is in accordance with our former statement that opposing courses of psychic processes can lead to identical results in ego organization.

OUTCOMES OF SATISFACTION AND OF FRUSTRATION OF DEMANDS FOR LOVE

The fact that opposite vicissitudes of the child's libidinal demands made upon the object may lead to similar situations in ego organization is more generally known.

The little child who has undergone a very rigorous training in cleanliness whose anal libidinal and aggressive tendencies have received insufficient satisfaction, may acquire a developmental disturbance. His ego is unable to master his drive demands sufficiently and he falls ill with a neurosis. However, the child who was subject to overindulgence, whose every wish for tenderness was satisfied, whose aggressive impulses could be acted out to a great extent, is also likely to acquire a neurosis. Both situations—too much gratification as well as undue suppression of drive needs—may lead to similar ego disturbances. The ego, then, has to put up with a neurotic distortion. Here, too, we encounter the same outcomes of drive demands. However, we must not overlook a difference between the two examples described above. The patient suffering from a work inhibition gave up masturbation in consequence of an inner process, without aid from the outside. In the second example, the suppression of drive demands was the result of an educational measure, an influence of the environment. However, the difference is lessened by the fact that the neurosis of the rigorously educated child usually comes to the fore only at an age when the prohibitions and demands from outside are already internalized. This means that the repression of anal tendencies has already been accomplished by the ego and superego. On the other hand, even in cases where masturbation is given up without support from outside, past experiences conceived as a prohibition of masturbation always play a role.

The patient who ended her masturbation struggle alone, with a victorious result, had never received direct prohibitions. However, she remembered being put to bed by her mother as a very little child dressed in pajamas. Though at that time she had not yet stopped masturbating, the analysis revealed that afterward, in the period of her struggle against masturbation, the patient took her mother's dressing her in pajamas as a signal of an interdiction.

Apparently it is of great significance for further ego development whether the decisive struggle to give up masturbation occurs with or without help from outside. I shall return to this point in later attempts at clarification. I now turn to another restriction of an ego function.

Potency Disturbance as an Inhibition Due to Different Outcomes of Drive Tendencies

Case 2

A young man, aged thirty, had been suffering from impotence for approximately ten years. There had been a very short period during which he seemed to have been potent. The patient suffered from a compulsion to look for perverse relations with prostitutes of an out-spoken, manly type. His attitude toward these women was gentle, loving, indulging, but desperate at the same time. The analysis revealed that the strong castration anxiety hidden behind his impotence which allowed him only masturbatory and perverse satisfaction was in fact a fear of retaliation. In every encounter, powerful aggressive tendencies against women were unconsciously mobilized and the patient feared punishment through castration during coitus. The prehistory of these aggressive impulses was to be found in his early childhood when they were directed toward his parents, who had subjected the child to a very severe education. The tantrums of the little boy gradually acquired the significance of a love scene and so served as a discharge of libidinal tendencies as well. The suppression of his rage became identical with a giving up of his sexual wishes. Afterward, the passive homosexual attitude, the strength of which was also a consequence of the castration anxiety, played an important role.

However, the successful suppression of the fused aggressive and libidinal impulses had to be paid for by the ego with a functional disturbance of the patient's sexual life. After he had recognized these connections, the patient expressed the idea that he would be potent if he succeeded in behaving energetically and even violently toward a woman, some time or other. In a certain phase of his analysis such a situation suddenly occurred. One evening the irritating attitude of his woman friend provoked violent rage in the patient. He allowed himself to express it. He flew into a tantrum; he raged and it came to blows and violence. Afterward he felt immensely relieved and freed; he was proud and content and convinced of his manly potency. The patient tried to have intercourse. However, he was still impotent, which surprised and horrified him at the same time.

We understood that the last occurrence, the acting out of the patient's aggressive sexual impulses, could not be tolerated without impairment of function. Only a gradual working through of the analytic material was able to bring about a kind of regulation of the discharge of drive energy which allowed this severely neurotic patient to regain some potency from time to time and in special circumstances which will not be discussed.

In this case we observe again that opposite vicissitudes of drive impulses may lead to similar functional disturbances, even in the same person.

ATTEMPTS AT CLARIFICATIONS

The Problem of Quantity

We will now try to learn something about the nature of these processes through comparison of the similarities and differences in the examples mentioned. We will not go further into the fact that in some cases we have to do with a restriction of an ego function (work inhibition, potency disturbance) and in other cases with a neurotic disorder of the personality as the final outcome. A neurosis, too, starts with the restriction of a normal ego capacity as a consequence of the necessity to ward off a drive impulse. On the other hand, an inhibition may initiate a neurotic symptom as well. For our purpose it is not important whether a simple curtailment of the ego emerges or whether the process leads to a compromise between ego and id and to the formation of neurotic symptoms.

We have already stated that the unrestrained expression of drive impulses can cause an ego disturbance. The same disturbance can be the result of the prevention of drive discharge. In other words, we get the impression that there must be a situation in which the influence of a drive impulse upon the ego leads to an optimal effect. We may see a parallel to the influence of certain drugs upon the body. We know that small quantities of certain medicines and chemicals may stimulate certain bodily functions, whereas larger quantities can bring about a paralysis or even a complete cessation of the same functions. It seems likely that in the problem of psychic processes we also encounter a question of quantity, of intensity. It is decisive for the ego what intensity of an id impulse is satisfied.

The discharged quantity is in itself dependent upon different factors, in the first place upon the absolute intensity of the drives, in the second place upon the opportunities given for a satisfactory discharge. The latter are determined by several factors; the environment as well as the inner conditions of the personality, the relative strength or weakness of ego and superego vis-à-vis the drive impulse, are decisive here. So in the final instance we are dealing with questions of (relative) quantities.

The problems of quantity seem to open a wide and very important field for research. They seem to play a predominant role in the understanding of mental processes.[2]

Unfortunately, this knowledge does not carry us far for the moment. We do not have at our disposal any means of measuring drive intensities.[3] For the time being we have to content ourselves with observation and description of the processes and with an assessment of the relations between the various forces *post factum*. In analytic work we always feel it to be an impediment that we cannot determine intensities and that we have to limit ourselves to impressions and estimations (valuations). We have already observed that abundant masturbatory discharge of drive intensities may lead to a work inhibition, because it can influence certain ego functions in a "toxic" way. However, this knowledge does not permit us to expect the lack of an inhibition where no masturbation took place. The patient with the work inhibition showed us that an excess of suppression of a drive impulse has the same paralyzing influence on ego capacities. We cannot yet decide where and when and with which quantitative relations between drives and ego demands an optimum of activities and freedom of the ego can come about. In our male patient, the severe suppression of his aggressive sexual impulses as well as their abundant discharge (which took place later on) caused a potency disturbance. It was impossible to decide beforehand which quantities had to be discharged in order to enable his ego to dispose freely of his potency. In analytic work, which aims at liberation of the ego functions, one is often impressed by the observation that mastery of drive processes, already made conscious, is a matter of the relation between id strength and ego strength. Apart from its significance for psychoanalytic practice, this aspect is of great importance for the study of child development and education.

Some decades ago Freud (1905c) pointed out that severe spoiling of a child as well as severe suppression of drive impulses can cause neuroses.

[2] L. Eidelberg (1935) develops interesting ideas in discussing the problem of quantity in the theory of neurosis. However, his ideas scarcely touch upon the questions put forward here.
[3] Bernfeld's interesting attempt to establish a "libido metrics" has not so far provided us with workable results.

Anna Freud warned explicitly against the danger in psychoanalytically oriented education of concluding from analytic findings that a child could be protected from developmental disturbances by avoiding prohibitions and demands. She pointed out that too much indulgence may cause neurotic and character disturbances in the little child. Analytic pedagogy had to take refuge in a compromise and advised the educators to choose a middle path between indulgence and frustration. In this endeavor, however, it meets with the same limitations as did the psychoanalyst, namely, with the impossibility of measuring quantities. In education it is equally difficult to assess the intensity of the drive impulse which is to be allowed satisfaction or prevented from discharge. Consequently it is impossible to predict the outcome of an educational measure in a satisfactory way. Only the result teaches us something about the processes involved.

Waelder[4] proposed a very fine and correct formulation, namely, that education has to maintain "a maximum of love and a maximum of burdening of the child's ego." However, it is very limited in its practical consequences. How can we determine the maximum of love and the maximum of deprivation which the child is able to endure without impairment? We can never know beforehand, and every educator has encountered many difficulties and is aware of how often our expectations have proved to be erroneous.

Summarizing, we may say: Analytic experience teaches us that the intensity of a drive impulse is highly important in its effect upon ego functions. We assume that an unmeasurable intensity (quantity) arouses an optimal result in ego functioning. Both more and less bring about disturbances or paralyses of the ego. It is a question not of absolute but of relative quantities, of the relation between ego strength and drive intensity. We do not forget that "strength" and "weakness" of the ego, too, are unmeasurable concepts and that they are meaningful only in relation to other factors and agencies. A "less" of drive intensity does not imply an absolute drive weakness; it may mean that only a small quantity is discharged.

With our girl patient, mentioned above, the ego was in a certain respect stronger than the id because it was able to prevent the drive

[4] Read at the Vierländertagung in Vienna, 1935.

discharge, to repress. However, the ego revealed its weakness vis-à-vis the id in so far as it had to tolerate the work inhibition. It will be clear that in an opposite case, where there is a great deal of masturbation, the inability to master drive impulses points to a primary relative ego weakness versus drive quantities.

A related problem seems to be worth mentioning here: what is the reaction of an already-constituted ego organization upon an increase of drive intensity? Such events occur in normal circumstances, for instance, in puberty, in menopause, and perhaps in other periods of life, as a consequence of bodily processes or certain pharmacological influences. We know very little about these events, so we can only put forward some assumptions. We are acquainted with the observation that in puberty and menopause an augmentation of drive intensity leads to changes in ego organization.

Anna Freud (1936) described some modes of behavior in adolescents, for instance, an oscillation between complete asceticism (not only in sexual life, but also in regard to every enjoyment of life) and dissolute self-indulgence, which she explains by a similar increase of drive quantities. In the menopause an intensifying of drive demands can cause a violent change of behavior in a normal person. It may also be responsible for the fact that during those periods of life neurosis or psychosis tend to break out and already-existing mental disorders are worsened. The ego has to react toward the intensified impulses either with more indulgence at the cost of distortions of the personality, or with a stronger defense which may lead to the outbreak of a mental disease. The aspect of drive quantities seems to be of significance in the explanation of slight psychotic states which may emerge out of "health" or on the base of a neurosis without any demonstrable precipitation from outside. The analyst is acquainted with cases in which after a prolonged analysis a hidden psychotic mechanism suddenly comes to the fore. These are usually paranoid mechanisms. One gets the impression that the analytic work has loosened the repression and liberated a certain amount of drive energy that the ego cannot manage at that moment. The former way of repressing is no longer open and so the ego is overwhelmed by the drive impulses. It has to choose a new tactic in turning against the outer world. The ego misinterprets the environ-

66

ment, for instance, by the mechanism of projection (as in a paranoid psychosis). In so far as this event is the result of a rapid and intensive influence of the analytic process, we may wait and expect the situation to be of short duration and not to spread outside of the analysis. In this case we are not dealing with a psychosis in a clinical sense.

However, I once observed a fifty-year-old woman, suffering from a hysterical neurosis, in whom a paranoid syndrome that came to the fore after two years of analysis and without an outer precipitation lasted much longer than usual. The patient produced an erotic delusion not restricted to the analytic situation and not completely soluble. Time and again the patient came back for an afteranalysis. A core of paranoid mechanisms continued to exist and the condition revived occasionally, though it never came into severe conflict with the outer world and the patient could maintain her position in society.

I think that in this case we are dealing with an intensification of the drives, in consequence of the menopause, which overwhelmed the ego and incapacitated it for healthy mastering as well as for neurotic repression. In such cases the analysis is sometimes able to take hold of the symptom and to ameliorate the situation even when it is unable to cure. Because of outer circumstances I could not follow the patient. Therefore I do not know whether the passing of the menopause brought about a change in her psychic situation or not. For the time being we cannot decide whether, in psychoses emerging in other periods when no physiological intensification of the drives occurs, we are also dealing with an increase of drive quantities, perhaps by somatic processes. It does not seem impossible. Rado (1926) and Simmel (1930) have discussed the effects of drugs upon the mental life, i.e., on addiction as well as on psychotic syndromes. Both authors present many important clarifications. They do not touch upon the problem of a possible increase of drives caused by drugs or of a "toxic" effect upon the ego.

We will now come back to our original theme and summarize our suppositions as follows: we assume that a given drive quantity exercises an optimal effect upon the ego organization when it is allowed discharge. A greater as well as a smaller quantity may cause a disturbance of ego functions. We do not forget that for the time being we are unable to measure the drive quantities.

Topographic Aspects

First I will recapitulate our observations, clarifications, and hypotheses brought forward so far.

We start with the relation of masturbation and work inhibition. It has already been mentioned that a person suffering from compulsive masturbation does not have enough libido (drive energy) available for other activities. This picture of ego paralysis does not change appreciably if the masturbatory act is replaced by conscious or unconscious fantasies. In addition to this simple explanation, we mentioned a second one concerning ego restriction through spoiling; i.e., overgratification of libidinal tendencies deprives the ego of every stimulus to activity. Freud repeatedly stated that the ego acquires impetus for higher cultural achievements through the tension of incompletely satisfied wishes. With overgratification this tension is lacking and therewith the stimulus to work as well. In the spoiled child still another factor is involved: the ego becomes fixated to the mode of overgratification, there is no more necessity for further development, a later emerging frustration encounters an unprepared ego, and an anxiety-provoking danger situation comes into existence. The latter, again, may lead to inhibition and neurosis.

If masturbation has become a symptom no longer sanctioned by ego or superego, the inhibition can be reinforced by anxiety and by a tendency toward self-punishment. Self-punishment may also occur if the individual has acted out aggressions to an extent intolerable to the superego.

In "*Inhibitions, Symptoms and Anxiety*" (1926) Freud explains a number of inhibitions of functions as being a punishment for sexual and aggressive impulses, which are *not* discharged in masturbation. In these cases the drive repression is the consequence of a superego demand. An inhibition can be the punishment for a carried-out masturbatory act as well as for a fantasied but repressed drive satisfaction. In other words, an inhibition caused by suppression of masturbation may be the expression of self-punishment, too.

The problem of quantities is complicated by one more factor. Until now, we have examined the relative drive intensity, that is, the relation of drive strength to ego strength. We have to add here the relation of ego forces and superego forces. Even if the ego is relatively strong vis-à-vis the id and successful in repression, a relative weakness vis-à-vis the superego may be able to compel the ego to renounce its function. In Freud's words, the ego foregoes its achievements *"in order to avoid coming into conflict with the super-ego"* (1926, p. 90). In the case of an erotization of function, the ego renounces its achievements *"in order to avoid a conflict with the id"* (1926, p. 90). However, the complication of the situation due to superego demands is less severe than it seemed to be at first sight, because the superego gets its severity from the id. The intensity of ego oppression by the superego is dependent upon the drive intensity. In summary: a relatively strong drive intensity (or a relative ego weakness) may inhibit ego functions. The way in which this happens is dependent on the topographical starting point. If the id is victorious in a direct way, "too much" drive discharge is observable. If the process makes a detour over the superego, we observe "too much" drive repression. A strong dependence on the superego has a prehistory in an extreme dependency on the objects and their love in early childhood. The little child's development, therefore, codetermines these processes. I shall come back to this point later. Freud described a second mechanism which leads to a general inhibition: the impoverishment of energy available to the ego. Here also two ways are possible: too much drive discharge (for instance, in frequent masturbation or in a fit of rage) deprives the ego of the energy necessary for work achievements; too intense repression of drive discharge (libido as well as aggression) demands so much ego energy that there is no more available for other activities. Here the same topographical aspect has to be applied. In the first instance, the starting point of the attack on the ego is the id; in the second instance it is the superego.

In the latter considerations we presupposed that the repression was demanded by the superego (with the little child, by the demands of the environment). In our analytic work we can often affirm this state of affairs. However, I think we sometimes meet with another complication. The superego (or its forerunner, the parental prohibitions) is not always the motor of repression.

In order to clarify this point I turn again to our girl patient with the work inhibition. I promised above to come back to the causes of the patient's complete renunciation of masturbation in her seventh year of life. I was able to learn of the following events. The patient did not remember any prohibition of masturbation. The analysis could not uncover one either. However, the attitude of the environment, the parents' secrecy regarding sexuality, had made the child feel that masturbation was something bad and prohibited. Her being dressed in pajamas had the same result. During treatment it became clear that these mild "prohibitions" were not sufficient to explain the child's desperate struggle against masturbation for such a lengthy period of time. After removal of guilt feelings and anxiety the masturbatory inhibition continued to exist. After prolonged analysis the deeper cause of this intense struggle emerged.

It proved to be the same motive which had led the little girl to renounce masturbation without any outside support, a motive described by Freud in "Female Sexuality" (1931b). It is the little girl's discontent with her own genital that brings about a devaluation of its function. In a number of analyses of female patients an inner animosity toward the genital because of the lack of a penis is found to be the ultimate cause for giving up masturbatory activities. It is always accompanied by feelings of inferiority. The analyst often gains the impression that an intense injury as a consequence of feeling incompetent paves the way for anxiety and guilt feelings.[5]

According to Freud, the little girl in this respect behaves like a wife who, being unfaithful to her husband, enjoys the happiness with her friend without feeling guilty as long as the relationship is undisturbed. The slightest disappointment, however, gives rise to severe guilt feelings. Analytic work reveals one more connection. In cases where the ego inhibitions were the result of suppression of masturbation in con-

---

[5] A personal remark of Freud's encourages me to point to a very often encountered fantasy of the little girl, i.e., "I was once in possession of a penis; however, I am deprived of it as a punishment for having masturbated." This fantasy is also encountered in cases where no direct castration threat was made. Many females cling to it tenaciously even after anxiety and guilt have been removed in analysis. The explanation is apparently that anxiety and guilt are easier to endure than the admission of being incompetent. A narcissistic injury seems much more difficult to master than the suffering of the masochistic fantasies of being castrated. Here we may perhaps find a way to a better understanding of the still unsolved problems of masochism.

sequence of feelings of incompetence, the inhibitions are more intense and much more difficult to remove than in cases where superego demands have caused the renunciation of masturbation. In the latter cases the superego can sometimes be softened and a therapeutic result can be achieved.

In our girl patient, anxiety and guilt could be removed. However, the work inhibition seemed to resist every therapeutic influence. Only after many years of analysis could the deeper cause for the giving up of masturbation, the discontent with the clitoris, be made conscious. The historical circumstances became clear at the same time. The little girl was extremely envious of a little boy playmate and refused to respond to his attempt to seduce her into sexual play. She was then present when other little girls gave in to him and our little patient repented and competed for his favor. However, the boy now refused her. Jealousy and hurt made her turn to a new period of frequent, stubborn, rebellious masturbation. This masturbatory period finally ended because of her strong penis envy. She felt she could never equal the little boy and so turned away from every masturbatory activity. In the unconscious the idea was maintained: "You cannot masturbate because you do not have a penis." Later on this notion was replaced by the following: "You cannot work because you do not have the real instrument for it." The uncovering of these ideas did not succeed in curing the patient of her work inhibition. During analysis she had to take up masturbation again after twenty years, though her female love life had already been restored and brought her satisfaction in an earlier analytic period. Only after she was able to experience a full orgasm through masturbation did her fantasy "You cannot work because you have no penis" disappear, and she became free to work.

In a number of cases such a result cannot be achieved, and the fusion of work inhibition with masturbatory incompetence proves to be unresolvable. Sometimes we can make an interesting observation in these cases. The little girl's reaction upon renouncing masturbation by her own efforts provokes a strong pride: "I have performed this grand achievement completely alone." This pride sometimes has grown into feelings of grandeur, which seem to make reparation and hide the "inferiority." It often alternates with depression and inferiority feelings. This

71

self-aggrandizement is of course nullified by the work inhibition in later times.

We may summarize: The drive repression leading to disturbances of ego functions is not always due to superego (or environmental) demands. In certain circumstances it can start from the ego, namely, if the process threatens the ego with a narcissistic injury. Again, the topographic aspect proves to be very important. Freud (1926) mentions two motives for the coming into being of inhibitions of ego functions: the ego's prudence which leads to avoiding (1) a conflict with the id and (2) a conflict with the superego. We now want to add a third one: (3) to avoid the confrontation with its own incompetence, which means, to avoid a disturbance of the narcissistic equilibrium. Especially in cases where the latter motive is present, a therapeutic influence is very tenaciously counteracted.

DISTURBANCES OF THE NARCISSISTIC EQUILIBRIUM

We must now face more questions. In our girl patient it was the narcissistic injury following her discovery of the lack of a penis which caused her masturbation inhibition and later on her work inhibition. The first question is: Is this state of affairs the individual fate of our patient, or is it a general occurrence? The second question is: Can we find similar connections between narcissistic injuries and inhibitions of function in men, and if so, what are those injuries?

The uncovering of the early infantile masturbation period in analysis is a laborious and difficult piece of work. Freud recently pointed to the importance of the details of the struggle between masturbatory impulses and defensive forces. The influence on ego development is different according to whether the struggle is successful or not, whether the suppression is the result of outer prohibitions or of inner motives, whether it takes place with or without support from outside, etc. These differences leave their marks in neurotic manifestations and especially in character formation. They can stamp adult love life as well.

There are still many uncertainties in this field just because the study of the details is so difficult. I was able to affirm Freud's discovery that in little girls the renunciation of masturbation is very often caused by their discontent with the clitoris. I also found in some cases that the inhibition of masturbation was the cause of a later work inhibition. Nevertheless, the observations are still too scarce, and the following tentative hypotheses are in need of further research. I have the impression, however, that, in women suffering from a variety of inhibitions, in the end we always come upon severe narcissistic injuries in connection with the lack of a penis. The struggle of the ego with drive impulses regularly touches upon it and it is decisive for the development of the personality. If the ego is victorious, an independent, active, and strong personality may develop. If the victory is only an incomplete one, an ego impairment may emerge. This damage may be limited to certain areas (for instance, work or sexual life) or it may appear only intermittently. In these cases, periods of free activity can alternate with periods of disturbances of functions accompanied by depressive moods. If the fight with the impulses is completely unsuccessful, a strong dependence of the ego on the id is to be expected. We most often encounter a compromise formation, especially if strong impulses and a considerable amount of activity (masculinity) are present. Of course we do not forget that the influence of the environment—prohibitions, etc.—plays an important role as well. However, as already mentioned, fear of the demands of the environment and guilt feelings are more easily removed in treatment.

We come now to the second question: What are the connections between inhibition of function and narcissistic injuries in men?

The comparison of the development of male and female children has taught us much about the similarities and differences between the sexes. Inhibitions in male patients are equally connected with sexual development and with the outcome of masturbation. Here we are interested in the cases in which an intensive suppression of it has led to disturbances. A comparison with female cases reveals first and foremost that they are less frequent in men. Freud mentioned that complete suppression of masturbation in adolescence occurs much more often in girls than in boys. Boys who are subject to strong castration anxiety, awakened either by threats from the environment or by observation of females, may renounce masturbatory activities, but usually less completely and for a shorter time than do girls. The little boy experiences castration as being a real danger. A little girl, showing anxieties which seem to be similar to a boy's, cannot take them as reality. Her anxieties are a reaction to her desire for a penis (which later on can become a masochistic desire to be castrated). So they are secondary factors for repression.

The difference between the processes in boys and in girls could be roughly described as follows: in the boy it is anxiety in the face of the threatening danger of a narcissistic injury, in the girl it is a present narcissistic disturbance which leads to the relinquishing of genital activity.

In my experience this difference is expressed in the fact that in pathological outcomes the consequent inhibition in women is more intensive, tenacious, and more difficult to remove. The man can recuperate more easily because the castration threat finally proves to be no real danger and his sense of inferiority therefore depends only upon his fears. This state of affairs is affirmed in cases where in the first days of life a circumcision was performed. When the little boy discovers the lack of the foreskin, he perceives a real mutilation of his genital, a perception which may then have consequences similar to the lack of a penis in the female child, though usually they are less severe. An operation on the penis at a later age sometimes leads to the same results.

In this connection, we must expect criticism from those analysts who conceive of the wish for a penis and of penis envy as acquired reactions and of secondary importance (Horney, Jones, et al.). We still have to wait for the final decision on who is right in this matter. However, in my opinion, analytic exploration in just these cases of inhibitions and impairments of function which are consequences of the fate of infantile genital activity show clearly how strongly and lastingly the narcissistic injury caused by the lack of a penis interferes with ego development. We should not forget that inborn or very early acquired bodily injuries have a lasting influence upon ego development and may lead to overcompensations and inhibitions. Adler's theory of organ inferiority is based on this observation. However, our observations teach us that the psychic reactions to these injuries are of much smaller significance than those to the narcissistic injury caused by the lack of a penis. I cite Freud: "The only bodily organ which is really regarded as inferior is the atrophied penis, a girl's clitoris" (1932, p. 65). So Adler has considered one motive, valid in female development, to be the basis for all mental processes (*pars pro toto*). Here the question arises whether there are other forms of narcissistic injury beside the lack of a penis which may bring about a devaluation of genital activity and an ego restriction. The answer is yes. In the analysis of patients of both sexes we regularly encounter the same monotonous complaints about childhood: the painful disappointment of being unable to fulfill all libidinal wishes toward the objects, of feeling the immaturity of the genital apparatus which the child seems to be aware of in comparing himself with adults. The little child wants to be "grown up," to do and experience what the adults do, and he continually meets with his powerlessness to compete with them successfully.[6] This injury is a general one to which every human being is subject. It is a consequence of the biphasic onset of sexuality. The first flourishing period of the drives is destined to decline. In the analyses of male patients one often finds this devaluating disappointment at the bottom of castration anxiety as a factor causing renunciation of genital activity. The stronger it is, the more tenacious is the change in masturbation and the more inaccessible is the neurotic disturbance consequent on it. In women the same process is fused with the disillusionment of lacking a penis. Both sources of narcissistic injury seem to be of paramount importance.

Nevertheless, in this general character of the impossibility of satisfying infantile sexual desires we have found a factor which may provoke an impairment of narcissism in men as well and which may lead to an inhibition of functions. In these cases we also observe a renunciation of the ego in order to avoid the experience of its own helplessness.

However, there certainly exists still another life experience which may cause a narcissistic injury to children of both sexes and have severe aftereffects. It is a trivial, well-known, ordinary experience. However, its explanation embarrasses us. It is the privation of love of the object felt by the little child even when surrounded by loving and devoted parents. This phenomenon is to be observed by every analyst and educator. We have to consider how to explain why this feeling of loss of love (because every delay of satisfaction is experienced as a loss) can

---

[6] See Horney (1932). In this paper Horney stresses a disturbance of the little boy's self-esteem. However, her view related to this point deviates considerably from mine.

lead to a narcissistic injury. According to Freud's early presentations (for instance, in "Instincts and Their Viccissitudes," 1915), object love emerges from the narcissistic reservoir in which all libido is stored in the beginning. A renunciation of the love for the object causes the libido to withdraw and to recathect the narcissistic position. After superficial consideration one might conclude that hostility toward an object would strengthen the narcissistic cathexis. However, in the little child we encounter just the opposite; a disappointment in object love disturbs the narcissistic equilibrium. This seeming contradiction is easily solved if we take into account the fact that the form of object love in a little child is different from its form in an adult potent man. The latter is a real, actively directed cathexis of the object representation. The little child's object attachment develops out of the infant's bodily dependence on the mother and is still a passively directed surrender. The child wants to be loved as it formerly was fed and cared for. In Chapter 2, I tried to point out that the inner struggle between libido and destructive drives forces the person to maintain his narcissism at a certain level in order to escape self-destruction. Apparently the child's narcissism, though quantitatively strong, is still unstable and free-floating in connection with the as yet feebly established ego organization. Moreover, a certain amount of libido is used to bind aggression aroused by disappointments. I further suggested that being loved leads to a strengthening of narcissism and that the first object ties are of a passive nature. Every disappointment, then, damages the drive equilibrium, and a striving to be loved comes to the fore again. To avoid misunderstanding I want to stress that a desire to be loved can be pursued by active behavior. This behavior, however, does not change the passive *aim* and its satisfaction strengthens narcissism.

The special nature of infantile love explains part of the little child's demeanor. He is strongly dependent upon this special form of love as well as upon the first object, which provides him with the satisfactions accompanying feeding and caring procedures, that is, upon the mother (or her substitute). Observations of infants confirm this state of affairs. The object tie with the aim of being loved, admired, cared for is later solved and exchanged for a new object which promises more satisfaction. There is only one constant attachment, the one to the mother. The weaker the ego organization is, the stronger must be the tie to the mother. Only the gradual consolidation of the ego organization permits a loosening of the passive form of love and prepares the way for the active cathexis of a love object. The final shape of active love does not appear until adolescence, when the love partner is taken possession of in accordance with the maturing of the genital apparatus.

The form of infantile love described here is at the same time the exquisitely female one. This is in accordance with the popular saying that a feminine woman is childish in her love life. Anatomy and the reproductive function of the woman determine her passive attitude and she finds in it a compensation for her damaged narcissism as well. Of course, active love toward her partner is also present, depending on the masculine trend in her development. A certain passivity is also maintained in the man's adult love life.[7]

To come back to early infantile development: the strong, passively directed dependence on object love is partly due to the relative weakness of the ego. At the same time the ego weakness is the cause of an oversensitiveness to disappointments, which may bring about intolerable narcissistic injuries. Frustrations are not merely painful losses of love, they may also disturb the inner drive equilibrium through narcissistic damage. As a consequence of lack of satisfaction from the side of the objects, drive processes may have a similar effect, for instance, the narcissistic injury connected with the discovery of the lack of a penis in little girls.

The point at which the drive frustration starts is highly important for the later development of the personality. If the disturbance occurs mainly between ego and object relation, we encounter anxiety about loss of love, which causes repression or renunciation. If the narcissistic ego cathexis is impaired, we have to expect more severe disturbances that are more resistive to any influence. It is a process similar to that of infantile masturbation. If masturbatory activity is given up under the impact of fear of the educators or of the superego, the ensuing inhibitions will be more accessible to therapeutic influence than in the case where mas-

[7] It goes without saying that this sketchy picture of certain vicissitudes of human love life does not cover all of the complicated and many-sided manifestations of love. I mentioned only some peculiarities which are relevant to the influence of disappointments on narcissism.

turbation is renounced as a consequence of the lack of a penis. We become aware of the fact that alongside the consideration of quantitative processes the topographic viewpoint is of equal significance.

This simple state of affairs seems to be more complicated in our analytic practice. There are only a few narcissistic injuries independent of object relations, namely, the inadequacy of the little child's genital satisfaction in general and the "inferiority" of the little girl's clitoris in particular.

The other narcissistic impairments already described are closely attached to object relations and often insolubly fused with them. During treatment we get the impression that the one group of impairments could come into existence only through the interference of the other group.

I come back once more to the history of my female patient. I want to stress again that the suppression of masturbation owing to her sense of having an inferior organ (the clitoris) became established only after a period of obstinate masturbation which followed her experience of being despised by her playmate. Here we have to ask a critical question: Are not those authors right who maintain that the little girl's penis is only secondary and overvalued in its significance by Freud and others? In our patient is not the feeling of being rejected the main motive for renouncing masturbation and not so much the penis envy as suggested by me? The question is rightly put. We know many cases of little girls in whom the two groups of factors merge, for instance, a case in which the female child has acquired her penis envy in the observation of a younger brother who she thinks is more loved by the mother just because he possesses a penis. Here disappointment in love and disappointment in having an "inferior" genital blend and the effects of the two events are almost indistinguishable.

In the endeavor to decide this question I nevertheless have to agree with Freud's view. In the analysis of my girl patient, I was strongly impressed by the little girl's reaction to the little seducer's rejection. However, the continued investigation of her childhood period, and also the patient's reaction to the different discoveries during analysis, indicated clearly that the penis envy was the decisive factor in her neurosis. After the period in which the little girl was rejected she took refuge in an intensified masturbation in which her feminine wishes were repressed and her masculinity was reinforced. She gave up genital activity only after she had gradually succeeded in accepting the fact that she would not get a penis. These connections were completely affirmed by the therapeutic results. In the first period of the analysis the experiences of seduction and rejection were brought to consciousness and revived. The working through of this material freed the patient from her sexual inhibitions and led her to a normal feminine love life. However, as already described, the work inhibition resisted any therapeutic influence. Only after long and difficult work in the analysis did the details of her masturbation period and the painful experience of feeling her bodily "inferiority" come to the fore. This narcissistic injury could finally be mastered. Only after this could the patient take up masturbation again, and next her work inhibition disappeared.

There are other experiences which seem to prove the fundamental significance of the wish for a penis in the lives of women. In the development toward complete and full femininity, the wish for a penis soon loses its importance. Where there is a clear masculine tendency, it is of great significance. The penis is the exponent of masculine, active tendencies and the lack of this organ hinders their discharge and damages the ego organization through injury of its narcissistic cathexis. We must mention in this connection that aggressive impulses (which are close to activity) are discharged in masturbation as well. In the "masculine" childhood period of masturbation my patient could live out a number of hostile impulses and vengeful feelings. The renunciation of masturbation then closed these outlets for aggression. The little child could thereafter do no more than turn these inhibited aggressions toward her own person. As I pointed out in Chapter 2, the aggressive tendencies turned inward threaten the inner equilibrium and the narcissistic cathexis of the ego organization. The passive dependence on the object (or superego) then becomes stronger and the danger of a new narcissistic injury through disappointment (or guilt feelings) grows. Nunberg (1932) described similar processes in a different context.

A last, but important, question is: When does a frustration from an object lead only to the experience of loss of love and when does it result in a narcissistic injury as well?

Apart from the already-mentioned quantities of drive demands, an age factor comes into play. If the frustrations occur in the first weeks or months of life, when the infant's ego organization is still very unstable, a narcissistic disturbance seems to be unavoidable. These privations can be of a somatic nature, for instance, hunger, severe illness, etc., or of a psychic nature if there is a lack of care, love, or tenderness from the mother's side. If the earliest infantile period is relatively undisturbed, healthy, and satisfying, a sufficiently strong narcissistically cathected ego organization and a sound ego development may come about. Frustrations and traumata occurring in later childhood are more likely to be experienced as loss of love and to be overcome more easily and more quickly.

Summary

In all mental drive processes a given though unmeasurable drive intensity seems to exercise an optimal influence upon ego organization. If this particular intensity is discharged, it allows the ego a maximum of functioning.

The discharge of a greater quantity of drive energy causes a "poisoning" of the ego, paralyzing a number of ego functions. The process is comparable to the poisoning of bodily functions through an overdose of pharmacological matter.

On the other hand, the discharge of too small a quantity of drive energy may result in a similarly paralyzing influence upon ego activities. Here we find a somatic analogy as well. We must expect disturbances of ego functions in all cases where the optimal discharge of drive intensity does not occur. Whether this happens or not is dependent on a number of different factors.

The first factor is the absolute drive intensity. If it is augmented by normal or pathological bodily processes (e.g., puberty, menopause, somatic illnesses), an overwhelming of ego functions may be the result. If the absolute drive intensity remains from the very beginning under a certain level, we see that a normal development of ego functions is not possible at all.

The second factor is the relative drive intensity, that is, the relation between id strength and ego strength. If the ego organization is a relatively feeble one, it is easily overwhelmed by the id. If a relatively

strong ego encounters the same id demand, we can observe two different results: (1) the ego is able to allow a discharge of drive energy that
provides an optimum of ego functioning; (2) the ego overshoots its
aim and represses too much drive energy, which causes disturbances of
functions. The ego can be brought to such an excessive effort, first, in
order to avoid a conflict with the id, for instance, in cases where the
given drive impulse is blended with a prohibited or painful tendency;
second, in order to avoid a conflict with the superego (because of guilt
feelings, fear of conscience); and third, in order to forestall a narcissistic disturbance or to deny a narcissistic injury.

Here we become aware of the fact that it is not only a question of
relative intensities that decides whether an optimal functioning of the
ego organization comes about or not. A third factor is the topographic starting point of the reaction to a given drive activity. This
factor is comparable to a somatic process as well. Several chemicals are
poisonous only for special body parts, for instance, particular regions
of the brain or the musculature of the heart, whereas they may be harm-
less for other organs. In the same way it may happen that a drive impulse could be mastered quantitatively by the ego if it did not start its
action on a special part of the ego organization, for instance, on the relation of the ego to an extremely severe superego, or on a point of special narcissistic vulnerability. According to our observations, this last
occurrence is of particular significance. We saw that a drive impulse
that provokes a narcissistic injury has to be warded off by the ego with
extraordinary force. Consequently it can be brought back to consciousness only with extreme difficulty and sometimes not at all. The ego often
has to pay for its victory with a severe impairment of its achievements.
Apparently a sound libidinal cathexis of the ego organization is the
first and most important condition for mental health. Of course, narcissism must not be a fixed, immobile one (as, for instance, in psychoses). The ego has to have at its disposal a certain quantity of mobile
energy in order to be able to communicate with the environment in an
undisturbed way. If this condition is fulfilled, the ego's undamaged narcissism allows the personality inner and outer freedom and independence. These qualities can raise the person to great and important achievements, if certain talents are present.

CHAPTER 5

Masochism and Narcissism

(1937)

It has always been difficult to understand masochistic behavior in men. The idea of pleasurable suffering is hard to accept. However, psycho-analytic observation reveals the fact that a pleasure gain from suffering does exist. It is inherent in masochistic experience. In the activities of masochistically perverted persons and in the masochistic fantasies of many neurotics, the pleasure gain is conscious. In persons suffering from unconscious guilt feelings and the need for punishment, we must conclude from their behavior that the chastisement is longed for and provides pleasure.

We may study the problem of masochism under two headings:

(1) The first centers on the question of what factors make a person look for unpleasure, suffering, and pain in order to find satisfaction.

(2) The second point is: how can we explain that unpleasure, suffer-ing, and pain can become pleasurable; how can this phenomenon be consistent with the nature of the drives?

It may be that the latter problem will never completely lose its mys-tery. Freud elaborates it in "The Economic Problem of Masochism" (1924a). In that paper Freud assumes a primary erotogenic masochism to be the basis of every masochistic experience. The latter is seen as biologically and constitutionally founded, as "an infantile physiologi-cal mechanism which ceases to operate later on" (p. 163); its explana-tion cannot be achieved without profound consideration. In the same

---

See also Chapter 26.

article Freud states his opinion that primary masochism may be "evidence of, and a remainder from, the phase of development in which the coalescence, which is so important for life, between the death instinct and Eros took place" (p. 164). According to this assumption, masochism should be seen as a portion of the destructive drive, still active in the inner world and fused with libido. As a consequence of this fusion it should have become a representative of the pleasure principle. These assumptions about the origin of primary masochism follow from psychoanalytic drive theory. As we are, for the time being, ignorant of the organic nature of the drives, we have nothing to add to this hypothesis.

Primary masochism or self-destruction is not observable in analytic practice. According to Freud, it works inside, silent and soundless. Masochistic behavior in infants is seldom or never seen. The infant reacts to pain and frustration with obvious unpleasure and tries to escape them. If the baby damages himself, it is usually because of his lack of knowledge about real dangers. Expressions of masochism which we can observe in analytic practice are outcomes of complicated mental processes. They belong to the so-called secondary masochism, in the shape of feminine and moral masochism. We may assume that the infantile form of primary erotogenic masochism, which Freud believed disappears later on, will not always or completely be subject to this fate. Apparently it can be preserved in a smaller or greater intensity. However, it is exclusively the secondary masochism which is open to observation by means of its psychic representations. The economic processes leading to secondary masochism are well known. Those portions of the destructive drive which are directed toward the outer world can be turned inward in certain circumstances, thus constituting secondary masochism. In what follows I will limit myself exclusively to phenomena of secondary masochism.

This leads us automatically to our first question: What factors make a person search for masochistic satisfaction, accompanied by unpleasure, suffering, and pain? In other words, at what moment and through what events does secondary masochism develop?

I propose to turn our attention to a masochistic fantasy often encountered in psychoanalytic work. Freud remarked that masochism has an especially intimate relation to femininity. It is therefore understandable that I choose a female's fantasy which we very often observe in little girls who have begun to notice the anatomical difference between the sexes. The fantasy accompanies masturbation, as I have pointed out in Chapter 4. It reads: "I was once in possession of a penis; however, I am deprived of it as a punishment for having masturbated." This fantasy can persist into puberty and often be retained long afterward. In the analysis of adult women it can resist every therapeutic influence with astonishing tenacity.

The devaluation of environmental prohibitions, the reduction of the superego's cruel severity, do not change the fantasy. We finally become aware of the fact that the masochistic fantasy, the painful idea of being punished for a misdeed, is less intolerable than the acceptance of a physical defect, of an always present inferiority of one's own personality. (Edoardo Weiss [1932] was concerned with the same problem.) The notion "I was deprived of my penis" restores the person's intactness in the past. This fantasy appears to provide some satisfaction. However, it is incapable of abolishing the present disappointment and the narcissistic injury resulting from the observation of the "defect." Apparently an additional pleasure gain is necessary for diminishing the unpleasure, and it is found in the pleasurable idea of punishment and suffering. Thus the little girl's masochistic fantasy has come into being to alleviate the pain of a narcissistic injury (the lack of a penis). In other words, the little girl gropes for pleasure gain from the idea of being punished in order to escape the much greater unpleasure of feeling injured. The drive process involved is the following: the narcissistic injury raises anger and rage, and these aggressions, which cannot be sufficiently employed in the outer world, are turned inward and used for masochistic pleasure gain.

This outcome is a very simple one. From the very beginning, psychoanalysis has observed a close relationship between narcissism and masochism on the one side and between masochism and femininity on the other side.

The study of the genesis of this masochistic fantasy provides the observer with still another very important insight: the significant role played by narcissistic injuries in mental development. The tenacity with which the fantasy of being punished is retained demonstrates the strength of the effect of a narcissistic injury and of the necessity to deny it or cover it up.

It seems to be significant in many respects that this injury originates in penis envy in little girls.

Here we must consider a critical question: Is not the origin of the little girl's masochistic fantasy simply the expression of a guilt feeling that results from prohibited aggressive and libidinal wishes discharging themselves in masturbatory activity? Many fantasies of being punished certainly serve the alleviation of guilt feelings. They were described by Freud many years ago in "A Child Is Being Beaten" (1919). In the little girl the fantasy reads: "I am beaten by my father." Here the idea of being beaten is the punishment for the libidinal oedipal wish as well as the regressive substitute for it. In analytic practice we learn that the effect of this masochistic fantasy, which may inhibit the love life of the adult woman, usually disappears if the analysis succeeds in lifting the repression of the oedipal strivings, in annulling the superego's prohibitions, and in removing the neurosis that is rooted in the oedipus complex.

The above-described fantasy, however, has a quite different origin, though it may happen that it provides the basis for the fantasy of being beaten by the father. The earlier fantasy of "I was deprived of my penis as a punishment for having masturbated" does *not* originate in the oedipal phase. It dates from the time of the preoedipal phase in which the superego was not yet established, and consequently fear of the superego was still lacking. At that time the conscience's forerunner, the fear of loss of love and of punishment, caused the drive restriction, and inner guilt feelings could scarcely play a role.

In the phallic phase of *pre*oedipal development, the little girl is concerned with her wish for a penis. Narcissistic needs are prevalent and the object which plays a role in this period is the mother. It is also the mother who is made responsible for the lack of a penis. "I was deprived of my penis" properly reads, "My mother has taken it from me." In contradistinction to the oedipal situation in which the tender father attachment is preserved, the outcome of this preoedipal phase is characterized by a strong hostility toward the mother and an abandonment of the mother as a love object. It is the stage in which the libidinal wishes are transferred to the father, thus preparing for the oedipus complex.

The idea of being castrated as a punishment for masturbation still serves to do away with the unpleasurable idea of being a defective person, and is not yet the expression of a loving surrender to the father. We must now ask how the different genesis of the two forms of fantasy reveals itself in analytic practice. The answer is the following: in our therapeutic endeavor, we learn that the fantasies of being punished that stem from the oedipus complex are relatively easy to influence. But the masochistic castration fantasies that serve to avoid narcissistic injuries are clung to tenaciously and often cannot be removed.

In Chapter 4 I came to a similar conclusion regarding therapeutic influence on neurotic inhibitions. There I pointed out that in cases where a neurotic inhibition emerged as a consequence of the ego's anxiety vis-à-vis superego demands or of the conflict between ego and id (for instance, in the case of sexualization of an ego activity), the chances for a therapeutic success are much greater than in cases where an inhibition comes about in order to avoid or to deny a narcissistic injury.

To summarize: A very early starting point (perhaps the first?) in the origin of masochistic behavior is the flight from a narcissistic injury. The unpleasure aroused by such an injury is greater than the unpleasure of punishment, suffering, and pain, and the former is softened by a masochistic pleasure gain. At the same time, this condition may be the reason for a tenacious clinging to masochistic behavior. Later on, when the superego has been established, the ego's need for punishment can reinforce the masochistic structure which originated earlier. In analytic treatment we discover how important it is to know which of the sources the masochistic phenomena are predominantly based on.

I have already illustrated these events with the fantasy of being punished in little girls; this frequently encountered fantasy reads: "I once had a penis; I have lost it as a penalty for having masturbated." The emergence of this fantasy can also be described as "the use of aggression turned inward in order to gain masochistic pleasure and to flee from the greater unpleasure consequent upon damage of the narcissistic libido position and upon hostility and rage which cannot be discharged sufficiently." Here I want to make the point that these

86

happenings are of general significance in the development of little girls. In normal development they may be present in small intensities and serve the mastering of penis envy. In this way they provide the necessary amount of masochism inherent in normal femininity. In cases where an excessive narcissistic vulnerability, perhaps combined with a strong "masculine," bisexual Anlage is present, this method of protection may fail to undo the injury. The outcome may be either a pathologically strengthened masochism followed by neurotic phenomena, sexual inhibition, perversions, and character disorders, or reaction formations like sadism and reinforced masculine behavior.

We now come to another question: Is it only in women that we meet with a narcissistic injury as an early source of masochistic phenomena? The origin of masochism in men is doubtless a more complicated process than in women. Masochism runs counter to normal male development. It is sadism that belongs to "masculinity." Nevertheless, we often observe masochistic fantasies, perversions, and behavior in men. We term it feminine masochism and connect it with feminine, homosexual tendencies. We are well acquainted with masochistic fantasies and acts developed out of the positive and negative oedipal constellation, especially in connection with passive homosexual love for the father. They express a need to be punished for prohibited libidinal and aggressive tendencies like the little girl's later fantasies of being beaten. However, in men we often find as a prestage of these oedipal fantasies an earlier narcissistic form, just as in girls. In one case I observed a male patient who experienced his circumcision as a severe narcissistic injury. The result was a flight into a feminine masochistic castration fantasy. We are not surprised to encounter the idea of a damaged penis as the starting point for the narcissistic injury. In other cases, different experiences, as for instance the boy's comparison of his penis and its erections with the father's penis or the unsuccessful rivalry with older boys in connection with urination and masturbation, may lead to a severe narcissistic injury. It is well known that similar painful events may cause feminine masochistic behavior in boys. The anxiety about not possessing a well-functioning genital, in short, "castration anxiety," is the factor which in its outcome runs parallel to the penis envy in little girls. It is possible that these processes are less common in men than in women. However, a third form of masochistic behavior, called moral masochism, can easily be observed in both sexes.

Moral masochism forces a person to behavior that leads to self-damage, to unsuccessful performances, to suffering and pain. In analytic treatment moral masochism causes the patient to react to a solution of a neurotic symptom with a worsening instead of an improvement of his condition. Freud called it the "negative therapeutic reaction." The patient is dominated by a need for punishment (an "unconscious guilt feeling"). It is a process which takes place between ego and superego. This need for punishment can be one of the most powerful enemies of therapeutic endeavor. It can resist every influence, notwithstanding the patient's brilliant understanding of the unconscious causes of his symptoms.

I have observed that with analytic exploration of the deeper causes of moral masochism one encounters differences in various patients' reactions. There are cases in which a prolonged and laborious analysis succeeds in removing the greater part of this need for punishment, restoring, at least partly, the patient's health. On the other hand, we encounter patients who resist every therapeutic influence; they are unable to renounce even part of their suffering. We then find the following explanation for the difference in result: the need for punishment stems from a tension between ego and superego, as already mentioned. The superego (conscience) inflicts punishment on the person in taking over the role of the demanding and prohibiting parental figures. However, it may prove to be much more severe and cruel than the parents ever were. We know the cause of this occurrence to be the process of turning inward aggressions which the child cannot discharge in the outer world. They lead to secondary masochism. A part of these aggressions, however, is invested in the superego, which now becomes cruel, torturing, and sadistic in its relation to the ego. The latter reacts masochistically toward the superego. The two processes, sadism of the superego and masochism of the ego, supplement each other, and finally lead to a need for punishment, self-damage and, in analytic treatment, the negative therapeutic reaction.[1]

The way in which the aggression turned inward is distributed is of

[1] Nunberg (1932) has drawn attention to this connection on several occasions.

great significance. The differences can be studied by looking for the intensity and the tenacity of the resistance in analytic treatment. Cases in which the larger part of the aggression is invested in the superego will offer much better opportunities for therapeutic influence. Sometimes a patient accepts the analyst as a substitute for parental and environmental demands. If the analyst then succeeds in softening the severity and cruelty of the superego, it may become possible to restore some of the ego functions, and a change in the personality and a beneficial influence on the patient's suffering may be the outcome. In cases where the inner aggressions are invested in the masochistically deformed ego, providing masochistic pleasure gain, every therapeutic attempt seems to be doomed to fail. Here the mitigation of superego demands and the removal of sexual prohibitions are unable to counteract the ego's masochistic pleasure gain. Therefore it is important to learn to distinguish between those circumstances which cause aggressions to produce a more sadistic superego and those which intensify the ego's masochism.

In some cases it might be a simple distribution in the following way: the superego's sadism emerges from the internalization of the parent's real cruelty and the masochistic ego comes into existence as a consequence of the child's own aggression turned inward. However, in other cases the process is a quite different one. I observed the case of a young man who had to spoil every success in his profession. The relentlessness of his superego in preventing any success did not correspond to parental severity. On the contrary, the parents had been full of understanding and very liberal with the little boy. His superego had doubtless absorbed a great deal of his own aggression and demanded the surrender of his ego. He had produced a fantasy in which the punishment was a regressive substitute for libidinal oedipal wishes (a process described by Freud in "The Economic Problem of Masochism"). Apart from surrender, the ego showed a strong opposition toward the superego as well. In the analysis the patient tried, with the analyst's support, to renounce the self-damaging attitude. The working through of both positive and negative oedipus complex finally brought about a change in the patient's behavior and a good deal of the longed-for success.

However, in two other cases which seemed to be similar ones, a male and a female case, I learned that although removal of guilt feelings attendant upon the oedipus complex was, to be sure, followed by the acceptance of generally more realistic moral demands, a change of the masochistic behavior did not occur. In the female patient I finally discovered the above-mentioned fantasy of the penis being cut off as a penalty for masturbatory activity, a fantasy which was adhered to in order to avoid the narcissistic injury of feeling that her body was defective. The ego's masochistic attitude toward the superego corresponded to the secret idea: "Unknown powers (or fate) punish and damage me; therefore I myself am not inferior or defective." The patient was, unconsciously, highly ambitious and tried to deny the painful failure of some of her daring plans in a way similar to her attempts to do away with her penis envy in childhood. In the male patient a similar process came to light. He suffered from a strong feeling of inferiority that had its origin in rivalry with an older brother in childhood. The brother already had erections at a time when the patient was not yet able to produce them. The patient never overcame this injury. Every failure of ambitious desires in later times caused equal pain, which could be alleviated only by imagining that he was maltreated by fate and by drawing masochistic pleasure from this idea.

In summary, I would like to say once more that in many cases of moral masochism we discover, behind the wish to be punished originating from the forbidden oedipal object relationship, a turning toward masochistic pleasure gain in order to escape an injury to the narcissistic libidinal position, with the accompanying rage impulses experienced as being dangerous. Renouncing this masochistic attitude would require a confrontation of these painful injuries and the realization of the powerlessness to undo them and to change reality. We know from analytic practice how difficult it is to achieve these requirements. In most cases the patient prefers keeping his painful masochistic behavior to exposing himself to the painful feeling of being powerless. His pleasure gain, then, is reduced to the dubious masochistic satisfactions.

We may conclude that a relation between masochism and narcissism is present not just in a single fantasy of little girls. We have to add that narcissistic disturbances are of etiological significance in many forms of masochistic expression in both sexes.

However, we started our investigation of this subject with the study of the little girl's masochistic fantasy connected with her penis wish and penis envy. It becomes clear that in studying mental developmental processes we time and again come upon the basic importance of the castration complex. A critical objection is whether it is not a blind one-sidedness to ascribe a central significance to penis envy in the woman's mental life. However, careful analytic observations invalidate this criticism. Of course a number of other narcissistic injuries befall the little child, for instance, situations in which jealousy is aroused, where feelings of not being loved and of being deserted emerge. All of them are highly important. The complicated object relationships of the preoedipal phase with its intense ambivalence are responsible for many developmental processes. However, the material invariably comes back to penis envy as a central point. It is from this point that the development into normal femininity begins. Its successful or unsuccessful solution determines whether the little girl will mature into a healthy woman or whether neurotic disturbances, an unmastered masculinity complex, or a masochistic attitude in life will come into existence. The inherent difficulty of mastering the narcissistic injury of the lack of a penis emerges not only in the analyses of our female patients; it also seems to express itself in the analytic literature. There have been many attempts to diminish the importance of the penis wish and penis envy in female psychic life. It is given a secondary place, or is avoided by attaching a greater significance to earlier or later experiences. Not only women but men, too, have participated in these endeavors to interpret the phenomenon differently. The resistance of men to accepting the importance of penis envy may be explained by the already-mentioned fact that in male mental life a comparable concern is of equal importance to the penis wish in females. It is a man's concern about the intactness of his genital, the vulnerable narcissistic estimation of his masculinity, in other words, the castration complex and its aftereffects. Man's castration fear apparently enables him to understand empathically the woman's penis envy. In both sexes it seems to be the castration complex which inspires the misinterpretation of the outcomes of penis wish and penis envy. It goes without saying that these assumptions cannot prove the correctness or incorrectness of the different theories. Freud, in a footnote to "Female Sexuality" points to the fact that in such cases "The use of analysis as a weapon of controversy can clearly lead to no decision" (1931b, p. 230).

The question why many of the most important normal as well as pathological mental processes often crystallize around the activities performed with the genital apparatus seems to be answered in principle by Freud. The contradictory interests of the individual and the species are manifested in the functions of the genitals. The species is preserved by propagation, which requires tasks running counter to the individual's own striving for pleasure and for the diminution of tension. As Freud puts it, "making use of libido in the service of the female function is most difficult to achieve, libido being an active urge in itself." Perhaps here we come upon the explanation of the fact that the development of women toward femininity is a highly complicated and arduous task.

CHAPTER 6

Considerations of Methodology in Relation to the Psychology of Children

(1939)

A little while ago an acquaintance of mine, the mother of a two-and-a-half-year-old boy, said to me: "I must tell you something quite extraordinary about my little son. For the last few days he has refused to put on his knickers and has kept on saying that he wants to wear a dress—a pretty dress, like Lini and Evi." (Lini and Evi are two playmates of his.) "Yesterday I went into his room and found him with flushed cheeks and sparkling eyes, playing with his indiarubber doll, which he had not taken any notice of for some time. He was tucking it into his blouse so that his body looked quite fat and then squeezing and pushing it out again, to the accompaniment of straining movements and noises, as though he were trying to defaecate." His mother, who had a great deal of insight, added: "I know why he was doing it. A friend of mine is expecting a baby quite soon, and I have often said to her that I should like to have another baby too. On those occasions Walter will look at me with great attention, and, now I come to think of it, with a certain amount of concern as well."

I asked my acquaintance what the child's attitude to his environment was. She told me that he was very much attached to her and nearly always preferred being with her to being with anyone else, but that lately he had now and then suddenly left her side and run to other people. She said: "When he is annoyed with me or feels that I have neglected him, he will go to his father or to our maid and behave in a very affectionate way to them." She went on to express anxiety about whether such behavior was not "abnormal." She had always understood that little boys loved their mothers and were their fathers' rivals. But Walter was behaving not at all like a little man, but like a girl. Was it possible that he would turn into a weak and effeminate person? All I could do was to tell her to be patient and to wait and see how the child's development progressed.

About three quarters of a year later the mother told me that Walter had changed to a remarkable degree. His games of pregnancy had completely stopped. He was ardently and passionately devoted to her, always wanting to escort her and to protect her. He behaved, in fact, like her *cavalier servant*. His father seemed to be merely a nuisance to him and he had lost all trace of his clinging tenderness toward him. He was disagreeable to him and hated him and was glad when he went away. As regards his body functions, he had become quite "grown-up." He despised the chamber pot and went to the water closet instead. The only thing was that he masturbated at night rather often.

Unfortunately, circumstances did not permit me to follow the further course of this little boy's history in a systematic way. I heard that he did well at school and achieved independence quite early. He reacted to the birth of a little sister a good deal later, when he was nine, by having an accident which nearly cost him his life; but he was affectionate with her and took care of her.

My readers will be wondering why I have troubled to give this doubtless instructive but quite commonplace story of a child. I have done so because I think that it illustrates and confirms very clearly certain findings which we have been able to make only as a result of long and hard analytic work with adults and older children.

I have in mind, among other instances, the case of a young man of thirty who came to me for analysis. He was highly intelligent and well educated, had had scientific training, and was very successful in his work, but he suffered from complete sexual impotence. He had never had sexual relations with a woman. After a long period of analysis and in the face of strong resistances, he produced the following recollection from his early childhood. When he was between two and a half and three years old he had a passion for putting on dresses belonging to his little girl cousins. He used to walk around in them with pride, and obviously not only behaved, but felt like, a girl. On the night before his fourth birthday—he could fix the date exactly—he had a dream, followed by certain experiences, which showed that some time after his "girlish" behavior he had harbored very intense and bold feelings of love toward his mother, but that they had ended in disappointment. The dream consisted of his performing the sexual act with his mother, and ended with his urinating in bed. The experiences consisted of being laughed at and made to feel ashamed by the others when he woke up next day, and of being threatened with punishment by his nurse for having been dirty and having wet his bed "like a baby." This experience caused him to give up his "masculine" attitude once more and to become a quiet, passive, and shy child with a strong inclination toward his father. My suspicion that the experience had had a fateful effect upon his subsequent development was confirmed by the following remarkable therapeutic success which took place in him. On the day after the recollection of the events of his fourth birthday had come up in his analysis (and this did not happen until much long and difficult analytic work had been done) he attempted to perform coitus and was successful. His analysis had various further results; and in the end he got married. He acquitted himself well as a married man, felt happy, and was able to cope with the external world which at one time had seemed to be full of insurmountable difficulties and demands. His feminine passive attitude hardly interfered with his life at all.

The similarity between the history of my patient and that of Walter is quite obvious. Both children passed through a phase in which they wanted to be girls; and in both this was succeeded by a phase of true "masculine" behavior, which was followed in the case of my patient by a return to a passive attitude later on.

I have presented these two accounts, which are not at all unusual, not only to describe the case history of an analytic patient with a parallel taken from direct observation of a child and to point out their similarities. My real reason for doing it is a different one and is connected with the occasion of the appearance of this birthday number of *The International Journal of Psycho-Analysis*. It seems to me that the best way of marking that occasion and of doing honor to Ernest

Jones is to pursue a line of thought which he himself has often followed in the course of his scientific studies.

Jones has made more than one important and felicitous contribution to our knowledge of the early developmental phases of the child. At the same time, he has been foremost in stressing the desirability of bringing out into the open as much as possible the differences which exist between our method of viewing the material which we obtain from the analysis and observation of children and the theories which we build upon that material; for in this way, he thinks, we shall be most likely to understand and clear up the points in dispute.

Accordingly, I should like in this paper to attempt to put before the reader a problem of this kind as plainly as I can. We are still, I think, very far from having solved every problem concerning the young child, and our knowledge is especially lacking in regard to the psychological events of the very first months of his life. We can, of course, find out something about the subject from a phenomenological point of view— by means, for instance, of nonanalytical child psychology, which sets out to record and collect all the child's reactions to every kind of stimulus, and so on. But we can at most only guess at the sort of instinctual manifestations that go on in the young infant and the sort of way in which his ego, as yet quite unfinished, reacts to those stimuli. This is not only because the infant is incapable of telling us in words about his inner life, but because his range of bodily expression is so incomplete too that what he communicates by means of play and action is very little indeed. Bodily expressions of this kind, which in slightly older children can convey so much important knowledge about their instinctual and affective lives, are limited in the infant. I think that a tremendous quantity of detailed and persistent observation of babies in the earliest months of life is needed before we can obtain a trustworthy picture of the situation.

My present contribution, therefore, is intended to take up a certain standpoint in regard to the methodology of the subject rather than to add any new facts to our scanty knowledge of the affective life of the infant. Fenichel (1926) and Waelder (1936) have already made some very important attempts to work out the differences of opinion that exist in this field of research. And although it is the methodological aspect which will principally be emphasized in this paper, we shall find many points of contact between the views put forward by those two writers.

The question which I should like to take up first is that of the relation between what we call the oedipus complex and that period of development which is known as the "preoedipal phase." The idea of the oedipus complex was established by Freud many years ago. He described it as "the fateful combination of love for the one parent and simultaneous hatred for the other as a rival" (1931b, p. 229), and places it in the phallic phase of libidinal development, that is, in that period of expansion of the infant's instinctual life which occurs somewhere between his fourth and sixth years and which is governed by the primacy of genital excitations. We see that Freud is very precise in his characterization of the nature and content of the oedipus complex. But the importance which he attributes to the development of the person does not prevent him from attaching equal importance to the instinctual occurrences and to the object relationships belonging to the earlier, pregenital phases of the child. (These phases, when viewed more particularly from the point of view of object relationships, were later on classed together as the preoedipal phase.) In those phases, in which the child's instincts obtain their main gratification from the oral and anal zones, he undergoes experiences which are equally important for his subsequent development. It is then, without doubt, that his relations to the objects prepare the way for that "fateful conjunction" of love and hate toward his parents as it appears in the oedipal attitude. The various phases are, of course, not sharply separated, with regard to time or the dominant themes. They merge into one another, each succeeding phase taking over something from the one before and each earlier one providing "precursors" for the next.

As we know, many analysts, in particular Jones and his colleagues (Melanie Klein and others), employ the idea of the oedipus complex in a different sense from Freud. They no longer mean by it the "fateful combination" of feelings in regard to the parents which represents the end product and climax of infantile sexual development, but assume that the oedipus complex starts much earlier than Freud supposed. They believe that it often appears as early as the first year of life—at a time, that is, when oral gratification still predominates and the primacy of the genitals has not yet set in, and when there is as yet no hint of the "fateful" fact of the simultaneous love for one parent and hatred of the other.

In the opinion of these analysts, the story of little Walter which we have given above would signify that at the early age of two and a half the child was already in the oedipal phase—at a time when, although he certainly chose his mother as his love object, he very easily turned to his father or the maid whenever he felt displeased with her, and when there was as yet no question of genital primacy. According to their views, if I have understood them aright, there would be no radical difference between the little boy's attitude then and his attitude six months later, when, as his mother said, he had become "totally changed" and had assumed toward her the typical role of a young man in love. Moreover, they "transpose back" the oedipus complex to much earlier stages even than those described in the case of Walter. They take it as far back as those quite early object relationships which are a necessary outcome of the physiological dependence of the child upon his mother.

The question I want to put is this: Are we justified from a methodological point of view in altering Freud's conception of the oedipus complex in the sense described above? My answer to this, I may say at once, is "No," and for the following reasons.

Walter's behavior at the age of three was, to use his mother's own words, "totally different" from what it had been at two and a half, both in regard to his object relationships (witness his altered love attitude toward his mother and his new hatred toward his father as a rival) and in regard to the manifestations of his instinctual life. Now there is no doubt, as we have already said, that this typical position of the small boy will contain traces and relics of what he has experienced on earlier levels. It was psychoanalysis which from the very first took special interest in genetic development and was always at pains to explain what existed in the light of what had gone before. But I think it is an error in method to assume that when there is a genetic connection between various events, those events are identical. The fact that A follows B does not mean that A is the same as B.

I should like to give a very simple example here to show how inadmissible such a method of argument is.

A man happened to tell a friend of his that he was very fond of big, high-colored tulips with long stalks. The next day his friend brought him some large tulip bulbs as a present. The man was very much surprised, but his friend was still more surprised at his astonishment. He tried to justify himself by saying that the fine bulbs would turn into wonderful tulips and that having bulbs or flowers in the room came to the same thing. All comparisons are to some extent inadequate, but this one does illustrate one or two points. The hungry baby who wants his mother's breast in order to appease his hunger and to obtain sexual gratification at the oral zone is not, after all, identical with the three- or four-year-old boy who tries to do the same things with his mother as his father does, who would like to kill his father, and who finds an outlet for sexual excitation in masturbation. The tulip bulbs contain all the forces and the material which will enable the flower to grow out of it; but this will happen only if certain conditions are fulfilled, such as that there shall be enough water, earth, air, and light. In the same way, the oedipal boy develops from the infant, but that development, too, depends upon all sorts of circumstances in his external world. Any changes or peculiarities that occur in those circumstances will exert an influence on his development, although its main lines are laid down from the beginning, just as in the case of the tulip its character, color, size, etc., are already contained in the nature of the bulb.

This procedure of "transposing back," or of equating the precursory stage with the final state, has not been confined to the conception of the oedipus complex. It has, I think, been made use of in many theoretical arguments. This is not only inadmissible as a method of thought but has led to a good many mistakes and false conclusions.

Many analytic writers, for instance, tend to "transpose back" the emergence of the superego. They are inclined to deny the fact that the superego springs from the extinct oedipus complex, as described by Freud, and attribute a superego to little children between the ages of one and two, or perhaps even younger. I believe that this procedure too is the result of a tendency to confuse the thing itself with the earlier stages out of which it has evolved. It is doubtless true that in the preoedipal stage children exhibit certain reactions which are similar to the reactions caused by the superego. A child who is being trained in cleanliness may, for instance, show signs of apprehension and look guilty if he is discovered making a mess; and, again, he may give up playing with his excrement, as he used to do with great zest a few months before. But can we fairly ascribe this behavior to the intervention of the superego? Unless we are prepared to apply Freudian terminology indiscriminately to different mental processes, we must reply in the negative. What Freud means by the superego is an agency which has separated off from the ego and which has come into existence through the introjection of object representations and which is already set apart from the real objects. The superego is an endopsychic agency acting more or less independently of the reality demands being made at the particular moment by the objects which are actually present. It may cause the individual to renounce an instinctual gratification without being required to do so by any real person, and even if no one in the external world is noticing whether and how the individual is doing it. However, a little child in the preoedipal phase gives up a gratification not because a part of himself demands this renunciation but because he is afraid of the reactions of his parents—that is, because he is afraid of punishment or loss of love. He may do "wrong" if he knows he will not be found out or if he is on bad terms with his love objects, not needing their love at that particular moment. A command from the superego has to be obeyed without regard to the object, and any disobedience will be followed by an intense sense of guilt and internal torment. If an instinctual renunciation is made because of fear of loss of the object's love, the resulting state is of course a precursor of the subsequent formation of the superego, but an important process of development must still be gone through before the superego can emerge from this early reactive behavior.

We might go back still further. We know that in the fertilized ovum which lodges in the wall of the uterus all the forces and all the preconditions are present which are necessary for the production of an individual belonging to the species of *Homo sapiens*. But we shall not make the mistake of calling that fertilized cell a human being. The same principle applies to the separate parts of the body and the mind. As regards the latter, there exists in each embryo an inborn instinctual disposition which can, under the influence of a variety of internal and external factors, give rise to extremely complicated instinctual constellations. In the same way we must assume that the embryo brings with it into the world the nucleus of a future ego; that the attitudes and forms of reaction of the ego, as it emerges, are subjected to the influence of the environment, until a distinctive personality finally takes shape. But, to return to our simile of the tulip, there is a great difference in actual fact between whether the bulb has reached the bud stage or whether it has grown into a full-blown flower. If the necessary preconditions are lacking, the bud will never become a flower, but only an incomplete and stunted one.

There is a strong temptation to equate a finished psychological phenomenon with the earlier stages out of which it has developed, and to transpose mental products back to a period of life when their existence is not susceptible of proof or disproof. The strength of this temptation is demonstrated by the fact that a good many analysts are inclined to take it as an established event that babies, when they are only a few weeks—or is it days?—old entertain such fantasies as "robbing the mother's body" or "getting out of her the father's penis which she has obtained from him in copulation" and other similar notions. Our analyses of children and adults have familiarized us with these and many other fantasies as they have been told to us in words and actions, and, in the case of children, in play. What psychoanalysis has endeavored to do from the very first is precisely to trace back fantasies, wishes, and affective reactions like these to earlier periods of development. I think that analysis has succeeded in this complex task. However, Freud has always insisted that in making the attempt we should produce confirmatory evidence for our conclusions, and he has always done so himself. In adult analysis we obtain evidence of this kind from our patients' recollections; and in the observation of children from their play. The two sources of knowledge are complementary and bear each other out. It is true that with infants we can, as has already been said, observe their reactions to stimuli, but so far we have no empirical knowledge whatever upon which to base a judgment about whether any such fantasies as the ones mentioned above are already attached to those reactions or not. We can observe that out of the suckling's need for nourishment there develops later on a psychological attachment to his mother, and we may perhaps be justified in assuming that the unpleasurable stimuli which he experiences, such as deprivation, pain, etc., give rise to aggressive trends in subsequent life. But here, too, we must not confuse a precursory stage with the final state, and we are not justified in equating the child's later fantasy of taking something away from his mother with his earlier reaction to a disturbing stimulus. A very important process of development has to take place before the one stage can emerge from the other.

Similar doubts and objections must be felt when we hear the affective states of little children given names that have hitherto been applied only to the gravest pathological conditions in adult persons. It seems to be more than a mere terminological inexactitude that the sorrow which a child shows when his mother leaves the room should be called a melancholia. Here again I think it is a question of confusing the rudiments or part of a thing with the completed whole. Melancholia is a very highly complicated pathological state of mind, which no doubt contains the affect of "mourning" and in which loss of love also plays a role. But nevertheless it is something quite different in its entity from the sadness of a lonely child.

Again, analysis may enable us to discover that a patient who is suffering from paranoia had, in the first years of his life, felt neglected by his mother and had thought her responsible for a great many of his troubles, but we should be making a great mistake if we said that the young child who brings unfair reproaches against his mother was suffering from paranoia or had a paranoid disposition. It seems to me that if we are not continually on our guard against equating later developments with their earlier stages we shall inevitably be led into imagining the existence of mental processes in early periods of life where we have no means of verifying our assumptions empirically. It is owing to this mistake that the genetic-dynamic method of research employed by psychoanalysis (which is legitimate in itself and has always been based on empirical principles) has been brought to a *reductio ad absurdum*, and that the Freudian discoveries concerning the development of the child's mental world have undergone distortions. It is quite evident that the described method of procedure must lead to similar consequences, for by equating early stages with later ones it passes over the developmental processes and thus proves to be a genetic-dynamic method only in appearance. When we study a developmental process we observe what happens to a given phenomenon under the influence of the most varied factors, both internal and external. To equate the initial product with the final one is to ignore the operation of those factors and of the dynamic process. As Waelder has pointed out, the adherents of that school of thought do not give due weight to the influence of reality. And I think we might add that they overlook the existence of a process of development within the individual himself. Just as preanalytic psychology denied that there exists an "unconscious," so do they deny the phenomenon of the dynamic developmental processes in the personality under the influence of external forces.

CHAPTER 7

The Preoedipal Phase in the
Development of the Male Child

(1946)

In the study of infantile development the data gained from the analysis of male and female patients were accorded different importance in the evolution of psychoanalysis. The first insight into neurotic mechanisms in general were derived from the treatment of women; in *Studies on Hysteria* (Breuer and Freud, 1895) only female patients were described. The case of Dora (Freud, 1905a) gave us the first insight into the impact of infantile events on development.

In a later phase, our knowledge of infantile sexuality was gained in the analysis of patients of both sexes; at that time, however, more was known about boys than about girls. The growth of the oedipus complex and its relation to the phases of pregenital libidinal development and the early object relation to the mother were first described in the male child, but the parallel processes in the girl remained obscure for some time. Similarly, the development of the superego as it relates to the termination of the oedipal conflict and the castration threat was understood as part of the boy's development before the

---

After the completion of this paper in Holland, I had the opportunity to read the interesting paper of Ruth Mack Brunswick, "The Pre-oedipal Phase of Libido Development" (1940), in which many similar problems are discussed. Since my own conclusions were arrived at independently during the war years, I did not try to discuss Brunswick's paper here.
See also Chapter 14.

sequence of analogous events in the development of the girl was understood.

In "Some Psychical Consequences of the Anatomical Distinction between the Sexes" Freud (1925) discussed some differences between male and female development and demonstrated that the latter is more complex. The castration complex of the little girl does not obliterate the oedipus complex; rather it proves to be its forerunner; the content of the castration complex of the girl, the penis envy, pushes her into her sexual position as a female. However, the earlier history of these developments remained obscure.

At this point in the history of psychoanalysis insight into the development of the girl came before that of the boy: the preoedipal phase was first studied in connection with female patients. In 1927 this author tried to point out that the female castration complex, and therefore the normal oedipus complex of the woman, was preceded by a negative oedipal constellation (Chapter 1). In these studies stress was laid on libidinal development, on the object relation toward the mother in so far as she is indispensable for the fulfillment of the needs and the desire for love of the child. Freud's study on female sexuality (1931b) taught us how full of content, how rich and decisive the preoedipal attachment to the mother is in the development of the little girl. We have since succeeded in gaining more detailed knowledge about this period, both in relation to the id of the little girl and to her ego development. In particular, many of the peculiarities of the woman's object relation and of her adult love life are now better understood.

This paper deals with the influence of the preoedipal relation to the mother on the development of the boy, especially from the point of view of the sexual life of the adult male. In approaching this subject we have two sets of expectations. First, since the earliest mother-child relationship is physically and mentally the closest possible between two individuals, traces of it must be found in adult life. Second, the difference between boy and girl must play a part in their development: the little girl has the more complicated development; she must abandon her early attachment to the mother in order to develop into womanhood, whereas the boy need not part from his original love object.

105

Thus we may expect that the influence of the preoedipal phase on the development of female sexuality may be more decisive and overwhelming than on the development of male sexuality. However, we may well expect this influence on male sexuality to be important enough to justify its closer study.

All further considerations must start from one insight: the direct development of male sexuality from the infantile oedipal attachment to the mother to the love life of the adult is threatened by the fact that a negative oedipus complex regularly exists in childhood in addition to the positive one. At one time or other in their development all boys develop a more or less intense loving attachment to the father and a more or less intense rivalry with and hostility to the mother. In this position the boys tend to behave in a way similar to little girls in their normal development. The attachment to the father is, as a rule, a passive feminine one (we can also speak of a homosexual attachment).

The existence of these passive libidinal tendencies must have a prehistory. Our findings indicate that during the preoedipal stage of development these passive libidinal tendencies are satisfied by the mother, who at the same time satisfies the boy's active strivings. In normal development these active strivings predominate and the passive ones are subordinated to them; it is well known that they are of great importance in the social adjustment of the normal male. In cases of pathological development these passive tendencies manifest themselves in three ways. First, they may influence the adult's sexual life as potency disturbances, in the guise of feminine masochistic behavior; or, in extreme cases, they may lead to homosexuality. Second, they may lead to neurotic tendencies. Third, they may cause abnormal character formation.

The analytic exploration of such cases shows that the continuation of the passive relation to the father is due to a fixation in the negative oepidus complex. In prolonged analysis we reach the earlier history of this fixation and we are able to observe the residues of the original passive attachment to the mother. We may therefore say that the passive feminine relation to the father is in the male a second edition of his primitive passive love relation to the mother, in a way similar to that of the girl. The difference is obvious. In the girl, passive attachment falls within normal development; in the boy, it contributes to pathological trends which may later disturb his normal sexuality.

There is still another consequence of the early attachment of the little boy to the mother which can be of decisive importance. Not only the negative oedipus complex, but also the positive oedipal relation has its forerunner in the preoedipal phase: in the active turning of the little boy toward the mother. A fixation at this stage or a regression to it has equally important consequences in the later development of the boy. His sexual life does not become a truly active and manly one; rather, it repeats his early relationship with the mother. Various signs of this relationship can easily be discerned. Its stigmata are the infantile aggressive forms of object relation, which is less libidinal and more narcissistic, intensely ambivalent, generally fluctuating. When passivity plays a considerable part, potency disturbances may occur. Peculiarities of pregenital libidinal development may be persistent. Oral and anal gratifications may be preferred and may lead to perversion. Males of this type behave like infants, whose love for the mother is egoistic, and claim indulgence of their own needs without respecting the needs of the partner.

A specific form of sexual behavior, the separation of sexuality from tenderness, which Freud first described, now seems easier to understand. Men whose behavior takes this form worship a woman whom they dare not possess as a sexual partner; their sexual partner must always be degraded. Freud explained the genesis of this attitude in the following way: the revered and unreachable woman is the beloved mother; since sexual activity has become degraded through prohibition and has become bad and dirty through its link to masturbation, the sexual partner has to be a degraded person. We can now add to this explanation: the admired and honored woman is chosen according to the mother image of the period of the oedipus complex. She is the heiress to the great love of little Oedipus for Jocasta. The degraded sexual partner, on the other hand, is the heiress to the image of the mother of the preoedipal phase; she has inherited the intense hostility that the little boy may have felt for her. That hostility, in turn, stems from his early ambivalence toward the mother and is reinforced by the fact that the mother has later become his rival in his love for the father. The adult man can vent his anger against the degraded sexual object; he can mistreat her, can force her to satisfy all his needs and desires, even perverse ones, and can compel her to attend to his wants as he wished his mother to do when he was a little boy.

At this point we are confronted with a specific question. How can we differentiate in analysis between the material pertaining to the oedipal period and that pertaining to the preoedipal period? This differentiation meets with considerable difficulty under certain circumstances. There are two reasons for this. First, all phases of infantile development overlap; second, a subsequent phase of development is always to a greater or lesser extent used to suppress residues of previous phases. And yet, on more detailed and precise examination of the material we discover many differences in the way in which the material is brought forth. In some instances even the body posture of the patient may be expressive: he may—as was the case with a patient of Paul Federn[1]— actually imitate the posture of the infant.

A young man who had undergone a successful analysis, which to a considerable extent had relieved him of his neurotic work inhibitions, came to me several years later because of a potency disturbance. He gave me an excellent exposition of his case history and of the results of his former treatment, which had revealed the development of his oedipus complex in all details. After some months of treatment with me the patient's behavior in analysis began to change.

During the first period of analysis he spoke easily and fluently, in a clear and loud voice, even when transference difficulties emerged, as, for instance, when he was compelled to re-experience his oedipal desires, and also when his transference resistance took other forms. In the second period of analysis his personality changed completely. He began to behave like an infant. His voice became high and childish. He no longer spoke as an adult does, but uttered incomplete and childish words and sentences. His emotions and his demands changed from one minute to another. He wept like a small child and clamored for my support and my love; the next moment he shouted and gave vent to the most intense hostility. This acting out in transference was amalgamated with bits of primitive fantasies, as ambivalent as we know the

---

[1] New York, personal communication.

emotional life of the child to be. These fantasies had an extremely passive content: I should handle him, feed him, nurse him, and satisfy immediately all his needs. These passive fantasies were interspersed with reaction formations: aggressive tendencies appeared and a wealth of suppressed anger and hate crystallized into reproaches and accusations. The slightest change in the tone of my voice, or any movement I might make in my chair, were used in order to produce love fantasies or were taken as occasions for outbursts of invectives. The love fantasies expressed oral and anal tendencies, wishes to be nursed and touched, demands for tenderness and for the satisfaction of exhibitionistic needs.

I gradually succeeded in persuading him that this change was natural and unavoidable. He became interested in the meaning of the change and succeeded in overcoming his narcissistic pride. He thus surrendered to the material which came from deeper layers of the unconscious. In the course of analysis his acting out in the transference was discussed, yet the patient occasionally manifested similar behavior patterns in his relationships with female partners. At the time when I primarily represented the mother whom, in identification with his father, he wished to love but whom he was not permitted to possess, he attempted partially to satisfy his preoedipal wishes in a relationship with a young girl of lower social status. During the period in which, in the transference situation, his early ambivalent mother attachment was revived, he turned adoringly to a much older woman of his acquaintance for a short time. Thus, most of the time his transference relationship to me shifted from one extreme to the other. However, gradually some historical events began to enter into his awareness: at the age of two he used to sit on his mother's lap in order to make her tell him stories and show him pictures. He spoke of sensations or feelings of warmth and delight, and expressed this in the childish manner that I have tried to characterize above; but he also remembered outbursts of hostility when his mother refused to repeat or to prolong situations which for him represented heavenly bliss. Memories from this period were scarce. However, the intensity and clarity of repetition in his acting out in the analysis made a convincing impression on both of us. The adult man who consciously had a strong desire to establish a family life was unconsciously seeking a woman who represented to him the preoedipal mother and who could revive all the details of his personal experience. Relationships that satisfied these unconscious perverse and hostile tendencies were to a certain extent disgusting to his adult personality. They disturbed the image of the adored mother of the later oedipal situation. It thus became impossible for him to reconcile love and sexuality. He had to prevent himself from marriage and even from potency with an approved sexual partner.

Another type of man who, in spite of a normal sexual potency, is constantly compelled to search for new women demonstrates a somewhat similar developmental disturbance. Such men, too, have an urgent desire for a quiet family life as a repetition of the infantile family situation; however, they are always forced to exchange one love object for another. They generally have infantile personalities and are fixated at the preoedipal phase of development. They are always in search of the mother of the preoedipal age, the mother who nursed them and toward whom they can behave as the spoiled child does. Either the adult part of their personality is frustrated in its manly aspirations or the infantile part of their personality is dissatisfied in its hopes and expectations. When in marriage a woman is able to fulfill the wishes of both parts of his personality—and this is possible only with women who have strong bisexual tendencies and a high degree of activity—the marriage can be successful. Otherwise divorces and changes of love objects follow each other. Needless to say, in the desires of these men oral and anal components play a considerable role, both directly in sexual behavior and indirectly in the urge to be fed and to be handled like a little child.

The case of another type of man, whom one might call the misogynist, is similar. Men of this type likewise show fixation points in the preoedipal phase; however, they usually have regressed to this phase because of the intensity of castration fear that they could not overcome. During the oedipal phase, in the eyes of the little boy the father is the castrator. In the analysis of this type of patient one discovers that in an earlier phase the boy was regularly extremely afraid of the mother. When he fails to free himself of his fear, he tends to make the

110

mother responsible for it. The boys who cannot overcome castration fear are, as a rule, those whose fear of their own passive tendencies is related to their *wish* to be castrated. Their hostility remains directed toward the mother. She becomes the actively hated object. Moreover, it is the woman who reminds these boys of the possibility of "being castrated"; she is feared and hated also because of this.

I should like to mention here a patient who had a good relationship with his wife, she being able to combine in her personality both mother images, the oedipal and the preoedipal one.

The patient came into analysis because of a work inhibition. After some time we discovered transient periods of disturbance in his relation to his wife. In the transference these disturbances expressed themselves in paranoid ideas; this proved to be a repetition of an experience that had occurred in infancy. As a little boy the patient had had a severe infection, and because of it had to be hospitalized for several months. During this period he developed the fantasy of being poisoned, so that he did not dare to eat; he remembered an intense hate of his mother, whom he made responsible for his suffering. The acting out in analysis seemed to show that this event was the second edition of an earlier one that had taken place after the birth of a younger sister. The patient was then one and a half years old and showed the well-known reaction of hostility to the unfaithful mother who had weaned him and given her milk to the other child.

Because of his wife's behavior, which enabled the patient to act out the different tendencies towards her, his marriage had not suffered. But the patient developed his work inhibitions as a substitute through which to express his conflict.

The influence of the preoedipal phase can also be studied in the formation of the superego. Where the sexual development is disturbed, the superego has not been consolidated. Traces of both father and mother images can easily be isolated, as well as traces of the identifications that are forerunners of the true superego formation. I intend to discuss this problem in another context.

However, I should like to mention here a case that shows clearly the fluctuation between father- and mother-identification, in behavior as well as in the superego functions.

The patient was a business man, though he had studied to be an engineer. He was nearly forty years old, very successful in his job, married, and the father of three children. The reason he came for analysis was, as he said, an interest in psychology, which time and again forced him to consider the possibility of changing his career. In these periods he wanted to study psychology in order to become a psychotherapist. He himself was astonished by this fantasy because he enjoyed his work. He wanted to establish a business of his own and knew he would be able to do so.

In his job he sometimes felt very independent. He then had excellent ideas and invented new plans to increase profits—ideas which were nearly always successful. Thus he was very much appreciated by his superiors. In other periods, he suddenly became inactive and lost his initiative. He then felt very dependent on the attitude of his chief toward himself. He had to watch carefully each remark, each change in the facial expression or voice of the latter, and was very much afraid of losing the chief's appreciation and sympathy.

The patient's history soon showed that this behavior was a repetition of the oedipal relation to his father. The latter, being a rich and a successful business man also, was the patient's example. The patient competed with and wanted to surpass him; but the moment he was successful he became guilty and had to punish himself by undoing his success, losing his initiative, and perhaps even the appreciation of others. He then had to reconcile his chief—father—and so behaved like a good dependent child. Thus he turned from the rivalrous, active, oedipal attitude to the passive feminine position. Thus far the analysis proceeded in the usual well-known way. But how could his sudden interest in psychological and intellectual problems be explained?

The family history showed that the patient's mother was a person of a cultural level quite different from the father's. Whereas he was a simple, crude, uncomplicated person, she was a refined, nervous woman, interested in science and art. The patient's scientific interest derived from an identification with his mother. However, this mother identification proved *not* to be related to his passive love for the father. As a very little boy he had understood that his father had no feeling at all for his wife's interests, and in the passive father attachment the patient's psychological aspirations played no role. His intellectual interests derived from an early mother identification, a primitive form of love attachment to her.

This preoedipal mother identification had various aspects. The mother had been suffering from a severe mental disease, for which she sometimes had to be hospitalized for several weeks or months. The patient was the only person in the family who had any understanding for this illness. As in early puberty he had heard something about psychology and psychoanalysis, he had become interested in it and produced the fantasy of curing his mother by it. However, in this fantasy the mother became the little child who was handled and treated and loved by him. The psychotherapeutic fantasy obviously was a later edition of very early mother-baby fantasies in which the patient alternatively played the role of the active (loving and aggressive) mother, and the passive child who wants to be handled and loved. These fantasies were revived in detail in an intense acting out in the transference.

For many reasons I cannot here go into detail. I hope I have succeeded in showing how the oedipal active-passive father relation, as seen in the patient's business life, was based on a preoedipal active-passive mother attachment that motivated his intellectual, mainly fantasied, interests. The patient's emotional life fluctuated between these two positions, each of them with a double foundation. His ability to identify with the active mother image was the basis of his later oedipal identification with the father and led to the normal manly part of his personality. The residues and continuation of his early passive mother attachment were partly transferred to a passive father relation and produced the split in his adult personality.

The superego formation showed similar discord. Traits of both father images and mother images could easily be found. In his moral attitudes toward others, for example, the patient fluctuated between crude, rough, ruthless conduct on the one hand, and soft, fine, sensitive behavior on the other. However, as mentioned before, I shall discuss these problems in detail elsewhere.

CHAPTER 8

On the Development of Ego
and Superego

(1947)

In resuming contact with psychoanalytic writing in other countries
after many years of separation enforced by the war, I am struck by the
varieties of directions in which research work has been extended. One
line of investigation, however, seems to me the most prevalent: there is
an increasing interest in the development of the ego and superego.
Many authors lay stress on the influence of environmental elements
connected with the formation of the ego. Psychoanalysis has shown
from the very beginning how important external experiences are for
the development of personality. But unfortunately many authors who
stress the importance of environmental factors seem to overemphasize
their influence and neglect or underestimate the importance of internal psychic processes. Sometimes they even go so far as to deny the
eminent significance of id drives,[1] especially of infantile sexuality, for
the ego and superego formation (Horney, Fromm). Our daily analytic
work regularly shows us the interplay of internal and external events
on the ego. These experiences force us to study the growth of personality as a biologically based dynamic process, which is certainly influenced by social circumstances.

See also Chapters 23, 24, and 26.

[1] I use the English word "drive" for the German *Trieb*, reserving the word "instinct" for the inborn mechanisms observed in animals, as for instance the nesting
instinct of birds, the food and fighting instincts of insects, etc. (see McDougall). I
hope to speak of this matter in another essay.

As far as I can see, the psychology of the social development of groups, of nations, and even of mankind in general must be regarded from the same point of view. Highly influenced by climate, economics, social life, and political circumstances, the development of mankind and its culture can only be understood as a dynamic process on a biological basis (N. Elias, 1939). Freud often pointed out that sexuality is the best-known part of the id, the psychic agency comprising the biologically rooted drives. We know that the genital organization of the adult is the result of a developmental process reaching back into early childhood. The phases of infantile sexuality, the oral, anal, and phallic stages in the formation of which libido and aggression participate, are the earliest and best-studied areas of psychoanalysis.

Early research work proved that the ultimate shape of sexuality in every person emerges from an interplay between the inborn nature of the drives and the influence of the environment. When we study a patient suffering from an obsessional neurosis we find a fixation of his libido on the anal phase of development owing to some traumatic events in his early childhood, on account of an anal disposition. Sometimes the first element is the more important, while the second is complementary (Freud's "complementary series").

We now turn to ego psychology. In the course of the development of psychoanalysis the ego was studied at a later period than the id. It is noteworthy that what attracts attention are the *functions* of the ego as they develop in dealing with the claims of the outer world. We spoke about a "weak" and a "strong" ego in its struggle with the id and the outer world, in its defense against inner and outer dangers. It was said by Freud and even more emphatically by Anna Freud (1936) that these defense mechanisms could become part of the character. However, the inner development of the ego has not been systematically taken into consideration. Yet we may observe in practice as well as in the study of the child that this inner development of the ego out of an inborn core actually takes place. This is parallel to the teaching of biology that in the fertilized ovum there lives the potential form of the whole highly complicated organism. In the id, which provides the mental power, the development of the drives is predetermined. We can expect the same from the ego. It is the task of the psychologist to study how the individual ego develops out of this inborn ego core. As a matter of fact, the investigation of the ego, or more precisely of the instrument with which the ego operates, the intelligence, has already been partially carried out. I refer to the developmental psychologies of Werner, Stern, Karl and Charlotte Bühler, Spranger, Piaget, etc. First and foremost, the work of Piaget (1936, 1937) seems to me of lasting value. In a series of accurate experiments he observes how the intelligence evolves from the hereditary reflex which is present at birth, as the sucking reflex, and shortly afterward in the form of the grasping reflex.

According to Piaget, the empirical intelligence is employed at the age of about one year; the systematic intelligence at one and a half to two years by the mechanisms of assimilation and accommodation. During this period real thinking in words begins; later on we see the constructive intelligence and the formation of judgment and reason. Psychologists differ in fixing the age when the child is able to judge logically, but certainly this function is not achieved before the third or fourth year (perhaps even much later). I do not intend to describe the whole of Piaget's research work. I only wish to point out the gradual autonomous development of intelligence.

I have just called "intelligence" the instrument with which the ego operates. The ego, it is true, uses it to get in touch with the outer world, groping for the environment and retaining its own observations as memory traces. We may say that the ego learns to observe by means of the intelligence and its forerunners; but at the same time it creates and develops them in executing its important function as an organ of perception. In later childhood and in adult life intelligence matures into different forms: one of them is the intellect, as for instance used in scientific work. However, other forms of intelligence are indispensable, e.g., common sense for judging situations, emotional processes in the inner and outer world, etc. There is still a large field of research work to be done in this direction. But now I will return to the study of the primitive ego. Its development—though partly an autonomous one— is at the same time highly dependent on the influences of the outer world as well as on the other parts of the person (id and later superego).

As I mentioned before, the functions of the ego are better known than its development. What are these functions? We have already spoken about the function of perception. A second function is the building up of the memory which enables the personality to progress toward the third and very important function of reality testing. Testing and judging reality, however, require intelligence of a certain degree, which, as we saw above, is only reached by the two- or three-year-old child. At an earlier age it exists only in a primitive form, as the environment and the knowledge of the infant are very limited. The ego functions of reality testing and building up of the memory, established during the first years, develop and grow during the whole life. A fourth important ego function is that of the "control of motility." The tendencies of the id try to find an outlet in actions which often come into conflict with environmental claims, so that the ego is forced to interfere. This intervention, however, is only possible if the child is able to master his muscular apparatus physically and mentally. In so far as the ego is a body ego, it has been formed in the earlier stage of childhood. The mental control of the motor discharge of tendencies and emotions follows and develops during the entire life, like other ego functions.

The growing intelligence and reason play an important part in the maturing of this capacity. They also show their influence in the fifth function of the ego, the so-called "synthetic function."[2] Though not entirely dependent on the level of intelligence and intellect, it is without doubt influenced by it. While in the id there is no question of a synthetic function, it is inherent in the ego from the very beginning of life. It develops, however, with the growth of personality and is perhaps as a rule more or less unfinished. Later on we shall speak about its origin.

We called the intelligence the instrument of ego capacities. But where does it come from? The intelligence itself is a highly organized mental process. According to Piaget, it develops out of hereditary reflexes. Perhaps we have to consider the instincts of the animals (instincts in McDougall's sense; see also Brun) as being the phylogenetic forerunners of human intelligence. (See the above-mentioned organized instinctive behavior of animals such as birds, insects, etc.) But it

---

[2] I was very pleased to discover nearly the same ego functions mentioned in Anna Freud's "Indication for Child Analysis" (1945).

is not the task of human psychology to state whether this idea is of any value or not.

We must now turn to another important question: what is the force or what are the forces which enable the ego to develop intelligence and its achievements? Piaget speaks about an "activity." The psychoanalyst can answer this question less vaguely: the ego originates out of the id, and in consequence must draw its forces from the same source. So it must be the energy of the drives, of Eros and aggression, which is used by the ego for its functions.[3] Freud's libido theory enables us to imagine the process. We know the ego is cathected with libido which we call narcissism, and it is taken for granted that the individual needs a certain amount of narcissism in order to function properly.

According to Freud, there must be a quantity of undifferentiated energy for the nonlibidinal mental processes, and he supposes this energy to be desexualized libido. Since we know the enormous role of aggression in mental life, we may amplify this opinion in describing a kind of sublimated aggression as the second contribution to this energy. The exploration and mastering of the outer world for the purposes of the ego take place through aggression sublimated into energic action and mixed with desexualized libidinal tendencies. However, in order to regulate this function a direct narcissistic cathexis is necessary as well as a balance between narcissistic and aggressive cathexis of the ego organization. This equilibrium is perceived as a satisfying feeling of self-esteem.

We may now summarize these questions in the following way: the ego as a part of the id develops out of an inborn ego core and has a development of its own. The process of the growth of the intelligence is well known to us (perhaps it is the basis of the "conflict-free sphere" of Hartmann). This autonomous development occurs under the influence of the contact with reality, with the id (and later on with the superego). In this development the ego functions arise, namely: (1) perception; (2) the building up of memory out of the traces of perception; (3)

---

[3] Here I wish to mention a remark made to me personally by Heinz Hartmann. He considers that id and ego both originate from a primitive, still undifferentiated state. I think it is merely a question of terminology. Phylogenetically, the id is older than the ego. Moreover, the id contains the biologically based drives.

reality testing; (4) control of motility (in the physical and mental way); and finally, (5) the synthetic function. An optimal narcissistic cathexis enables the ego to accomplish this task, which is many-sided and very complicated.

It is well known that in consequence of these various differentiated functions the ego is threatened by a great many dangers.

The ego is the servant of the id, the outer world, and the superego and it has to satisfy these three masters, as Freud described it. As the claims of the environment and the id are often in conflict, the ego frequently has to mediate. As far as the outer world is concerned, it tries to do so by its knowledge and experience. In the period in which these capacities are still small, i.e., in childhood, the person is very dependent on the outer objects (primarily the mother). It learns from them how to master reality. Here the mechanism of identification with the objects is used, and this is a very important process that we shall discuss later on. If the help of the mother, however, does not suffice, or if the mother herself is a part of the outer world which makes all these demands, the child must defend himself against these claims. Then the ego mobilizes one of the well-known defense mechanisms (A. Freud, 1936). Here denial plays the most important role.

On the other hand, the satisfaction of the id claims is not less difficult. The id requires satisfaction according to the pleasure-pain principle. In many cases these demands run counter to the claims of the environment. The ego tries to modify the id wishes, but when it fails to do so it must defend itself against these tendencies too, and mobilizes various defense mechanisms against them. These mechanisms are known as repression, isolation, regression, reaction formation, undoing, projection, introjection, sublimation, etc., well described by Freud, Anna Freud, and others. The ego is impressed by them. Thus, little by little, the ego organization becomes formed by these reactions and the child's character takes shape.

Observation teaches us that the choice of the special defense mechanisms is determined by an inborn factor, a tendency of the ego core, though also influenced by internal and external experiences of the child.

At a later period, when the superego is formed, its claims bring the ego into a third dependency, and, of course, equivalent actions and de-

119

fense reactions become necessary and influence character development. Later on I shall speak about these processes. First I should like to turn to a fourth dependency of the ego, which has been less studied.

As I mentioned before, the ego organization needs a certain amount of narcissistic cathexis in order to function properly. Especially in the earlier stages of ego development, this libidinal position is very vulnerable. There are many experiences, disappointments, and frustrations which are injurious to the ego's self-esteem and thus disturb the integrity of the ego cathexis. In Chapter 4 I described the danger to the ego when it is forced to defend itself against them. If the ego cathexis is hurt by the exorbitant claims of the outer world or overwhelmed by strong urges of the id, the ego is unable to develop its capacities and to behave normally. When it is injured in its libidinal position it will be disturbed in its autonomic functions, as already described.

In clinical work we can observe these processes if we turn our attention to ego analysis. When we study a patient suffering from hysteria, we can see, in dissolving his symptoms, that he has rejected an id impulse, at the command of the superego, by the mechanism of repression; the id tendencies cannot find normal discharge; the libido is partly regressed to the phallic or perhaps oral phase. But what about the ego? It is unable to function normally. In the first place, the memory is disturbed. There are gaps in its functioning. Sometimes the mastery of movement is interrupted, e.g., in hysterical paralysis control of movement is inhibited. In other cases perception is disturbed, e.g., in hysterical scotomization. In all cases the synthetic function is deranged; there is no more harmony in the personality. In other diseases, e.g., the obsessional neurosis, intelligence—though its level may be high in general—has partially regressed to a primitive level such as the magic phase, a forerunner of logical thinking. Here the split in the personality is much more obvious than in hysteria. The most far-reaching regression of the ego can be observed in the so-called narcissistic neuroses and the psychoses. Here the ego is really split up, the synthetic function has disappeared, reality testing is falsified or, in serious cases, almost totally disrupted. Judgment of the outer world has vanished in favor of primitive wishful thinking, etc.

As so often happens in psychoanalysis, the study of pathology teaches us how normal development takes its course. We suppose, in the case of a serious neurosis or a psychosis, a regression of the drives accompanied by an ego regression. And we can understand what has happened. The pathogenic process has damaged the narcissistic position, which was either too weak because of its predisposition, or has been weakened by this process, or both. In the case of a character disturbance, we can observe the same process in a part of the ego. There are persons whose ego functions normally in several capacities, but who show pathological behavior at one single point; as regards one particular claim their judgment of reality may be disturbed and they project their own feelings onto the outer world. These persons, who can think very logically and who usually act absolutely correctly, form in certain situations the erroneous idea that the environment hates them and is trying to counteract their activity. I have called that the "personal delusion" of nearly normal individuals. Studying this phenomenon in ego analysis, one always arrives at a narcissistic injury in childhood which has produced the feeling of being powerless. We know this process very well from the little girl who lives under the wounding disadvantage of lacking a penis and who feels inferior and powerless because of it. However, the little boy, too, suffers from feelings of impotence toward the mighty father and in earlier stages even toward the mother who originally is almighty in his view. In this connection we must do justice to the old theory of Alfred Adler. His "will to power" is really an important tendency in the life of mankind, but it is merely a part of childhood development and by no means the only one. Moreover, Adler was unwilling to see the great part played by libidinal components in this longing for power, which has to strengthen or restore the narcissistic cathexis of the ego.

When we have the opportunity of studying so-called normal adults we realize that almost always survivals of primitive ego reactions are to be found. There are very few, if any, totally integrated persons whose synthetic function has succeeded in constituting a really harmonious personality, whose reality testing enables them to think and judge in each situation in an objective and rational way, and whose self-esteem makes them act according to their own needs as well as those of their fellow men. If we study the personality of the leader of a group we learn that his exceptional influence on others is based on a strong narcissistic cathexis. Unfortunately, this quality is often misused. His aggression is not sublimated into a socially advantageous activity but is used in a more or less primitive way for the satisfaction of his own craving for power.

There are still many questions and problems in this field of research open for study.

We might now look at the third part of the personality, the superego.

As part of the ego, the superego takes over some of the ego functions. In normal cases there is unity between them. However, we know how often a conflict exists. At earlier stages of human development this unity cannot yet be observed. Therefore it seems justifiable to turn our attention to the growth of the superego.

From analytic observation we must conclude that the superego develops in the same way as the id and ego. Still, there are some differences: the id is present from the very beginning of life; the ego develops from the infant's entry into the outer world, that is to say from birth on, though we had to assume the presence of an ego core in the id. The superego arises only after some years, as an heir of the oedipus complex. As is well known, some analysts place its origin earlier, but I prefer to distinguish between the forerunners and the superego proper. A gradual maturation necessitates complicated processes of identification and introjection. So we must accept a developmental phase of which the superego is the main achievement. We assume that the construction and the mechanisms of the subsequent superego are to some extent predetermined. We observe, e.g., that the intensity with which infants take over the orders and prohibitions of their parents differs in different children. The acceptance of orders is primarily an imitation of parental behavior. By means of the mechanism of identification, however, it becomes an inner part of the psychic personality. Therefore, the capacity for identification is of paramount importance for the building up of the superego, and it certainly differs in nature in different individuals. Though the contents of the superego claims are dependent on the influence of the parents, the mechanism of identification is inherited. Moreover, we know from Freud that the severity of the punishing superego also depends upon the intensity of the child's hostility and his ability to turn aggression toward himself. Thus through this mechanism the superego is also partly independent of the parental image.[4]

Up to now we have spoken of the judging and punishing superego. But we must also consider another superego function, that of ideal formation. Observations teach us that this ideal formation occurs very early. As a matter of fact, in the harmonious adult these two parts of the superego, the ego ideal and the judging superego, are homogeneous and form a unity. But I think we must follow Alexander and some other authors, e.g., Flugel in *Man, Morals and Society* (1945), in separating them while we are studying their development. The ego ideal plays an important role in maintaining the narcissistic position of the ego organization. I have already mentioned that this position is indispensable for a well-balanced functioning of the personality. When the self-respect is wounded the child satisfies his narcissistic needs in creating and introjecting his ideal. At first it is formed after parental images. Later on, other examples are added to them, until finally social, moral, scientific, and religious ideals are created. It is an important support for a man's mental balance if his ego ideal functions well, if its level is not too high but high enough to strengthen self-respect. Therefore the first identifications are of lasting significance for the entire development. Stimulating the process of identification without exaggerating it is an important educational method and may offer suitable ideals. The same principle holds for the formation of the judging superego. Here acceptable orders and prohibitions should be offered to the child. In describing the influence of education we must not forget the intrinsic force of the developing superego, as we know the mechanisms and the strength of the aggressive impulses to be inborn qualities. Moreover, the superego is intimately connected with the id, as it becomes fixated after the oedipal situation has passed. Therefore it not only revives ancestral images but also inherits part of the immobility and immutability of the instinctual drives. On the other hand, one can observe how changeable and unstable identifications can be in earlier periods of development, and it often happens that this instability remains throughout an entire lifetime. These antagonisms represent the two factors of

[4] According to a personal communication from Dr. Tibout, it is possible that the superego is established only after the aggression is turned inward.

123

Freud's complementary series: disposition and environmental influence. Many people remain at an early stage and do not succeed in developing an independent and adjustable superego.

So far we have spoken mainly about the mechanisms at work during the formation of the superego in the widest sense (thus including the ideal), as a psychic organ. But what about the creation of the contents? In the individual they are partly taken from the environment and therefore very much influenced by the family constellation and later on by the actual social, economic, and political circumstances. In so far as they are taken from inside—that means from the earliest identifications with norms and ideals of the parents whose own moral system was based on the requirements of an older generation—they contain precipitates of former superego formations and therefore represent residues of earlier periods and former cultures. The question arises whether phylogenetic laws exist in accordance with which morals and ethics have been built up. This question raises another one: are the tendencies of the superego inherent only in the id and ego mechanisms, such as the intensity of aggression, the mechanisms of identification and of turning aggression against the self, or is there also a specific factor inherent only in the superego? This is a wide and difficult problem for detailed research with which I cannot deal now.

We will make only two remarks in this connection: (1) in prohibitions the demand for the renunciation of satisfaction plays an important role. In this connection I am thinking particularly of aggression which disturbs the social relations of men. To check it, reaction formations against it have to be developed, e.g., overcompensation in loving one's fellow men. We know how often people fail and fall back upon open or hidden hostility. To use a popular expression, the question is whether love can remain stronger than hatred. (2) In the creation of ethics and ideals the narcissistic need must be satisfied. At the same time the needs and interests of our fellow men have to be respected and included in our satisfactions. From a social point of view it is dangerous if men remain at the primitive phase of self-satisfaction and longing for power without adjusting their needs to a higher social level. It is also unfortunate if they try to compensate their lowered self-esteem by excessively worshiping another person, an idea, a deity. Can an equilibrium be achieved between self-assertion on the one hand and a due regard for the community?

It seems justifiable to suggest that well-balanced compensation of aggressiveness by love and acquisition of self-assertion through ideals are the driving forces of the religious, ethical, and scientific achievements of mankind.

CHAPTER 9

The Origin and Development of Guilt Feelings

(1947)

In various discussions among psychiatrists and psychotherapists in Holland there has proved to be a confusing misunderstanding because of an insufficient differentiation between the concepts of "guilt" and "guilt feelings."

When trying to define the term "guilt" one enters the sphere of valuations. During the age-old history of the development of mankind a great number of normative systems, religious, philosophical, ethical, social, have come into existence. Different definitions of the words "guilt," "good and evil," are to be found in each system. It is very remarkable that within a given social or religious community definitions change in the course of time, from generation to generation, under the influence of economic, technical, geographical, and other conditions. Therefore one can speak of "guilt" (objective guilt) only within a certain community in a given space of time. Thus limited, the definition is useful and necessary in community life. In practice, each community needs norms and values in order to be able to protect itself against individuals or groups that might become a danger to its organization.

A psychologist who is working scientifically will put the question as follows: What are the causes of the development of *this* special conception of norms, in *this* very period in *this* very group of men? He will have to take into account social, economic, technical, geographical factors as well as biological and psychological ones in the light of their own development. It seems almost impossible for one single person

126

to master all those sciences. The future will teach us whether modern teamwork will succeed in solving this problem. First and foremost the psychologist has to occupy himself with the psychological aspects, without neglecting the influence of the other factors mentioned above, of course.

In his daily work the psychoanalyst does therapeutic and research work with his patients at the same time. He is often accused by outsiders of being exclusively interested in the individual and of neglecting the urgent problems of mankind in distress. In my opinion this reproach is unjust. Each individual constitutes part of some community or other. Each community is composed of individuals. Without knowing the laws of psychic life of individuals one will never be able to get to the bottom of the problems of social psychology. It is unnecessary to emphasize that this does not imply that concepts and theories gained by exploring individual mental life should be applied to groups without further discrimination.

However, psychoanalysis has revealed many general human laws and trends which are of outstanding importance for sociology and social psychology. The pioneering work of Freud in this field is well known. Psychoanalytic science, however, is still penetrating more and more into the structure and dynamics of mental life, so that further contributions to social psychology are to be expected.

It is noteworthy that the very persons who disparage psychoanalysis as one-sided and narrow-minded expect it on the other hand to solve all the mental problems of mankind. The impossibility of realizing this expectation is in turn used as a reproach against psychoanalysis.

Reverting to the problem under discussion—guilt and guilt feelings: I have mentioned the divergence of views on "what is guilty" in various communities in different periods. Society defines "guilty" in its juridical laws. A person is "guilty" and therefore punished when he acts against these laws.

The normative systems, e.g., the religious ones, have created more or less dogmatic commands and prohibitions, norms of "good" and "evil." Within such systems a person acting in contradiction to the norms of "good" is considered to be "guilty."

Many dogmatists are convinced that they have the only real judg-

127

ment of "good" and "guilt," referring to an inner feeling of evidence. Naturally a follower of another religious or ethical system is not satisfied by this statement, he himself pleading for his own conviction by a similar inner sentiment. Here the scientist can only make the highly interesting observation that in all of those different valuations similar mental processes are operating.

In the psychology of the individual, "guilt feelings" play an important role. The phenomenological description of those feelings is given in different terms, according to the religious, philosophical, or ethical persuasion of the given person.

Some people speak of "sense of guilt," of "consciousness of guilt," of "an existential experience of guilt," of "a metaphysical guilt," and so on.

The psychoanalytic study of human mental life has taught us to describe "guilt feeling" as a (mostly unpleasant) tension within the personality. This tension is likely to become conscious as a feeling of being "bad," "guilty," as a feeling of discomfort, of dissatisfaction with oneself, as a shortcoming, as a vague anxiety, etc. We regard all of these feelings as falling into the group of guilt feelings, because they are tensions that come into being through similar inner processes, one being able to substitute for another.

This intrapsychic tension is localized between two parts of the psychic personality, the ego and the superego. The superego, it is well known, is a psychic structure that comes into existence during the development of man. The newborn infant has no function of conscience. He has many needs and wants: whenever these needs are satisfied the infant is tensionless and quiet (content, as the mother says); whenever they remain ungratified for a longer or shorter length of time, the baby shows an inner tension by being uncomfortable, by crying, etc. Not until the baby has achieved a psychic relationship, an attachment to the mother, does he begin to perceive what the mother desires, what she disapproves of, what she feels is "good" or "bad." In order not to lose the mother's love and approval, on which he is highly dependent, the young child will learn to renounce forbidden and bad wishes. The toddler, though already aware of the mother's valuations, quietly does forbidden things whenever there is no chance of his being punished or of losing the mother's love. In this period anxiety is the only factor to control the infant's behavior and to determine his being good or naughty. There is no inner voice of conscience, defining what is good or bad, and consequently we cannot speak of the infant's having guilt feelings in this phase.

Later on, the fear of punishment and of losing love is transferred to the father, educators, teachers, social institutions, etc. It always remains part of the directives for behavior in the life of man, though variable in quantity in different persons.

However, older children and adults may feel guilty and renounce forbidden wishes when they need not fear punishment or loss of love and approval. These persons really have an inner conscience. There has been established an authority in their ego organization that judges good and evil. Sinning against this conscience produces a real feeling of guilt.

This newly organized part of the ego has come into existence through the process of identification with the parental images and their valuations. This process is a complicated psychic event and the final stage of the intensive and highly important development of the small child's instinctual and affective life.

During this development the mechanism of identification comes into existence. At first it produces only unstable and changing trends in the child's ego. It is the same period in which the child becomes aware of the mother's demands and valuations and is influenced in his behavior by his fear of the mother's disapproval, as we described above.

However, at the end of the first developmental stage before entering the latency period, part of the child's ego produces a real, stable change by internalizing the parental images, claims, and judgments, and it thus creates the inner conscience, the superego. The parental judgments have now become part of the child's own mental inventory.

Sinning against the superego gives rise to guilt feelings and must be paid for by self-punishment in the form of the inner grief of self-reproach, self-torment, penance, and sometimes even self-mutilation. Guilt feelings develop out of the ego's fear of the superego claims and have their forerunner in the ego's fear of the claims of the environment.

In many persons the regulation of their social behavior occurs mainly through the fear of environmental commands, as already mentioned above. Other persons develop a severe superego and a strict conscience. Both regulating principles are always to be found, their mutual relations varying from case to case. It seems worth while to describe some peculiarities of the different types resulting from the various mixtures of the two principles.

Adults in whom the superego is poorly developed generally do not have a stable opinion about morals. They behave socially mainly out of fear of prison or some other punishment. They call "good" and "evil" what is defined as "good" and "evil" by the momentary authority in their environment. They know that they are "guilty" when they act against the law, but they do not *feel* guilty. Whenever another authority comes to power they easily take over the new opinions and act according to the changed laws. In this way they behave like small children. We may say that their mental development has been inhibited in the stage before the superego is stabilized. People with well-developed superegos have acquired the ability to create opinions of their own. Originally, it is true, they have taken over the parental judgments. But maturation and mental growth involve development of the superego to more or less independence and originality. The persons in question have their own opinions about morals and behave according to the inner voice of their conscience. When they act against their conscience, they become subject to real guilt feelings. When authority and law change, they keep their own valuations.

This description of independent development may be called too idealistic, it is true. However, I have already mentioned that in practice both regulating principles are always to be found. I have only described extremes in both directions. Another complication arises when an inhibition in development takes place not *before* the establishment of the superego as I described above, but soon after its formation. This inhibition can cause an arrest of the development of the superego. It becomes fixated to the parental opinions and remains rigid, unable to grow into an independent personal mental structure. Extreme inhibitions in this direction are to be considered as belonging to the field of pathology. I shall come back to this later.

Next we will turn our attention to two striking peculiarities of guilt feelings.

(1) Some people suffer from an extraordinarily powerful sense of guilt without ever having done anything really bad. In these cases there are impulses to be observed which are labeled by the person himself as extremely bad ones. He judges himself as severely as a real judge would do when confronting a real delinquent. Here we encounter the remarkable unconscious phenomena of psychic identification of thought and deed, the "omnipotence of thought," usually found in primitives and children. I shall return to the origin of this primitive desire to be "almighty" later on.

(2) Some people deny every feeling of guilt (or the counterparts described above), although they behave as if they were guilty. They are constantly harming, punishing, tormenting themselves, or provoking harm and injury from others or from the state. We say these people are suffering from unconscious guilt feelings or, to put it more correctly, from an unconscious need for punishment. Evidently the conflict between ego and superego is repressed in these persons. However, it forces its way out into a neurosis or a neurotic attitude toward life. In both cases we enter the province of pathology.

The sound, integrated personality has established an equilibrium between the claims of reality and superego on the one hand and the needs, desires, and capacities of ego and id on the other hand. The diseased personality, however, has not been able to solve his inner conflicts and therefore has failed to find an equilibrium. Psychoanalysis tries to find out in which cases the pathological guilt feelings remain unconscious and where they force their way to the level of consciousness.

Now we encounter another important question: What is it that sometimes makes the superego so extremely powerful and tormenting? Where does this intensity come from? I mentioned above that the superego in its origin represents an introjected image of the parental behavior. It takes over the commands and prohibitions of the parents and at the same time the severity of their claims for obedience, but this process is not the only one. A very striking observation teaches us that many children with weak and indulgent parents develop a severe and

131

sometimes cruel superego. This superego not only treats the ego as the parents used to treat the disobedient child; it also behaves toward the ego as the disappointed, vengeful child wished to behave toward the parents. How vengeful and destroying a child's wishes sometimes are can easily be observed in children who are educated in a free and not intimidating way. They ventilate the most harmful, damaging, and destructive fantasies toward siblings as well as toward the parents, either directly or in play activities. Severe disturbances like obsessional neuroses and melancholic depressions are characterized by the influence of an extremely severe superego. When analyzing patients suffering from these diseases we realize that these same destructive strivings existed in their infancies. An intolerant education of course furthers the process of repression in the infant and stimulates the inner process of self-punishment. On the other hand, I have already mentioned how often a mild attitude in the educators cannot prevent the building up of a pathologically severe superego. In order to understand this phenomenon we will consider the child's development in respect to these details.

Originally the infant regards himself as the center of the world. He does not know of any outer world but is exclusively aware of his own wants and needs. When he discovers a world outside of his "self" that does not afford direct satisfaction at every moment, he experiences disappointment and mortification, which provoke his hostility. The small, powerless child is unable to discharge his hostile, destructive impulses. On the one hand he must fear the parents' punishment, but when the parents are mild and tolerant the main point is that the hostile feelings come into an insoluble conflict with strong love for them. We understand that the above-mentioned "omnipotence of thought" makes the child feel as if he really had damaged the parents, and therefore robbed himself of their protection and love. The child becomes afraid of his own destructive tendencies. This so-called "ambivalence conflict" leads to repression, to a turning against the self of the aggressive impulses. At the end of the period of the child's flourishing instinctual life, which, though only lasting for a few years, is very intense and of paramount importance to the full development of the personality, the attachment to the parents is definitely internalized and the parental

132

images survive in the superego. However, this process is attended by an introjection of the hostile impulses toward them. One part of this aggressiveness is taken up by the superego, which now behaves in a severe and sadistic way with respect to the ego. The ego begins to fear the superego. The other part of the aggressiveness is drawn on by the ego, which becomes servile and masochistic in its relation to the superego. The tension between the two parts of the personality is perceived later on as a strong guilt feeling. These two processes always take place side by side but in various proportions. In pathological cases it is of importance for therapeutic success whether the greater part of the aggression is finally established in the ego or in the superego. Pathological guilt feeling (need for punishment) is always hard to influence. However, the masochistic ego is still more resistant to therapeutic attempts than is the abnormally cruel superego.

Summarizing, we are justified in stating that guilt feelings of adults, experienced in different ways and phenomenologically described in various terms, originate from the fear of the superego. They are differentiations of this superego fear.

I have already mentioned one of the forerunners in the child's development: fear of the claims of the environment. We now have to add a second one: fear of his own destructive impulses. Here I should like to face an old critical question. Is it really possible to fear one's instinctual drives? Perhaps the drive becomes a danger only through the prohibition of the environment? Many investigators (including some psychoanalysts) answer the second question affirmatively. The relations at issue are hard to penetrate indeed. The child works up each disappointment, each privation, into a penalty for a forbidden desire. However, it is obvious that there are situations in which a given ego constellation can be too weak to meet a certain demand of a drive without fear. Here the ego can neither tolerate the discharge of the drive impulse nor master the striving in some other way. One may observe this in a small child if a given drive is provoked prematurely before the child is prepared to meet it, e.g., in cases of seduction by older children or grownups. This traumatic situation can apply to sexual as well as to destructive drives. It depends on the momentary relation between id forces and ego forces whether the trauma can be mastered normally or not. The destructive drives, however, involve another specific danger.

The imperative life impulse of the infant and his actual helplessness cause his dependency upon the mother's love and care. The child has to love the mother in turn. Life as well as love are threatened by the destructive and hostile strivings. When the infant develops an impulse to damage or to destroy those whom he loves and wants to preserve, he must experience anxiety.

Fear resulting from the tension of the ambivalence conflict could be termed the biological root of guilt feelings. In the course of development, fear of the outer world comes into existence. Later on the fear of the superego is experienced as guilt feeling (or as one of the various equivalent sentiments described above). Here we encounter the social-psychological background of guilt feelings.

We will turn now to the events provoking the infant's destructive tendencies. One group has already been mentioned above: disappointment, privation, unsatisfied longing for love provoke hostile impulses toward the object in question. There is another very important source to be found, however, from which aggressive strivings arise: injuries of self-esteem, of the craving for power, or to put it in other words, primitive narcissistic injuries.

The newborn infant is originally unaware of an outside world; he imagines his "self" as the almighty center of the world. The discovery of his own lack of power is a shattering injury to his self-esteem. The infant tries to undo this injury by using the fantasy of the omnipotence of thoughts and wishes. However, this mechanism is foredoomed to failure and consequently it is followed by a wave of rage and aggression. At first the mother is made responsible for each sort of injury, and consequently the destructive forces of the child are directed toward her. Now the child's love of his mother is endangered, destructive tendencies have to be turned against the self, and the above-described process runs its course.

In our therapeutic work with patients we must know the sources of the fear of their own aggression (and guilt feelings); e.g., states of severe depression generally cannot be influenced without working through this early conflict of ambivalence.

Sometimes the view is met with in outsiders that psychoanalysis considers each guilt feeling as a pathological phenomenon. Another view often held is that psychoanalysis aims at destroying the patient's superego. Naturally both views are equally absurd. As soon as a community arises there is a need for laws and norms, the interests of individual and community often being in conflict. The internalization of the norms (the foundation of the superego) is a normal mental process in every child. It is one of the consequences, and a very important one, of the development of mental life in mankind. The superego not only represents the prohibiting authority; at the same time it enriches the personality with ideals, the mental and moral possession of men. In Chapter 8 I expounded my view that it is advantageous to have a separate look at the development of the judging conscience (superego in a narrower sense) and at that of ideal formation. There are persons who develop a pathologically severe superego (they have to torment and punish themselves perpetually), but in whom ideals and ethics are on a low level. On the other hand, there are people of a high ethical and ideal standing who do not possess an excessively punishing superego. Guilt feeling is a normal psychic phenomenon as well. It is an alarm signal of disturbed inner harmony between ego and superego, parallel to anxiety which signals the danger of a disturbed equilibrium between ego and id or ego and environmental claims. The forms and contents of the ideals as well as those of the prohibitions are borrowed from the outer world and therefore are as varying, multicolored, and changing as the different circumstances make community life. Which general function they are fulfilling in a given community at a given moment is a most interesting question within the psychological and sociological fields of research.

As already stated, the psychologist generally cannot possess the deep knowledge of other sciences (sociology, anthropology, history of religion and economics, etc.) necessary to answer this question. From the psychological point of view, a few remarks may perhaps be of value. As social and individual interests often collide, a community has to protect itself against possible individual opposition. Therefore it has to create prohibitive laws. Now, bodily and mental power are different in various persons. Thus it occurs that the prohibitive laws are more and more used by the persons or groups in power to protect their acquired authority (they call it their "rights") and to suppress the powerless people. This comes into conflict with the original purpose of the regulating and prohibiting measures, namely, to protect the survival of the community. The laws become more or less the servants of the needs and wants of a relatively small group of men in power. The result can sometimes be the disintegration of the given community. A similar process can be observed in regard to ideals and ethics. Various sources of suffering and misery make men grope for solace in religious and ethical pursuits. Strong ideals can cement the relations between the members of a community. But the men in power often begin using the idealistic force to dominate their weaker fellow men. They tend to rob them of their sources of consolation by threatening them with severe punishments before or after death when they refuse to be obedient. So religion and ideals may be degraded to weapons for suppressing fellow men. The oppressors are most successful when they manage to use both laws and ethical claims to fix their power.

We have been able to study the origin and development of guilt feelings in the individual. It is not surprising that, as usual, pathological cases were the first objects. However, the same psychic processes operate in normal development. It is decisive for the person whether he will succeed in creating and recreating an inner harmony between ego, superego, and id within his special environment. When considering the almost immeasurable number of problems in the inner and outer worlds, one will understand how extremely difficult it is to grow into a harmonious integrated personality. One of these many problems is that of guilt feelings, the tension between ego and superego. We laid stress on the observation in our daily analytic work that pathological guilt feelings can be transformed into normal sentiments only by working through all the developmental stages without forgetting the underlying, biologically founded ambivalence conflict, i.e., the conflict between erotic and destructive strivings.

Sometimes we encounter a tendency in therapists to deny or to devaluate the destructive drives in man. It would be easy and pleasant if they were actually lacking. Men would not have to suffer so much under the difficult task of solving the conflict of ambivalence. Moreover, one could ignore the unpleasant feelings of impotence that are raised by this conflict. One could feel "all good" and "almighty." However, denial has very seldom given a lasting solution to a conflict. It seems to be more appropriate to face the problem. The direct discharge of destructive and aggressive tendencies usually clashes with the claims of the mighty principle of life: love. Life itself offers numerous ways to transpose aggressive strivings into activity. The active mastering of the sources and forces offered to mankind in its struggle for life has created high technical achievements, mental and moral possessions of paramount importance. It is astonishing to observe how often people prove to be unable to grant each other and themselves the undisturbed enjoyment of these high values. But here we pass from the individual problem to one of the community.

Every community has to create moral norms, as mentioned above, for a variety of reasons. One of them, perhaps the most important, is that destructive and egoistic omnipotent strivings of the individual have to be suppressed (or at least greatly restricted) in order to produce security for the community. We need not emphasize again that the community up to now has shown very poor success in trying to do this. One out of many causes for this failure, however, is to be found in the denial (or at least the undervaluation) of the force of destructive tendencies and of wish for omnipotence. Denial excludes mastery.

When these destructive natural forces in mankind are recognized, accepted, and mastered, the conditions enabling man to create productive instead of destructive activity are given. Better social and economic circumstances may result from this process. Sublimating destruction into productive activity may satisfy part of man's craving for power and may simultaneously free the other partner in the conflict of ambivalence: love. Perhaps some of mankind's misery and grief could be reduced by the creative power of love.

CHAPTER 10

Neurotics, Delinquents, and Ideal Formation

(1949)

It is a pleasure to contribute a paper in honor of the work of August Aichhorn, who opened new ways to our understanding and treatment of youthful delinquents. His famous book, *Wayward Youth* (1925) is not only an invaluable source of practical experience in dealing with problem children but also our first psychoanalytic orientation in the etiology and theory of delinquency.

Aichhorn considers delinquency the result of two types of faulty development in the child's libido structure. The first type occurs in the process whereby the pleasure principle is converted into the reality principle. The second is a malformation of the ego ideal. Both are problems of libido and ego development.

According to Aichhorn, a characteristic symptom of the dissocial child is his inability to meet the demands of reality. His ego cannot give up the pleasure principle and he meets such demands of his environment with obstinacy or revolt. This is the result of two extremes of faulty training, either of which may prevent him from an adjustment adequate to his age level. If he is treated with either excessive indulgence or excessive severity, the result may be the same. Our own clinical experience confirms this claim. Delinquent children all show the same inability to give up immediate gratification, and almost in-

---

See Chapter 8.

138

variably they have been brought up by someone (parents or guardians) whose methods were extreme. Either they were too severe and did not compensate the child for frustrations of love or other gratifications, or they spoiled the child until he was incapable of bearing any disappointment, or they oscillated between the two attitudes so that the child became too confused to be able to make any adequate adaptation.

But since these parental behavior patterns are found not only in the histories of delinquents but also in those of neurotics, the question arises what determines whether a child becomes neurotic or delinquent?

There has been much discussion of this point. Although psychiatric literature generally classifies waywardness and delinquency as psychopathies, a clear and uniform definition of this term is still lacking (see Rümke et al., 1947). It is very difficult to give such a definition because delinquent (psychopathic) behavior almost always reveals evidence of neurotic trends, and because both kinds of symptoms, delinquent and neurotic, show similar developmental disturbances.

H. G. van der Waals (1943, 1946) in his studies on the problem of the psychopath distinguishes between "dispositional" and "developmental" psychopathies, though he admits one must always allow for a complementary series of factors (Freud) in these as in the case of neurotics.

Although many psychiatrists tend to regard the neurosis as an acquired, the psychopathic state as a congenital disturbance, van der Waals concludes that "it is probable that the genesis of the psychopathic condition is identical in the main with that of the neurosis."

I agree with this author. The study of both neurotic and problem children usually reveals that their parents used faulty educational methods because of their own difficulties or neuroses. Therefore we tend to consider them responsible for the child's pathological development. Yet we sometimes meet cases of both categories whose parents were obviously normal and whose training was both understanding and free from the errors of extreme severity or indulgence. In such cases we are forced to postulate an abnormal disposition, although we must still be cautious lest we have overlooked some influences of earliest childhood.

139

We would therefore say that the genesis of both neurotic and dis-social disturbance lies in the interplay, in varying mixtures, of dispositional factors and environmental influences.

Yet this similar genesis should not blind us to the striking differences between neurotic and delinquent behavior. We must still be specific about these differences and attempt to find their causes.

Both neurotic and delinquent children show the same inability to harmonize their instinctual drives with the demands of their environment. We realize that in both cases it is a symptom of their faulty ego development. But the neurotic tries to solve the conflict by repressing id impulses while the delinquent ignores the social demands and acts out his primitive desires as far as possible. He refuses to give up immediate gratification and prefers to jeopardize his relation to his environment. In contrast, the neurotic's anxiety prevents him from risking a conflict in his relationship to his environment and so he has to bear the pain of giving up direct gratification. To put it differently, the delinquent's object attachment is not strong enough to act as a barrier against his instinctual needs and therefore his ego cannot achieve an adaptation to reality, whereas the neurotic is too dependent upon his object to permit the id more than a limited degree of instinctual satisfaction. Needless to say, we are using these quantitative terms in a relative sense only.

The delinquent who has made himself relatively independent of his environment is then proportionately more dependent on the gratification of his instinctual drives.

Since the neurotic is able to free himself to some degree from the imperative demand for immediate gratification, he, in turn, is correspondingly more dependent on the love he receives from his environment. Thus we see that the neurotic's ego is strong where that of the delinquent is weak and vice versa.

Let us at this point return to Aichhorn's second type of faulty development in the child's mental structure, the malformation of the ego ideal.

During the course of its development, one of the functions of the child's ego is to take over the demands and prohibitions of his parents. Thus starts the development of the superego, which later becomes a part of the ego organization by the introjection of these parent images. This introjection is theoretically completed and the superego established with the beginning of the latency period.[1]

The foregoing description of the neurotic's and the delinquent's reactions to their environments is now further complicated by the demands of the superego. An inadequate or disturbed relationship to the parents also disturbs the development of the superego, which manifests itself in a defective social adjustment.

Aichhorn (who uses the terms ego ideal and superego interchangeably) describes various types of delinquents whose behavior demonstrated their inability to form a socially acceptable ego ideal. He describes two groups.

In one group, the mechanism of the superego, or ego ideal, functioned well but the introjected parental norms were dissocial ones, that is, the parents were themselves criminal, so that the child who took over his standards from them inevitably came into conflict with society.

In the second group, it was the early relationship to the parents which had been disturbed, so that the process of ego ideal formation could not take a normal course but resulted in dissocial behavior.[2]

Let us specify at this point, parenthetically, that we consider an ideal social adaptation one in which the inner equilibrium between ego, id, and superego enables the personality to realize its own needs and capacities without preventing others from doing the same. Since individual needs often differ from the interests of a group or society, this adaptation is often hard to achieve.

Aichhorn, then, in discussing his second group of dissocial personalities enumerates various situations in early childhood which can cause faulty development of the ego ideal. Such is the case if a child is an orphan or semiorphan, or an illegitimate child who is placed in a succession of institutions or foster homes. He therefore has no one to

---

[1] Following a proposition of Hartmann and Kris (1945), I shall, in order to make the terminology more precise, use the word "maturation" instead of "autonomous development" and reserve the term "development" for the processes of growth predominantly dependent on the environment.

[2] Here I should like to stress the fact that social adaptation is not identical with uncritical submission to every passing demand of a given society. There can be and often really are circumstances in society which require a condemnation of prevailing norms and a rebellion against them.

whom he can form a sound and stable attachment or with whom he can make a real and lasting identification. In such cases there is either no way of establishing an ego ideal or it is defective and too weak to regulate conduct in later life.

Aichhorn describes other abnormal family situations that can have similar consequences, but they all demonstrate the same formula, namely, a defect or absence of object attachment causing a defect or absence of an ego ideal. Both a normal object relation and a sound ego ideal are necessary for an adequate social adjustment, and where either factor has been abnormal, delinquency may result.

Let us examine these same processes in neurotics.

The anamneses of neurotics also show disturbances in object cathexis and ego ideal formation. It seems probable that neglected children, who have not had a mother's (or parent's) love seem more predestined to delinquency. Though my own experience with delinquency is too limited to justify an opinion, I am sure that lack of motherly love and severe frustrations can lead to a neurosis.

But this still does not illuminate our question about differential factors since most of the cases we meet show a combination of symptoms. The delinquent reveals neurotic trends, and our neurotic patients show tendencies toward more or less dissocial behavior. Therefore we have to confine ourselves to the quantitative aspect in making our diagnosis. Where the dissocial behavior predominates we speak of a delinquent with neurotic symptoms, and where there is a reversed balance of factors, we speak of a neurotic personality with (often concealed) delinquent features.

Although it is difficult to separate abnormal psychic manifestations from each other, careful observation sometimes enables us to gain insight into the origin of our patients' different behavior patterns.[3] Aichhorn describes types of delinquents who commit their dissocial offenses because of a need for punishment (an unconscious sense of guilt). Such cases force us to assume a severe superego (see Freud, 1916). Yet we repeatedly observe that a too severe superego causes

---

[3] Needless to say, we must always realize that clinically these various phenomena overlap and merge. Perhaps it will prove to be true that in each individual, whether "ill" or "normal," some trends of delinquency (psychopathy) are to be found.

neurotic symptoms. Can we discover what factors determine whether a strong and cruel superego leads to delinquency or to neurosis?

Since a punishing superego (like punishing parents in early childhood) makes one suffer, individual differences in the capacity to endure suffering, pain, or discontent must play a role in the problem. A person who cannot bear such tensions not only develops an inadequate adaptation to reality but, unlike the neurotic, will not endure self-punishment. He tries to escape it by mobilizing his rebellion against the outer world as a means of acting out the tension caused by his guilt feelings.

Why does the neurotic not do likewise? Perhaps his ability to endure suffering is greater, yet this means of relieving it would benefit him also. Must we conclude that his punishing superego is stronger than that of the delinquent? I do not believe so. The delinquents whose offenses are due to a sense of guilt show an intensity of purpose which hardly justifies this conclusion. It seems to me that another formulation may afford a deeper insight into this problem (see Chapter 8).

Up to this point, I have used the terms ego ideal and superego interchangeably as does Aichhorn. I now propose to make a distinction between them, as have Alexander, Flugel, and others.[4]

The superego is established through a dual process of development. The infant identifies himself very early with both parents and wants to be or to become like them, and to incorporate their ideals as well. ("I want to be like my parents and have their ideals.") At the same time the child also takes over his parents' orders and prohibitions, and by introjecting them builds up the inhibiting (and punishing) part of the superego. ("I must or must not do this or that.")

The ideal formation in the ego of the young child has a special function apart from that of social adjustment. It might be said to fortify the ego. These ideals serve the child as compensation whenever he feels hurt or incompetent in comparison with older children or adults. They strengthen his self-esteem by counteracting narcissistic injuries and frustrations. During maturation these ideals expand into all kinds of social, ethical, religious, and scientific norms. Even for adults, high ideals, if not

---

[4] In the English translation of Aichhorn's book, *Wayward Youth* (1925), the translators also mention this tendency in psychoanalytic literature.

exaggerated far beyond the personal level of attainment, are of great value to their self-esteem.

The young child's judging superego has the function of supervising his instinctual gratifications and curbing his passions through punishment whenever they threaten to conflict with external demands. This function of the superego, therefore, often injures the narcissistic position of the ego and hurts his self-esteem.

Where there has been a harmonious development, both parts of the established superego work together toward inner and outer equilibrium and finally form a unity. But if the development of either the ideal formation or the punishing part of the superego is disturbed, the two may diverge. We can understand this process better if we study the forces behind them.

We know from Freud that the severity of the superego does not correlate exclusively with the parents' attitude. The cruelty of the superego corresponds more closely to the strength of the child's own aggressiveness. During the period when the child's superego is being established it uses that part of the child's aggressiveness which is turned toward the self. This takes place after the period of active instinctual life has terminated with the ending of its last phase, the oedipal situation.

When development is normal, the part of aggressive energy which is turned toward the self serves to secure the fulfillment of the ideals and thus strengthens the ego's self-respect. The remaining part of free, aggressive energy is used for mental, intellectual, and bodily activities in the outer world, for learning, adapting to, or changing the environment. It is "sublimated" into activity.

Unfortunately this difficult, complicated, and dual process is frequently disturbed. Often too much aggressiveness is turned toward the self. This aggression then becomes sexualized and the whole relation between superego and ego ceases to be a judging, regulating function in the service of normal adaptation. Instead it becomes a sadomasochistic relationship. The result is an obstinate tendency to self-punishment, an arrest and restriction of ego development and of the formation of the ego ideal.

On the one hand the ego is threatened by the cruel superego which

144

has become as *triebhaft* as the id, and on the other the ego receives no support from the ego ideal because the ideal formation has been both damaged and restricted.

Moreover, when the two processes of the formation of an ego ideal and of a sadistic superego diverge, this divergence is itself another inhibiting force to the growth of the total personality.

When the aggressive energy used for developing normal activities cannot be adequately sublimated still another disturbance results. Either repression and inhibition are increased or the aggression is expressed in a direct, primitive manner. If it combines with sexual energy it can lead to various other forms of abnormal development.

Neurotics as well as delinquents may show a driving need for self-punishment. I now claim that the differential factor between neurotics and delinquents is to be found in a developmental difference of their ego ideal and superego formations.

Where there has been a strong ideal formation in early childhood which later was disturbed by an oversevere superego, its effect is to inhibit ego development and to prevent the sublimation of aggressive energy into activity. The strong ideals forbid the expression of any aggression toward the outside world and it therefore turns toward the self. The result is the well-known vicious circle of the neurosis.

If in the young child there has been a weak ideal formation which later is disturbed by a sadistic superego, the result is self-punishment and also defective ego development. But in such cases the weak ideal formation is unable to prevent the aggression from discharging and the superego's aggression is acted out against the environment. This results in dissocial behavior or delinquency.

There are interesting instances of mixtures of these two processes. Thus, for example, one may observe persons who, in one area of their lives have high ideals to which they may either be making a good adjustment, or if blocked in attaining them, react with neurotic symptoms in this special field. But in other areas they may be utterly lacking in ideals and norms and behave quite dissocially. Careful examination of many delinquents often reveals a similar mixture in their personalities, with a few areas dominated by high norms and fine social feelings.

The ideal formation which begins in early childhood and uses the

145

mechanism of identification is probably a difficult and vulnerable process.

Since it would seem that almost everyone, be he as "normal" as possible in ordinary life, has a small "neurotic" nucleus and sometimes an almost undetectable "personal delusion," he probably also has a minor "psychopathic" spot in his makeup (Chapter 8).

I regret that the scope of this paper prevents me from presenting illustrative cases. Instead, I should like to discuss here two additional problems.

What are the prerequisites for a sound and lasting ideal formation? What is the source of this overpowering and ungovernable aggression which partly threatens the self and partly the environment?

I would say that there are two prerequisites for ideal formation. There must be a capacity for identification, innate and capable of being stimulated by experience. There must also be the right objects with which the child can identify. If these are lacking or inadequate, the process is correspondingly restricted.

There are children who succeed in building high ideals and norms in spite of having either no parents, or unsound or unstable parent figures. It may be that this astonishing achievement of some unloved children is the result of their need to compensate for the narcissistic injuries which this lack of adequate object gratification caused them.

But when a child is not loved in his early years the more frequent result is an impaired ideal formation. The child's narcissistic needs are then doubly frustrated through lack of love as well as through imperfect ideal formation. This formulation brings us once more to an awareness of the importance of a child's first love objects.

To return to our second point, namely, the source of the overpowering aggression: Observation of children convinces us that even a young child's aggression can be and generally is mobilized by the frustration of a bodily or mental need or wish.

The same is true in regard to sexuality. The infant at first seeks gratification of his sexual urges through his own body (thumb-sucking, friction, anal play, masturbation, etc.). It is the mother who introduces the child to sexual pleasure. By offering her breast and by caressing the baby while nursing him, she excites the baby and provokes his libidinal attachment. We know how important maternal "seducing" proves to be for the child's sexual development and how an excess of "seduction" may cause a variety of disturbances. It is true that in normal development the baby's discharge of aggressive energy by means of his own body is seldom noticed. The normal tendency toward the preservation of life ordinarily masks the signs of these aggressive urges. But occasionally aggressive urges reveal themselves unmistakably in cases of self-damage (by scratching, etc.).

In obviously pathological cases, however, severe self-mutilation has been observed.[5] But we hold to the truth of our previous statement, namely that acts of aggression are in the main provoked by "frustration" as are sexual ones by "seduction." These facts guide our educational procedures and make us say: A child needs love but too much gratification may be experienced as seduction and can be as harmful as lack of love.

Our knowledge that frustration stimulates aggression leads us to say: The child must have opportunities for discharging a part of his aggression, but stimulating his aggression by too much frustration will have damaging results. All of us who deal with children are aware of this danger of steering from Scylla into Charybdis.

Since too many frustrations provoke an excess of aggressiveness, the child must be compensated by love so that he can make a sound love attachment and a tenable ideal formation.

There seems a tendency in the literature to neglect the topic of aggressive, instinctual urges in life, because of the fact that we only notice the aggression which follows frustration. We would be in a similar position were we to ignore the need for sexual object attachments because they arise only after stimulation. The fact that some authors have never observed acts of genuine aggression hardly justifies this omission. In the same way, in the early days of psychoanalysis, the existence of infantile sexual urges was indignantly denied by the pediatricians, educators, and parents who had never observed them. Although the analogous observation of aggressive urges is far more difficult, it seems possible that further investigation will broaden the observer's views.

[5] See the case in W. Hoffer's paper on "Mouth, Hand, and Ego-Integration" (1949).

Some authors seem to neglect this topic of instinctual aggression because of their doubts about Freud's theory of a biologically founded death instinct. In my opinion, biology has not yet gone far enough either to affirm or deny Freud's hypothesis. Should it be proven erroneous, psychoanalysis must discard it. This would leave us without an answer as to the origin of aggressive energy until we can formulate a new and more tenable hypothesis. But meanwhile we cannot afford to overlook the manifestations of both sexual and aggressive drives in mankind.

From the social point of view it is vitally important that mankind does not deny the existence and intensity of genuine aggressiveness. Denial always leads to blindness and therefore to disturbed reality testing and adjustment. Some people seem to have a deep-rooted fear of admitting their own aggressive drives and therefore deny them in all human beings. Not until the role of the aggressive drives in the individual and in society has been accepted can we conceive of finding ways and means of overcoming the menacing manifestations of aggression and destructive behavior in mankind.

Among the major purposes of any educational program must be the aim of providing compensating love, constructive ideal formation, and suitable methods for sublimating aggression into fruitful activities.

In one chapter of his book (1925, pp. 167-185), Aichhorn describes an attempt to re-educate a group of juvenile delinquents in an institution. Their aggressiveness was so overwhelming as to segregate them from all other groups. Though he himself points out how, in his handling of this group, he was still groping for technique, and though today he might have used other methods, one is nevertheless struck by his intuitive understanding of their problems.

And we can recognize in this pioneer attempt at group re-education his awareness of the balance of factors and his endeavor to change the hitherto misdirected processes which have been the subject of this paper.

CHAPTER 11

Some Remarks on the Development of Psychoanalysis During the Last Decades

(1950)

Psychoanalysis, like every science, has been continually developing during the more than fifty years of its existence. Development implies the possibility of enlargements and modifications of the original form. The object of psychoanalytic study is human psychic life, its theory is based on observations of the manifestations of this psychic life in both "normal" and "abnormal" persons. Since the observations have steadily increased and become greatly refined in the course of decades, the theory has gone through an evolution, has adjusted over and over again to the increase in knowledge, as is the case with all sciences. Where psychoanalytic psychology touches biology, notably where the biological substratum of the instinctual drives is concerned, the theory has, for the time being, a more hypothetical character.

It may be expected that a growing biological knowledge will either corroborate Freud's biological theory of the drives, or entail the necessity of modifying it.

Psychoanalysis is often blamed for not being concerned with the so-called *Geisteswissenschaften*, which are engaged in the determination of values and norms (ethics), in philosophical speculations (such as, e.g., in the systems of Heidegger et al.), upon creeds, such as are to be found in the various religious systems, but—remarkably enough—on the other hand it is often said that analysis intends to affect or even to destroy norms and values, the "conception of life" of individuals and sometimes that of mankind itself.

Both reproaches are apparently rooted in a misappreciation of the empirical-scientific character of psychoanalysis. Psychoanalysis wants to observe, to gather knowledge, and to detect certain rules. Its relationship to the normative, speculative, and religious systems mentioned before can only be such as to take such systems—as manifestations of human emotional and mental life—for its objects of study, which has already been done by Freud and others. The objection that analysts do have a "view of life" and that consequently psychoanalysis has one too sounds very naïve. Every person who lives in a community with others, and therefore the analyst too, needs values and norms, has a "conception of life." It stands to reason that enrichment of knowledge and extension of insight affect the conception of life and the determination of values. This has always been found to be true throughout the ages. Man, in our present civilization, no longer conceives of his genesis as a lump of clay which was molded, nor does he regard the earth as the center of the universe. It would be a wrong way of thinking, which no longer needs to be refuted, to conclude from these facts that the conception of life and the determination of values of one or of a number of analysts proves that psychoanalytic *science* embraces a conception of life. It cannot and will not represent a conception of life.

I would like to discuss a condition which has often given rise to these errors in thinking. It lies in the fact that the analytic method of treatment is often mistaken for psychoanalytic science. Whenever two persons meet they will influence each other, however brief the encounter may be and even though the influence may be infinitesimal. An exchange of emotions may take place even without spoken words. If a patient applies to a doctor for help in combatting his neurotic symptoms, his psychic disturbances and disharmonies, and if the two of them decide upon a psychoanalytic treatment, they start upon this procedure with the conscious purpose of striving for a "value," which they have determined together, i.e., the patient's health. In doing so, the knowledge provided by psychoanalytic psychology is utilized, to wit, that neurotic symptoms or disturbances can sometimes be removed by tracing their genesis of which the patient is unaware.

By making the unconscious conscious, by reconstructing, remembering, and especially by once more *living through* and *working through* the conflicts that arose in previous developmental stages, a disturbed development can be modified and, if the patient is willing, it can be corrected.

In every encounter necessary for this purpose an exchange between analyst and patient takes place. Since the latter is usually helpless as a result of his illness and disequilibrium, he will be very susceptible to influence (unconscious or conscious), he will desire it and often even provoke it. The analyst, however, will try to utilize the patient's openness to influence for the sole purpose of making him accomplish the difficult psychic task, described above, which is a prerequisite for realizing the common goal (the "value"), i.e., to return to the patient his "health" and his own personality, if possible.

The analyst will regard every attempt at transferring the contents of his ethical, religious, or philosophical norms or concepts to the patient as taking advantage of the patient's openness to influence, a state which is temporarily raised by the therapeutic situation. Only with children, and with some adults who have remained very infantile and who have not developed a sufficiently normal personality, does one sometimes have to avail oneself of such a pedagogical influence in addition to the analytic treatment. Experience has taught us, however, that every such intervention is attended by a disturbance in the dynamic psychic process (to wit, the discovery and re-experiencing of the warded-off unconscious) which automatically arises in the analytic situation and the undisturbed course of which offers the best chances of recovery. Therefore one will avail oneself of these interventions as *rarely* and as *sparingly* as possible, and one will have to realize over and over again that in using them one runs the risk of adversely affecting the chances of recovery and development.

Now I have come to our subject proper: the development of psychoanalysis during the last decades. I want to distinguish three themes: (1) the development of the scientific theory; (2) the development of the technique and the therapeutic possibilities; (3) the influence of psychoanalysis on other branches of science, such as psychiatry, academic psychology, sociology, anthropology, ethnology, pedagogy, etc.

151

The Development of Psychoanalytic Psychology

As has been said before, the psychoanalytic theory has been developed in the course of years and modified whenever necessary in the light of the experiences which increased owing to the growing refinement of the technique of exploration of mental life.

But Freud's fundamental discovery that neurosis arises whenever a psychic conflict cannot be solved in a normal way still maintains its validity. The neurotic patient displays, in a very obvious way, psychic phenomena (actions, thoughts, behavior) which are alien to his conscious personality. These observations made it necessary to accept a stratification or structuralization in the psyche and to distinguish between a conscious and an unconscious psychic life. This distinction could not be a merely descriptive one. Experience taught that one could make the unconscious conscious only by a certain psychic effort after overcoming the counteracting forces (resistance). Consequently one had to assume various systems in mental life, between which an interplay of forces takes place. Thus in addition to the topographic viewpoint, a dynamic viewpoint became necessary in the theory.

The study of hysterias and compulsion neuroses (and also the study of some paranoid states) soon revealed that certain startling events concerning the emotional life and certain urges, tendencies, and wishes which could not be tolerated or gratified by the conscious personality, were not only "forgotten," but were repressed to the unconscious, warded off, and, by the mobilization of certain forces, prevented from entering consciousness; these are the very forces which, as I described before, manifest themselves as resistance in treatment.

The repressed urges were usually found to originate from the sexual sphere, and the startling events were found to be especially traumatizing when they occurred in early childhood, thus encountering a weak, undeveloped personality.

I will regard these early developmental stages of psychoanalysis as common knowledge and will leave it at this brief picture. I will only call to mind how the experiences on the instinctual and emotional life of the young child necessarily resulted in an extension of the concept of sexuality, which until then had practically been equated with adult sexual life. Adult love life turned out to be a final product of a long developmental course of sexuality from birth onward. This sexuality was found to go through a flourishing early period in the first years of life, during which it passes through various developmental stages (oral, anal-sadistic, and phallic phases), to flourish again in puberty after a latency period, and ultimately to result in adult life.

Certain traumatizations or excessive instinctual demands proved to be capable of disturbing this normal course of events, while the concomitant object relationships were also disturbed and neurotic symptoms arose; now the dynamic viewpoint could also be better circumscribed in the theory. The interplay of forces was opposed by the sexual drives on the one hand and by the drives of self-preservation on the other. Quantitative factors required a third viewpoint in the theory: the so-called economic one. Quantitative relations between the various forces and in the various systems were decisive in regard to the final outcome of the conflicts in which constitutional factors and environmental influences were always found to play a part (Freud's "complementary series").

The biologically prescribed, autonomous development of infantile sexuality turned out to be subject to being influenced, stimulated, or inhibited by the attitude of the first love objects, originally the mother (or nurse), afterward also the father and other members of the family. At the height of the phallic phase a certain constellation of the object relations is found, i.e., the so-called oedipal situation, consisting of a positive attitude (love for the parent of the opposite sex and rivalry and hate as far as the other parent is concerned) resulting in normal sexual development, and a negative oedipal situation (love for the parent of the same sex, rivalry with the other one), tendencies of which are gradually desexualized under normal conditions and sublimated into social relations. They may play an important role in pathology; however, I need not go further into this subject here. Freud's discovery that the oedipus complex constitutes the nuclear point of the neuroses can still be endorsed at present. We do know now, it is true, that the oedipal instinctual and emotional constellation is already the finished product of a greatly differentiated developmental process in the so-called preoedipal situation.

I will now briefly describe the developments that the various as-

153

pects of psychoanalytic theory have gone through. I will first examine (a) the structuralization of the mind, and then (b) the theory of the drives.

Topography or Structure of the Psychic Personality

The division into conscious and unconscious psychic life (Freud's *Pcpt.-Cs.* vs. *Ucs.* systems) soon proved to be insufficient to allow the ever-increasing numbers of differentiated psychic phenomena to express themselves. It was found to be possible that processes which were at first counted as belonging to the system consciousness were repressed to the unconscious in a later developmental stage, etc. Freud suggested denoting the agencies between which the psychic processes take place as "id" and "ego." The id represents what has been carried in the germinal cells and comprises among other things the instinctual life (the drives); it is the source from which all subsequent features develop. In the id the so-called "pleasure-pain principle" prevails. Pleasure is striven for in an imperative, rigid way, and pain is avoided. The mode of action of the id is the so-called "primary process," well known from the study of a normal psychic phenomenon, the dream, and extensively described in Freud's *The Interpretation of Dreams* (1900).

The ego is that part of the psychic personality which develops from the id under the influence of the outer world, and acts as an intermediary between the demands of the id and those of the outer world. To fulfill this task the ego develops a number of functions. It derives its power from the id and draws on the store of possibilities, capacities, and potentialities which are present at birth and are ever further developing. The ego modifies the pleasure-pain principle under the influence of the demands and restrictions imposed by the environment into the so-called "reality principle," which gives up the original rigidity, learns to tolerate pain to a certain extent and to renounce immediate gratification of pleasure. The mode of action of the ego is the so-called "secondary process"; in the mature ego this is an ordered, structured process, governed by thinking. As the ego gradually develops from the id, the development from pleasure principle to reality principle and from primary process to secondary process is a gradual one too, while transitions are always to be found.

154

As long as, for instance, the child's sense of reality has not yet developed, i.e., as long as the child cannot adequately distinguish between himself and the outer world, the reality principle cannot come to full development and action. In this case the mediation between the id and outer world is a deficient one for the time being, and the ego can respond to many stimuli and demands, both from the outside and from the inside, only by escape (repression, resistance, or denial) instead of by adequate handling and control.

Not only does the development of the sense of reality gradually take place, but all functions of the ego have to be developed from a primitive stage. The possibility of observation of stimuli, perception, the formation of memory traces and memory images, the control of the steadily developing motility in order to make it subservient to the discharge of instinctual tensions and to the exploration and conquering of or adaptation to the outer world, the testing of reality—all these psychic functions the ego has to learn gradually. Intelligence, speech, and thinking also undergo a process of maturation from very primitive stages (see also the developmental psychology of Piaget).

At the same time the person needs not only discharge of instinctual tensions but also gratification of the strong desire for love, consequently a good relationship with the objects. These objects do help the child in the development of all his capacities, but on the other hand they make demands, impose restrictions upon the child, and cause frustrations the child is often unable to cope with. These difficulties can inhibit or even prevent the development of the various functions.

The ego produces mechanisms of defense and reaction formations against the instinctual tendencies which can become fixated and play a role in determining the character. Ultimately the ego strives for an inner unity and equilibrium. However, the synthetic function (integrative faculty) comes into existence comparatively late. From the very beginning this function can be damaged by disturbances in these infinitely complex, early, and labile developmental stages.

In contradiction to academic psychology, psychoanalytic psychology has paid a great deal of attention to the dynamic processes. Both in the analytic exploration of the first years of childhood and in the direct observation of very young children it has found an abundance of material enabling the study of the effect of instinctual life on ego development. Without utilizing this dynamic viewpoint the genetic psychology of the young child remains incomplete and results in a misconception of infantile psychic life.[1]

In neuroses and other faulty developments not only is a regression to an early fixation point of instinctual development to be found, but likewise a regression to an earlier stage of ego development. Inasmuch as reactive and defense mechanisms toward instinctual tendencies are concerned, there is a correlation with the corresponding libidinal stage. But all primitive ego attitudes may be mobilized again, and disturbances in certain functions occur in the various clinical pictures, such as hysteria, compulsion neurosis, paranoid states, etc.

I will now mention a very important process in ego development, described by Freud nearly thirty years ago, i.e., the formation of the superego. I may presume that it is well known that the superego is part of the ego, that it arises early in the latency period as a kind of precipitate of the oedipal object relationships which have been replaced by identifications. Through these identifications the modified part of the ego has assimilated the norms, commands, and prohibitions of the parents and at the same time the ideal images the child has made of them. Examples from the much wider social environment are added later on. The superego has become, as it were, the conscience of the child: it exercises criticism, it demands and prohibits, and simultaneously it has become the ego ideal (see Chapter 10).

In normal development, ego and superego harmonize with each other. The ego adapts itself to ideals, norms, and prohibitions, the superego adjusts its demands, if necessary, to the capacity of the ego. It is well known, however, how often this harmony is disturbed, leading to a gap arising between them.

The development of the superego is gradual, and correspondingly one also encounters precursors or, to put it otherwise, primitive developmental stages in the superego.[2]

[1] In the scope of this paper I cannot go into further detailed descriptions, and must refer to the analytic literature on these problems which has been published in various countries in the past few years (see Chapter 8; also A. Freud, 1936, 1945; A. Freud and D. Burlingham, 1942, 1943; Hartmann, Kris, and Loewenstein, 1946).

[2] For a different view of superego development, see Melanie Klein (1932, 1948).

The ego already uses the mechanism of identification at a very early stage, first, as a mechanism of defense against fear of loss of love, secondly (besides imitation), to learn from the object, to develop, and third, to form an ideal. By means of this form of identification the child also adopts prohibitions; this is very clearly observed in the anal phase of development. The child has already accepted, to a greater or lesser extent, what is permitted and what is not permitted; the ideal formation runs a parallel course. Normally a fusion of ideal ego and judging (prohibiting) superego is established only in the ultimate formation of a superego agency at the onset of the latency period.

This superego shows a further development throughout life and it obtains a greater or lesser autonomy by modifying the initial imperative parental norms in accordance with its own insight and experience. Nevertheless, in so-called normal people too, some residues of the infantile superego, acting in a compulsive way according to parental norms, are still to be found. Furthermore, it is my opinion that an even earlier precursor of the superego can be observed. In the earliest period of life, when the child begins to distinguish between "inside" and "outside," the unpleasurable, the painful, the "bad" are projected onto the outside world. The pleasurable, the "good," remain inside. Later on "bad" and "good" obtain entirely different meanings, but in many people this primitive "What is within me, what I am, is good; the other is bad" is often found again in their subjective conviction that they have "the" truth, know "the" revelation, advocate "the" good or "the" right, while misappreciating the subjective values of others. Here again a brief mention must suffice.

Many problems of ego and superego development are still unsolved, and so are their interrelations and their relations to various neurotic processes.

The Development of the Theory of the Drives

Originally Freud was of the opinion that psychic conflicts, which can be studied most sharply in pathological phenomena in view of the larger dimensions assumed there, were caused by a clash between opposing instinctual drives which he conceived of as being linked with the two different systems, designated at that time $Cs.$ and $Ucs.$ He distinguished self-preservative or ego instincts from sexual drives. When, however, it was found that the ego too may become the object of sexual drives, that the ego has a libidinal cathexis, the so-called narcissistic cathexis, the distinction between the different groups of instinctual drives could no longer run parallel to the division into structural systems (or agencies). In the meantime Freud had also discovered that destructive and aggressive behavior could not be attributed to a certain transformation of the sexual drives, but that it was the manifestation of a destructive (or aggressive) drive which could be observed, being linked with and mixed with the sexual drives. In certain pathological cases, but notably in young children, an abundance of pertinent material is found on careful observation (see, e.g., A. Freud, 1949a). The new theory of the instinctual drives, which is still dualistic, distinguishes between erotic and destructive (aggressive) drives, which can act in conjunction (alloyed), but also separately.

Originally the drives are part of the id (in the widest sense). Aggressive drives accompany sexual ones on their way through the various developmental phases (oral, anal, phallic, and in adults the genital phases). In recent investigations attempts have been made to study the forms of expression of aggression in the various stages (see, for example, Hartmann, Kris, and Loewenstein, 1949). Especially in the first years of life one can observe how libido and aggression may be discharged simultaneously and separately. We meet, then, with instinctual ambivalence, which in turn entails emotional ambivalence. This ambivalence often continues throughout life; it may prevent the integration of the personality and may result in neuroses and/or character disorders.

During development the ego derives energy of both kinds of drive from the id. Partly the ego neutralizes or sublimates drive energy and it uses this neutralized energy for the many psychic functions and activities which it gradually develops during life. Yet a direct instinctual cathexis of the ego continues to exist throughout life. A certain level of narcissistic cathexis of the ego is found to be a precondition for normal functioning. Both excessive narcissistic cathexis, resulting in inadequate or faulty object relations, and a too small amount of narcissism may give rise to diseases or disorders. In the complexity of human existence in the present civilization, an optimal condition does not seem to be easily attained.

Optimal sublimation of aggression into active control of the outer world is also a difficult task. Far too often activities turn out to be more or less purely aggressive deeds. Here we are confronted with a new task of the ego. Besides the functions of acting as an intermediary between id and environment, developing its functions, developing defense and reactive mechanisms, and building up a harmonious unity with the superego, the ego is also called upon to maintain a narcissistic cathexis, which is an indispensable basis for all its achievements. Injuries of this cathexis (so-called narcissistic injuries) also entail consequences for the development of the personality and may give rise to disharmonies (neuroses, deformities of character, etc.).

The legitimate need to find a biological basis for the forces that operate in psychic life (drives) caused Freud to construct a working hypothesis, in which he conceived of the vital process as an interplay of two different forces, the connecting (Eros) and the dissolving or destructive force. (The designations "life instinct" and "death instinct" are not a fortunate choice, in my opinion.) The erotic and aggressive drives, manifestations of which we observe in psychic life, would be expressions of the primal forces operating in all animate nature.

This hypothesis is rejected by many people, among whom are psychoanalysts, although it may offer explanations for a number of phenomena for which a better or more elucidating hypothesis has not been advanced by any of its opponents. Such a speculative working hypothesis can never be proved from psychological knowledge, nor can it be refuted. It remains for biology to substantiate, reject, or modify this hypothesis.

The psychological theory of the drives, as it is presented to us today, is capable of explaining the dynamics of psychic phenomena fairly well. In this brief survey I cannot discuss the multiplicity and complexity of the various forms of expression to their full extent, of course.

159

THE DEVELOPMENT OF THE PSYCHOANALYTIC TECHNIQUE
AND THE THERAPEUTIC POSSIBILITIES

The increase in knowledge of mental life has greatly affected the technical process of psychoanalytic treatment. Conversely, the refinement of the technique has made us familiar with many more phenomena and has taught us to explain them more thoroughly.

Originally, Freud developed a technical procedure to make the repressed unconscious of a patient conscious because experience had taught him that neurotic phenomena sometimes could be removed by this process.

The discovery of the forces counteracting this process (resistances) made it necessary to go beyond making unconscious contents conscious and to find psychological means of handling these forces and to learn to control them. This required a finer technique and a slow working through of all positions, traumatic events, and fixation points in the past.

Our increased knowledge of the maturation and development of the ego gradually made it possible to develop a technique to treat not only the cases where the disturbance lay in conflicts between the instinctual life and a relatively intact, adult ego, but also those in which the ego had become involved in the disease and had been disturbed and inhibited in its own development. Not only were regressions to former stages of the libido made conscious, but ego regressions to early points of arrest in development were exposed, defense mechanisms and reaction formations were traced, inasmuch as they had assumed pathological forms, and thus the patient was given an opportunity to make up the deficiencies in his ego development. Pathological reactions of the superego were also made conscious and worked through, owing to which morbid reactions of guilt feeling and tendencies toward self-punishment can sometimes be abolished. Moreover, the knowledge of instinctual life makes it possible at present to remove not only disturbances in the sexual sphere but also pathological manifestations and modifications of aggression, which play so great a part in, for instance, inhibitions, disturbances of the capacity to work, depressions, etc. The discovery, referred to above, of the early history of the oedipus complex, the preoedipal attachment to the mother, and our detailed knowledge of the pregenital developmental states of the libido (Abraham, 1921, 1924a, 1924b, 1924c) enabled us to revive traumatic events of even the earliest childhood.

The psychoanalytic technique had to undergo a real change. The material from this primordial period does not rise to the surface in words, in memories, dreams, or fantasies, but by way of so-called acting out, the re-experiencing of infantile events, feelings, emotions, etc., in the analytic situation. Here again the modified and more refined technique provided us with new data on psychic events and on early ego development.

The increase in knowledge and the refinement of the technique have also widened the range of applications of psychoanalytic therapy. While at the onset only hysterias, compulsion neuroses, and some paranoid states could be treated, at present we can also employ psychoanalysis in the so-called narcissistic neuroses, depressions, deformities of character, delinquency, developmental disturbances in children, and various mild psychotic states. Naturally this does not by any means imply that all these morbid states can always be entirely cured or that it is possible to make a perfectly harmonious, integrated personality out of every disturbed human being. Just like every medical therapy, psychoanalytic therapy has its limitations and restrictions. It is very remarkable that, in many people, even in doctors and psychiatrists, one encounters the idea, and the demand, that psychoanalysis must be able to remove all psychic disturbances. Although nobody blames a surgeon or a specialist on pulmonary diseases for not being able to cure a number of his patients after a careful and patiently continued therapy, a great fuss is often made when psychoanalytic treatment does not always yield the desired success.

In the event of a failure, the analyst can only take comfort in the idea that he has increased his knowledge by which other patients may benefit, and that he may have learned to realize where the limitations of therapeutic influence lie. I will not go further into this question here, since it would lead us too far from the subject under discussion. I will merely point out another field where the progress of psychoanalytic technique and science must be regarded as of importance.

There are many patients with whom one does not want or is not able to apply psychoanalytic treatment, for internal or external reasons. In order to make these patients fit for life, to a certain extent at least, one resorts to one of the forms of so-called "brief therapy." This used to be based (and this is still often the case) on an uncontrolled, so-called intuitive treatment of the patient. Our increased knowledge of psychic conflicts enables us occasionally (and probably will do so even more in future) to attack only certain conflicts or to displace them to fields where they are less disturbing in the patient's life situation.

Owing to our refined technique we are better able to see how we can and ought to utilize the relation between doctor and patient in order to help the latter in solving certain conflicts. The detailed elaboration of the technique of these "brief therapies" is still in the making, but it is being further studied by various analysts and in various institutions in Europe and the United States.

I want to point out one danger to which brief therapy is exposed to a much greater extent than is analysis. The improvement of the patient's condition arising in consequence of a displacement or of a merely partial solution of his disturbances can be undone again in later years. It very often happens that a patient, after having undergone one or more psychotherapies in the course of years, all of them attended with some success, ultimately does turn to the psychoanalyst, when middle-aged or older. The analyst then has to regard the chances for recovery in this period of life as much poorer than they might have been at an earlier time. It may even happen that an attempt to start an analysis has to be given up entirely, for instance, with women in the climacterium whose main talents lay in being a wife and mother and who would consequently not be able to do very much with their regained health.

As already indicated, I am of the opinion that psychoanalytic (and psychotherapeutic) treatment must remain a procedure which aims at tracing the causes of certain (mental) diseases and at trying to cure them.

An opinion which is often voiced at present, that the therapist should introduce a certain conception of life or of mankind into the treatment, is not only a nonmedical and unscientific one, but moreover limits to a great extent the group of people that can be reached.

162

Experience has taught that with psychoanalysis one can help people of different races and nationalities, with the most divergent creeds, conceptions of life, and social convictions. Exercising influence in philosophical, religious, or political directions is the field of the philosopher, the pastor, the pedagogue, or the propagandist. When the psychotherapist is prepared to give up the narcissistic satisfaction of transferring his own values and convictions to his fellow men, he will be able to handle the human relation with his patients in order to restore the health of as large a number of people as possible.

The "ideal" that I am defending here is a medical-therapeutic one in the widest sense of the word.

Should it be indispensable in very infantile patients, as I remarked, to exercise more personal influence, one must always remain aware of the fact that one has added a second goal to the medical-therapeutic one. Our knowledge of psychic life enables us to make these finer distinctions and to dose the measure by which the patient is influenced.

THE INFLUENCE OF PSYCHOANALYSIS ON OTHER BRANCHES OF SCIENCE

Psychiatry and psychology have been more or less consciously adopting the discoveries of psychoanalysis for decades. This is denied by many, although one continually encounters the influence of analysis both in theory and in practice. This denial has undoubtedly affected psychiatry rather unfavorably. Sometimes psychoanalysis is said to be accepted. However, it often happens that this "acceptance" is limited to an injudicious and distorted utilization of technical terms, in which the unbiased observation of the phenomena has fallen into the background.

In practice one often encounters a conscious rejection together with an unconscious utilization of psychoanalytic psychology, which usually does not yield profit to the patient. The use of a method not mastered by the therapist may be very dangerous, as in every medical therapy. Where analysis is not consciously rejected, but where the therapist has not acquired the technique by personal experience in living through and working through his own conflicts, it is often observed that the so-called analytic treatment is limited to labeling certain conflict situations, preferably in theoretical terms. The dynamic character of the

163

therapeutic process may be misjudged; the detection of his very individual experiences and the working through of his special conflicts in his own sphere and language may be withheld from the patient.

However, in view of the growing interest in psychoanalysis (especially in England and the United States but also on the Continent), it may be expected that a more objective, scientifically critical attitude of psychiatry will gradually prevail. Such an attitude would make a more judicious use of the findings of psychoanalysis and at the same time would further the efforts to fill the many gaps still present.

The influence of psychoanalysis on sociology and anthropology[3] started very early. This influence began with Freud's own work, as is well known. (I merely refer to *Totem and Taboo* [1912-13] as a classical work.) During the last decades sociologists and anthropologists, especially in America, have often appealed to psychoanalysis. The analysts, too, have made attempts at elucidating sociological problems with the aid of analytic psychology. The difficulty is that in general sociologists are not sufficiently schooled in analysis, while analysts are not sufficiently in touch with the many facts to be found in the fields of sociology and anthropology.

Since a thorough knowledge of the development of the relations between men and of all aspects of mankind, social order, etc., does not seem to be possible without a profound knowledge of the individual, one may assume that teamwork will develop in the future, as it is already operating in America on a small scale.

Analysis has been of great significance in education, beginning at a very early date. Besides the application of the method to children, the so-called child analysis, it has greatly influenced the pedagogical attitude of adults, both in normal and in pathological cases, in connection with the enormous increase of knowledge regarding the development of the child.

I will not go further into this matter, but I want to stress the fact that the pioneer work of Aichhorn (1925) with dissocial and delinquent youth has been built up on the foundations of psychoanalysis.

[3] In order to prevent misunderstanding, I will point out that "anthropology" is used here in the sense it had of old and still has almost everywhere in the United States, that is, the natural history of mankind, and not in the philosophical sense of Heidegger et al.

Before concluding, I will point out that psychoanalysis, apart from the many discoveries it has made and the deep insight it has afforded into human psychic life, is still a growing science. Many psychic phenomena are not yet fully understood and further correlations and interdependencies must be studied.

In this brief survey I have endeavored to outline some trends and possibilities for the development of psychoanalysis, but I am fully aware of the fact that it is far from exhaustive.

CHAPTER 12

Discussion on Evolution and Present Trends in Psychoanalysis

(1950)

The title of the subject under discussion embraces two different approaches to the developmental aspect of psychoanalysis. "Evolution" means organic growth, theoretical amplifications, and revisions as a consequence of the increase of empirically gained data, whereas "present trends" refer to applications to allied fields of work. In regard to psychoanalysis, applications both to other sciences and to therapeutic procedures are to be considered.

The four opening speakers give interesting illustrations of these two aspects.

Maurice Levine presents valuable examples of applied psychoanalysis. He gives an idea of the deep influence psychoanalysis has exercised on psychiatry, general medicine (psychosomatic medicine), social problems, child guidance, etc., and on some psychotherapeutic methods in America. (For a European analyst it is quite fascinating to learn the great extent to which psychoanalytic training is demanded in official psychiatric departments and medical schools of various American universities.)

But Levine does not fail to lay stress on possible dangers resulting from those applications. The penetration of psychoanalysis into the

---

This paper was read at the Symposium, "The Evolution and Present Trends in Psychoanalysis." For the Proceedings of the Symposium see *Congrès International de Psychiatrie, 5.* Paris, 1950.

afore-mentioned disciplines is not, in the first place, due to an inner evolutionary process. It was born out of a need of those other fields of work, and that need sometimes gives rise to incorrect modifications of psychoanalysis for some practical purpose or other. Levine speaks of the danger of "dilution."

Real examples of evolution are brought forward by Anna Freud. She describes some modifications of theory introduced by Freud as a consequence of the process of internal evolution. The study of mental development during the first years of life produced advances in knowledge which led to a broader insight into: (a) the biological basis of psychic life, to wit, the interplay of two biological forces, the life force and the destructive force; (b) the development of the structured psychic life itself, to wit, the development of the ego organization (ego functions, defense mechanisms, superego, etc.).

Anna Freud advocates more experimental work, especially in child psychology, in order to stimulate further evolution.

The organic evolutional modifications of psychoanalysis naturally do not fail to influence the field of work to which it is applied. Conversely, data gained in related disciplines can be utilized for the development of analysis, *at least when the process of evolution remains undisturbed.*

In the course of applications, parts of analytic theory are lifted out of the whole structure over and over again. This method is a legitimate effort. However, it often occurs that the chosen parts gradually come to be handled as if they were representatives of psychoanalysis as a whole. In the allied disciplines they become isolated from the evolutionary process which takes place in analytic work, and then psychoanalysis is often attacked as a rigid, antiquated doctrine. A further consequence may be that other, essential parts of analytic theory are rejected or neglected.

Sometimes it is difficult to decide whether a proposed modification is correct or not. However, partial revisions that neglect essential knowledge based on observations, as for instance the knowledge of sexual development, cannot be fertile as far as evolution is concerned. They are bound to find their limits in themselves, and may lead to violation, mutilation, or "dilution" of psychoanalysis.

Levine and others are looking for the danger of "dilution" in the popularization of analysis among nonanalyzed research workers. However, similar events can be observed in psychoanalysts themselves. I should like to cite a few condensed examples out of the many that could be given.

A very interesting and far-reaching application is that to sociology. The topic lies beyond the scope of today's discussion. I only want to mention that several analysts working in this field tend to see the source of all personal as well as social misery in environmental influences, neglecting the importance of inner conflicts originating from the nature of the instinctual drives and the complexity of structures, both in individual and in social life.

But I must turn to a theme of today's discussion.

For the time being the work of Franz Alexander and his coworkers concerning so-called "brief psychotherapy" holds the limelight of therapeutic interest. Psychotherapy is as old as the history of mankind. Alexander's attempt to base brief therapy on a scientific, psychoanalytic theory deserves great interest and the appreciation of every socially minded therapist, since neuroses and mental disturbances are widespread maladies and severe dangers for men and society. It is undoubtedly a social disadvantage of psychoanalytic treatment that it can be performed only with a limited number of patients.

However, it is astonishing to see how, in order to recommend his therapy, Alexander has to make use of a devaluation and distortion of both analytic technique and knowledge.

The limited scope of this communication permits taking up only a few points:

(1) Alexander proclaims as the aim of treatment a better adjustment of the patient to his environment, a "reconditioning," a practical, valuable goal indeed and sometimes attainable in brief therapy. But Alexander neglects the fact that the goal of analytic treatment goes further. It aims at liberating repressed forces originating from the instinctual life in order to enable the patient's ego to realize its capacities, making use of its own forces.

(2) It is perhaps in connection with this misunderstanding of the psychoanalytic goal that Alexander considers practical arrangements,

such as, for instance, daily sessions and the patient's being placed on a couch, etc., as the essential characteristics of analytic technique. Actually, they are merely tools promoting the dynamic analytic process.

(3) In my opinion, however, Alexander's greatest error is to be found in his reasoning for rejecting analytic treatment with very dependent patients. Too much dependency is caused not only by faulty education and wrong parental attitudes. It is the result of a strong infantile fixation on early levels of instinctual and ego development (passive-feminine attachment to the parents, oral fixation, conflicts with aggressive urges, etc., and incomplete ego organization). That means that it is the result of an interplay of both *external and internal* factors.

Of course the therapist's active display of an attitude opposite to that of the patient's parents can have an influence, but it does not enable the patient to get through the psychic work necessary for a lasting change in his personality. Alexander does not seem to have noticed that he is merely substituting one form of dependency for another.

(4) A remarkable counterpart of the tendency to neglect the role of instinctual drives in therapy manifests itself in Alexander's new psychosomatic "surplus" theory of sexuality. The role of sexuality is reduced to a secondary one, a kind of waste of energy. The problem of where the energy of emotions and tensions comes from is eliminated. His theory has regressed to a preanalytic phase.

I now come to the report of Raymond de Saussure. It presents a most interesting research in the field of ego psychology and especially of the development of two ego capacities, (a) that of thought, and (b) that of mastering emotions. The attempt to connect psychoanalytic data with Piaget's findings is, in my opinion, a very stimulating evolutionary trend in our research work. I myself initiated this idea some ten years ago. It would be tempting to discuss the abundance of problems and suggestions stimulated by de Saussure's lecture, but time is lacking.

It is disappointing, however, to learn that de Saussure, too, could not escape the danger of overvaluating new points of view and mutilating analytic theory. For by proposing, for instance, "to oppose in psychopathology the prelogical or hallucinatory thinking to the rational or assimilated thinking rather than to preserve the opposition of the id, the ego, and the superego," it is clear (a) that de Saussure locates the origin of neurotic disturbances exclusively in ego development and eliminates the role of the instinctual drives, and (b) that he neglects the fact that prelogical thinking itself is already a complicated product of development. It is striking and interesting to see that in all the cases mentioned it is the theory of instinctual drives (sexuality) that is repudiated, just as happened in the earlier days of the psychoanalytic movement (Jung, Adler, and others).

I now come to the final question: What are the lines along which further evolution of psychoanalysis can be expected? For the time being I should like to make the following suggestions:

(1) In regard to the evolution of psychoanalysis proper: (a) In the field of instinctual life: developmental stages of aggressive (destructive) urges and their interplay with libidinal tendencies should be studied in detail. (b) The study of ego development, not only of thought but of all capacities and functions, including superego and ego ideal, requires further elaboration. Here wide fields for research are still unexplored. (c) Finally, the interaction and mutual influence of instinctual development and ego (superego) development have to be studied in chronological order.

(2) In regard to applied psychoanalysis: (a) Continued application of scientific and therapeutic data to the afore-mentioned fields of work. (b) Experimental research on young children in order to elucidate, verify, or, if necessary, revise psychoanalytic theory.

It should be kept in mind that the entire research work can be productive only if the tendency to take the part for the whole and to reject and neglect well-founded parts of the theory is counteracted and eliminated.

In summary: Evolution of psychoanalysis is still based upon experimental work. Neglect of present knowledge and well-founded theory has to be avoided. New insight has to be obtained, for instance (a) in the field of instinctual life (developmental stages of aggressive drives and their interplay with sexual tendencies); (b) in ego development; and (c) on the mutual influence of ego and instinctual development. Anna Freud presents examples of real evolution. In applications to other sciences or to psychotherapy, psychoanalytic theory is often mutilated when parts of its knowledge are treated as if they represented the whole theory. Alexander, for instance, in his application to therapy, underestimates the importance of the internalized conflicts and devaluates the role of the instinctual drives, aiming only at the patient's better adjustment to the environment. Alexander's attitude leads toward dilution of psychoanalysis. De Saussure, in his most valuable attempt to enlarge the knowledge of ego development, unfortunately also devaluates the role of instinctual life.

CHAPTER 13

On Masturbation and Its Influence on General Development

(1950)

I

In 1912, the Viennese Psychoanalytic Society published a symposium on the topic of masturbation. Freud (1912) concluded his own contribution with the statement: "For we are all agreed on one thing—that the subject of masturbation is quite inexhaustible" (p. 254). Today, after a lapse of thirty-eight years, I think this statement is still valid. However, we may be able to contribute some additional information to some of the outstanding points in the 1912 discussion.

Freud summarizes, among other things, those points on which there existed a general consensus among the discussants and those on which opinions differed.

The discussants agreed (a) on the importance and meaning of the fantasies accompanying or replacing masturbation, and (b) on the importance of the guilt feelings connected with masturbation.

Today we can confirm these findings; moreover, we are now better informed concerning the origin, development, and fate of the fantasies.

One of the points on which at that time opinions differed concerned the origin of the guilt feelings. This particular uncertainty has since disappeared; the various sources of the guilt feeling are now rather well known to us.

The other differences in opinion at that time centered, to be exact, around one question: "Can the masturbatory activity per se be harmful?" This question was answered, more or less passionately, by some discussants in the affirmative; by others in the negative as regards any direct somatic impairment.

To Freud, who belonged to the first group, this problem was intimately connected with his concept of the "actual neurosis." Freud maintained his first conception that a number of neurotic symptoms were caused by the toxic effects of undischarged or inadequately discharged quantities of instinctual energy, and thus created a nucleus for the psychoneuroses, caused by psychological conflicts.

The symptoms of neurasthenia—constipation, headaches, fatigue— were thought to be the consequence of (excessive) masturbation, the anxiety neurosis "at bottom a small fragment of undischarged excitation connected with coition" (p. 248). In the discussion at that time, Freud retracted his original idea that the " 'actual' symptoms" could not be influenced by psychoanalytic treatment (p. 249). However, he then considered the cure of those symptoms as a secondary effect of the treatment. He assumed that the psychoanalytic treatment effected a greater tolerance of the "current noxae" or that it enabled the patient, through alteration of the sexual regimen, to avoid these noxae. At what point and according to what mechanisms the direct organic (toxic) impairments of masturbation occur was not known, in Freud's opinion. He also emphasized at that time that one must separate these direct impairments from "those which arise *indirectly* from the ego's resistance and indignation against that sexual activity" (p. 253).

It would be wrong to conclude from these concepts that Freud always considered masturbation a harmful activity, although this conclusion frequently has been and may still continue to be drawn. Thus even at that time he pointed out that there are times in analysis when we must consider masturbation as a sign of therapeutic progress. He was referring to those cases, as in hysteria or compulsion neurosis, in whom, masturbation previously having been repressed for neurotic reasons, it then recurs during treatment.

At present we can neither prove nor disprove the existence of toxic impairment due to masturbation or frustrated excitation. On the one hand, we know how important a normal sexual life is for mental health and how greatly periods of life with physiologically increased instinctual demands, like puberty and menopause, predispose the person to psychological disturbances. On the other hand, our growing psychoanalytic experience has taught us how frequently neurasthenic complaints can be dissolved and how analogous they are in this respect, and also in respect to their causation, to hysterical or psychoneurotic symptoms.

It may be that today the question whether instinctual (sexual) energy could have a toxic effect (on the psyche) has lost its importance.

The investigation of the interaction between psychic and somatic disturbances has been very much in the foreground. It appears that certain organic pathological manifestations, asthma nervosum, colitis ulcerosa, ulcus ventriculi, skin diseases, hay fever, etc., may be caused by psychological conflicts similar to those underlying various psychoneurotic symptoms. Some of these somatic complaints have even been influenced, indeed cured, by psychoanalytic treatment (psychosomatic medicine). Careful observation has shown the frequency, even in healthy persons, of organic reactions to psychological stimuli—reactions, for instance, of the vascular system, of the intestinal tract, of the sensory apparatus. On the other hand, we have to presume an organic correlate as the basis for all psychic processes, even if its existence cannot be proved directly. It is improbable that this organic correlate is to be looked for only in the manifestations of sexuality. I will not elaborate on this interesting topic, or on the hopeful expectation that somatic and psychological therapy will be combined to an even greater extent when in the future our information about these interactions increases more and more.

I will return now to the subject of masturbation. I want to emphasize that so far my remarks have referred to the masturbation of adults. By masturbation I meant any manipulation of the genital apparatus (or of erogenous zones substituting for it) for the purpose of gaining pleasure. But we have to take into consideration that generally masturbation is indulged in from early childhood, at a time when any other discharge of instinctual tension is not yet possible because of physical and psychological immaturity. It has been ascertained that *all* children masturbate during their first years of life, that most of them masturbate during puberty, and that masturbation sometimes occurs during the latency period as well. By this means sexual as well as aggressive instinctual excitations are discharged.

I think we may describe masturbation as a normal activity of childhood for the purpose of discharging instinctual tension. It may fulfill the same function with adolescents or adults whenever the instinctual gratification of a physical and emotional relationship with a lover is not or not yet possible in a form more appropriate to adulthood. In the so-called civilized societies the latter situation frequently occurs, because the individuals have usually reached sexual maturity, physically and mentally, long before it is made possible for them to satisfy their emotional love needs in a permanent relationship and in the foundation of a family.

Masturbation may be accompanied or followed by neurotic disturbances of many kinds. There may be physical ("neurasthenic") or emotional symptoms. The latter may consist of depressions, nosophobias, inferiority or guilt feelings, or self-torment. But whatever these manifestations, we are certain that the masturbatory act did not cause them but that we are dealing with neurotics who, as we know from psychoanalysis, acquired their disharmonies in early childhood and now connect their complaints with the masturbatory act. Therefore there is no sense in limiting the meaning of masturbation, either in psychology or in psychopathology, to the physical manipulations of the genitals or of the substituting erogenous zones. The decisive factor for health or sickness lies in the conscious or unconscious fantasies, feelings (guilt feelings), and impulses which accompany the masturbatory act.

This brings us to the two points mentioned above on which, according to Freud's summary, there existed a consensus among the Viennese discussants. However, we want to add that masturbation fantasies and (guilt) feelings not only are of importance but are of *essential* significance for psychic life.

Among the Viennese participants, Stekel more than anyone else argued against the concept of the injuriousness of masturbation. We are in accord with him as far as the physical actions are concerned.

On the other hand, we definitely dispute his statement that "all people masturbate" even if we take into consideration that Stekel includes herewith the disguised forms of masturbation. Emotionally healthy grownups will seek ways (and will usually find them) to satisfy their sexual needs in a normal love relation with a partner; they may occasionally use masturbation but only temporarily in periods of transition. Adults who *permanently* resort to masturbation (whether they choose it as the exclusive form of satisfaction or retain it in addition to sexual intercourse) are persons, more or less disturbed in their development, who have remained fixated or have regressed to that infantile form of sexual activity.

II

I now want to turn our attention to the psychological manifestations accompanying masturbation and trace certain vicissitudes of these fantasies, impulses, and emotions. Let me emphasize again that, when I speak of masturbation in what follows, I am referring to the *whole complex* of physical and emotional manifestations. We will see that both components may join in following the same path or may also be separated. Wherever this separation occurs, psychoanalysis can always demonstrate that in the unconscious they belong together.

Masturbation, especially in young people, often gives rise to an oppressive burden of emotions. Feelings of anxiety, guilt, sin, inferiority, and depravity as well as fears of sickness, insanity, spinal disease, impotence, etc., may all be connected with masturbation.

It is well known that a very important source of all these horrors lies in various layers of society, in the attitude of those responsible for the child's upbringing. Parents, teachers, clerics, and often doctors too, in speech and writings, often very forcefully attempt to convince the young that masturbation is the most dangerous and sinful of vices.

Yet it is remarkable that in spite of these ominous threats and punishments so many people finally attain a normal sexual life. Whether in defiance of all intimidation they continue to masturbate until they achieve adult sexuality with a partner, or whether they give it up, the end result can be a healthy love life.

On the other hand, there is a frighteningly large number of persons who react to these prohibitions and threats with mild or severe psychological disturbances. One encounters cases which range all the way from mild disturbances of potency, inhibitions or difficulties of adjustment, to severest impotence, neurosis, and impediments of development. Where there is no severe impairment, frequently simple reassurance about the harmlessness of the activity and enlightenment in case of ignorance may produce relief and may lead development into normal channels.

However, where such a procedure is of no avail, it is evident that the intimidations of the environment were not the sole cause of the neurotic illness, but that they affected an already sick or disturbed person, and that one has to seek for the causes in his childhood.

Masturbation, as I said before, already occurs during infancy. The infant plays with or rubs different parts of his body. In the beginning the mouth zone plays a very important role, sometimes perhaps in consequence of feeding, i.e., through stimulation by the breast or bottle. However, according to a number of observations by physicians and nurses, some infants, even before the first feeding, suck their fingers, which may lead to a facial expression of satisfaction and to quietly falling asleep. The sucking reflex seems to point the direction here. After some time various other body zones are rubbed and finally the genitals too. Some observations on infants up to the age of one seem to indicate that a kind of acme may be reached which could be considered as an early infantile form of orgasm. Perhaps more frequently this playing is quiet and uninterrupted, and seems to lead to a diffuse kind of satisfaction. In Spitz's interesting and important article, "Autoerotism," in which he records observations on 196 infants from birth to fifteen months, he calls such activity "genital play" instead of masturbation (1949).

A widespread opinion, already represented in the Viennese discussion in 1912, contends that the bodily care of the infant is in effect a seduction by the mother or nurse and that the child is led to genital activity in this way. In contrast to this view, Spitz believes that it is not the physical rubbing or friction which teaches the child the genital play but the emotional relation to the mother (1949).

I agree with the author when he writes in the introduction of his paper: "A really unimpeachable study would have to offer continuous 24-hour observation of the infant during the whole of the first year of life" (p. 85). It also seems to me that his experimental conditions—the observation of each child at *weekly intervals* and during only *four hours per week*—are very far removed from the ideal conditions mentioned.

I therefore think that the conclusions and hypotheses of Spitz, interesting as they appear to be, should be viewed with the greatest caution and that many observations under more favorable conditions will be necessary to give them validity. Thus, for instance, I question whether the autoerotic gratification of rocking only occurs because the child is unable to establish an object relationship due to "the inconsistent, contradictory behavior of the mother." From a few but intensive observations I have gained the impression that rocking also occurs with a strong object relationship. (The latter can be neurotically tinged on the mother's part.)

On the other hand, it is a tempting hypothesis to assume that the infant's activity and thereby also his genital play is not only learned through mechanical stimulation but that the emotional relationship to the mother (or mother substitute) is an indispensable factor. It seems certain that infants treated without love (even though adequately nourished) deteriorate physically and are psychologically hampered in their development as well. Intelligence, emotional life, motility, instinctual life, and ego functions are interfered with in their maturational processes and show more or less retardation. From his observations, Spitz concludes: "When this [the mother-child] interrelation is at its best, genital play will be general in the first year of life and general development will surpass the average" (1949, p. 103). This is marvelously in accordance with Freud's concept, laid down in 1905 in his *Three Essays on the Theory of Sexuality* (1905c).

In the section on object choice, Freud describes that every object choice of the adult is a "refinding" and a continuation of the relationship of the infant to the mother (nurse) who not only stimulates and satisfies the child through his erogenous zones but also supplies him with emotions which originate in her own sexual life, etc. And further:

> As we know, however, the sexual instinct is not aroused only by direct excitation of the genital zone. What we call affection will unfailingly show its effects one day on the genital zones as well. Moreover, if the mother understood more of the high importance of the part played by instincts in mental life as a whole—in all its ethical and psychical achievements—she would spare herself any

178

self-reproaches after her enlightenment. She is only fulfilling her task in teaching the child to love. After all, he is meant to grow up into a strong and capable person with vigorous sexual needs and to accomplish during his life all the things that human beings are urged to do by their instincts [1905c, p. 223].

Whether it results in an acme or in a diffuse gratification, masturbation plays a normal part in the development of a healthy infant's instinctual life, as well as supplying him with pleasurable activity of various bodily zones. A good, loving attachment (close relationship) is a precondition for sound development. What form this mother relationship takes is a different question. The emotional attachment develops gradually out of the biological, physical, mother-child unit. Just when or how this occurs, is, in my opinion, still unknown.

Melanie Klein concludes from her numerous and particularly impressive observations that during his first weeks of life, the infant already forms a wealth of complicated fantasies, of a loving as well as an aggressive nature. According to Klein, the infant wants to possess the mother, wants to penetrate her, wants to incorporate her and to dismember her, to rob her and to destroy her depending on his feelings about the mother as a "good" or "bad" object. The infant then supposedly is tormented by guilt feelings because of his bad fantasies and during the first months of life already has a severe and punitive superego (M. Klein, 1928).

It seems to me a large and arbitrary step to conclude that all these complicated fantasies are already present in the infant merely from the observations that satiated and contented infants smile at their mothers and that hungry ones or those suffering from painful sensations scream, struggle, or show expressions to be interpreted as anxious. It seems much more plausible to assume that intense primitive excitations, sensations, and impulses may exist in the infant which may be directed toward the mother, but that these are only elaborated into complicated psychic formations, as the above-mentioned fantasies, after the psychic apparatus reaches a certain level of development. We are aware that such excitations and impulses also exist in domesticated animals without concluding that they form similar fantasies. Ego development has not yet begun in the newborn child even though an innate nucleus of the ego exists. It still takes a rather long time before the infant develops his ego functions and before he is able to achieve an even primitive coordination of some of these functions. However, only after such an achievement is one justified in speaking of a primitive ego. The differentiation in the ego, which leads to the formation of the superego, belongs to an even later phase of maturation.

To make a simple equation between primitive id impulses and psychic formations involving ego and superego hardly seems a service to scientific attempts at clarification. This method ignores the fact that psychic life undergoes a process of development—of dynamic maturation. However, it would be premature to postulate more exact data for the individual stages of development. Let us console ourselves with the fact that many more thorough observations will be necessary for the clarification of these conditions.

However that may be, we may assume that the infant in his first year of life provides pleasure and gratification for himself by playing with various parts of his body, and that in this gratification the genital apparatus has an important role. Moreover, this gratification is closely connected with the mother-child relationship which accompanies and shapes the child's entire development.

When at the end of his first and in his second year the child enters the anal phase of libidinal development, this playing begins to be concentrated on the anal zone and its productions. It is quite certain that a high intensity of instinctual energy is disposed of here. But genital play and the stimulation of other body zones frequently continue during this period as they did during the preceding oral phase, although perhaps with less intensity. It is well known that Freud's classification of the three phases of infantile libidinal development is schematized and that an overlapping of the different phases occurs, with remainders of earlier phases coexisting with elements of later phases to a greater or lesser degree. In the final phase of early libidinal development, the phallic phase, the instinctual discharge occurs primarily via the genital zone. The sexual activity of the child now reaches its peak in masturbation, which may be accompanied by erections and which frequently culminates in an acme.

The fantasy activity, in the meantime, has blossomed along with the entire infantile personality. Intelligence, many ego functions, the fore-runners of superego in ideal formation and moral demands, have taken shape. The child has learned to differentiate between his self and the environment to a greater or lesser degree; he has gathered knowledge of the external world and has developed a reality sense which some-times is still incomplete, but which is frequently amazingly correct and keen. The fantasy life as the expression of intense instinctual and emo-tional strivings has followed its own course of development. That does not mean that the elementary force of the instincts has not exerted great influence upon infantile ego development. This influence may be a stimulus. Thus, for instance, the awakened sexual curiosity may lead to efforts at exploration and discovery which may foster the knowledge of reality. The child's craving for power arouses the desire to be big and, in his rivalry with the grownups, may support his intellectual unfolding and his desire to learn.

However, if for external or internal reasons the fantasy life consti-tutes a danger, a reverse influence may occur, resulting in an inhibiting and sometimes even destructive effect on the entire ego development.

It is well known that this second outcome occurs only too often, on the one hand because of the frequent and severe condemnation and punishment of infantile masturbation by persons in charge of the child, and on the other hand as a result of the many instinctual and emotional conflicts to which the child is exposed. As a consequence of these experiences we encounter neurotic disturbances, inhibitions of development, and character deformities. Before we take up the fate of the masturbatory activity and of the fantasies which initially, at least, accompany them, we will first say something more about the origin and content of fantasies during the anal and phallic phase.

The child's fantasies become well known to us as soon as he is able to verbalize them. This scarcely occurs before the age of one and a half or two years, even if one has learned to understand the child's primitive language. Yet we can hardly question the existence of a form of repre-sentation without words. This is proved by adult dreams in which de-sires, impulses, and emotional strivings find a plastic representation. We have learned from Freud's *The Interpretation of Dreams* (1900) that this representation is an archaic one belonging to the primary process. The primary process is the psychic mechanism which dominates the psychic life of the young child before he is able to develop the secondary process. In addition, the one-year-old child, who has already developed certain psychological and physical abilities but not the ability to verbalize, demonstrates in his play and actions manifestations which we can only interpret as expressions of desires followed by symbolic gratification. In place of many illustrations I have only to cite Freud's observation of child play which he describes in *Beyond the Pleasure Principle* (1920a). This description also shows us the difficulty of interpreting such play and how cautious one has to be in interpretation since it is probable that many different impulses are discharged in a single action. The affectively charged games and activities of the one- or two-year-old child must be considered as the predecessors of fantasies at a later period which, in the phallic phase, are known to us as oedipal fantasies. Sometimes we are able to follow them through the latency period and watch them break through again with great intensity in puberty, even though they have been modified by development and the broadening of the world of experience.

Verbalized fantasies have become a dependable source of psychoanalytic knowledge. Sometimes the psychoanalytic treatment of adults yields us deep insight into the primitive forerunners of the fantasy world of the child. When a patient, during the psychoanalytic session, temporarily renounces his adulthood and presents the attitude, mimic behavior, crying, struggling, and stammering of a young child, he re-experiences, often with intense vividness, the impulses and sensations of this archaic period. Such an acting out resembles a real psychotic episode. The disadvantage of these observations during treatment in psychoanalysis compared with the direct observation of children lies in the difficulty of differentiating early from later material; this sometimes may represent a special technical task. However, the inner conviction with which, after this acting out, some patients are able to account for that immediate emotional experience is a valuable confirmation (or correction) and a pointer for the further task. The young child, of course, is unable to give such an account. Therefore the child observer lacks an important instrument for evaluating the correctness of his interpretations.

Let us now try to collect whatever we know so far about these primitive predecessors of fantasy life. From the beginning the child tries to get rid of unpleasant bodily tensions which are connected with imperative bodily needs (need for nourishment, excremental needs, etc.) and which are soon accompanied by psychic tensions or cause these tensions. Sexual and aggressive drives take part; passive and active strivings coexist; the impulses are awakened in the mother-child relationship and aim at the one and only object, the mother or her substitute. In rough outline there is a primacy of focus, shifting in succession from the mouth to the anal and finally the genital zone—although during all these phases there is also activity on various other parts of the body. Finally this whole complex of excitations, impulses, and emotions merges into the (relative) end phase of the oedipal constellation of instincts and emotions. This oedipal constellation lends to the whole personality a more or less stable structure, a pattern for the final shaping of the personality in adolescence.

In normal development the oedipus complex is distinguished by the fact that genital masturbation has become the only (or almost only) act of autoerotic gratification. At this point a boy's desires and instinctual impulses are expressed in fantasies whose abbreviated content is: "I want to take father's place with mother." The comparative simplicity of the strivings and fantasies in the oedipal situation is in contrast to the manifold diffuse impulses, strivings, and aims of the preoedipal period. However, on close inspection we notice that a great number of manifestations of the preceding period are preserved, in more or less disguised form, by the youthful Oedipus. These are just the ones which come to the fore in the infantile acting out of the patient during the psychoanalytic situation described above. Most striking are the strivings and desires with passive aims. The child desires to receive everything passively from the mother, not only to be fed but also physical gratifications in forms of caresses, fondling, affection, and admiration, and all this with a child's well-known insatiability as the exclusive love object of the mother. These passive desires may be expressed in oral, anal, and phallic fantasies. During or after the oedipal phase these passive fantasies are displaced from the mother onto the father. Thus the passive-feminine father relationship (negative oedipus

183

complex) develops in the boy, whereas in the girl it leads to the normal positive oedipus constellation which serves as a pattern for her later, grown-up femininity. Strangely enough, active as well as passive fantasies are discharged through masturbation.

Abraham (1924a) pointed out that in each of the three developmental phases one may distinguish two chronologically separate tendencies toward the object. These are the tendency to take in and to retain and its opposite, the tendency to expel and to destroy. They represent the instinctual and emotional ambivalence (libido-aggression and love-hatred). Abraham's work has greatly enhanced our understanding of the development of the child and of pathological conditions like melancholia, mania, compulsion neurosis, and paranoia. However, I believe that at that time not enough attention was paid to the coexistence of active and passive strivings. I also believe that in consequence the chronological succession postulated by Abraham becomes a schematization which does not completely correspond to observations. Tendencies to (passive) incorporation and (active) ejection always exist simultaneously during all three phases, although in individually different intensities.

In the newborn we find, together with the passive tendency to be nursed, also a clearly noticeable active tendency to search for the breast, to take possession of it, and to suck it. Even in the newborn one observes strong differences in *constitutional* activity and passivity. Furthermore, the personality and attitude of the mother—the other partner of the initial mother-child unit—has, of course, great influence on the further development of these strivings. During the anal phase also, active and passive attitudes coexist rather than succeed one another. One is always surprised anew by the observation that in psychic life passive experiences precipitate activity and active attitudes are followed by passive desires. Keen observation of healthy adults reveals that they too show a succession of these alternating tendencies which are immediately evident in pathological conditions (most extreme in the manic-depressive).

The child's activity is initially to a large extent still an expression of instinctual ambivalence; i.e., discharge of the unsublimated aggressive or destructive drive, especially where it has been awakened by the frustration of passive desires. (The tendency to destroy the object in the cannibalistic phase and in the first part of the anal phase, as described by Abraham.)

The combining of aggression and libido and the sublimation of both drives results in the postambivalent phase, that of object relationship which Abraham presupposes, albeit as an ideal, for the final genital phase.

Marie Bonaparte, in "De la sexualité de la femme" (1949), broadens Abraham's scheme of early infantile instinctual development by giving great importance to the passive and active instinctual aims. Her extensive and very interesting report on female sexuality is particularly valuable. But in her description of early childhood processes, Bonaparte likewise presents as a chronological succession what, in my opinion, exists simultaneously. Though she acknowledges the phallic activity of the little girl, Bonaparte believes that the girl passes through a preceding passive phase during which she experiences pleasure sensations at the anal zone (called by the author "cloacal zone" in analogy to the biological embryonal development). The author also believes that these sensations attain a special "feminine" character through the fact that during clitoral masturbation the girl often accidentally reaches the introitus and thus becomes acquainted with her own vagina.

I agree with Bonaparte that little girls may masturbate at the introitus and labia minora more often than had previously been assumed by Freud. We know that reddening and catarrh of the introitus have been observed in little girls and may have been caused by masturbation. However, it seems questionable to me whether these observations should be evaluated differently from similar anal play of the boy. It is absolutely certain that children of both sexes develop the most active aggressive games and fantasies with anal gratification; one could say with anal masturbation or masturbation of the introitus or of the labia. We also know that in the oedipal or postoedipal period, strongly passive-masochistic fantasies are discharged through penis—or clitoris—masturbation. I believe it is misleading to equate in a child vaginal masturbation with passivity or femininity and to identify phallic masturbation exclusively with activity and masculinity.

It seems improbable to me that a little girl is ever able to reach the fundus of her vagina at which the real orgasm of the adult woman originates. But even if this should sometimes occur, for instance after seduction, it has little significance in regard to the passivity or activity of the child's fantasies or experience. Passive and active forms of experience accompany the physical masturbatory activities of children of both sexes throughout the three main phases of development before the genital apparatuses actually gain primacy. In normal development, it is only after the recognition of the sex difference has had its effect that the active (penetrating) desire is tied to the male and the passive (receptive) desire is associated with the female organ. This occurs after the castration complex has taken effect. For the boy the passive-receptive organ is the "hole" which he has seen in the girl and which, in accordance with his anatomical knowledge and his own experience, can only be the anus. For the little girl it may be anus, labia, or introitus, but never the fundus vaginae.

Although the parallel drawn by Abraham between psychological and embryological physical development (a parallel also assumed by Bonaparte) is very interesting, one must not carry it too far.

In the first place, by the time psychic life begins, the sex of the person has long since been physically established. Secondly, the development of the highly complicated psychic processes is influenced by so many internal and external factors that it quite certainly also follows a course of its own.

To prevent misunderstandings I want to stress that it is far from my intention to prove that little boys and girls are identical in their psychological make-up. While the ratio between active and passive strivings varies in each person, it also certainly varies normally more in favor of activity in the male, and more in favor of passivity in the female child. Nor may one underestimate the importance of the parents' attitude. The mother ordinarily seeks to foster masculinity in the son, the father, femininity in the little daughter. However, in my experience the shaping of the sex does not take place in the individual child before the peak of the oedipal constellation has been reached. This is the very point when the development of boys and girls parts ways. In the boy the active sexual strivings will become victorious and passivity will be sublimated and becomes socially applied (of course, together with that part of activity which is withdrawn from direct sexual life). In the girl, activity is subordinated to passivity. Now at the end of the oedipal period, that forceful repression takes place (initiated in the boy under the pressure of castration anxiety) which leads into the latency period. All the restrictions and prohibitions of instinctual gratification which the child experienced from the mother (later from both parents) are now fused into one prohibition: you must not masturbate. This prohibition will be introjected and lead to the formation of the punishing part of the superego. The danger of castration as a threat to narcissism, the danger of losing the love of the parents and soon after the love of his own superego, cause the boy to renounce masturbation or at least to reduce it and to repress the accompanying fantasies. If he does not succeed in giving up masturbation, it will be practiced with anxiety and guilt feelings. Frequently the fantasies disappear from consciousness only to maintain a kind of isolated existence in the unconscious. Often, however, the opposite occurs: physical masturbation is renounced but a blossoming fantasy life persists.

The little girl's development runs a different course: the narcissistic injury due to her awareness of her being "castrated" causes enmity to the mother whom she holds responsible for this "defect." Her phallic activity toward her mother becomes unpleasurable and she turns toward the father with passive desires. The repression of instinctual life is not as imperatively effective, since castration anxiety is lacking. However, the repression-effecting threat of punishment by the parents (and the superego) is strongly reinforced by the very feeling of having an "inferior" genital with which one cannot really masturbate. And thus girls more often give up masturbation during the latency period than do boys. But then fantasy life (now most frequently directed toward the father) continues to flourish. Yet in girls also masturbation may break through the latency period, and be accompanied by conscious or unconscious fantasies.

Masturbation almost always re-erupts during a boy's puberty, less regularly in that of the girl. The fantasies frequently are real sexual images involving a partner; they may also be prolonged daydreams which begin to resemble stories or novels. Close inspection and analysis reveal more or less clear traces of the early infantile fantasy and impulse life.

I have given only a brief summary of the phallic-oedipal period of both sexes, since this phase and its importance for adult sexual life have been repeatedly and thoroughly described. I would now like to comment on the various vicissitudes both of the content of fantasies and of the masturbatory act, and finally on the influence of these vicissitudes upon character and personality development.[1]

In addition to the oedipal fantasies which are positive and active fantasies of taking possession of the mother, the boy in the phallic phase may also express other, more or less forceful, passive desires toward the father (negative oedipal constellation). These passive feminine (homosexual) strivings, which culminate in the desire to take the mother's place with the father, demand as a precondition the renunciation of the penis and are therefore dangerous for the child's masculinity.

If they cannot be sufficiently repressed, they frequently seek a way out in the return to the preoedipal object relation, in which the little boy lets himself be loved, taken care of, fondled, caressed, admired, fed, cleaned, even given an enema, and nursed by the mother. In this form of passive gratification the danger of castration no longer threatens him. Moreover, the mother herself participates intensively in these kinds of gratification, a fact which the child then experiences as permission or even seduction. Naturally, he also experiences many limitations and prohibitions, because the desires of the child are insatiable, and training and education demand adjustment to the norm, restraint, control, or renunciation of instinctual impulses altogether. The weaning from the breast, control of excretion, suppression of finger sucking, anal play, aggressive outbursts, etc., may arouse anxiety which may become the forerunner of castration anxiety. However, in comparison with castration anxiety, which concerns the most highly estimated part of the body, the penis, this anxiety is mild. Regression to the preoedipal period is mainly fostered by three factors: (1) a comparatively strong passive constitution; (2) forceful and extremely severe suppression of instinctual expressions by the parents; (3) a dominating, aggressive mother who (because of her own penis envy) is not able to tolerate masculine activity in the boy and who seduces him into passive

[1] On its inhibiting influence which leads to neurosis, see Chapter 4.

behavior, the child thus representing her own lacking penis which she unconsciously wants to fondle and caress (masturbate).

However, the *active* oedipal desires also may regress to the pre-oedipal phase. Castration threats, experienced or only expected, from the father arouse extremely intense anxiety if the child's aggressive drive is especially strong. Aggression becomes an internal danger through the attitude of severe parents (or a severe superego) as well as through the ambivalence conflict which makes simultaneous love and hatred, directed toward the same person, gradually intolerable. This aggression has to be suppressed and thus a sublimation of aggression into constructive activity is prevented. The entire development falls back a step and the boy escapes to the preoedipal mother with both his active as well as his passive desires.

The interesting aspect of this is that the drives may or may not take part in this process. Where the drive participates, in some cases a permanent regression of instincts occurs, whereby (sometimes only gradually) genital masturbation is given up completely and there is recourse to anal, oral, or other primitive discharge, sometimes in disguised or displaced forms. This for instance may be the case in compulsion neurosis, where the symptoms, the compulsive acts, may gradually replace masturbation. However, genital masturbation often continues without interruption up to adulthood, but the fantasies find expression in the language of preoedipal desires and experience. One finds this among hysterical neuroses, anxiety conditions, and phobias. But what is of greatest interest to us is the mode in which these fantasies, inhibited in their development, are built into the personality structure and into character formation.

In "The Preoedipal Phase in the Development of the Male Child" (Chapter 7) I described some forms of the love life of adults who have remained fixated to the preoedipal mother imago, or who returned to it, while their potency was only mildly disturbed. For instance, men who remain dissatisfied in their marriages and compulsively engage in one relationship after another are frequently looking for the image of the preoedipal mother from whom they demand the gratification of their infantile desires. Or men who compulsively devaluate and debase their wives may project on them the hatred belonging to the preoedipal ambivalent period, etc. I also mentioned in that paper the influence which the preoedipal mother fixation may have on superego formation.

In the same way we can also observe that a remaining with or returning to the preoedipal fantasy life may inhibit the *ego* (or parts of it) in its development. This leads to the so-called infantile personalities. Sometimes the development of intelligence is not inhibited but some of the ego functions may be partially or entirely arrested, as, for example, the sense of reality.

An adult who, in his unconscious fantasy, lives to be fed, indulged in, and cared for by his mother, expects the same situation in real life, demanding of his environment protection and affectionate handling, and will frequently be unable to realize and accept the sober reality and the necessity of building an independent life. The final outcome of this inhibition of development depends on the extent to which the sense of reality is impaired. If the greatest part of the ego remains in this infantile constellation, a psychotic condition may result. If a part of the reality sense remains intact, adjustment difficulties, inhibition of emotional contact with others, frequently even failure in work and professional life, will result. The objective evaluation of people, situations, political events will be impaired, because the formation of judgment is merely "self-related" and is tinged and distorted by narcissistic needs. A second important factor which leads to such defective evaluation of the real world lies in the fixation to the emotional ambivalence which is normal for the young child. In harmonious development, aggression and destruction are gradually bound by libido; they are partly sublimated and used for constructive activity and partly turned inward and used for self-criticism and self-control. If one or several of these mechanisms fail (e.g., in cases where frustration, disappointment, and injury are not overcome), the aggression may be indiscriminately turned against the external world. Then judgment and critical evaluation of the environment (persons, events, and situations) cannot be objective. The "other one" is bad and worthy only of contempt. From this description we also see that fixation and regression to the world of preoedipal experiences likewise inhibits another ego function, namely the synthetic (or integrative) one.

If one part of the personality, as for instance intellectual development, reaches the level of the actual chronological age, but the reality sense and the judgment formation connected with the inhibited emotional development correspond to the age of a young child, a disharmony, sometimes even a split, in the personality results.

Even the ego function of control and use of the motor apparatus may be impaired if the unconscious fantasy demands the gratification of being an infant with whom the necessary actions are performed by the mother. Some persons, because of anxiety due to their own aggression, either avoid any motor activity or at least inhibit it.

I have described some of the many inhibitions of development which may be caused by regression to the fantasy life of the preoedipal phase, and which in the male are due to the unconquerable anxiety of the oedipal situation, that is, to castration anxiety.

Similar infantile character formations may be found in the female who may take similar flight to the preoedipal mother. As we have said before, in the female the cause of this flight is not castration anxiety. It is the concurrence of her oedipal disappointment in the father with a sometimes insuperable narcissistic injury caused by her awareness of her own genital, which she considers defective.

This is the point, as mentioned before, at which the development of the two sexes takes radically different directions. Sex differences may have been noticeable before this time so far as differences in emphasis and intensity between active and passive attitudes go, but neither the physical modes of gratification nor the fantasies showed essential differences.

Since I wish at this point to elaborate once more the different vicissitudes of the masturbatory act in boys and girls respectively, I have to make a brief recapitulation.

During the latency period the boy rarely gives up masturbation completely. Masturbation will be suppressed, on the one hand owing to the comparative calm of the instinctual life, and on the other hand owing to the anxiety caused by the forbidden incestuous desires. But from time to time a discharge of the sexual urges through the masturbatory act may occur. The fantasies are concerned with being big and grown-up; in the center of the fantasies is the ambition to be a powerful man both in a heroic love life and in all other life situations.

The maturation process, an active and progressing development, runs its course, to be most heightened in puberty and then gradually to merge into adult life. Masturbation, which was regularly practiced in puberty, gives place to normal sexual life; the ambitious narcissistic fantasies are replaced by full object love.

Disturbances of this course of development may occur if prohibitions and castration threats are so severe or have such a strong effect that masturbation is given up completely and the fantasies are completely repressed. These repressed fantasies may then lead their own life in the unconscious and, as mentioned above, may sometimes be cloaked in preoedipal forms. The instinctual life may regress.

Instead of elaborating on the neuroses thus caused, I want to present two other fates of such repressed fantasies.

(1) If a boy has developed a marked negative oedipal constellation based on a strongly bisexual constitution, and in consequence of a specific family constellation combined with specific experiences in early childhood, his castration anxiety will become exceedingly strong. For the gratification of these passive desires castration is a precondition, and therefore they are a threat to his masculinity. They enhance anxiety and force repression of both fantasies and the masturbatory act. At the same time they sometimes paralyze activity in other areas and inhibit the maturation process of the entire personality. Escape back to a preoedipal fantasy world and the preservation of the passive father attachment of the negative oedipus complex support each other in an inhibitory effect.

(2) The other important factor, which, in combination with the two just mentioned, may prevent normal maturation, is evident in those boys who turn inwardly an extreme amount of aggression during superego development; the passivity involved in this mechanism is then secondarily erotized and is turned into masochism. We thus encounter beating fantasies which have been extensively described in all their various phases and forms by Freud (1919). I will not elaborate on them but only mention that these fantasies are always of a sado-masochistic nature; i.e., the author of the fantasy always figures both

192

as the beater and the beaten—while the act of beating is often replaced by fantasies of being overwhelmed, damaged, debased, or castrated. The nucleus of these fantasies is always the fantasy of parental coitus, regardless of whether or not it has been observed in reality. In this fantasy the child in turn plays the role of the father and the mother and the content is tied to the preoedipal fantasies. These sadomasochistic fantasies may increase both the fear of and the struggle against masturbating. Masturbation will seem more evil, forbidden, and dangerous than ever. I mentioned at the beginning of this paper that it is of utmost importance to the adolescent whether the struggle against masturbation does or does not succeed. When it succeeds, it produces an enhancement of self-estimation which in pathological cases may range from an abnormal increase of ambition to megalomania. If the struggle fails, feelings of inferiority, depression, and pathological ideas of self-devaluation and self-abasement result. When these abnormal ideas of grandeur or of inferiority are chiefly the result of the threats of the adult world, they are frequently accessible to simple psychotherapy. Reassurance and enlightenment may be miraculously effective and may undo inhibitions in the development of the entire personality. But if the disturbance has been caused by early inhibitions of development as a consequence of strong passivity, strong sadomasochistic tendencies and fantasies, preoedipal fixations and therefore defectively developed ego functions, the resolution of these developmental disturbances is very difficult and time-consuming and attainable, if ever, only by a correctly conducted psychoanalysis.

The difficulties are most intense in the areas of maximum influence on ego development where consequently the disturbances of adjustment originated (A. Freud, 1949b). Let me select only a few from the many examples.

(1) A child who in his latency period completely gives up masturbation under duress of castration threats remains in a strong and mainly sadomasochistically tinged dependence on the adults. Whenever the urge to masturbate threatens, he has to reinforce his submission toward the prohibiting persons. In adolescence this process repeats itself and the young man is incapable of becoming independent. He remains, as we term it, an infantile personality.

193

(2) The complete suppression of masturbation due to external prohibitions may also lead to opposition against all adults. "Being good" in sexual matters is compensated for by indiscriminate "wanting everything different." This type always and everywhere desires the opposite of the environment as it is. The objective evaluation of other people and situations is also greatly impaired in such cases.

(3) The success in the struggle against masturbation by one's own power enhances self-esteem, but it may lead to feelings of grandeur, which then stamp the entire personality. A lack of self-criticism, overbearing behavior, and overestimation of the self then result. These qualities go back to the early infantile feeling of omnipotence, and they disable the personality in adjusting to the real world.

(4) If the struggle fails, self-accusations, self-torment, and inferiority feelings ensue which may impair the development of all other qualities and talents, and compulsive masturbation may paralyze all other activities of the person.

(5) Very frequently the struggle succeeds only partially with periodic breakthroughs of masturbation. Then we find a vacillation between megalomanic and inferiority fantasies, the one type always precipitating and increasing the other.

(6) Most frequent are the mixed forms of all these types. All of them lead to adjustment disturbances. In cases with more marked inhibitory tendencies, ego deformations and ego constrictions result in addition to neuroses. In cases in which eruptions of instinctual impulses (primarily aggression) lead to external acting out, we encounter delinquency.

Only by the thorough presentation of individual life histories could one do justice to the manifoldness and intricacy of the various combinations of possibilities, a goal beyond the scope of this paper.

So far, I have mainly presented the various vicissitudes of the masculine developmental process. Naturally most of these phenomena are also found in the female. However, I want to draw attention to some particularities in female development.

I mentioned above that the complete suppression of masturbation during latency, and perhaps during puberty also, is a much more frequent occurrence in girls than in boys. This is the case even when the external prohibitions and the threats of punishment are the same for both sexes. The normal oedipal situation demands of the girl the renunciation of active-phallic desires, of the boy the renunciation of his passive strivings. It appears that with an equally strong bisexual constitution the subordination of passivity to activity is more easily effected than the reverse process. Instinctual life has an essentially active, driving, urging quality. Moreover, the danger of castration, which once had seemed to the boy overwhelmingly great, is and remains only an anxious fantasy which never becomes reality. If the passive constitution and with it the desire for castration is not too strong, the conquering of castration anxiety is effected without too great difficulty.

The girl, however, is convinced without redress, by her observation of the sex difference, that she will never obtain the once ardently desired male genital even though for a long time she still retains the fantasy that it will grow on her. This narcissistic injury is a decisive factor in taking the pleasure out of masturbation, and in renouncing it.

With a normal feminine constitution, these two processes, turning to passivity and the acceptance of the lack of a penis, are successfully accomplished either during latency or puberty. The active strivings are sublimated and employed for other ego functions as well as for intellectual development. However, this process remains more difficult than the analogous one in the boy.

The girl's passive situation in the oedipal father relationship seems to favor the renunciation of masturbation. At least, one can observe that it is the girl with a strongly bisexual constitution who fails in the struggle against masturbation. At first glance this appears strange, since it is the girl with strong active desires whom one might expect to be most injured and disappointed by her lack of a penis. One would expect her to withdraw from the manipulation of her "defective" genital at the earliest time. The explanation for the contrary fact is given by the fantasy world of these little girls. In the fantasy the lack of the male genital is regularly denied: it is hidden in the vagina and one day it will come out or will grow. The heroes of her daydreams or unconscious fantasies are frequently boys or young men and are easily recognizable as the ideal image of herself. Or the little girl repeats her

195

fantasies of the parental sexual life (in various alterations, of course) whereby she simultaneously plays both roles, the active and the passive. Also, there is often a fantasy of being the father's penis or the penis of the phallic mother. Geleerd (1943) describes a case in which compulsive masturbation, which gravely inhibited the little girl's development, was accompanied by many such fantasies.

Frequently, also, manipulation of the genitals, whether clitoris or introitus, is given up and displaced onto other parts of the body (playing with the nose, mouth, ears, hair, breasts, rubbing of the legs, etc.).

A further particularity of the fantasies of the constitutionally active girl is that they are sadomasochistically tinged. In "A Child Is Being Beaten," Freud (1919) points to the fact that beating fantasies occur more frequently in women than in men. The passive "letting oneself be beaten" (letting oneself be overpowered) is, according to some authors, part of femininity. However, in normal femininity it plays a role only to the extent of a capacity for physical submission. If there exist strong sadomasochistic elements we are already dealing with a deformation of healthy femininity which is the consequence of a marked active-aggressive constitution. Aggression is partly turned inward; but where masochism is apparent psychoanalysis regularly reveals strongly sadistic fantasies. These fantasies substitute for the renounced masculinity and simultaneously take revenge on the envied male or on the mother-woman who is held responsible for the patient's sex.

Thus the active type of girl, like the boy, does not easily succeed in renouncing masturbation. Where the environment has enforced its prohibitions, the reactions and character formations are also similar; yet if the suppression of masturbation is forced by severe threats of punishment the girl, too, may develop into the "constant rebel" type, or she may remain the dependent child who cannot grow up.

Suppression of masturbation by her own efforts may also produce megalomanic ideas and overbearing behavior in the girl, whereas feelings of inferiority may be awakened by the temporary failure in this struggle.

For the development of sound femininity, the gradual renunciation or reduction of masturbation during latency seems to be most favorable, at least in our present civilization. A mild relapse during puberty with preference of introitus or vagina may serve the transition to adulthood. However, in many cases there is little or no masturbation at all in puberty. This may be an escape from the above-mentioned fantasies, originating in the masculinity complex; it may be caused by guilt feelings and anxiety, thus having a neurotic basis. But it may also be a preparation for the healthy submission to adult sexual life, during which normal vaginal orgasm is experienced for the first time, and the remainders of the infantile fantasies are adjusted to adulthood and thus enter the realistic world of the woman, in her behavior in family life, and in her other social or professional tasks.

CHAPTER 14

Re-evaluation of the Role of the
Oedipus Complex

(1952)

During recent decades psychoanalytic research work has yielded a series
of experiences regarding the development of the child in the first years
of life. The significance of an undisturbed course of the preoedipal
phase has been demonstrated by direct observations on children. Disturbances in the first mother-child relationship (which is based upon
the biological mother-child entity) result in physical and psychical de-
partures from normal, ranging from slight neurotic fears to grave inhibitions in instinctual, emotional, and ego development, to paucity of
affect, pseudo debility, etc.

Study of the genesis of neurotic and developmental disturbances
during analytic treatment has likewise shown, more and more clearly,
that fixation points in the preoedipal phase, or regressions toward this
developmental period, are responsible for the various symptoms or
character anomalies or at least play a very important role in their genesis.

Such observations justify the question how we, equipped with our
present knowledge, must evaluate the role of the oedipus complex. In
the initial period of psychoanalysis Freud defined the oedipus complex
(the "fateful" love attachment to the parent of the other sex and the
hostile rivalry with the parent of the same sex in the phallic phase) as
the central point of the healthy and the neurotic development, as the

198

example for adult love life, both in the normal and in the abnormal. Freud's view was soon extended to cover the reverse feelings to the parents, which also belong to the oedipal situation. The concept of the oedipus complex had to include the negative oedipal constellation.

Can we still agree with this concept? Or does the stress at the present moment lie upon the preoedipal attachment to the mother in the anal or oral developmental phases? The oedipus complex does undoubtedly develop from the early attachment to the mother. We also know that each subsequent stage contains residues from earlier stages, that subsequent stages overlap, and that the "archaic" is elementary and powerful. On the other hand, what is the fatefulness by which Freud was struck at so early a date?

In order to answer these questions we propose (1) to consult our clinical material, obtained during the analytic process; and (2) to avail ourselves of the new theoretical insights regarding this problem.

MATERIAL SUPPLIED BY THE STUDY OF THE ANALYTIC PROCESS

Although all persons go through identical developmental stages prior to attaining the capacity for becoming adult, stabilized personalities, we know from our experience how different a course the process of growing up may take in different persons. Two large groups of factors are responsible for this: (a) environmental influences; (b) the dispositional factors which determine the possibilities and limitations of the complicated structure of adult personalities.

Psychoanalysis has pointed out from the very beginning how important are the attitude of the environment and the environmental factors for the child's development. The environment is supplied at first by the mother, who is herself likewise a product of her own environment. The influence of the family as a whole is soon added, and of its social conditions which are in themselves likewise dependent upon position, status, group relations, economic situation, national and racial peculiarities, etc. In the first phase of an analysis, these factors as well as the specific peculiarities and capacities of the individual himself come to the fore. They give the analyst an unforgettable impression of the variegation of the individual paths of life. Strangely enough, it is nevertheless possible to observe a more or less typical course in the analytic process. The

199

general human problems begin to manifest themselves. This applies to the gravely neurotic patient who is presenting his unsolved conflicts, as well as to the approximately "healthy" analysand, who wishes to become acquainted with the special form and structure of his own personality. While endeavoring to bring to the fore some points of this typical course of the analytic process, we wish to point out with emphasis that, naturally, deviations from it may occur, and that they are not exceptional. *In psychic processes no rigid schematization is ever possible.*

The typical course of events is to be observed most clearly in analyses of children in the latency period. At this time of life the core of the personality has already been formed; the superstructure, however, is less complicated than it is in adults, the environment being still limited for the most part to family and school. A "typical" child analysis brings to the fore first the rivalizing attachment to the siblings; next, the phallic phase and the typical emotional relationship with the parents from the oedipal constellation. The oedipal tendencies and fantasies are linked to the problems of masturbation, sexual curiosity, and the infantile fantasies regarding the parents' love life. But they are charged with and distorted by pregenital representations. Not until then does that stage come up for analysis in which the early infantile attachment to the mother and the pregenital developmental phase indirectly repeat themselves, and can be dealt with.

On close scrutiny we shall be able, as we said above, to observe a similar course in most analyses of adults, although the persons of siblings and parents have been replaced by other persons and the rivalry will be acted out with friends, collaborators, colleagues, or superiors, and love will already have been directed toward spouse or lover.

The observation of the typical course here depicted is occasionally hampered during an analysis, because confusing periods, called by Helene Deutsch "chaotic" periods, occur in every analysis. In these chaotic periods divergent material from differing developmental stages is presented without logical sequence. It cannot be unraveled moment by moment. However, a correct psychoanalytic treatment is a *dynamic* process. If only we succeed in *accompanying* the analytic process and in supporting it by our interpretations of defense and content at the right moment without disturbing it by untimely interference, the typical phases mentioned above will gradually unfold themselves.

The most surprising feature is that, in an analysis which is running a favorable course, toward the end, a fourth phase begins to manifest itself. This is the convergent phase. The material which has led to working through and revising the early mother attachment is replaced by material converging once again toward the phallic phase and making possible another re-experience of the oedipal parent relationship, but now in a normal form, freed from pregenital fixations. In favorable instances a process of detachment from the parents and an after-development into normal, adult love life takes place. The latter yields an optimal therapeutic success.

Here we must stop for a moment and once more occupy ourselves with a question that has been asked repeatedly: How is it possible to recognize whether the material stems from the oedipal phase or from the period of the early mother attachment, the preoedipal phase?

We have already said that it is not always possible to answer this question in the chaotic period. In the convergent phase of clearing up, it is completely possible. The fact that a first light was not shed upon the preoedipal mother relationship of the little girl until in the late '30s clearly shows that this encountered great difficulties at the outset. Helene Deutsch and I were able to bring some typical facets to the fore. These observations were affirmed later on by Freud and others, and elaborated further.

Parallel studies on the rich variegation of the early mother attachment of the little boy were published afterward by Ruth Mack Brunswick and myself. In Chapter 7 I presented some examples and also described some criteria for recognizing oedipal and preoedipal material. I will here repeat only two of these criteria, which are in my opinion the most important:

(a) In contradistinction to the oedipal material, often presented in fantasies and reminiscences, the preoedipal expresses itself exclusively in the form of *acting out*.

(b) When the analysand presents the preoedipal material, his personality changes during the analytical hour and his behavior greatly resembles that of an infant or very young child. It manifests itself in attitude, voice, behavior, motility, mimicry, and other primitive means of expression. As a matter of fact the patient re-experiences the prehistoric time of the first years of childhood (see Chapter 13).

We will now occupy ourselves with a second problem.

Since we are so much impressed, during the analytic process, by the various typical phases in which the material presents itself and by the differences in the nature of the early mother attachment and the oedipal relationships, the residues of these differences must necessarily manifest themselves in the adult object relationships. Thus it is indeed. Out of the complexity and the many shades of these greater and lesser differences, I will select only a few in order not to exceed my time limits.

The adult woman orients herself in her love life with her male partner and in the problems of nursing and educating her children, basing herself for the most part on the example of her own child-father and child-mother relationships. Her husband inherits, as it were, the oedipal love for her father, the children receive the love she herself once got from her mother. We say that the normal woman finds her object relationships by way of the healthy identification with her mother. Her attitude toward her husband must, however, be different from her attitude toward her children.

Where a feminine surrender is indispensable for a healthy love life, the bringing up of children requires a strong activity, a harmonious blending of active and passive behavior. In other words, toward her husband the woman makes use of her identification with the oedipal mother image. She experiences love in the form of passive surrender, as she formerly did toward her father.

In regard to her children, who are in need of the actively and passively caring and loving mother, the woman utilizes the attitude resulting from identification with the preoedipal mother image. We can actually observe these various identifications expressing themselves in the family life. I need not say how often these relationships are disturbed because they are utilized inadequately. How far the family life is a harmonious one depends greatly on the right distribution of these two mother identifications.

In Chapter 7 I described some cases in which the residues of the preoedipal and oedipal attachment to the mother clearly manifested themselves in the life of the adult *man*. In the normal development of men much less of the preoedipal relationship is left than in women. The little boy does not change the love object in the oedipal period as the girl is forced to do; it is only the nature of his love that changes in consequence of the process of growth. In the life of men a real repetition of the situation of the archaic child-mother entity never takes place, in contradistinction to the woman's life, wherein she becomes a mother herself. This may be the very reason why a neurotic fixation of the little boy on the early mother attachment often has a particularly disturbing effect on his adult love life.

I will add a few observations to the examples cited in the afore-mentioned paper.

Men who state that their married life is on the whole satisfactory sometimes complain that they occasionally experience obsessive impulses to visit prostitutes. Sometimes they merely speak to such women and leave it at that, or merely walk through the districts which prostitutes frequent; sometimes they look for an actual sexual outlet, yet without obtaining a real psychic satisfaction. Sometimes normal coitus does take place, but generally masturbation and various perverse acts are preferred. Analysis shows us that a split has taken place between the oedipal and the preoedipal mother image. The latter is occasionally longed for in an obsessive way. The prostitute unconsciously represents the preoedipal mother image, who actively gratifies all archaic (oral, anal, urethral, sadomasochistic) tendencies through the perverse acts and repeats the nursing and handling of the infant. If this archaic period is worked through in analysis, the preoedipal fixation may be removed and the two mother images united, thus bringing about the harmonious afterdevelopment and integration of the love life. One often hears the view expressed that man and woman cannot really understand one another in their love life. Many factors are responsible for this, but part of the explanation lies in this twofold origin of the object relationship. The wife cannot understand her husband's assurance to her that his infidelity has nothing to do with his love for her. The husband on the other hand cannot understand the grief of his wife, who has invested the whole of her capacity for love, coming from both the preoedipal and the oedipal phases, in marriage and family.

203

The typical course of the analysis, depicted here, shows us over and over again:

(a) how important is the preoedipal development for the ultimate formation of the oedipus complex;

(b) that the oedipus complex is the final product of the preoedipal development, but of a specific nature. Its ultimate shape is decisive for the normal as well as for the pathological love life of the adult;

(c) that disturbances in the preoedipal phase can cause abnormal shapes of or weaknesses in the oedipal constellation. Thus they further regressions toward early fixation points and give rise to neurotic and defective development.

When the fourth phase of the analytic process, the handling of the material which converges once more to the oedipus complex, is not at all or only partly successful, the therapeutic result of the treatment remains unsatisfactory. These failures have taught us which of the many responsible factors is the central one. It lies in the castration complex. If the castration anxiety of boys, which is linked to the oedipus complex (with girls it is the masculinity complex), cannot be overcome, a regression takes place toward certain fixation points in the preoedipal phase.

In the course of analytic work such regressive flights are repeatedly observed whenever a new quantity or intensity of castration anxiety is mobilized.

The preoedipal phase—as is well known—has its own sources and forms of anxiety. Whenever tensions arise because of ungratified needs, they are capable of producing anxiety reactions. As soon as the mother is recognized and loved as an object outside the self, fear of losing the mother's love will arise in the face of conflicts between instinctual life and the mother's wishes. An important source of anxiety is given in the ambivalence conflict. The child, simultaneously loving and hating the mother, finds himself in an *inner* conflict situation. Anxiety arises which can be diminished or reinforced, but not removed, by the mother's attitude. In the oedipal period love is directed toward one parent, whereas the other parent receives the child's hostility. Consequently the love for the mother obtains (in the boy) a much less varying and a more permanent character. The same applies to the rivalizing hostility toward the father. In this consolidation of the affect relationship lies part of the fateful nature of the love of the little Oedipus. The preoedipal forms of anxiety contribute to the formation and intensity of the castration anxiety in the oedipal period. However, the latter (anxiety over the possession of the penis in the phallic period) has a very exceptional character:

(a) as a result of the biological function of the sexual organ and its narcissistic significance for the self-esteem of the individual;

(b) because of the impossibility—acting as a narcissistic injury—of leading an adult love life, which is due to the immaturity of the child; and

(c) because of the bisexual disposition of all persons. In the boy the passive tendencies threaten his masculinity and are to a considerable extent the cause of his castration anxiety. In the girl the active (masculine) tendencies constitute the biological substratum of the factors deciding for normal or pathological development and determining the form of the castration complex. The linking of the oedipal situation to the castration complex is a second facet of the fateful character of this period of life.

Here we must lay emphasis on the fact that especially in the girl the negative oedipus complex can be of the greatest importance in this connection. The question may arise whether there are cases in which the positive father attachment fails to develop.

We now arrive at:

THE NEWER THEORETICAL INSIGHTS OF THE LAST FEW DECADES

Among these, the following are of importance for our theme: (a) our increased insight into the development of the instinctual life in the preoedipal phase; (b) our knowledge regarding the early ego and superego development.

(a) The instinctual life we now know to be an interplay of erotic and aggressive instinctual drives. The manifestations in the various preoedipal developmental phases bear the marks of both groups of drives. However, not sexuality alone passes through developmental stages; aggressive drives seem to do the same, and thus to influence the object relations. I will cite one instance out of many:

The strivings for power and rivalry originating from the aggressive drives attain a certain acme in the anal period and color the object relationships. A great deal of them is preserved in later life, but in normal growth they are raised to a different level and merge, for instance, into a nondestructive ambition and a productive "trial of strength."

In the phallic phase the boy's relationship with the father is dominated by rivalry and aggression. However, the ambivalent relation develops and results in an identification with the father, and becomes the basis for normal masculinity. The girl emulates the mother; her identification with the oedipal mother image results in healthy femininity.

(b) Our knowledge of the early ego development is equally important for the understanding of the preoedipal and oedipal object attachments. The ego is still undifferentiated in the newborn. It gradually develops a number of qualities and functions. By means of some of these it becomes acquainted with the outer world; it learns to distinguish between within and without and to perceive the inner world. The ego must appropriate the control of certain instinctual demands as well as of other desires and needs, in order to bring them into harmony with the demands of the outer world. It must partly permit these needs and instinctual desires to be gratified, partly leave them unsatisfied or postpone their gratification or modify them in their ends. The ego must effect in part an adjustment to the outer world, in part it must try to modify the environment in accordance with needs and desires. In order to be able to accomplish all these tasks, the ego develops its intelligence, its thinking, its knowledge, etc. It produces reaction and defense mechanisms against intolerable instinctual tendencies and demands of the environment that cannot be satisfied.

It refines its capacity to distinguish between outer and inner world; it tries to integrate wherever there are contradistinctions (see Chapter 8).

The mutual influence of instinctual and ego development is discussed in another symposium at this Congress.

For our theme the following seems to be of importance:

Object attachments are the expression of instinctual needs that are related to a person or object in the outer world. Since the ego is the intermediary between inner and outer worlds, it is obvious that the nature of the object attachment is also determined by the developmental level of the ego. E.g., as long as the ego has not developed its faculty to distinguish between inner and outer worlds, an *object* love in a real sense, i.e., a love for the mother "on her own merits," is out of the question. The attachment to mother or to the mother's breast is still a biological and not a psychic one. The infant aims at satisfying his needs and expects this gratification from his mother in the same way as from his body. Therefore we call this earliest attachment a narcissistic one, in contradistinction to the real object attachment from later periods. It is well known that the growth of the narcissistic into the object-libidinal attachment is very gradual. Even if the object is already recognized as something outside the self, the character of the attachment is still for a long time predominantly "narcissistic."

A great deal of this early attachment is preserved in the adult love relationships as well.

A certain amount of narcissistic gratification obtained from objects is indispensable for the health and the normal functioning of man. However, a sound relationship presents a considerable amount of actual love for the object, with respect and appreciation of the personality of the other. This latter form of object attachment seems to be prepared for during the preoedipal developmental phase, but it does not flourish until the phallic, oedipal period. In this period the ego has actually acquired a sense of reality, naturally in an interplay with the instinctual development and under the influence of the environment. The ego has overcome magical thinking and the magical attitude toward the outer world to a considerable extent; it has also developed its integrative powers to such an extent that ambivalent attitudes are no longer directed toward one single object, but can be divided between father and mother; it has formed the necessary reactive and defense mechanisms, which have transformed or warded off such instinctual tendencies as disturb the object relationship.

In the meantime, the *affective* life has also gone through an important development. Originally affects are attendant phenomena of instinctual manifestations.

Before the period of differentiation between id-ego and inner-outer worlds, and thus before a primitive structuration of the personality, we can only attempt to describe the affects as diffuse phenomena. It is, however, part of the task of the growing ego gradually to get acquainted with the affects, to learn to register the instinctual processes of the id, to control the affects and ultimately to take possession of them. It is a triumph of the ego over the id, if, at last, the personality is capable of saying: "I feel something," and no longer "There is a feeling within me." This process, too, is not effected until a comparatively late stage, and it is never completely accomplished. The affects that are attendant upon the erotic drives are usually classified under the heading of love feelings. Affects covering aggressive drives are classed with the feelings of hate. In the infant the affects are not yet differentiated; they are elementary, passionate, and violent. Gradually a process of differentiation and refinement of the affects takes place.

In adults we find in the gamut of love a multiplicity of feelings, e.g., kindness, sympathy, friendship, compassion, admiration, adoration, etc. The series of feelings of hate comprises hostility, antipathy, spite, jealousy, revenge, contempt, and others.

The capacity for differentiating the affective life is dependent upon instinctual processes as well as upon the qualities of the ego. The greater the ability of the ego to understand the inner world, the more mature its knowledge of the outer world, its possibilities of learning from the environment, the richer will be the development of the affective life. This means that the affective life will present an increasing resemblance to that of the adult.

As the mother is the first example from which the child learns and with which he identifies himself, it is self-evident that the mother's personality is of paramount importance for the ultimate formation of the child's affective world. A healthy, loving, and emotionally balanced mother will be promotive of a normal affect relationship in the child. A sick or inharmonious mother will greatly interfere with the growth of the infantile emotional ties.

As long as the ego is undeveloped, however, this identification can only be a primitive one. It stands to reason that, after the first years of life, the personalities of the father, of other members of the family, and of persons outside the family, too, are of great importance for the affective development.

I have already pointed out that the *oedipal* object attachments and the love and hate *feelings* bear a very great resemblance to the adult love relationships. The instinctual drives are directed toward the possession of the beloved person and the removal of the rival, just as in adult partners. However, the *shape* of the *sexual* representations is still an infantile pregenital one. The latter is connected with the somatic immaturity of the child as well as with the interruption of the instinctual development at the onset of the latency period, as already mentioned. In consequence of this interruption the instinctual development is one stage behind the affective maturation.

We will now turn to a particular developmental level in the construction of the ego, i.e., to the genesis of the superego.

As a result of the inhibition of the instinctual development at the onset of the latency period, the oedipus complex is repressed in its typical fateful shape, and it does not emerge until puberty, as a transition to adult love life.

Ego and emotional development proceed, but at a different level, no longer directly linked with a flourishing instinctual life. According to Freud's oldest formulations, the superego would arise as a residue of the oedipus complex, *an agency in the ego organization*. It takes over and represents the commands, prohibitions, norms, and ideals of the parents through identification with the oedipal objects. We have to face the question whether our knowledge of the prehistory of the oedipus complex does not require a revision of this concept regarding the genesis of the superego. We have already said that the process of identification plays an important role in the preoedipal phase, as regards both the ego functions and the growth of the affective life and the object relationships. It is obvious that in the preoedipal phase the child forms ideals through identification with an image of the admired parents. In the very period during which wishes for omnipotence and magical thinking are flourishing, ideal formation takes place. Disappointments at one's impotence and frustrations are compensated for by fantasies of omnipotence dealing with an ideal and identifying oneself with the "almighty" ideal. The formation of an ego ideal begins in the preoedipal phase. What about the judging and prohibiting superego, the conscience? In the beginning the young child puts up with restrictions of his gratifications and disappointments for fear of punishment or of loss of the mother's love. Nothing of a judging agency or an inner prohibition can be perceived. When, however, the development has advanced so far that the child begins to identify himself with his mother, he also starts to take over her prohibitions and commands.

A differentiation takes place in the ego, owing to which the child learns what is permitted and what is not permitted. Now he is more or less able to determine his behavior himself, along these lines, so as to prevent painful experiences. This process bears a certain resemblance to the training of animals, and may obtain the character of the conditioned reflex. A good example is bowel training. Many children, trained in cleanliness, lose this acquired capacity rather easily under changed conditions: e.g., if the mother is absent or lessens her demands, or if in the inner relationship between the child's emotional life and his acquired ego functions new conflicts arise, which often occurs in consequence of the birth of a younger child, etc. According to a communication from Anna Freud it might also happen, however, that the internalized command of cleanliness can no longer be undone in the anal period, not even at the emphatic wish of the mother. If, for instance, the anxious mother should try to force her child, who is seriously ill, to deposit his urine and feces in bed, it may become obvious that the child is no longer able to do so. However, a conditioned reflex in an animal also continues to exist for a longer stretch of time, although it finally disappears. It might be interesting to investigate whether in the special group of children in the anal phase referred to by Anna Freud this inability to dirty themselves will continue to exist even if the demands of the educator are not renewed, or whether it would ultimately disappear. Such an experiment would be hampered by the progression of the development toward the next, the phallic phase and the oedipal constellation, as a result of which the conditions are entirely different.

However this may be, the internalization of a certain command in the anal phase does not by any means appear to be identical with the existence of a conscience function, and a self-judging agency. The affects of the successfully trained child do not present—in a conflict situation—the differentiated character of the later guilt feelings. They

210

rather resemble generally the primitive anxiety reactions of the animal that has dirtied the floor. It seems likely that here individual differences occur in connection with a more rapid or a slower maturation of the personality. Although we should not speak, therefore, in the anal preoedipal stage of a superego with the function of an inner conscience, we have to envisage this early, unstable internalization of commands as processes that constitute examples for the postoedipal identification processes resulting in the formation of the superego. They are—as it were—the precursors or primitive stages of the superego.

The superego itself displays a very definite structure that is not essentially changed even though the contents and the shapes of the norms are subject to modifications under the influence of growing up. The boy's ego ideal, which had been selected originally in accordance with the example of the mother (although it was the phallic mother) obtains more definitely the image of the father at the time of superego formation. The commands and prohibitions, mainly received from the mother, are attributed to the father and introjected in connection with the latter's person. Although archaic forms always persist—to a greater or lesser extent—the process of structuration and of conscience formation in accordance with the image of the father can be clearly followed in normal cases. In the girl it is the identification with the image of the preoedipal mother that causes the earliest ideal formation and the first internalization of commands. At the time of superego formation the imago of the oedipal mother, i.e., the mother as the father's wife and as the girl's rival, is the one to put its stamp upon the superego.

Formulating the matter in other terms, we may say:

During the preoedipal development primitive forms of ideals and internalized commands arise via identifications; they are consolidated in the oedipal phase into a superego and ego ideal of a structure, determined by the oedipus complex.

Summary

In the preoedipal phase a psychic object attachment to the mother develops from the biological mother-child entity. The form of this attachment is dependent (1) upon the nature of the mother; (2) upon the hereditary factors in the child; (3) upon the instinctual and ego development; (4) upon the maturation of the affects; (5) upon the early identifications (precursors of the superego); and (6) upon the mutual influence of all these different factors.

The structured and stabilized product of this varied and eventful development is the oedipus complex, which is to be placed in the phallic phase.

The oedipus complex is the example for the adult love life and, because it is linked with the castration complex, it is the starting point for the "coming into being" of neurotic disturbances in children in the latency period, adolescents, and adults. As the oedipus complex carries along with it its previous history, the preoedipal phase, the events of the latter period determine the shape of the oedipus constellation and thus play an important part in the ultimate formation of the personality.

Severe preoedipal disturbances may *hamper* the process of ripening, *weaken* the phallic position, and distort the *oedipal* constellation. In such cases the infant's anxieties cannot be overcome, castration anxiety becomes overwhelming and causes regression toward preoedipal and pregenital positions and fixation points.

In conclusion we may say that:

Neuroses and other psychic disturbances may arise from several nuclei of maldevelopment, to be found in the oedipal *and* in the preoedipal phases.

CHAPTER 15

Depression and Aggression

A CONTRIBUTION TO THE THEORY OF THE INSTINCTUAL DRIVES

(1953)

DIFFERENCES IN THE PSYCHIATRIC AND PSYCHOANALYTIC APPROACHES TO
THE PHENOMENON OF "DEPRESSION"

In psychiatry, the term "depression" is often used in a diagnostic sense. A subdivision is made into different clinical pictures, such as reactive depression, psychogenic depression, hysterical depression, endogenic depression, etc.

Some authors distinguish between endogenic depression and melancholia, others seem to equate the two terms, but they all agree that endogenic (melancholic) depressions are constitutional diseases based on an innate predisposition.

Reactive depressions, on the other hand, are considered as reactions to external, traumatic events in otherwise almost normal persons, while the term psychogenic or neurotic depression is used for depressive disturbances developing in the course of life, on the basis of childhood neuroses.

From a descriptive point of view, these differentiations are justifiable. Many phenomenologists offer very fine and detailed pictures of the inner experiences of depressed patients.

See also Chapters 24, 25, and 26.

As far as the psychoanalyst is concerned, however, the phenomenology is the starting point for his investigation. Some patients give as colorful and detailed a description of their depressive states as many phenomenologists have done in their writings. The analyst, however, wants to know far more. He is interested in the structure and genesis of the psychic deviations from normal; he searches not only for the immediate causes of the outbreak of the disease, but for the deeper causes as well. It is common knowledge that psychic disorders invariably arise from a conjunction of constitutional and developmental factors (Freud's complementary series). As regards the field of the depressive states, this implies that a fundamental separation of endogenic from exogenic depressions is impossible. *All* depressive clinical pictures contain endogenic and exogenic factors. Naturally, it is of practical, therapeutic importance to know at which end of the complementary series the syndrome in a given patient must be placed.

A psychotic patient presenting a grave melancholia with delusional ideas, having hardly any affective contact with his environment, is not amenable to psychotherapeutic or to analytic therapy in this stage. Yet Abraham (1924a) has pointed out that, not infrequently, manic-depressive patients can be treated in the interval periods, sometimes even successfully.

It is my experience that there are cases of "endogenic" depressions where analysis is possible and, though the technique has to be slightly modified, rather significant results can be obtained. The periodic cyclothymic variations of mood mostly continue to exist, but the amplitude of the oscillations has decreased so much that they are sometimes hardly perceptible any more to the environment. Such experiences impel us to be very careful with our indications for shock therapy in depressions, the more so as the damage done by shocks to the subtle psychic functions can be very considerable.

The so-called reactive depressions may sometimes disappear spontaneously or with superficial therapeutic help. Whenever it is possible to observe them analytically, it becomes clear over and over again that they arise only in persons who have already gone through inconspicuous depressive changes of mood. The latter can regularly be tracked down into early childhood. Many of the differences between mild and grave depressive states, so great from the phenomenological viewpoint, prove to be based, genetically, on economic, i.e., quantitative, factors. The active psychic mechanisms are the same, however.

Psychoanalytic Knowledge of Depressive States

Psychoanalysis does not look upon depression as a separate disease but as a syndrome that may occur in nearly all neuroses. Fenichel speaks of "that most frequent and also most problematic mechanism of symptom formation, depression" (1945). And next: "To a slight degree, depression occurs in nearly every neurosis (at least in the form of neurotic inferiority feelings); of high degree it is the most terrible symptom in the tormenting psychotic state of melancholia."

We know that depressions occur in combination with hysterical symptoms, with obsessive-compulsive symptoms, with perversions, and also with all kinds of character deformities and developmental disturbances. The depressive mood is the expression of an injury to the self-esteem, ranging from slight inferiority feelings to a total loss of self-esteem. The latter is often attended by feelings of depersonalization; the patient has become estranged from his surroundings or from himself (once a patient used the expression: "I suddenly feel I have lost myself").

Sometimes an intense anxiety is experienced, sometimes it is suppressed, but during analysis it invariably manifests itself. This anxiety signals the great danger of the "ego loss," of the impoverishment in narcissistic libidinal cathexis, which is indispensable for a normal self-esteem.

It is also well known that self-reproaches may alternate with blaming others. The patient feels bad or guilty, the ego is no longer loved by the superego, as Freud puts it.

The ego tries to reconcile the superego by means of self-accusations, self-vexations, penances, etc., for the feeling of being loved again increases self-esteem. The latter also applies to the surroundings. In every possible manner, the patient demands that the persons in his environment supply love, care, sympathy, help, etc., because he feels permanently wronged. To quote Fenichel: "These patients are love-addicts."

In other words, the patient's affective relationship with the environment as well as the relationship with his own person is not on an adult level; he does not love objects on the basis of their own merit; he has regressed to an infantile stage of love life.

The classic work of Abraham's referred to above moreover presents us, in a way still unsurpassed, with a picture of the regressive libidinal processes to be observed in depressions as well as in manic-depressive psychoses. The author found a combination with compulsion-neurotic phenomena in the mild forms of depression as well as in the interval of the manic-depressive psychosis. Therefore he was forced to accept a regression toward the anal phase. In the more severe and psychotic forms, however, the process of regression was found to have proceeded to the oral phase. Abraham holds this deeper regression responsible for the psychotic character of the disorder. In such cases, the representative of the object is introjected, in consequence of which the relationship with the environment gets lost. The more complete this process, the more deeply psychotic the patient becomes.

Abraham also assumes that such regressions may occur under the influence of traumatic events (e.g., the loss of beloved persons, etc.) in those persons who are predisposed by a fixation at the pregenital developmental stages. Constitutional factors may play a role here, but also the so-called "primal depression" of earliest childhood, which may arise from a lack of gratification of the primitive bodily needs as well as from a deprivation of love.

Abraham's subdivision of the three libidinal developmental phases (each of them further divided into two phases), explains some peculiarities of the ambivalent affective attitude of the depressive patient toward the environment. However, a number of questions remained open at that time, some of which can now be answered, in connection with the increase of our knowledge about the development of the ego and the development of the aggressive urges. Although Abraham's clinical material presents an abundance of aggressive and destructive reactions, both against others and against the own person, he speaks only of anal and oral sadism (or masochism), and no attempt is made to study the specific role of aggression.

At the present time we consider the following points as two of the most important problems of psychoanalysis: (a) how have we to en-

216

visage the coexistence of erotic and aggressive instinctual manifestations; and (b) what is the mutual influence of ego and instinctual development.

Concerning (a) I should like to recall to mind that no human relationship is free from ambivalence. In the greatest happiness of two loving partners a certain hostility, however deeply concealed it may be, is never entirely absent. One often gains the impression that living out a certain amount of aggression, provided that it is used in the right form and at the right moment, may increase the feeling of felicity. It is common knowledge that a wrong dosing or timing may disturb or destroy the entire experience of love. The very fact that erotic and aggressive feelings and urges are so closely interwoven renders our study much more difficult.

Concerning (b) I wish to recall to mind the fact that communications about instinctual urges only reach us via the ego. What we actually observe are instinctual derivatives in which we must recognize, by means of analysis, what portion was original instinctual urge and what modification this urge has undergone because of the responses of the ego. This is also valid when the whole of this conglomerate of drive-ego reaction has been repressed and, in the analytic work, has become conscious only after a resistance has been overcome. Uncontrolled, instinctual impulsive actions, in which the ego has been taken by surprise, provide us with a more direct picture of the instinctual event. This can become abundantly plain in certain psychoses. In more or less normal persons it is observed for instance in outbreaks of rage or under the influence of alcohol or other intoxicants. The observation of very young children who have developed only a very few ego functions is particularly instructive in this respect.

I am of the opinion that the study of the depressions may shed some light on the two problems mentioned under (a) and (b). Since analytic treatment of depressive patients can take place only with those patients in whom some of the ego functions have remained intact or, at least, are functioning enough to permit cooperation of analyst and patient, we always have to contend with the difficulties mentioned above. Therefore we must be very cautious in our attempts at distinguishing the shares of the erotic drives, the aggressive drives, and the

217

ego functions in the psychic event. We are always dealing with a total personality. Observations of young children, such as were made by Anna Freud in the Hampstead Nurseries and such as are taking place in many American institutions, provide us with valuable, complementary data and corrections.

THE ROLE OF AGGRESSION AND OF EGO DEVELOPMENT IN DEPRESSIONS

I shall present a few examples from the abundance and variety of the material gained from thorough personality analysis in order to illustrate the facets that are of significance to these two problems. The gloomy mood of a depressive patient, which he often accounts for by declaring himself to be inferior, bad, stupid, incompetent, figures prominently among his complaints.

We have already described that these complaints express an inner psychic conflict: the ego feels itself to be bad when confronted with a strict superego which acts condemning and punishing. But there is more to it: in every patient with strong inferiority feelings, analysis one day reveals the existence of superiority feelings, fantasies of grandeur and omnipotence.

The patient cannot love another human being on his own merit, because he is unable to give. He only wants the other *to be his*. In other words, the object is, to the patient, a complement, an extension of his own person. He can only love the other in the form of possessing him. It is a craving for power, an enlargement of his own power through that of another. In childhood, this wish for power is concerned with the parents who, in the child's fantasy, are omnipotent. In a certain phase of infantile development the feeling of omnipotence arises from an introjection of the images of omnipotent parents. The fantasies of omnipotence are well known in the obsessive-compulsive neurotic who performs "magic" in words, thoughts, and compulsive acts. In magical thinking and acting we recognize ego functions at a primitive level. However, these processes are, at the same time, manifestations of a twofold instinctual event. The need for love is satisfied through the union with the object, but at the same time the process serves as a means of increasing power. The existence of the object has become insignificant at the very moment the craving for power predominates.

218

In some cases of depression the fantasy of devouring the object entirely (introjecting it) and destroying it gets the upper hand. Freud described this phenomenon in grave melancholias at an early date.

We are accustomed to linking the feelings of omnipotence which have to compensate for the experience of being powerless, so intolerable to many sensitive children, to the anal and oral phases of libidinal development. It is one of the earliest analytic discoveries that the young child's emotional attachment to the mother in the periods of breast feeding and bowel training is accompanied by a somatic sexual gratification and consequently by a discharge of libidinal tension. It did not become clear until much later, however, that the aggressive instinctual energy also may find an outlet in the struggle for power, in processes of conquering the object, wanting to possess it, keeping or destroying it.

The Interrelationship of Erotic and Aggressive Drives

Freud's original conception reads that, normally, we are dealing with a blending, a fusion of erotic and aggressive drives, while in pathologic cases a defusion can take place. This applies to the aggression turned against the outer world as well as to the aggression directed against the own person.

When observing an uncontrolled outbreak of anger or a temper tantrum in a child, we are struck by the enormous quantity of aggression that can be discharged. It is quite probable, to be sure, that such an event is accompanied by some discharge of libidinal energy. Freud pointed out, at an early date, that every important somatic process, such as, e.g., pain, may act as a sexual stimulus. However, in the outbursts of impotent rage the discharge of aggression is clearly predominant, in contradistinction to, for instance, what happens in a lust murderer, in whom sexual and aggressive (destructive) drives are discharged with nearly equal intensity. The latter also applies to the sadistic (and masochistic) masturbatory fantasies.

A patient suffering from depressive states, feelings of derealization and inferiority, once depicted the great difference in subjective experience. In the course of some years' analysis, an abundance of sadomasochistic fantasies had been worked through. The early infantile material

219

next emerged in acting out. Desperation and impotent rage manifested themselves in crying, yelling, trampling, kicking, and beating on the couch. In the subsequent discussions the patient was greatly impressed by the intensity of his destructive urge. When I tried to find a connection with his sadistic fantasies, in which he used to humiliate and beat his objects, he replied: "That's something entirely different; with those fantasies, long drawn out in bed at night, I had erections and sexual gratification. What I experienced now was merely: 'wanting to smash, to bite, to destroy.'" I gained the impression that the patient was right.

After all, the patient had not really destroyed anything, neither myself, nor the furniture, nor some property of mine. What had put this destructive need in check prior to its realization?

In the analytic situation, the patient's ego had temporarily abandoned some of its functions, such as, for instance, self-control, but it was still functioning enough to preserve part of the reality sense and to leave part of the control of motility intact, and therefore actual destruction was given up. It goes without saying that this was due to a conjunction of various motives, e.g., under the influence of the moral system, of guilt feelings, and especially of anxiety.

We are interested, however, in the question of what happened here in the instinctual sphere. (a) Has the discharge of the aggressive energy simply been interrupted? (b) Has a fusion with libido, modifying the destructive urge, come about? (c) Has something happened to the aggressive instinctual drive itself, i.e., has it become an aim-inhibited urge, has a sublimation taken place?

Inhibition of the discharge has undoubtedly taken place, as is shown by direct observation. But surely more things have happened: as far as the processes of fusion with libido and of sublimation are concerned, the subsequent course of the analysis will shed some light on that. We might briefly describe this course as follows:

After an aggressive outburst such as the one described above, we see the patient regaining, more or less gradually, a positive attitude toward the analyst. At first this often occurs under the pressure of an enormous fear of retaliation on the part of the analyst, a fear of losing his love and appreciation. In this period of the analysis it is the analyst's often difficult task to deprive the patient, by a great deal of quietly waiting patience, understanding, and invariable kindness, of the possibility of rationalizing his anxiety by an actual danger situation.

He learns to understand that the danger was real in his early childhood but has become superannuated now and, in various circumstances, such as the analytic situation, no longer exists in reality. When the patient has repeatedly had this experience we see, after new aggressive explosions, the positive, libidinal attitude come into existence spontaneously, automatically as it were.

The more successfully the inner instinctual conflict is solved and the anxiety about the aggressive and destructive urge is overcome, the sooner the patient will be able to abandon his self-vexations, his raging against himself, i.e., his depressive symptoms.

I wish to add here that, naturally, this healing process can be accomplished only in some cases. As I discussed above, it is self-evident that one cannot embark upon an analysis in a grave melancholia where the representation of the object has been entirely, or almost entirely, introjected, where the patient has consequently turned nearly all aggression and destruction against his own person, and where there hardly exists any affective contact with the environment. In an interval, or with grave depressions on a more or less obvious endogenic basis, it is sometimes possible to bring about the process described above, although it may take many months and runs a monotonous course.

As I pointed out in the introduction, the result is often limited to a reduction of the amplitude of the oscillations; this however, may represent a very important improvement from the therapeutic viewpoint.

A practical difficulty may be encountered in the fact that, as is generally known, the self-destructive tendency may become so strong, in grave depressions, as to entail the danger of suicide. It is often very difficult, then, to decide whether the patient must be hospitalized or whether one may venture to continue the analysis. If the libidinal attachment to the analyst is strong enough to carry the patient over all aggressive and self-destructive tendencies, one may book a success in return for one's pains. But there are cases in which the analyst's courage, tact, and patience are of no avail.

I revert to the cases in which the healing process described does materialize. In addition to the aggressive discharges experienced by the patient as destructive urges, other forms of aggression can be observed in some cases. They are described by the patient as a wish to control, to get hold of, to gain possession of. In fantasies the object (the analyst) is belittled and humiliated, it is true, but it is not destroyed. These ideas and experiences, too, are clearly distinguished by some patients from their sadistic and masturbatory fantasies.

The events taking place here during the analytic process remind us in many respects of the observations of babies and toddlers by various authors, e.g., Anna Freud in the Hampstead Nurseries.

Anna Freud (1949a) describes the baby's first emotional contact as presenting the same characteristic quality of aggressive insatiable greediness that he displays toward food. And afterward: "In the oral stage the infant destroys what he appropriates (sucks the object dry, tries to take everything into himself)" (p. 40). She depicts the toddlers' "peculiarly clinging, possessive, tormenting, exhausting kind of love which they have for their mothers," etc. And, "We understand that on these pregenital stages it is not hate but aggressive love which threatens to destroy its object" (p. 40). The author describes elsewhere (1951) a form of "autoaggression" (head-knocking) as "the aggressive equivalent of autoerotism" and later on "as one of the rare representatives of pure destructive expression where fusion of the drives is incomplete, or after defusion has taken place" (p. 28).

Thus, in order to explain the phenomenon of "aggressive love," Anna Freud uses Sigmund Freud's theory of a fusion or mixture of the erotic with the aggressive drives. It is certainly distinctly observable that the infant, sucking, biting, laughing, and whining, is developing an erotic attachment to his mother's breast (and afterward to his mother). Tearing up and smashing toys, attacks on pet animals are, at the same time, the child's expressions of love just as the struggle for power and the toddler's wish to domineer are in the anal phase.

But it remains an open question whether this coexistence of aggression and erotic play is a real fusion of the two drives and whether, e.g., the substitution of a striving for power, or an urge to dominate, is to be solely attributed to an admixture with libido.

Another possibility urges itself upon us. Prior to going further into this subject, I shall briefly discuss libidinal development. We readily follow Freud's conception that the sexual drives may have different aims. However, we must clearly keep in mind what we must understand by this concept. The general description given by Freud in "Instincts and Their Vicissitudes" (1915) runs as follows:

> The aim of an instinct is in every instance satisfaction, which can only be obtained by removing the state of stimulation at the source of this instinct. But although the ultimate aim of each instinct remains unchangeable, there may yet be different paths leading to the same ultimate aim; so that an instinct may be found to have various nearer or intermediate aims, which are combined or interchanged with one another [p. 122].
> The aim which each of them [the sexual instincts] strives for is the attainment of 'organ-pleasure'; only when synthesis is achieved do they enter the service of the reproductive function and thereupon become generally recognizable as sexual instincts [pp. 125-126].

We can fully endorse the first sentence of this description. The aim of a drive is *gratification,* relief of tension, or, in other words, the personality aims at a discharge of tension (energy). The question remains, however, whether this discharge takes place at a body zone functioning as a specific source for a given instinct. We would rather assume that instinctual discharge takes place at different zones of the body, having an exceptional significance in certain developmental phases in relation to the body's needs, but not necessarily being the "source" of the instinctual energy.

These zones vary according to the person's maturation as well as his development under the influence of the environment (i.e., the educators' attitudes and demands).

We no longer speak, at present, of the instinct of self-preservation but regard the striving for self-preservation as an ego function. The first, most elementary need is the intake of food. The first libidinal discharge takes place at the mouth (the oral zone). Later on, it is the processes of digestion and excretion that are attended by sexual gratification (anal phase). Ultimately, in adult sexual life, an ejaculation of sperma, accompanied by an orgasm, provides a complete discharge of tension.

The "intermediary aims" are gratifications at the various erotogenous zones (apart from mouth, anus, and genital, the skin, the respiratory organs, and other parts of the body may also act as such). Thus we speak of organ pleasure, which is probably comparable to the more or less diffuse gratification the young child provides himself in masturbation and is undoubtedly different from the orgasm attending the ejaculation of the sexually mature male.

We shall now revert to our considerations of the aggressive drives. As far as they are concerned, we also assume that the ultimate aim is *gratification, discharge of tension.* Temper tantrums, etc., demonstrate this *ad oculos.* It does not seem unlikely, however, that the aggressive drives are not so rigid as Freud originally believed them to be, but that they, too, can reach the ultimate aim (gratification) by "various ways." A destructive or aggressive act can be directed against animate as well as against inanimate objects. The discharge of aggressive energy observable in an outburst of rage might be compared with the sexual discharge in a complete orgasm (see also Brunswick, 1940). It is my impression that "gaining possession of," conquering, mastering, getting hold of an object should be regarded as variegated ways of discharge providing some kind of gratification. The object (animate or inanimate) is not incorporated (i.e., destroyed), then; its survival is tolerated and sometimes guaranteed. Gaining possession of the object serves the increase of the subject's own power.

The problem of the aims of aggression has already been touched upon by Hartmann, Kris, and Loewenstein (1949). These authors write:

> What should we assume the aims of aggression to be? It has been said that they consist in total destruction of objects, animate or inanimate, and that all attempts to be "satisfied with less," with battle with or domination of the object or with its disappearance, imply restrictions of the original aims. It seems that at the present stage in the development of psychoanalytic hypotheses the question concerning the specific aims of the aggressive drive cannot be answered; nor is a definite answer essential [p. 67].

In my opinion, this formulation of the question is not the right one. As I said before: *the aim of a drive is gratification, discharge.* (The authors cited above assume, just as I do, that aggressive discharge per se may be experienced as pleasurable (p. 77) and that the pleasure does not necessarily arise from "narcissistic components.") *The ways by which discharge can be effected may differ*, but no one is "superior" or "inferior" to another. A given form of discharge is not a "restriction" of another form, either. Nor does an aim inhibition of the drive take place. The different modes of discharge are manifestations of *instinctual development*. The various ways of discharge can be used concurrently, e.g., an urge to gain possession of the object can be accompanied by a destructive urge. A specific mode can also be abandoned and replaced by another one. This is, e.g., clearly to be observed in a child as a reaction to the object's attitude. If, for instance, the mother resists the child's striving for power, if the child feels disappointed or hurt in some fashion or other, a tendency toward revenge will arise and provoke the destructive impulse.[1]

The question whether the *quality* and *intensity* are the same in the different forms of gratification should probably be answered in the negative. But in this respect there is no fundamental difference from the possibilities for sexual gratification.

The sexual gratification obtained at the oral or anal zones, or experienced by the little boy playing with his genital, certainly differs quantitatively, and probably also in intensity, from the orgastic experience attendant upon the ejaculation of the adult male, as I pointed out before.

We revert once more to the problem of the relation of libidinal and aggressive energy to certain *zones of the body*. Observation, especially of children, has taught that the sequence of oral, anal, and phallic developmental stages of the libido is not a constant one. For instance, genital stimulation takes place in the infant (masturbation in infancy), i.e., long before the phallic phase. Oral and anal phases overlap. The anal stage in particular is greatly subject to the influence of educational measures as regards its duration, form, and significance. In this connection I refer to a communication by Anna Freud in "Observations on Child Development" (1951) viz., that she was in a position to observe an extremely intense penis envy in one-and-a-half

---

[1] I feel justified in concluding from a personal communication of Hartmann's that he, personally, is inclined to accept a diversity of aims (perhaps he also means a diversity of modes of discharge?) of the aggressive drives.

to two-year-old girls, following a particularly intimate bodily contact with little boys, such as perpetually occurs in nurseries.

According to many authors, the relation of the aggressive drives with certain parts of the body would be such that these organs are not places of stimulation, but serve as instruments of discharge of tension. Remarkably enough, one of the first organs to be used for the discharge of aggression is the mouth, the very organ where sexual stimulation and discharge takes place. I do not venture to discard the possibility that the stimulation of the mouth (lips and jaws) caused by sucking the breast may also be able to serve as a stimulant for the aggression, which is then discharged in "sucking out," biting, "swallowing up," and crying.

When the musculature develops further, it is especially the muscles of arm and hand, in addition to the muscles of mouth and jaws, that become instruments for the discharge of aggression.

It is likewise an open question whether muscular tension per se may function as a stimulus for aggression (often in the form of an urge to gain possession of the object.) The so-called pleasure in functioning, i.e., the immense satisfaction a child may display when successfully utilizing muscular functions he has recently learned (e.g., walking), is certainly an expression of a saturated "possessive instinct" (power over his own body), apart from the sexual gratification it may represent.

Although differences in the development of libido and aggression cannot be discarded, we come to the conclusion that they are likely to be smaller than they appeared at first.

AGGRESSION, EGO DEVELOPMENT, AND OBJECT ATTACHMENTS

We shall now turn to the following questions: Under what conditions do the aggressive drives search for discharge in the one mode or in the other, by this or by that way?

It has become clear from the above that this depends upon the stage of maturation of the person, and upon developmental factors under the influence of the environment. The development of aggression partly follows libidinal development, partly the growth of the body, partly the psychic and emotional maturation, and it is especially correlated with the maturation of the ego.

226

In the process of growing, the ego gains mastery over motility, i.e., the use of the muscular apparatus which is the instrument for the discharge of aggression. In the oral developmental stage the object is captured and destroyed by "eating." It stands to reason that this does not imply, as is sometimes said, that the infant sucks the mother's breast "wishing" or "intending" to destroy it. As long as the baby cannot distinguish a world outside his own self he cannot have a "wish" regarding such a world. He does not suck out of "love" or out of "hate" or because of his "wish to destroy." Sucking is a reflex movement stimulated by hunger. But this activity apparently offers, at the same time, a possibility for discharge of libidinal and aggressive instinctual tensions; therefore sucking is continued even if the stimulus of hunger is no longer operating.

A need, a wish for gaining possession of the object (the mother's breast) cannot arise until the child can distinguish an outside world from his own self, i.e., after a certain degree of ego development.

Only when the object is recognized as a prerequisite for the gratification of needs does a libidinal attachment come into existence. And only when the child has learned that destruction of an object means loss of what is indispensable (or beloved) will he replace the destructive urge by a striving to gain possession of the object, sparing its existence.

It is easy to observe this phenomenon in a toddler who smashes a favorite toy with blissful satisfaction, who is then surprised and unhappy on perceiving that it does not function any more, is broken or gone, and who ultimately learns to "possess" the beloved doll or animal while leaving it intact.

We mentioned above that disappointments and injuries may provoke destructive impulses again, e.g., in the form of a wish for revenge. In other words, part of the development of ego functions, e.g., the capacity to distinguish between outside and inside, acquiring a reality sense by means of experience, but also the magic form of thinking (the basis for fantasies of omnipotence and grandeur) are preconditions for being able to replace a certain mode of discharge of aggressive energy by another one.

A second process, the development of a psychic object attachment, also plays an important role. The object perceived at first as indispensable for the gratification of bodily needs becomes essential as a source of love later on. The feeling of being loved is a gratification of the self-esteem which is so easily hurt in the child, who feels utterly powerless when confronted with demands of the environment as well as in regard to his own wishes for power. The tragic conflict lies in the fact that being hurt or disappointed is likely to mobilize a destructive urge against the very person whom the child cannot do without as a love object. It is self-evident that the attitude of this person (at first the mother) may exert a great influence on the intensity of this conflict. Since, however, in consequence of the peculiar complexity of man, his protracted immaturity and dependence, a life without any frustration or feeling of impotence is impossible, the conflict is fundamentally unavoidable.

Thus we see alterations taking place in the forms of discharge of aggression, actuated by maturation and ego development on the one hand and consequent upon the libidinal object attachment on the other hand.

We shall now revert to our earlier question. Could this not be explained simply by the theory of the fusion of erotic with aggressive drives? Clinical observation leads me to regard this event, at least partly, as a developmental process of aggression which runs its course alongside the libidinal development, in addition to the process of fusion of aggression and libido.

I return to our depressive patients and the distinction, already described, in their experiencing of sadomasochistic urges or fantasies and aggressive or destructive bursts of anger. The striking point is that a clear-cut difference between the therapeutic possibilities in regard to influencing the two phenomena can be observed. In sadistic and masochistic acts and fantasies, a fusion of libido and aggression is unmistakable. Hurting, humiliating, or destroying in perversions or masturbatory fantasies *is* gratification, and vice versa.

We all know how difficult it is therapeutically to affect the sadistic and masochistic perversions, as well as the morally masochistic attitude toward life. There are depressions, however, that are comparatively easy to cure and they are the very depressive states where there is less sadism involved but where one is chiefly concerned with aggressive (destructive) urges and with possessive tendencies. I have the impression that an intimate fusion with libido under special circumstances can fixate the aggressive drives in such a way as to render them invariable, whereas, remarkably enough, an aggressive urge operating more or less independently of the libido can be liberated from repression and eventually integrated into the personality. The nature of those special circumstances should be further explored.

The question how integration may take place leads to the problem of *sublimation,* which I have avoided so far and on which I will be brief.

Sublimation was described by Freud as an instinctual vicissitude of the libido. More than once I have expressed the view, and I am in agreement with many other authors, e.g., Hartmann, Kris, and Lowenstein, that aggression can likewise be sublimated (see Chapters 8 and 10).

Possessive urges, besides sexual curiosity, provide an important contribution to exploring the world, acquiring knowledge, controlling nature, creating social achievements, etc. Such activities may become constructive for personality and fellow beings. Destructive tendencies, too, *can* be used in a constructive form; I refer to the well-known example of the surgeon who cuts up in order to cure; of the decomposition of substances in laboratories which can be used productively in chemistry and engineering; of analyzing man and social conditions, etc., etc.

In the person himself, some of the sublimated aggression, together with sublimated (or desexualized) libido, is used for the structural differentiation of the psychic apparatus.

Hartmann prefers to speak of neutralized energy in this connection. Does it make sense to distinguish between neutralized and sublimated instinctual energy? Both expressions refer to aim-inhibited energy. However, to the term "sublimation" we attach the idea that the energy is drained off in actions valued as being "socially higher." Thus in distinguishing between the two terms we introduce the element of evaluation. Experience has taught us how defective sublimations frequently are, both in the individual and in the community.

We now return to the therapeutic possibilities with depressive patients. Apart from the observation that it is difficult to affect libidinally fixated aggressive tendencies, we have to consider the greater or lesser capacity for sublimation (or neutralization) as playing a most important role in the therapeutic procedure, in addition to a number of other ego functions which I shall not discuss now.

Finally, however, I wish to stress the fact that the form of discharge of aggression predominantly present in a certain patient may be of importance. If the mode of *destruction* of the object prevails—i.e., if the instinctual regression to a very early stage has taken place, if, to cite Abraham's words, the "primal depression" is localized in the earliest years of childhood and caused or enhanced by traumatic events such as the mother's death or a particular lack of love on the mother's part, while moreover the patient's ability to neutralize energy is not very great— a grave melancholia is more likely to occur than in a patient in whom other possibilities for discharge of aggression have already come into existence, in whom no malign fixation has arisen from fusion with libido and in whom there are ampler and more extensive possibilities for sublimation.

I feel justified, however, in mentioning one other experience. Though it is sometimes possible to cure a patient afflicted with a grave depression, it is definitely *not* possible to do so when one does *not* succeed in uncovering and bringing to consciousness the various ways used by his aggressive urges in the course of his development. For only this process, if successful, can offer the opportunity of effecting an after-development, of sublimating and of integrating those urges into the whole of his personality.

And only if this is done can a harmonious interplay of sexuality, aggression, and ego achievements become possible. Such harmony seems to be a precondition for a constructive attitude toward environment and society as a whole.

CHAPTER 16

Problems of Psychoanalytic Training

(1954)

It is remarkable that the four speakers of this symposium concentrate mainly on two fields of training activities: (1) the selection of candidates, and (2) the problems of training analysis.

The other part of the program, the theoretical and practical teaching in lectures and seminars and the supervision of treatment, are left out of consideration. This fact demonstrates that there is general agreement about the overwhelming importance of the candidate's personal analysis in the training procedure.

Though I share this opinion completely, I think that we should not altogether neglect the value of an efficiently composed program of courses on theory. Instead of giving positive suggestions, which would take up too much time, I want to mention only two difficulties which might impair the efficiency of the theoretical teaching, one on the part of the students, the second on the part of the teachers.

Many students join the courses expecting that they will be able to learn the whole of psychoanalytic theory during this teaching. I think it is necessary to fight this misconception by stressing over and over again the fact that courses are only able to stimulate the candidate to serious study of the analytic literature.

This paper was read as an Introduction to the Discussion of the Symposium on "Problems of Psycho-Analytic Training." For the prepared papers, see M. Balint (1954), Heimann (1954), G. L. Bibring (1954), Gitelson (1954).

Some teachers tend, from the very beginning, to present to the students criticisms of and deviations from psychoanalytic theory. Such teachers seem to be afraid of being called "orthodox Freudians." They overlook the fact that the students usually become confused by this teaching. The Dutch Training Institute therefore decided to present to the students, in the first two years, the development of Freud's theory, the basic concepts and writings. Not until the last year are differences and deviations brought forward and broadly discussed.

Supervision, too, is an important part of training, not only to teach technique, but also as a means of judging the candidate's capacities and progress. I cannot go into further details here.

Before entering into the problems of the training analysis, I want to say a few words about the first point: the choice of candidates for admission.

Two of the four speakers in today's symposium take up the problem of the suitability of students.

Heimann presents us with seven criteria for the acceptance of candidates. I can agree with all of them, though I share Balint's opinion that the rules of admission of training are rather vague, intuitive, and "haphazard," as he puts it. Nevertheless, I want to add one other (vague) point to Heimann's: in my opinion, integrity of character is indispensable for the future analyst. I am aware that I shall be blamed for bringing moral principles to the fore. However, as analysts are treating human beings therapeutically, their behavior has to be guided by medical ethics. It is a pity that we do not possess an objective criterion of a person's integrity. Our inability to define objectively the suitability of psychoanalysts for the profession is inherent in the nature of that profession, which works with feelings, needs, impulses, values, in short, with human mental processes.

Although only Heimann gives a list of criteria for admission, all the speakers seem to be in agreement about the necessity for serious selection. Gitelson stresses the difficulty of the problem that in many Institutes a large and ever-increasing number of students are applying for training, wishing "to get through with it as rapidly as possible," and pretending to be "normal." Perhaps Grete Bibring is right in saying that this may be a more pronounced problem in America. Nevertheless, there are also European groups contending with the same difficulty and, as in some American Institutes, the temptation to capitulate to the pressure of the multitude of applicants is great. It seems highly questionable whether it is advisable to yield to this pressure. The Dutch Institute, for example, which originally welcomed the increase of applications, is experiencing more and more the disadvantages of having accepted candidates who later proved to be more or less unsuitable for analytic work. The Training Committee has now abandoned this mistaken atttitude. For the sake of psychoanalysis as a science and as a therapy, as well as for that of the student himself, we prefer to reject an applicant rather than to educate inefficient persons. A small group of efficient workers is more valuable than a large group of mediocre ones.

We now come to the main theme of the symposium: the training analysis.

All participants in the symposium agree that the training analysis is the most important part of the training, but that it is full of difficult problems. There is also agreement on the three following points:

(1) The technique is in principle the same as in a therapeutic analysis.

(2) The training analysis has different aims. It does not terminate when neurotic symptoms are removed, as a therapeutic analysis usually does. It has to go further, "deeper," as Heimann puts it; it tends toward a "supertherapy," as Balint says; it must be a "character analysis," to use the words of Gitelson and Bibring.

(3) A special difficulty of the training analysis is that it takes place under conditions quite different from the well-known setup of the psychoanalytic situation. These conditions are consequences of two sets of circumstances: (a) the analysand occasionally meets his analyst in courses, seminars, and meetings, and he knows a good deal about his personal circumstances, peculiarities, and scientific convictions; (b) the analyst has to judge his analysand's suitability and capacities and decide at what point in time he can be allowed to start the theoretical and practical training.

In a lecture at the Amsterdam Institute, Anna Freud once presented a clear and colorful picture of the different ways in which the training analyst is bound to offend against the classic rules of technique.

Today's speakers also give their views on this difficult point, which undoubtedly has to be considered seriously.

I personally agree with Heimann and Bibring that the problems concerning the encounter of analyst and analysand outside the analytic situation are minor ones. It is more of a problem and a burden for the training analyst as it demands the latter's skill, self-knowledge, and self-control to help the analysand to overcome the resistances awakened by and attached to the extra-analytic encounter. The major difficulty seems to lie in the analyst's task of deciding on his analysand's status and progress in training. This problem was strongly felt by some members of the Dutch group as well. However, as the analyst's opinion of the student's capacities and personality proves to be indispensable for judging the candidate's suitability, the only possible way of meeting this problem seems to be its most careful and rightly timed handling in the analytic situation. It may happen that a candidate's distrust and oppositional hostility cannot be overcome. The analyst should then look for a disturbing element from his side and eventually send the analysand in question to another training analyst. In case of another failure with the second analyst, I think we are entitled to assume that the analysand is unsuitable for the psychoanalytic profession. We ought then to have the courage to reject him as a candidate.

I now come to the most problematical point: the special aims of a training analysis and its differences from a therapeutic analysis as a consequence of these aims.

Balint has pictured the changing claims made upon the future analyst's analysis during the development of psychoanalysis. Experience has taught that neither the curing of neurotic symptoms nor the additional demonstration of psychic mechanisms in a short analysis are sufficient preparation for the future analyst's task.

What more do we have to do? What does a "deeper" analysis, a "character analysis," a "research analysis" mean?

I suppose most of us have almost the same aims in mind, though the descriptions may be different. We are not content with merely liberating the warded-off instinctual and affective life of our analysand. In addition, we want to supply him with the most thorough knowledge of his personality structure, his capacities, peculiarities, and limitations. This means that we shall have to bestow great care on his ego analysis. We shall try to pursue the development of the ego, of its capacities, its reactions, its mechanisms of regulation, adaptation, and defense in connection with the influence of the environment and the demands of the instinctual drives, both in the normal and the abnormal. We shall have to pay special attention to fixations on and regressions to early stages of ego development because these processes cause ego restrictions and distortions which often produce blind spots and handicaps in analytic work.

In this part of our training work we encounter a special problem, a magnified difficulty of ego analysis in general, already described by Anna Freud (1936). In analyzing id contents, the analyst can count on the patient's cooperation, because impulses and affects strive to penetrate into consciousness. In ego analysis, the patient begins to refuse each corroboration, defending the position of his reaction formations and defense mechanisms in order to protect himself against anxiety raised by inner and outer danger situations. In a therapeutic analysis we handle only the ego attitudes involved in the neurosis and constituting a hindrance to the patient's recovery. In the training analysis we have an additional task. We try to give the candidate insight into the development of all ego attitudes, peculiarities, and deformities of character, etc., even when he does not suffer from them. It is quite clear that without the stimulation of suffering, the resistance to cooperation with the analyst is still much stronger than it is in patients who suffer severely. Consequently, the analytic work in a training analysis may be more time-consuming, calling for still more patience and for uninterrupted contact within the analytic situation. Therefore the indications seem against reducing the number of weekly sessions or their length, as is sometimes recommended.

I am quite aware that I have put before you an ideal situation, and I think you will blame me for making such high demands on our poor students. It really seems necessary to reflect upon this situation, to ask ourselves whether it is advisable to run after ideals that will never be realized, and to question whether it would not be wiser to return to the period of pure instruction in the analyses of candidates.

Though this would certainly be the easier way, I think it is our duty not to yield to this temptation, but to continue to strive for a most thorough ego analysis in spite of the knowledge that an ideal solution will never be reached. A justification for this striving is found in our daily observations of our patients, of our students, of our control cases, and last but not least of ourselves.

Time and again we encounter failures in analytic work due to the circumstance that the analyst reacts to the analytic situation with unresolved conflicts of his own, with a blind spot resulting from unknown ego attitudes, fixated unconscious defense mechanisms, and the like. Those difficulties may present themselves as an uncontrolled countertransference, as pictured by today's speakers (and also by Annie Reich in a very interesting paper [1951]), or simply in a limited understanding or dull incomprehension of certain psychic events.

Every normal reaction formation and defense mechanism can grow into a pathological limitation of personality. One example, for instance, is to be found in the process of denial, so common a defense in a child exposed to strong anxieties. An analyst who has not mastered his own mechanism of denial is limited in his recognition of reality factors. Consequently he is unable to see his patient's lack of reality sense in its real proportions.

Instead of continuing the long list of ego limitations possibly disturbing to analytic work, I want to depict one other psychic situation that may lead to fateful failures.

A very frequent reaction to disappointments and narcissistic injuries in a child is the mobilizing of fantasies of grandeur and omnipotence. We call these fantasies normal mental products at a certain stage of development, the stage of magical thinking in ego development, corresponding with and reacting to the aggressive craving for power from the side of the id, in the preoedipal (anal) phase. The same is valid for the ambitious fantasies of puberty. Only when the infantile feelings of grandeur have become unconsciously fixated do they prevent an adult person from seeing reality and acting accordingly. The overvaluation of the self is then used as a defense mechanism not only against disappointments from the environment but also against inner feelings of inferiority. The fixated primitive form of this mechanism acquires the character of a delusion. The person in question feels offended, maltreated, persecuted, and reacts with hostility and aggression. When it covers only a part of the personality and leaves part of the reality sense intact, it causes no severe disturbance. But it remains a danger, as it usually strives for extension. This psychic process is especially dangerous for the analyst. I remind you of Freud's words: "Analyzing spoils the analyst's character." The analytic situation, in which the analyst is the leader, the patient's confidant, the object of the patient's love, admiration, and infantile adoration, is a real temptation to the analyst to mobilize his own feelings of grandeur and to overrate himself. Therefore it seems to be of extreme importance for the analyst to know his own personality in its actual proportions, his capacities as well as his limitations and his faults.

I have returned to the high demands made upon the training analysis of future analysts. In the meantime you will certainly have thought that these claims should not be addressed primarily to the students, but in the first place to the training analysts. I am in full agreement. In organizing our training we should first of all look for competent training analysts. The training analyst has to live up to the demands of self-knowledge as far as possible. Here I come very close to Bibring's remarks on this topic. She recommends that the training analyst should accomplish this task by means of a self-analysis. This is certainly good advice. However, I think we cannot expect too much from it. "The drawback of self-analysis is really the countertransference"; this means that self-love easily prevents us from seeing our own shortcomings. Each of us has his own particular blind spot.

In my opinion, training analysts would be wiser to hold to Freud's advice (in "Analysis Terminable and Interminable," 1937) to resume their personal analysis from time to time. In addition, and in cases where outer circumstances prevent the training analyst from resuming his own analysis, he should take every care to examine his own behavior, to recognize his wishful thinking, his strivings for grandeur, his character peculiarities, etc. By seeing his own limitations clearly, the training analyst on his part creates the most favorable situation for making the best of the cooperative work with the future analyst.

CHAPTER 17

Group Discussions with Stepmothers

(1954)

*At the time this communication was published in the Dutch periodi-
cal for mental health, an extensive literature on group discussions and
group therapy was already available from the Anglo-Saxon countries
as well as from the Continent, and had been studied by me. I did not
refer to those publications, intending merely to survey my own observations and to present a few ideas stimulated by them. Therefore I do
not claim any priority for the explanations and thoughts brought forward in this short article.*

The data of my communication are derived from twenty-one weekly
discussions with a group of nine mothers in whose families lived one
or more stepchildren. The discussions lasted for one hour and fifteen
minutes and continued for nine months. The mothers were clients of
the Amsterdam Child Guidance Clinic (Prinsengracht 717), of the
Youth Psychiatric Department of the Communal Health Service, and
of the Child Guidance Clinic of the *Hervormde Stichting* (a Protestant
institution) in Amsterdam. The staff members of these various institutions worked hard in searching for the most suitable cases. The discussions took place in the Psychoanalytic Institute of the Dutch Psychoanalytic Society.

The objectives of these discussions were twofold: (1) a social one;
(2) a scientific one.

(1) The social aim was to give support to the mothers, who had come

to one of the three above-mentioned institutions for advice in connection with difficulties they experienced with the stepchildren in the family situation.

(2) The scientific aims were several. I wanted to try: (a) to investigate the special problems of the stepchild within a family constellation; (b) to gain some insight into the relation between educational problems specific for the stepchild and problems inherent in the upbringing of children in general; (c) to get some idea of the relation of group discussions on the one hand and group psychotherapy and individual psychotherapy on the other hand; (d) to find out what psychic mechanisms and dynamisms come to the fore in group discussions.

Concerning (1), I shall start with a brief survey of the course of the various sessions, fragmentary and incomplete as it will have to be.

During the first interviews all participants were present. Later on there were usually one or two absent as a consequence of their children's illnesses. The winter was cold and wet and many children got colds and minor diseases; sometimes the mother herself was ill, and on some occasions she had not been able to find a friend or relative who could take care of one of the smaller children and babies. Usually there were five or six mothers present, occasionally only three. A few times a baby accompanied the mother when she had not been able to leave him elsewhere.

The complaints which had caused the mothers to seek help consisted of neurotic phenomena in the children, i.e., enuresis, anxieties, learning inhibitions, etc., as well as behavioral delinquent problems, i.e., "troublesomeness," tantrums, lying, stealing, pilfering, baiting and teasing, and "sexual misbehavior." The various institutions had prepared the mothers for our discussions. The first gathering served the purpose of getting acquainted with one another. The mothers did not know each other and I myself was a stranger to them. I started by welcoming them and stressing how difficult it is to handle and educate stepchildren. We were coming together in order to try to understand some of the problems and conflicts involved and to find out how to meet them. It was remarkable to observe how soon the ice was broken. After one mother had started, the others could scarcely wait for their turns to speak and to pour out their hearts. They told their troubles not only in connection with the stepchildren, but also with their husbands and their own children. In some families there were only one or two stepchildren, in others children from previous marriages of the father or the mother were present, as well as illegitimate ones and those of the present marriage.

During the first interviews I remained very passive. I listened and limited myself to a few words of understanding and encouragement in order to gain confidence. Later I had to answer questions and give explanations. After a short time most of the mothers became highly interested in the problems of the other members of the group. They tried to understand each other and then became eager to give advice.

The levels of intelligence and psychological insight were very different. After three or four sessions some of the participants left, either because the material was beyond their comprehension or because of a lack of emotional understanding. In this group were the "narcissistic" types. They demanded to be in the center of attention, they could not listen and were continually disappointed that their special problems were not always in the limelight. After the sessions they tried to have a personal talk alone with me. Usually I said a few words to them, trying to give some support. However, they were unable to enter into a group relationship, finally lost interest, and stayed away after some five or six sessions. The others came very regularly apart from the already-mentioned occasions of illness, and a strong group relationship was established.

The problems that gradually came to the fore could be divided into two groups: (a) general problems; (b) individual problems.

Prominent among the general problems was the never-failing fear of being a "real," that is, a "bad," stepmother as pictured in fairy tales. All the women were from the working class or from the lower-middle classes and without exception they had entered into the marriage with a strong intention of becoming a very good mother to the "poor" stepchild. The stepchild was to be pitied because his real mother had died after a long and painful disease, or because she had been a "bad" mother, neglecting her child and deserting the family. The stepmothers intended to replace the real mother completely, sometimes with a conscious or unconscious idea of surpassing her and of being a much better mother to the poor child. One of the participants had been a stepchild herself, and had suffered severely from her hostile stepmother. Now married for a second time, she favored her husband's little son strongly above her own little daughter whom she brought with her from her previous marriage. The little girl was by far the most disturbed in the family. The woman suffered so much from a fear of being prejudiced against her stepchild that she did harm to her own child. The discussion of this situation and the woman's experience of being understood by the group members brought her relief and she was able to become much more tolerant and much nicer toward her difficult little girl. I shall come back to these problems later on.

Another general problem centered on if and at what moment the stepchild should be told about his actual relation to his stepparent. Only one mother was in favor of withholding the truth from the child. All the others agreed about the desirability and even the necessity of speaking openly about the family relations, though some of them clearly showed a strong fear of actually doing so.

In connection with this point the difficulties of the stepchild himself were open for discussion. A good understanding was finally achieved of the suffering of a child deprived of his own mother, making for mistrust and suspicion in certain circumstances. The fact that a mother has a special bond to her own child, in connection with biological ties, which is lacking in the relationship to a stepchild was discussed repeatedly. With some of the group members it resulted in a more natural and softer attitude to the stepchildren's disturbances and behavioral difficulties, which was then followed by a relief of tension in the total family. A number of friendships among the members emerged from the group discussions, which had a favorable result. Especially did the knowledge that all of them were struggling with identical problems bring great relief. I explained that though there are doubtless special problems in a family with stepchildren, the upbringing of children in an ordinary home is one of the most difficult tasks laid upon parents (at least in our society and culture). This explanation also provided reassurance.

I myself always tried to focus attention on the general problems of the stepchild. It was, however, remarkable to notice that from the second session onward the individual problems and the personal family situations came ever more to the fore. There were meetings where nearly every mother tried to present her own conflicts, normal as well as neurotic ones. In these cases the difficult or disturbed stepchild was not mentioned but the other family members and their reactions were discussed. It was especially the husband who was spoken of. A number of complaints about his behavior were put forward, i.e., "If my husband had not spoiled his child so completely . . . "; "If only my husband were not so hot-tempered toward the children . . ."; "If my husband had shown more understanding of my problems, and if he had only supported me, then . . ."; etc. Gradually a number of confessions about the mother's personal disturbances, as for instance anxieties, compulsive actions, frigidity, sexual abnormalities, tantrums, etc., were brought out.

The reader will understand that little by little we ended up in group *therapy* instead of group *discussion*. Though originally we had started with "discussions on the stepchild situation," I thought it better not to counteract the spontaneous course of development and to go along with the needs of the participants. Thus the "therapeutic" element could not be completely eliminated.

In using the word "therapy" I have to stress the fact that a real, uncovering (psychoanalytic) therapy was out of the question and was not even aimed at. From time to time a single neurotic symptom or mode of behavior was removed or diminished, sometimes bringing about a change in the mother's attitude toward the stepchild or toward other family members. Occasionally this led to a decrease of tension which influenced the children's difficulties to a certain extent. I shall present two examples.

Some of the mothers had been stepchildren themselves, as I have already mentioned. They had entered marriage with high ideals, trying to support the poor stepchild and be a better wife to the widowed or deserted husband. However, every one had suffered disappointments with the consequence that she either tried spasmodically to regain the lost illusion, or unconsciously repeated her own childhood situation as a lonely and embittered stepchild. This state of affairs sometimes caused manifest or suppressed hostilities that disturbed the family bond and unfavorably influenced the neurotic or antisocial behavior of the step-child. In the mother, strong guilt feelings, inferiority feelings, and anxieties were evoked.

A second example concerns a mother who in one of the later sessions confessed that she suffered from frigidity and sexual aversion. She had been brought up with great severity. In adolescence she had suffered from a suspicious mother who had prohibited every outing, being afraid of her daughter's "going with a boy." In reality the daughter had been completely uninterested in boys. At the present time she could allow her fourteen-year-old stepdaughter scarcely any kind of freedom. In the long run the group succeeded in providing the woman with some kind of insight into her envy of the pretty young girl who was enjoying life, with the consequence that the sensitive woman tried very hard to change her attitude toward the handsome stepdaughter.

I cannot go into more examples. However, I shall try to summarize some of the unconscious mental mechanisms in the mothers which sometimes could be favorably influenced by our discussions to a certain extent. This brings us to a tentative and very incomplete answer to the questions formulated above.

Concerning (2a), the stepchild situation gave rise in some women to (1) an excessive neurotic guilt feeling; (2) a too strong feeling of being injured in connection with disappointed expectations and hostility aroused by them; (3) envy of the stepchild who was felt to have a much better life than the mother had had herself; (4) pathological jealousy toward the husband who was felt to favor his own child above his second wife, and jealousy toward the child; (5) some anxieties and mild neurotic symptoms.

It is well known that similar psychic factors may sometimes be influenced in individual (psycho) therapy. We have to consider whether some such brief therapy is to be preferred or whether one can expect a better result from group discussions or group therapy. This brings us to our next points:

Concerning (2c) and (2d): as far as my experience goes, I should like to formulate the following impressions:

The problems of neurotic guilt feelings can sometimes be discussed with relative ease and success in a group. Giving a hearing without

243

prejudice to a participant's self-accusations may provide relief. However, the very fact that many other people in a group suffer from similar difficulties is even more releasing. One could say that "shared guilt is half of the guilt." In our group it was undoubtedly important that the leader-doctor was a mother figure, understanding, unprejudiced, listening, and explaining. However, of equal significance were the group bonds, sometimes developing into real friendships and actual mutual assistance. In connection with these interpersonal relationships some of the jealousy situations, disappointments, and injuries could be recognized and tolerated more easily, with the consequence that advice from other group members was accepted and assimilated to a higher degree.

A restriction of therapeutic possibilities in a group seems to lie in the fact that only the most superficial of anxieties and symptoms can be reached. Early and strongly repressed and warded-off material cannot be touched upon. Reaction formations and neurotic behavior patterns which have come about as a defense against fears and neurotic conflicts cannot be changed. If one tries to discuss or interpret a particular defense mechanism, the participant who is using this mechanism most intensively will put a limit to the explanations. If one goes beyond his capacity for using the explanation, the resistance can only become stronger with the possible consequence that one or more of the group members will run away. The group bond is then disturbed. Moreover, a similar interpretation may cause the mother to act out her conflicts in the family to a much higher degree than she did before, and the family may suffer considerably from this.

Concerning (2a) and (2b), I should like to comment: the special problem of the stepchild situation in regard to the mother lies in her recognition of the fact that (1) the tie to a stepchild is always different from that to her own child; (2) in connection with this state of affairs it is necessary to be sincere and to provide the stepchild with complete information. At the same time, the stepmother should have full understanding of the difficulty for a sensitive child to accept his position in the family and she should be loving and tolerant toward his behavioral disorders; (3) the stepchild situation is likely to provoke jealousy and rivalry in connection with the husband (father of the child) and the child's own mother, requiring a good deal of self-control on the step-mother's side; (4) her own children's upbringing is a difficult task as well; therefore the stepchild situation is *not* responsible for all of the conflicts and difficulties in the family.

Finally, I should like to make a few remarks on the question whether there was any success in the group discussions from the social side. Were our talks able to provide some support? A single experiment can merely give some tentative impressions. I myself think that one should not see the results either too optimistically or too pessimistically. Something undoubtedly happened in our group; tensions were relieved and displacements of conflicts occurred within the family relations which sometimes influenced the family ties in a favorable way. However, fundamental changes did not take place, either in the mother or in the child. In cases where one or the other was severely disturbed, there was scarcely any transformation, as was to be expected. It remains an open question whether the favorable influences have lasted and if so, for how long. However, the same problems are encountered in the infrequent (weekly or biweekly) contacts of individual mothers with, for instance, a psychiatric social worker, in casework, and even in "brief therapy." In a follow-up discussion with the staffs of the child guidance clinic and the other institutions, it became clear that some of the women who had originally benefited considerably from the discussions had come back after a longer period of time with the same or other complaints. Apparently the weekly active participation in the group had been a necessary condition for being able to keep to the changed attitude and to the improved family relationships.

This does *not* mean, however, that all of the affective ties to the group had been broken. I mention only one example out of many: more than a year after the termination of our meetings one of the participants asked my advice about a certain problem. She thanked me in a letter, in which she wrote in addition, "I was so impressed and grateful that you, Dr. Lampl, still knew the name of my stepdaughter. It is a proof of the fact that our discussions were extremely intimate. . . ."

Among the many questions raised in our final staff discussion, one should be mentioned particularly: "Are group discussions generally preferable to individual contacts, or is the reverse a better approach?"

My tentative impression is that in cases where the mother is not severely hampered by her own neurosis the group ties may be so significant that they may make the group discussions more successful. For more gravely disturbed women, individual contact may be preferable.

CHAPTER 18

The Theory of Instinctual Drives

(1956)

Freud's early libido theory, set forth as a working hypothesis in order to clarify certain problems of the genesis of neurotic disturbances, had to be enlarged and modified several times in connection with the increase of psychological material needing to be explained. A good survey of the development of Freud's theory of the instinctual drives is given by Edward Bibring (1936). The most exciting, remarkable, and at the same time disputed modification is known as the theory of the life and death instincts. It was first mentioned in *Beyond the Pleasure Principle* (1920). Some psychoanalysts were very much impressed by the new theory and embraced it enthusiastically, others rejected it more or less vehemently from the very beginning. A third group was skeptical and neither accepted nor rejected it. This conspicuous reception of the new hypothesis seems to prove that it was not welcomed objectively as a scientific contribution to be tested by further investigation, but was felt by many to be a disturbing and confusing burdening of human emotional life. Today, thirty-five years after Freud's first presentation, the attitude toward the theory of life and death instincts does not seem to have essentially changed. An affective response on the part of outsiders toward one or another theory of Freud's is quite familiar and understandable to psychoanalysts. But a similar reaction from analysts themselves calls for a serious inquiry into the phenomenon. Does it prove that the theory itself is not a workable hypothesis? Or are there factors independent of its value to be held responsible for these various reactions?

247

First I want to make a few remarks on the second point: the attitude of psychoanalysts toward the "death instinct" theory. In an article in *Psyche*, R. Brun (1953) makes an attempt to prove its falsity. He gives, among other things, a review of the psychoanalytic literature on the topic, and draws the conclusion that most of the authors who originally accepted the theory as a valuable working hypothesis changed their minds at a later period (between 1931 and 1941). He states that thirteen authors (he mentions only twelve names) arrived at an "uncompromising rejection." One of the names mentioned is my own. Now for my own sake I must emphasize that the conclusion Brun draws from my paper "Masochism and Narcissism" (Chapter 5) is based on a misunderstanding or a misinterpretation. I there tried to give some explanations of clinically observable phenomena of masochistic behavior, and I stated explicitly that in psychological events we are dealing with what is called secondary masochism. The so-called primary masochism, later on used by Freud as equivalent to the "death instinct," is not psychologically observable in clinical material. My paper does not in any way deal with the biological theory of drives. It is neither a proof nor a disproof of its correctness. I must confess that Freud's latest "drive theory" always impressed me as a far-reaching and consistent endeavor to form a connection between psychological and somatic biological data, in other words, to look for a biological basis of psychological phenomena. This endeavor was by no means the first in Freud's scientific life. In 1895 he wrote a manuscript (published in 1950, eleven years after his death), the "Project for a Scientific Psychology," in which he developed a highly interesting theory, trying to depict psychological events as quantitatively determined by conditions of material elements of the brain (see also Jones, 1953). Although Freud soon afterward discontinued his search for the brain-physiological basis of mental processes, he always used to say that at some time the connection between psychology and somatology-biology would need to be re-established. In Chapter 22 I have tried to connect findings in modern brain physiology, cybernetics, and ethology with psychoanalytic data and theory. In today's presentation I must refer to many ideas laid down in that paper. There are remarkable analogies to be observed between Freud's ideas set forth in "Project" and many of the theories of the scientists working in those fields, though the terminology is different. I cannot pursue this interesting connection further here. However, in pursuing the train of thought that seeks to find the somatic foundation of mental processes, we inevitably encounter the necessity of dealing with the underlying forces at work.

In psychoanalytic psychology the forces providing mental energy were called *Triebe* (drives).[1] The drive energy undergoes different changes during growth and development. The fact that many interests of the individual as well as of the group run counter to a direct gratification of the instinctual drives brings about sublimation or neutralization of the drive energy. With some simplification we can say that the unconscious (mainly the id) works with direct, the conscious (mainly the ego) with neutralized drive energy.

From the very beginning Freud tried to localize the sources of the drives. He observed, e.g., oral, anal, phallic, and genital sources and components of the sexual drives. The source of the aggressive drives he localized in the musculature. With regard to the somatic, physiological processes from which the *forces* providing the mental energy originate, he confined himself to more general statements in his later works. In the *Outline* he says: "The forces which we assume to exist behind the tensions caused by the needs of the id are called *instincts* [*Triebe*]. They represent the somatic demands upon mental life" (1940, p. 19). In other places he speaks of "original forces" ["*Urkräfte*"]. In using the term "forces" Freud points to the physical origin of the drives. The same seems to be valid for his reformulation of the definition of *Trieb*. Originally the concept of *Trieb* was a psychological one. It covered the sexual needs of man and animal on the one hand and the need for self-preservation on the other (sexual and ego drives). In "Instincts and Their Vicissitudes" Freud explicitly states that the theory is "merely a working hypothesis, to be retained only so long as it proves useful" (1915, p. 124). Though in this essay he repeatedly points to a somatic basis for the drives, e.g., to chemical processes underlying sexual func-

---

[1] Elsewhere I have proposed translating the word *Trieb* by "drive" and not by "instinct," because an "instinct" seems to be an already complicated behavior pattern. Animal instinct is perhaps a phylogenetic forerunner of human ego devices, as it deals with the outside world. Hartmann has dealt with the problem in a similar though slightly different way.

tions, the somewhat different definition of the *Urtriebe* or *Grundtriebe* as derivatives of "forces" appears only in his later works.

Here Freud comes upon two forces, working in different directions. One force tends to bind, to constitute ever larger unities, the other to dissolve connections, to destroy unities. The question arises whether such forces operate only in the living world. The inorganic world was formerly considered to be eternal, indestructible; physics calls it a closed system, where a tendency toward increase of entropy reigns, and in which states of equilibrium are reached. But modern astronomy and physics teach us that in many parts of the universe unifying and resolving forces are at work. This holds true for atoms, molecules, and elements as well as for planets and stars. More complicated and higher elements and atoms originate from simpler ones, e.g., helium from hydrogen. In the solar system there is an augmentation of matter that may lead to organization and to the formation of new celestial bodies. On the other hand, a constant disintegration of matter and the disappearance of small and large bodies is observable. Unifying (constructive) as well as dissolving (destructive) forces are at work. I must emphasize that the words "constructive" and "destructive" are not used here in the sense usual in psychology, that is, charged with a connotation of *value* (good and bad, or desirable and undesirable, etc.). They indicate simply the *direction* of the forces at work in the process of unification and dissolution. Though the inorganic world as a whole is a closed system, it also contains open systems with decreasing entropy. From a scientific point of view we must consider living matter as having originated out of lifeless inorganic substance. According to biology, there exist particles, simple viruses, which can be crystallized, and are to be considered as transition phenomena between the inorganic and the living worlds. We are, it is true, still quite unaware of how the birth of life comes about. But it seems quite reasonable to expect that similar forces or tendencies are at work in both the inorganic and living world. A critical question arises here. In the nonliving world the dissolution or destruction of one body can be followed by the formation of another; one form of energy or matter is replaced by another; after destruction, new construction may occur. What of this in the living world? The individual life, it is true, is definitely destined to disappear.

The phenomenon "life," however, does not disappear so long as certain environmental conditions are fulfilled. Life as we know it on our planet may be expected to cease when conditions of temperature, atmosphere, etc., change. It will certainly do so when the earth, perhaps after millions of years, comes to be destroyed as a whole. We do not know, however, whether life exists or will in the future exist on some other planet. In spite of our complete ignorance on this matter for the time being, we are, I think, entitled seriously to consider such a possibility. Be this as it may, as a matter of fact we see the opposed forces easily at work in somatic processes. In living cells and bodies we observe forces or tendencies directed toward binding and growth as well as forces or tendencies toward dissolution and decay. It is well known that metabolism provides the necessary energy (chemical, physical, and electrical) for these processes. We may find further support for these considerations in modern biology. The organic world is only *one* instance of an open system with decreasing entropy. Though total equilibrium is reached only in death, a tendency toward minimum entropy production, the so-called homeostasis or steady state, is at work in vital phenomena. But it is at work in every open system, and therefore in some inorganic systems as well. Ludwig von Bertalanffy (1950), e.g., states that the so-called equifinal behavior, considered by Driesch and others as "an extraordinary performance to be accomplished only by the action of a vitalistic factor and therefore a proof of vitalism," is *not* limited to vital processes. "Equifinality is found also in certain inorganic systems which necessarily are open ones." Prigogine is of the opinion that the second law of thermodynamics, formerly so defined as to apply only to closed systems, is an "admirable but fragmentary doctrine." He says: "It is necessary to establish a broader theory comprising states of non-equilibrium as well as those of equilibrium." This means a theory comprising organic as well as inorganic processes. To quote von Bertalanffy once more: "Not only must biological theory be based upon physics, the new developments show that the biological point of view opens new pathways in physical theory as well."

In our language we are accustomed to call the process of growth and organization in an organism "life," that of decay and disorganization "death." Now why should we not speak of life forces and death tendencies at work in the living organisms? We must certainly be aware of the fact that we cannot define the essence of the term "force." But in physics "force" is a hypothetical term as well. Enigmas are still to be found in the lifeless as much as in the living world.

We will now turn to *mental* life, a very special and late developmental product of life, it is true, but still part of life. The assumption that representatives of the constructive and destructive biological forces are at work in psychic processes is inevitable, though we must be prepared to encounter them in a different shape. I think Freud had these points in mind when speaking of the necessity of a scientific psychology, of the physical basis of psychic events, and finally of a somatic-biological theory of mental forces.

We have now to ask the question: What is the psychical reflection of or correlation with these somatic processes? From a scientific point of view we have no reason to think of mental processes as mystical or supernatural events, entering into the human individual from outside, as do some philosophical and religious systems. Science considers body and mind as a single entity. I have earlier (Chapter 12) adopted this standpoint, though I explicitly stated the limitations, for the time being, of physical and physiological approaches to mental events. Now, as Freud described the mental forces providing the energy for psychic processes as *Triebe* (drives), we come back to the question why it proves to be so difficult to see Freud's conception of Eros (life instincts) as the psychological *representatives* of the organic life forces and the destructive drives (or death instincts) as those of the organic destructive forces in the sense mentioned above. One of the most striking observable differences between the drives and the underlying forces seems to lie in the fact that the drives are charged with the psychic quality of sensations, feelings, affects, as I point out in Chapters 12 and 22. The feelings may be experienced as tensions (e.g., with needs), as pleasure and unpleasure, and in higher development in a variety of most differentiated and differently colored affects. It is well known from analytic observation that in the unconscious the drive representations do not lose their affective charge.

I should like to mention a few factors out of many that seem to me to be responsible for the difficulties of understanding Freud's latest drive theory, though of course they do not give us information about its validity. I ask myself whether some of the impassioned opponents may perhaps have failed to take into consideration the extension of the concept of drive inherent in the theory. Perhaps it may be called an omission on Freud's part not to have announced this extension explicitly. Freud's rather humorous reference to a "mythology" in connection with the drive theory, too, may have promoted some misunderstanding. I wonder, however, whether the psychological concept of drive is any more mythological or mysterious than the concept of "force" in physics?

The earlier theory of the drives embraced the psychic manifestations and vicissitudes of the sexual drives. Sexuality, however, is only a part of the life process, though a very important one. The highly complicated development of the total psychic life seems to hamper the *observation* of connections with the bodily processes, not only for outsiders, but for analysts themselves. On the one hand we know for certain that the connections do exist, on the other we are aware of the fact that the underlying somatic forces are not observable directly and unchanged in psychic events. In these circumstances seem to lie many possibilities for a lack of understanding. I will mention one factor out of many: human beings, scientists included, tend to be proud of their highly complicated mental life. A deep-rooted narcissistic need often leads them to hold on (unconsciously) to primitive ideals and grandeur fantasies in one or another higher developed form. Where scientists do not embrace philosophical or religious systems, they can satisfy this need by (unconscious) glorification of some psychological theory or other. In our field the "drive theory" seems to be a very suitable one for this purpose. To see the drives as mysterious, supernatural powers seems to satisfy the pleasure principle in the form of a narcissistic gratification. In this connection I feel we should take Freud's above-cited remark about the drive theory as "mythology" as something of a warning against this pleasurable but unscientific tendency.

Be this as it may, a passionate uncritical adherence to the theory may be caused by such an affective need for idealization. But the reverse can occur as well. It is especially the part of the theory concerning the destructive drives, the death instinct, that may lead to an uncritical rejection, rationalized by the faulty supposition already mentioned that the death instinct has to be observable directly in clinical material. Brun, for instance, is of the opinion that the scarcity of suicides can be used as a proof against the theory. I will come back to this topic afterward. Flugel (1953) in his very interesting paper states: "The concept of the death-instinct is embarrassing not only emotionally but also intellectually, for its relations to the other more generally acceptable features of psychoanalytic theory are often far from clear." I wonder whether we really have to distinguish between emotional and intellectual embarrassment. What seems to be intellectual evidence may be in reality an overlooking of the extension of the concept of drive. Now the very fact of extending the meaning of a concept is nothing uncommon in psychoanalysis. More than half a century ago the concept of sexuality was enlarged by Freud to include the whole of infantile instinctual and affective life, an enlargement by now accepted by every psychoanalyst. The refusal to accept a similar extension of the concept of drive to make it embrace the underlying somatic forces as well is not likely to be based on intellectual, logical considerations, but rather on affective motives. Nevertheless, in order to facilitate the understanding of Freud's theory, we may propose a reformulation of the terminology used in the drive theory for practical purposes. From this practical point of view we suggest that the word "drive" be reserved for psychic phenomena, and differentiated from those forces or tendencies of a more general nature that underlie them and are closely related to them, in other words, that we distinguish between the purely psychological and the biological-physical concepts. While I accept Freud's idea of this close relatedness, the inclusion of both these series of factors under the same term may lead to ambiguities. Thus I propose to speak of sexual or constructive and destructive or aggressive *drives* on the one hand, and of life and death tendencies or *forces* of a more general nature on the other. Such a distinction carries in itself the danger of furthering the desire of many people to separate body and mind and to forget that in reality body and mind are one entity. However, as for the time being we are not able to indicate the organic correlate to each psychic event observed, we might accept the distinction until further notice and until progress in science enables us to unify the two theories in a less disputed form.

254

We can benefit by this distinction in our practical psychoanalytic work. It at once becomes clear that in studying psychic phenomena we have neither the possibility nor the need to search for a "death drive." As Freud put it, the death instinct works silently. At the present time no human being is able to perceive psychically the metabolic processes of dissolution in the body cells. Neither can he experience the opposite processes of upbuilding. What we perceive are tensions, needs, longings, and so on. From the very moment of perception these phenomena are already psychic processes, though originally in a very primitive and simple form. That in the course of development they become complicated mental events and lead to a variety of refined reaction formations, etc., is sufficiently known. The ways by which the transformations and reactions take place are not always thoroughly clear. The investigation of these problems has to be reserved for future research.

I completely agree with Flugel and many others that a longing or wish for death is seldom experienced by human beings, whereas the wish to continue life is markedly more frequent. This observation does not prove anything in favor of or against a biological theory of the forces at work. It merely tells us that human individuals in their mental and affective life perceive the phenomenon of "life" as a property they want to preserve. This seems to be a particular developmental outcome of a special vicissitude of narcissistic drives. Where a longing to die is observable, it is the expression of complicated psychic processes, influenced by mental, bodily, and environmental factors.

Another striking phenomenon is a strong fear of death so often encountered in human beings. We know from our observations that it too has a complicated structure. Freud showed its close connection with castration fear. But it is obvious that this fear has other sources as well. Kurt Eissler (1955), in full acceptance of Freud's "thanatology," as he calls it, gives a number of highly interesting reflections on "death" as subjective experience, on the longing for and the fear of death. However, he does not differentiate adequately between the subjective experience "death" in the human mind and the biological organic forces terminating the individual life. I regret that I cannot discuss his valuable study here.

255

The very existence of the fear of death is perhaps a second factor responsible for the emotional embarrassment vis-à-vis the theory of the death drives, mentioned by Flugel. The use of the intellectual knowledge of the inescapability of death for each individual is so much hampered by the wish for eternal continuation of one's own personality and consequently by the fear of one's own death, that even scientific considerations of the origin of destructive mental forces are very difficult to pursue. If my ideas should prove to be correct, we should once more have an example of the well-known fact that emotional embarrassment can impair the intellectual judgment in scientific procedure. In order to avoid misunderstandings I must emphasize once more that the very fact of emotional involvement vis-à-vis the drive theory does not prove anything in favor of or against it. Whether it will finally be accepted or rejected as a workable hypothesis lies with future research.

A last remark here will concern another practical consequence for our daily psychoanalytic work. Freud was of the opinion that the understanding of the phenomenon of "aggression" was facilitated by the new theory. I think all psychoanalysts agree about the correctness of the observation that aggressive and destructive acts whether directed toward other persons or toward the self (in the most extreme form in homicide and suicide) are usually provoked by frustrations and severe disappointments. It seems much more difficult to search for the *forces* that enable men to commit murder and suicide. As Eissler puts it: "The . . . occurrence of suicide is not the decisive factor; rather, that every human being possesses during most of his lifetime the capacity of committing suicide should be made the center of investigation" (1955, p. 67). (See also the important contributions of Karl Menninger, and a footnote in his paper, "Regulatory Devices of the Ego Under Major Stress," 1954.)

From clinical observation we know that in a suicidal act many psychological factors are involved. Freud considers the fantasy or impulse to murder an ambivalently loved (or hated?) object as a very important determinant. Another fantasy may be equally decisive, namely the idea of returning to and being united with a once deeply loved dead person.

There are still other psychological factors which may be involved in suicide, and various forces have to work together in order to provide the energy necessary for the performance of the act. As a matter of fact we frequently encounter suicidal fantasies and impulses, whereas the carrying out of the *act* occurs relatively seldom, at least in our Western culture (compare Brun). From this we must conclude that the tendency to live and the forces directed to the continuance of life are remarkably strong. On the other hand, whenever suicide actually takes place, it proves that the force directed toward the discontinuance of life is still stronger at that particular moment.

Many psychoanalysts cease their investigation after the statement that destructive actions are provoked by environmental circumstances. But the very fact that such a provocation can be successful points to the presence of forces providing the energy for the deed. And what sounds more plausible than to expect these to be psychological tendencies (or forces) attendant upon the somatic-biological forces constantly at work in the organism?

Summarizing, I would say:

(1) Science has to presume similar constructive (unifying) and destructive (dissolving) forces in the lifeless universe, in living bodies, and in mental life, though in different shapes.

(2) For practical purposes we can, for the time being, propose a terminological revision in the drive theory so as to reserve the term "drive" for psychological and the term "force" or "tendency" for the underlying somatic phenomena.

(3) Aggressive and destructive acts have to be studied psychologically as regards their various determinants, but the capacity to perform the acts is to be found in the underlying general forces.

In conclusion: Freud's theory of the "life and death instincts" (sexual and destructive drives), seen in *this* light, is no more "mystical" or "embarrassing" than any other hypothesis in any field of science. Further investigation will have to decide its value as a working hypothesis.

CHAPTER 19

Psychoanalytic Ego Psychology and Its Significance for Maldevelopment in Children

(1956)

From the very beginning, the term "psychoanalysis" has had a twofold meaning. According to Freud, the term covered (a) a specific therapeutic method capable of curing or at least improving certain forms of psychoneuroses, and (b) a psychological theory which not only accounted for the genesis of neuroses but in addition was able to elucidate the dynamic, psychic processes in patients as well as in "normal" persons.

Observations on neurotics and on certain mental phenomena in "healthy" persons (e.g., dreams, parapraxia, etc.) necessitated enlargements, additions, and modifications of the theory. Conversely, theoretical deepening of knowledge gave rise to an extension of therapeutic possibilities. It goes without saying that psychotherapeutic and analytic influence both have their limits.

Psychoanalytic knowledge has proved to be of significance for other disciplines too. One of these areas is the bringing up of children. I want to start with a very short survey of the development of the psychoanalytic psychology of children. The newborn enters the world as an instinctual creature, as Freud put it. The infant has a variety of needs, originally of a somatic kind, which categorically demand satisfaction. Since the human child is completely dependent upon motherly care for a long period of time in order to survive, he soon makes an intense attachment to the mother. In addition to the bodily tie, a psychic tie comes about very early. The need for food is a particularly urgent necessity, but at the same time the needs for warmth, care, and bodily sensations demand immediate satisfaction. When a psychic tie to the mother has been established, this object relationship creates new needs and dependencies. The object bond provides new possibilities of gratification; however, it becomes a source of disappointments, frustrations, and suffering at the same time. Freud very early described the development of the child's sexual instinctual needs from birth to adulthood. I will not go into the different stages of sexual development here. Later, Freud pointed to the equal importance of aggressive drives and tendencies. In infants we observe love and aggression operating simultaneously and intermingled with each other, though sometimes separately as well. They may be directed toward objects as well as toward the self.

From the very beginning Freud opposed to the instinctual part of the personality, the id, another agency, the ego. He had observed the personality developing in and around conflicts. The ego, or ego organization, is the psychic agency which has an integrative (synthetizing) function; it mediates between inner and outer world. Later on the ego has to take into account the demands of the normative agency, the superego, as well. The superego, or conscience, comes into being in the little child when he encounters the demands and ideals of the parents and the wider environment. This process starts at an early age and consolidates in the fifth to sixth year of life, at the end of the phallic phase. However, superego continues to develop throughout life with modifications of norms and ethics. The first principles of analytic ego psychology were laid down by Freud; they were further developed by a number of his coworkers after his death, e.g., by Anna Freud, Hartmann, Kris, this author, and many others. The extensions of ego psychology are still based upon observed phenomena. The hypotheses used to account for newly discovered material are re-examined and retested time and again. During the last decades a new field for research was found in direct observations of young children. The so-called "longitudinal life histories," observations from birth until adulthood, have provided very significant material and suggest the possible elucidation of many uncertainties and obscurities in the near future.

A Short Survey of Present Psychoanalytic Child Psychology

Before presenting the disturbed development of a three-and-a-half-year-old little boy, I want to give a short and necessarily incomplete presentation of the complicated ego development of the infant.

The newborn comes into the world with an archaic psychic heritage called by Freud "the id in a wider sense," by Hartmann "the undifferentiated phase." Out of these undifferentiated innate dispositions the different maturational stages of the instinctual drives (the id in a narrower sense) and the ego functions develop gradually during the first years of life. Some ego functions develop in a relatively autonomous way (Hartmann, 1939a), as a consequence of the general processes of growth and maturation. One example is the intellect. Academic developmental psychology describes the different stages of intellectual development of the little child (e.g., Bühler, Stern, Piaget). However, we know that many ego functions develop in interplay with and as reactions to drive processes. In mediating between the inner and outer worlds the ego makes use of adaptation mechanisms. It has to acquire knowledge of the environment, to learn to use it or to adapt to it. Many of these ego functions can become secondarily autonomous. This may happen after a certain amount of drive energy has become indifferent energy (according to Freud, sublimated or desexualized energy). Following Hartmann, we now speak of deinstinctualized or neutralized energy since observations have taught us that not only sexual energy but aggressive drive energy too can be neutralized (deaggressivized). However, all of these ego functions can again be instinctualized through certain experiences so that they revert to earlier modes of sexual and aggressive satisfaction, impairing the course of development. A clear example can be seen in many learning disturbances of young children. If, e.g., reading or counting secondarily regains a sexual or aggressive meaning, the further development of these achievements may become disturbed or paralyzed.

The infant's drives have to be tamed. Whether and in what way the feeble primitive ego succeeds in doing so or not is dependent upon a number of factors: (1) the nature of the drives, the instinctual disposition; (2) the capacities and inborn factors out of which the ego organization develops; (3) the demands and influences of the environment, the mother's attitude; (4) the continuous mutual interplay of the factors named under (1), (2), and (3). Observations on infants have revealed that a harmonious development is dependent not only on the nature of the mother's demands and educational measures, nor merely on their severity or leniency, but first and foremost on the developmental stage in which they are imposed upon the little child.

Though there exist individual differences of instinctual needs and ego capacities, we can nevertheless point to some factors which are not to be neglected in the endeavor to encourage a harmonious development: (1) in every developmental phase the little child should get a certain amount of direct drive satisfaction; (2) the possibilities for these satisfactions should be offered to the child for a certain (long enough) time. In the first year of life the infant is in need of a quantity of oral pleasure as well as of pleasure on other body parts, e.g., on the skin and on the motor apparatus, both in a passive and in an active way. Apart from the satisfaction of hunger, sucking at the breast provides pleasure, as do thumb sucking and sucking on other objects. Infantile sexual tensions are discharged by these activities. Skin erotism and passive needs as, for instance, being caressed, being lovingly handled, etc., have to be satisfied as well. In motoric movements, e.g., grasping, crawling, walking, etc., aggressive energy is discharged alongside libidinal energy. During the same period the infant's "ego" acquires knowledge of the outer world, it develops the functions of memory, of mastering motility and of using it for particular actions. Furthermore, the functions of differentiating between inner and outer worlds and of reality testing come into existence.

When the excreta come into the center of the child's interest, he experiences anal and urethral pleasure. If education in cleanliness is started too early, the result may be either a mechanical compliance at the cost of disturbed development, inhibitions, and anxieties, or a stubborn opposition followed by ego and character distortions. We assume the age of approximately one-and-a-half to two years to be the optimal one for starting training cleanliness in our culture. Too frequent and too long-lasting soiling resulting from too much indulgence may cause similar developmental disturbances and inhibitions.

Similar considerations are valid in connection with masturbatory pleasure gain, in the infant as well as in the child in the so-called phallic phase, in which the manifold oedipal relationships to the parents emerge. The aggressive drives and their later derivatives, e.g., the urge to conquer, also must find an adequate discharge in movements, in the handling of objects, and in play (which is the child's "field of work").

THE HISTORY OF A LITTLE BOY

Tonny is brought to a child guidance clinic by his mother at the age of three and a half years. The mother is very much worried because her son does not speak, never plays alone, and is not able to do anything at all. He usually sits down silently in a corner of the room, he wets and soils his pants. He is unable to put on or take off his coat. He cannot bring a spoon or a fork to his mouth and has to be fed by his mother. He makes the impression of being a severely retarded child, nearly an idiot.

The first interview in the clinic seems to confirm completely the mother's statements. The psychologist trying to test the little patient is unable to make contact with him. After some time, however, she becomes aware of Tonny's casting a sudden glance at her and in saying good-by she gets the impression that he has perceived and retained some events. The former diagnosis of severe retardation is doubted and a longer period of observation is initiated.

The first interview with the psychiatrist starts in the usual way. Tonny sits down in a corner of the room and does not do anything. He is invited to play, there are trains, cars, dolls, little houses, etc. Tonny does not react and remains silent. The psychiatrist sits down himself and begins to play with the railroad cars, lets the train go in different directions, and does not pay any attention to Tonny. After some time he casts an inviting glance at the child, who does not react. The same situation is repeated without success. After some thirty minutes the therapist speaks to himself, saying softly, "I think Tonny fears that he is not *allowed* to play with the train. That is a pity, because the toys are here for Tonny to play with and it would be so nice if he would dare to do so." Tonny seems to listen, after some minutes he moves a little bit, very slowly. The therapist repeats his former words and looks at the boy encouragingly. Tonny sits down near the toys, stretches his hand in their direction, stops, and looks at the therapist inquiringly. Finally he seizes a car. He glances at the toy and at the therapist alternately and undecidedly. All of a sudden he puts the car down and lets it run. Tonny is playing. He gradually moves toward the other toys, hesitantly and with wooden movements, but with growing attention and finally with an unexpected intensity, which very much surprises the therapist. He lets Tonny go his way, does not interfere, and only answers the boy's inquiring gaze with a friendly smile. After fifteen more minutes the session is at an end. Tonny's pale face is flushed with excitement, he smiles and is happy. The moment the mother enters into the room, Tonny is pale and motionless again; only a slight angry twitching in his face is observable. The mother wants to put on his coat. He stares at her, suddenly he stands up, snatches his coat out of her hands and tries to put it on himself, in which he succeeds after some unsuccessful, clumsy attempts. This time the mother is startled. She says to the therapist, "But Tonny cannot put on his clothes all alone." The therapist calmly answers: "Apparently he can, Mrs. X." Then he makes another appointment with Tonny.

I cannot describe the course of Tonny's further treatment in detail, but wish to emphasize only this much: in every succeeding session the little boy starts to play more and more freely, he gradually becomes ever more skillful, and he initiates conversations with the therapist. In the beginning his childish speech is hard to understand, but in a remarkably short time the therapist and the patient are able to communicate with each other quite satisfactorily. Tonny listens with greedy interest to the therapist talking about Tonny's anxieties and fears, and every time it becomes clearer that Tonny has a good mental grasp and a correct comprehension of the doctor's explanations. The diagnosis of retardation is abandoned.

Though nearly all of Tonny's ego functions had been arrested in their development at a very early stage, most of them were after-developed in an astonishingly short time. After six months of treatment Tonny was able to enter kindergarten and to adjust to the situation.

We must now concern ourselves with the question of what factors were responsible for the little boy's very severe developmental inhibitions. We once more let the mother narrate: Tonny had been a very normal, lively baby, feeding and growing well. Not until the end of his first year of life did the mother notice changes in his behavior; he became quieter, detached and absent. Crawling started late and walking was not learned until the age of two and a half years. Speech was never mastered; he merely stammered a few unintelligible sounds. He obstinately opposed bowel training.

Naturally the mother was asked several times whether something unusual or startling had occurred around his first birthday. She denied this and could not think of any extraordinary event. After several weeks, however, the mother, who came regularly for interviews, had gained more confidence and began to speak more intimately about her own problems. One day she related the following story. At the age of ten to eleven months Tonny had been a very lively, fidgety child. The mother, being very busy in her household, put him in a pen, often for many hours on end, to "protect him" against possible injuries. Once she found him playing with his genital and she was extremely frightened, thinking it was most dangerous. She pulled his hand away, hit it repeatedly, threatened the child, but nothing was successful. He continued his genital play. After the mother had heard about his supposed retardation, she was secretly convinced that this was the outcome of these terrible deeds. As prohibitions and punishment were of no avail, the mother fastened Tonny's hands to the pen's bars. She was convinced that she had saved her boy in "curing" him of masturbation. This procedure of fastening his hands continued for some six to eight weeks. Afterward Tonny did not masturbate any more. However, he was incapable of all other activities and motor actions, ordinarily learned by a one-year-old. Tonny could not gain any pleasure satisfaction, neither an infantile sexual nor a motoric aggressive one. In addition, the emotional tie to the mother became severely disturbed. We must assume that in this special period of life genital play was Tonny's main source of pleasure, as well as the basis for the unfolding of motor actions and activities in general. The complete suppression of pleasure gain and activity development, occurring at a too-early age and too rigorously, had apparently paralyzed the growth of all ego functions. He was unable to learn anything new from that time on.

At the early age of ten or eleven months there is not yet any question of castration fear, which does not come to the fore until the phallic phase in connection with oedipal wishes and strivings. The little boy believes in the danger of castration only when he experiences his various oedipal conflicts and after he has observed that creatures (girls or women) without a penis do exist. With Tonny the genital play was merely a form of pleasurable activity. The mother's rigorous restrictions and punishments were the result of her own neurotic inhibitions and anxieties. To the infant a loving relationship with the mother is indispensable for his growth. As Tonny's mother attachment was so severely damaged, a stimulus from this side was lacking as well. Thus every progress in development had become impossible.

We had to come to the opposite conclusion from the mother's. It was not active masturbation which had caused Tonny's "illness," but the forceful impediment of the necessary activities which brought about the little boy's pseudo retardation.

In treatment the therapist gradually removed the prohibitions, with the result that the interrupted development was taken up again and could be continued more normally.

CHAPTER 20

The Role of Identification in Psychoanalytic Procedure

(1956)

By the term "identification" we denote a normal mental process which leads a person in some way or other to become like another person. Identifications make use of the mechanism of "introjection" (or "incorporation"). The person "introjects" the image of the other person, he "takes over" some or many of the latter's characteristics. In normal growth "identifications" express themselves in different contexts during the various phases of maturation and development. In this short paper I have to limit myself to the description of only a few of them.

As identification is a form of relationship with an object, it can only manifest itself after some (primitive) differentiation between self and object has come into existence.

In *Group Psychology and the Analysis of the Ego*, Freud defines identification as "the earliest expression of an emotional tie with another person" (1921, p. 105).

In normal development the process of identification serves different aims. I will mention three of them:

(1) Identification is one of the ways to secure the satisfaction of bodily and psychical needs, provided by the object.

(2) It finds a place in, and promotes, the process of learning. The little child acquires intellectual knowledge, he learns to speak, to read, to handle toys and tools, to test reality as well as to master emotional situations, and to adjust his instinctual life to the demands of the environment in large measure by identification with parents, siblings, and

other persons. All these learned skills may be called ego achievements.

(3) Identifications form the base of the ego ideal. In the preoedipal, magic phase of development the little child identifies himself with the images of omnipotent parents in order to feel as powerful as they are imagined to be.

In normal development the ego ideal unfolds and widens its contents through new identifications with other persons, examples in social life, etc., a process continuing throughout the whole lifetime and constituting one of the normal outcomes of so-called narcissistic identifications.

It is a sign of maturity when ideals and norms are freed from primitive magic features; that means, when the person in question has learned to accept that neither omnipotent parents nor other almighty persons exist. However, every human being preserves remnants of early developmental stages. More of those relics persist in disturbed personalities such as our patients. This brings us to the question of what role identifications play in psychoanalytic procedure.

I shall try to depict some aspects of a patient's identification with the analyst during treatment. With a view to a clearer presentation I will distinguish between "normal" and "pathological" identifications, though in reality, of course, they are intermingled, and a clear-cut distinction is not always possible.

"Normal" Identifications in Analytic Treatment

From the very beginning of treatment the analyst is an important person in the patient's life. No wonder that the patient tries to identify himself with that person as he does with teachers, superiors, authorities, heroes, celebrities, social or religious leaders, etc. The patient wants to know the ideas of the analyst, his outlook on life, his norms and ideals, his personal circumstances. But the analyst's task does not allow him to satisfy the patient's desire to obtain insight into the analyst's personal life and views.

There are two good reasons for this on the analyst's part:

(a) It is well known that psychoanalysis aims at furnishing the most favorable possibilities for the patient to develop his personality along the path of his *own* capacities and circumstances, and therefore at avoiding his being molded after the picture of the analyst.

(b) Only after the patient's desire to take over his analyst's views of life is frustrated does the uncovering of the infantile, archaic, pathogenic forms of identification become possible.

There is perhaps one limitation to the strict application of this rule, namely when the analysand is a future colleague. A "normal" "adult" identification with the analyst's professional personality may promote the acquisition of technical skill in the young analyst. However, as the first task of a training analysis is always the removal of neurotic symptoms, blind spots, and other ego restrictions and distortions, we have to behave in the same way as we do with patients, at least for a considerable part of the treatment.

The danger that acquired technical knowledge may be used to ward off neurotic or archaic patterns is strong, especially with the candidate.

For the analyst a danger lies in the temptation to yield to his analysand's wish in trying to model him after his (the analyst's) own ideals.

"PATHOLOGICAL" IDENTIFICATIONS

We now come to what we may call "pathological" identifications.

(a) I mention only briefly the process of identification used by the ego's defensive organization as one of the various defense mechanisms, e.g. in hysterical symptoms.

Hysterical identifications are regressions of forbidden oedipal object relationships toward earlier forms of a bond with an object. An example is Freud's famous case of Dora. Some of the somatic complaints of this hysterical girl proved to be based on an identification with her father, to whom she was strongly attached with sexual fantasies. When analysis runs a favorable course the hysterical symptom and with it the pathological identification disappear after the interpretation and working through of the connected material, which is, at least partly, transferred to the analyst.

I will not go further into these forms of identification.

(b) I now turn to the so-called narcissistic identifications, of which we have to distinguish between (1) identifications in the ego ideal, and (2) ego identifications.

Identifications in the Ego Ideal

As suggested above, we have to deal in analytic treatment with the pathological parts of the ego ideal, that is, with its archaic features. Sooner or later every patient idealizes his analyst. This means that he projects upon him the persisting images of omnipotent parents, simultaneously, of course, with the reactive counterpart: extreme devaluation. Sometimes this is a regressive phenomenon; however, one often gets the impression of its being related to areas of the ego ideal that never reached a more mature level. They are fixated relics of the preoedipal magic phase. The usual interpretations reveal that the patient clings tenaciously to the images of omnipotent parents as well as to his own infantile fantasies of grandeur. Both groups of fantasies still have to compensate for the daily narcissistic injuries, once experienced by the child when he came upon his own powerlessness. They are still unconsciously at work in the patient's actual life circumstances and neurotic complaints. In many cases the analyst finds that analytical interpretations alone do not make for the patient's recovery. Here an aftergrowth, a re-education, sometimes has to take place.

In early days Freud remarked that psychoanalytic treatment comprises a kind of re-education. By this he did *not* mean to recommend the imprinting of new ideals and norms upon the patient's personality. On the contrary, we should avoid doing this. But what the analyst *can* do to stimulate the patient's maturation is to convince him of his unrealistic conception of the analyst's personality. It is sometimes difficult to show the analysand that the glorification of the analyst is a product of his (the patient's) own wishful thinking, that in reality the analyst is an average human being, to be esteemed for his merits, but with limitations and weaknesses similar to those of all other persons. It depends greatly on the attitude of the analyst whether the patient succeeds in forming a normal reality-adjusted ego ideal or not. Something similar is valid for our second point.

The Archaic (Pathological) Ego Identifications

When analytic procedure has liberated repressed forces by the undoing of the various warding-off practices, every patient has to find new ways to use those forces, and to revise many of his ego activities and reactions in life. Patients with a relatively well-structured ego organization (and, of course, with not too strong and rigid drive forces) find those ways spontaneously without too great difficulty. Patients with very unstable, primitive, archaic ego structures, however, not seldom prove unable to do so. They behave like children. Here analysis may take advantage of the afore-mentioned fact that the learning processes run very much along the path of identifications.

Needless to say, the analyst has *not* to deal with the patient's learning of intellectual and other skills. We are concerned here with the aftergrowth of the patient's emotional and instinctual life. The liberated drive forces have in part to be allowed to find direct gratifications, in part to be neutralized and used in sublimated activities. Where the inborn capacity for neutralization of drive energy is minute, psychoanalysis will have very little success.

In cases where the capacity for sublimation is sufficiently present, the patient has to learn how to provide enough direct gratification on the one hand and how to handle the neutralized energy on the other. He can make use of identifications with his analyst for the aftergrowth of his infantile emotional life. Once more I would repeat that this process is not accomplished through verbal suggestions for actual new activities, forced upon the patient. It depends considerably upon the analyst's attitude whether the patient can profit from his identifications or not.

Unconsciously by means of empathy the patient becomes aware of the analyst's tolerance and warm understanding, and of his firm and quiet mastery and control of affects and impulses, which the patient tries to provoke in the analyst through acting out.

The analyst's behavior, his timing of communications, his facial expressions, a number of imponderables, last but not least the tone of his voice, are extraordinarily important here, perhaps much more so than the words he actually uses.

It seems of significance to mention one other special danger situation for the analyst himself. Empathy is necessary for the understanding of the patient. As empathy is based upon the identification mechanism, the analyst has to identify himself with his patient to a certain degree. Now the danger arises that the identifications with the analysand unconsciously become too strong or mixed up with old patterns from the analyst's own past life. Those identifications are bound to disturb instead of to further the favorable course of the patient's development.

Finally, I want to stress a particular point of great importance for the patient's recovery, though this may involve us in a number of difficulties. The point in question concerns aggression and the concomitant guilt feelings. It still seems uncertain whether aggressive energy is less suitable for neutralization than is libido. In every case liberated libido finds new ways for employment more easily than aggressive energy does. This holds true for the period of the upbringing of children as well as for that of the aftergrowth of our patients, at least in the circumstances of our culture, where very little aggression can be directly satisfied.

The analyst's attitude toward direct aggressive outbursts as well as toward more hidden aggression, as, e.g., in jealousy, rivalry, competition, etc., is of considerable value here. With many patients we get the impression that they will never master primitive aggressive impulses in a constructive way. They mostly have to turn them to the self, with many disastrous consequences. Sometimes, however, patients succeed in finally controlling and neutralizing aggression, in which process identification with the self-evident, natural behavior of the analyst can play a very stimulating part.

Time forbids my going further into this interesting area of exploration. Only one final remark to avoid misunderstanding:

The attitude of the analyst as here described is in no single way in contradiction with the classical technical rule of the so-called neutrality of the analyst. This rule is often misunderstood. The analyst, it is true, has to provide the patient with the possibility of projecting and transferring his (the patient's) own feelings and strivings onto a clear screen in the analytic situation. This does *not* mean that the analyst should be an absolutely neutral, emotionless creature. Apart from the fact that such a creature does not exist, it would be inhumane to try to live up to such an artificial automaton. Freud's technical devices clearly show that the rule aims merely at preventing the analyst's acting out of his own feelings instead of analyzing those of his patient and at guarding against his impressing his own stamp upon his analysand.

Freud used to stress the significance of the integrity of the analyst and of his being a humane, decent, and harmonious personality.

In this presentation I have tried to throw some light upon areas in analytic procedure where the patient's re-educational aftergrowth may go in a favorable direction under the influence of identification with an analyst, who is himself a well-balanced personality.

CHAPTER 21

On Defense and Development:
Normal and Pathological

(1957)

In studying the concept of defense one is confronted with much confusion in psychoanalytic literature about a great many problems. To name only a few of them:

(1) Is "defense" in itself a pathological phenomenon or are we entitled to speak of "normal" defense mechanisms and defensive processes?

(2) What is the relation of childhood neurosis to the defense mechanisms?

(3) We may turn our attention to the chronology of defense mechanisms.

(4) What is the role of defensive processes in the total ego organization?

(5) We could examine the different analysts' views regarding the practical question of whether or not every defensive process has to be dissolved during analytic treatment.

More questions could be raised. In this communication I shall limit myself to the presentation of only a few ideas on some of the points. I begin with the first problem mentioned above.

Can we speak of "normal" defense, or does every defensive process belong in the realm of pathology? What conception of defense is most

273

fruitful in analytic theory and practice? There is no doubt that Freud first made use of the term defense in connection with psychopathology (1894, 1896). It seems that many authors tend to retain this early employment of the term and want to reserve it for neurotic and other forms of maldevelopment. They do so in spite of the fact that at later times, e.g., in *Inhibitions, Symptoms and Anxiety* (1926), Freud clearly showed the connection between "normal" and "pathological" defense mechanisms.

Speaking of the relation between "repression" and "defense," Freud (1926, p. 163) recommends the rehabilitation of the latter term as "a general designation for all the techniques which the ego makes use of in conflicts which may lead to a neurosis." "Repression" is to be viewed as one special defense mechanism.

In his contribution to the Symposium on Defense, Hoffer (1954) mentions this statement of Freud's, and further adds that many authors consider defense mechanisms to have "their own history and sources." He continues: "they [the defense mechanisms] may be traced back to their origin in the primary processes, e.g., in displacement and to the genuine mechanisms which the growing ego successively develops from inborn patterns, that is to the autonomous ego functions; they are often highly developed, very complicated structures of the mind" (p. 194).

Hartmann (1939b) has shown how important it is to view mental processes not only in their interplay with mental conflict but also from the point of view of the part they play in adaptation. Hoffer cites a number of other authors, who point out that defense mechanisms may be used "regressively" or "progressively"; they may "protect" the ego or "destroy" it (Eissler, 1953).

Nevertheless one repeatedly encounters the idea that defense mechanisms are pathological phenomena. Fenichel (1945) considers only sublimation to be a normal one and regards all others as pathogenic.

Anna Freud, in her book *The Ego and the Mechanisms of Defence* (1936), describes different defensive attitudes of which she says that they can also be seen in normal reactions. She includes them, however, under the heading "Preliminary Stages of Defence."

We should like to find a way out of these confusions. With this purpose in mind, I propose to examine two well-known defense mechanisms encountered in severe psychic illness: projection and identification.

Projection may be used in paranoid psychosis, identification (based on the mechanism of introjection) may, e.g., lead to severe symptoms in a melancholic patient.

When we turn to observations of infants, however, all of us assume that processes of projection and introjection play a considerable role in every infant's normal growth. None of us would think of a severe pathological process in this context. Therefore it may be confusing when Melanie Klein and others use certain terms taken from clinical psychiatry—e.g., "depressive position" or "persecutory anxiety"—to describe early processes in normal infants.

When we turn our attention to the newborn's behavior we see a somewhat different picture. The newborn responds at first merely somatically to outer and inner stimuli. To the shortness of oxygen during birth the infant reacts with putting into motion the respiratory organs, in order to "incorporate" oxygen. When hunger and thirst stimuli arrive the newborn will drink; this means he incorporates fluid food by sucking the mother's breast. Incorporation of oxygen and food as well as egestion of carbonic acid and excreta are normal regulative reactions to the metabolic processes tending to maintain a physiological homeostasis.

In this connection, experimental psychologists and ethologists speak of mechanisms of regulation and adaptation. There are other adaptive processes in the human newborn (though fewer than in newborn animals), e.g., the adaptation of the skin capillaries to stimuli of cold and heat, the closing of the eyelids when too strong a light stimulus reaches the eye, etc.

We assume that the first primitive awareness that inner and outer world are separate entities arises in connection with the different bodily responses to inner and outer stimuli.

It still is difficult to decide at what point we are entitled to begin to speak of psychic phenomena in the infant and at what moment the body "self" is enlarged with a mental "self." Among many factors the maturational state of the central nervous system apparently plays an im-

275

portant role. But we may take it for certain that the psychic life develops on the base of somatic reactions or, to put it more precisely, in interplay with them. This is one of the expressions of psychosomatic entity.

In a theoretical discussion in a small work group in Amsterdam, Bastiaans, referring to observations on psychosomatic patients, made the suggestion that every neurotic defense mechanism could be traced back to a normal somatic regulation or adaptation mechanism, and would represent a quantitative variation of the latter.

There is one early definition of Freud's (1905b) which points to what one could call a "psychosomatic" viewpoint. It runs: "Defensive processes are the psychical correlative of the flight reflex and perform the task of preventing the generation of unpleasure from internal sources" (p. 233). It points to the correlation of body reactions to dangerous stimuli (flight) and mental reactions guarded by the pleasure-pain principle.

When a little child projects unpleasurable drive stimuli and sensations upon the outside world and simultaneously introjects images of need-satisfying objects, the mechanisms of projection and introjection are not used merely for "flight" (and "fight"), but at the same time as regulative and adaptive processes.

A physically healthy child growing up under favorable circumstances, with a loving, understanding, and tolerant mother, presents himself as a friendly, gay, charming, and harmonious little creature. We are naturally aware of the fact that every person's growth proceeds on the basis of conflicts. But we should not overlook the fact that in these so-called "normal" children the conflicts result for the time being in a regulation of the emotional and instinctual needs and an adaptation to the outer world. I hasten to add that I am certainly not of the opinion that thereby these well-balanced little children would be prevented from acquiring neuroses in later times. There are too many examples of harmonious children finally developing more or less severely disturbed personalities.

What I wanted to suggest, however, is that we view the neurotic defense mechanisms as pathologically exaggerated or distorted regulation and adaptation mechanisms, which in themselves belong to normal development. One might raise objections and say that this formulation is merely a terminological variation. I do not think that is correct. I believe that apart from decreasing some of the confusions mentioned above, my formulation has the advantage of stressing the connection (or the continuum) of physiological-biological and psychic processes, both in the normal and in the abnormal. Last but not least, it may prevent us from overlooking normal developmental processes in our children as well as in our patients. I agree with Brierley (1947) and Hoffer (1954) that "our closer association with mental disease . . . has often hampered our dealings with normality" and that "the personal integrity of the patient [may be] impaired by the omission of the normal aspect of the rôle of defence in mental functioning." For the "normal aspect of the rôle of defence" I should like to substitute "the role of adaptation and regulation in all processes that deal with mental conflicts."

I realize that one could justifiably reproach me for speaking loosely of "normal" and "pathological" and of "health" and "disease," without giving clearer definitions. I cannot solve this problem in its complexity, and will remind you of the well-known, though stale statement that "normality" and "health" as well as "disease" are merely practical conceptions which so far defy scientific definitions.

We may nevertheless try to throw some light upon one special function which is indispensable for a person's psychic health—the synthetic or integrative capacity—precisely by using the viewpoint of the psychosomatic entity. The infant uses the inborn and the learned regulation and adaptation mechanisms to establish physiological homeostasis in metabolism. The little child does the same to attain psychic equilibrium. We know that it is the task of the ego to develop a synthetic, integrative, harmonizing ability.

The little child's growing, but still primitive and unstable, ego organization has to learn with the mother's help how to regulate its drives and affects, its needs, etc., as we mentioned before. In the first years of life the mother is indispensable for both normal *bodily and mental* growth. However, she remains indispensable much longer for mental development.

When the mother-child symbiosis succeeds in establishing and promoting a synthetic, regulative ego function and when in addition the

277

mother is able to further the child's independence in the subsequent development, the outcome may really be a well-balanced personality. Or, examined from the reverse side, we may say: since every normal infant's instinctual needs come into conflict with the outside world, which can offer only limited satisfaction and always has to demand restrictions, the regulative ego functions cannot develop in a harmonious way when one or both of the partners of that early mother-child bond fail in the cooperative interplay. Such a failure impairs the normal growth of the still weak ego organization and threatens the ego with being overwhelmed by the drives and affects; thus inner conflicts are added to the outer ones, signaled by anxiety.

When the mother is aware of the child's emergency situations, she may be able to furnish the necessary support for the child's ego growth and a new balance may come into existence. When she fails to do so, the way is open for more or less severe neurotic disturbances in the child. The same may happen when the other partner in the mother-child relationship, the little child himself, falls short of his task in the cooperation, either through an unfortunate instinctual disposition (e.g., untamable drives, too much ambivalence, too strong clashes between libido and aggression or active and passive strivings, etc.) or through a lack of indispensable inborn ego capacities.

I will choose the process of identification to illustrate the pathological use of mental mechanisms. In normal development identifications play an important role in learning. When identification is used to ward off danger situations, it may go so far as to overwhelm the child's total ego organization. The child's personality "melts together" with the image of the mother. The resulting loss of one's own identity is experienced with strong anxiety and may lead to a severe damage of further development. I shall come back to this point later on.

Now I should like to give an example of a favorable collaboration between mother and child in a relatively normal boy of two years nine months. The boy was a lively, well-balanced child. Toilet training was accomplished in a quiet, natural way around the second year. After the birth of a new baby when the boy was two years two months old he wet his bed only two or three times. About half a year later the bed wetting suddenly reappeared. At first his mother did not understand what had happened. Nothing extraordinary could be discovered in the family situation. Then, however, the mother became aware of the fact that the boy was masturbating and having erections much more frequently than before.

On an appropriate occasion she spoke with her little son about his erections, apparently in a natural, reassuring way, with full acceptance of his masculinity and his right to pleasure and masculine pride. The next night everything was all right. After several weeks the enuresis came back, but only for a short time. Following this period it has never recurred up to the present time. The boy is now three and a half years old.

In the meantime, his ego development had also advanced in other respects, as I should like to demonstrate in an occurrence the explanation of which I owe to Anna Freud. When the boy was three years one month old he was taken on an excursion during which he traveled by car over a very long bridge. He admired it very much and was impressed by the many cars passing over it at the same time. Some hundred meters away lies a second, a railway bridge. When the boy was told that trains were running over this second bridge, he said: "But *cars* are running over it, *too*." To the answer: "No, that one is only for trains," he replied with the utmost conviction: "But *formerly* there were cars running over that bridge, too."

I did not understand the meaning of this statement, but Anna Freud gave a fascinating explanation of the event. She thought the boy wanted to say: "Formerly all pleasurable experiences were allowed to be made everywhere." She is of the opinion that the boy's statement indicated his readiness to accept limitations. This acceptance and the distinction between former and present times represent an achievement of the ego's development. Some months later this explanation was confirmed by a second experience.

The boy is the owner of a number of small toy cars. He is especially fond and proud of a Chevrolet. During another excursion the boy again traveled over the long bridge. This time a train was just passing over the railway bridge. He was happily excited and said: *"Formerly* when I was driving in my Chevrolet I passed by that bridge the way the train is doing now."

I would sum up the successive events in the following way. In the inner conflict, caused by an increase of masculine, genital sexuality that for a moment had threatened his inner balance, the still weak ego had made use of the mechanism of regression to an earlier phase and produced the symptom of bed wetting. With the mother's support the ego succeeded immediately in discontinuing the regressive process. The boy returned to the former state of ego achievement in mastering again the excretory functions and in developing new ego capacities: the distinction between past and present and the acceptance of the different possibilities of satisfaction.

Such regressive phenomena occur very often during the period of the little child's growth, just as do other defensive attitudes in conflicts which provoke anxiety. Should we speak of a neurosis and of defense mechanisms in this connection? This question brings us to the second point I mentioned in the introduction of this paper: When should we speak of childhood neurosis and what processes have to be considered as normal developmental ones?

The answer apparently does *not* lie in the nature of the mental mechanisms used by the growing ego in its reactions to conflicts. We have already mentioned that projection and identification are normal regulative and adaptive mechanisms. By making use of them the ego learns to distinguish between inner and outer world, to develop reality testing, etc. Identifications especially play a paramount role in learning processes, in acquiring different skills, in learning how to handle emotional and instinctual needs.

Regressions and anxiety never fail to appear in normal development. Isolation of past and present events furthers the orientation in time and so stimulates the phase-adequate development. I think the answer is better to be looked for in the examination of the *ways* in which the different mechanisms are made use of by the child's ego.

If, at first with the help of a kind of auxiliary ego borrowed from the mother, the ego succeeds in making use of the various mechanisms in their regulative and adaptive aspect, the conflicts may be solved in a way that stimulates balance and growth. If, however, the ego has to fight too strongly against the drives, it has to use all available forces for the maintenance of its still weak, just established organization. In this case there is a greater opportunity for a lasting disturbance in balance and for an arrest in development.

This idea gives rise to the question of what causes the child's ego to go the one or the other way. I think that among the many ego capacities necessary for a favorable solution of these conflicts, there is one of the utmost, perhaps decisive, importance. It is the ego's capacity to deal with the child's aggressive drives. Or, in other words, the child's capacity to neutralize (and sublimate) aggression. I remind you of Freud's suggestion to view mental conflict in regard to aggression. Every conflict, whether between child and environment or between ego and id, provokes free aggression. And it is precisely aggression that is least tolerated in free discharge, that is most dangerous for the developing ego organization when turned inside, and that in many cases is more unsuitable for neutralization than is libido. Even in conflicts in the sexual sphere it might be the fate of the simultaneously provoked free aggression that becomes decisive for the final outcome.

In the analysis of one of my adult patients it ultimately became clear that the aggressive, mocking, and sneering way in which his mother had rejected the little boy's exhibitionistic genital wooing had provoked his own overwhelming aggressive response with the final result of a rigid standstill in his ego development.

Among other factors, the switching off of the normal learning processes by means of identifications, of which I spoke before, here played a decisive role. The little boy's sexuality was reduced to a passive surrender toward the father. He identified with the passive mother image to such a degree that he lost his own identity. In his adult sexual life every approach to a woman meant a "melting together" with her. To escape the danger situation of losing his self he had to summon up nearly all his strength. The result was an inhibited personality with very restricted ego capacities.

Such observations point at the same time to the paramount importance of the mother's attitude toward the little child's aggression. In my patient every attempt to master aggression was counteracted by the mother. A well-balanced mother, on the other hand, is a well-suited object for identification and may thus come to be of very great help to her child in his effort to learn the controlling of aggression, to

281

neutralize aggressive energy, and to use this energy in the building up of the ego organization.

Returning to our question of what constitutes neurosis in childhood, I should like to summarize as follows. Mental mechanisms, which may later be used as neurotic defense mechanisms in adult neuroses, are normal developmental mechanisms in early childhood as long as they serve and promote the ego's regulative and adaptive capacities.

I remind you here of Anna Freud's well-known statement (1945) that, in the assessment of childhood disturbances, we should make use of the criterion of an unimpaired advancement in ego development. In full agreement with this view, I should like to continue: regulative and adaptive functions of the so-called defense mechanisms are particularly endangered when the capacity for neutralization of aggression is not sufficiently present. Furthermore, we should speak of a real childhood neurosis only when the defensive function of the mechanisms outbalances the regulative function *and* holds up the continuation of the process of growth.

Here a critical remark is in order. In every child's development there is one phase in which the first condition—the prevalence of the defensive aspect of a special mechanism—is a regular and normal occurrence. This is the oedipal phase, in which the mechanism of repression predominates. In our culture every child has to repress his sexual and aggressive strivings inherent in the oedipus complex. However, after a more or less *"normal"* solution of this complex, the ego development receives a great impetus for further unfolding, and no neurosis develops. Precisely because the defensive function in repression of oedipal conflicts is indispensable, the preconditions for the coming into existence of a real neurosis become stronger in this phase. These considerations are in accord with Freud's very early view of the oedipus complex as the nucleus of the neuroses.

Perhaps we really could keep to this view for the average child. While preoedipal developmental disturbances may contribute to a particular unfortunate shaping of the oedipus complex, it is still the fate of the ego's development during and after the oedipal phase itself which decides whether a more or less fixed neurosis will originate or not. Only in infants who from the very beginning show severe disturbances, caused either by inborn factors or by serious deprivations, do we observe fixed neurotic symptoms in the preoedipal phase. We could assume in these cases that either the ego was lacking every possibility for advancement in development or that it was exposed to a precocious and therefore heavily endangered development, so that a regulative and adaptive use of the available mechanisms was eliminated from the beginning.

Be that as it may, in the preoedipal phase it is more often the mother's neurosis or other environmental circumstances that cause usually reversible disturbances in the little child. After the decline of the oedipal phase, when a preliminary shape of the child's personality and the establishment of his superego have taken place, the child's circumscribed neurosis takes a certain fixed shape.

In this context I merely want to mention the fact that an obsessional neurosis arises only in the latency period. If repression in latency and adulthood fails to be sufficient for defensive purposes, other mechanisms are used in the attempt to ward off the returning repressed contents; among them are mechanisms that formerly served regulation and adaptation, as for instance projection, identification, isolation, turning inside, etc. I will not name them all because they are well known from Freud's and Anna Freud's works.

It would be fascinating, however, to pursue the vicissitudes of the different mechanisms from the viewpoint of, on the one hand, their adaptive, regulative aspects, and on the other hand, their defensive aspects during the personality's development from birth to maturity. This brings us to our third point: the chronology of defense mechanisms. In following the chronology of specific mechanisms, we might really discover that all pathological defense mechanisms seen in the neuroses and psychoses of latency and adulthood are the very same mechanisms that served normal ego development in early childhood and that at a later stage were used simultaneously in a distorted way to ward off the re-emergence of the insufficiently repressed strivings. It is possible that some mechanisms become fixed only after the superego has been established, as for instance the turning of aggression against the self. The regulative, constructive side of this process furthers the consolidation of social norms and ethical values, whereas its defensive function operates in a destructive way and may lead to severe pathological guilt feelings and self-damage. Usually this mechanism of turning aggression inward is not observable in infants, though there are cases described of self-injuries in early childhood. However, it is probable that the ways in which defense mechanisms work in the service of the superego have their forerunners in relation to ego activities.

I leave this theme for further investigation and now turn to our fourth point: the place of the defensive processes in the total ego organization.

I speak here of defensive processes because in the course of development the ego, making use of different mechanisms, builds up a complicated defensive organization. From latency onward parts of this organization can be mobilized to ward off other parts of it. This may happen when the latter part proves to be endangered in new stages of development, in which additional demands are made upon the ego. I give one example out of many.

In the preoedipal phase the little boy's passive strivings toward the mother may be countered by the growing ego through a specific regulative and defensive mechanism, namely, through activation of active tendencies. In the oedipal situation the normally increased masculine urges may become a danger in connection with rivalry with the father. The boy now remobilizes passive strivings to ward off his masculine fantasies. Whether the boy finds a normal solution of his oedipal conflict or not depends upon the ego's capacity to save his active strivings from repression (or from being warded off) and upon the degree to which the ego succeeds in neutralizing energies and in sublimating these active strivings into constructive activities. In our neurotic patient this faculty of the ego proved to be too weak in relation to the instinctual urges, hence the result was a feminine sexual relationship to the father. In the course of further development such a father attachment can again be warded off and covered by a distorted, pseudomasculine behavior in life.

It is clear from the foregoing that the ego's defensive activity constitutes a very important part—yet, it is true, only one part—of the totality of ego functions. Instead of examining in detail all ego activities and achievements, I will only stress once more the importance of considering the normal regulative-adaptive functions of the various mechanisms and processes, and their influence upon the development of other ego capacities, both on the intellectual and on the emotional level. I have illustrated this process in regard to the mechanism of identification.

Finally, I want to mention again a specifically significant point. According to one of Freud's definitions, neuroses are disharmonies in the ego organization. Among the many factors that are responsible for those disharmonies, we have already referred to one of particular importance: the personality's capacity to neutralize aggressive energy. This capacity is dependent on the one hand upon the quality and intensity of the drives, and on the other hand upon very specific ego properties whose development may be stimulated or counteracted by objects in the environment.

Turning to our fifth and last point, I think we can do away with a frequent misapprehension expressed in the demand that psychoanalytic treatment should attempt to demolish the ego's defensive organization. For many of us it is self-evident that we should not, and even could not, succeed in our endeavors to live up to this "requirement." Nevertheless we often encounter pronouncements such as: "The patient's defense mechanisms have not disappeared, therefore he is not yet cured." Or: "You should aim at doing away with your patient's defenses," etc.

Keeping in mind that every defense originally has a regulative-adaptive function, we can correct these remarks. In analysis we should try to give the patient's ego the opportunity for abolishing the pathological, rigid employment of the mechanisms in the neurotic conflicts, and we should try to open ways for their regulative, constructive use in order to promote a harmonious afterdevelopment and unfolding of the total personality.

CHAPTER 22

Psychoanalysis and Its Relation to Other Fields of Natural Science

(1959)

In this paper I shall endeavor to set forth some ideas on psychoanalytic theory, regarded in the light of findings in other branches of science. Freud developed his conception of the "complementary series" in the early stages of his study of neuroses. It is said that neuroses emerge from an interplay of innate dispositional factors and experiences, due to the environment, undergone during a lifetime. This conception may be extended to mental development in general.

We already know a great deal about the processes of development from infancy to the adult stage; an increasing tendency toward tracing the earlier phases, to study the very young child and the newborn infant, may be observed in recent psychoanalytic research. In the course of these endeavors it is inevitable that we come up against innate factors. Several psychoanalysts, for instance Kubie, Masserman, Szekely, Ostow, Brun, and many others, have therefore in recent years turned their attention to predispositional factors. It is my impression that there are three particular fields of science which demand our special attention: (1) modern cerebral anatomy and physiology, which assist us in achieving a better understanding of the physical basis of mind; (2) modern physics and mechanics, which stimulate our knowledge of the way in which the brain functions; (3) animal psychology, especially ethology, as this teaches us a great deal about instinctive behavior and its development from the innate mechanisms of the various types of animal life.

In these branches of science I am myself a layman, and am therefore able only to develop a few tentative trains of thought which doubtless will require verification, revision, or both.

We all know that modern neuroanatomy, neurophysiology, and neurosurgery have taught us a variety of things about the construction of the central nervous system and its physical activities.

We know that the human brain contains approximately 10,000,000,-000 neurones—nerve cells—and countless nerve fibers as well as afferent and efferent fiber tracts, which conduct stimuli into the brain and out of it. There are also the associative tracts which connect the different parts of the cortex. We know that the stimuli which activate the sense centers are carried on to other parts of the cortex. The same is the case with the inner stimuli, which reach the brain by means of the blood supply and the nervous pathways. Scientists tell us that the living brain contains electric potentials which are constantly at work and are able to vary their speed and rhythm: Adrian (1946), for instance, says that there is "constant transformation of energy in the brain." We have long been acquainted with the manner in which reflexes in the central nervous system operate (Pavlov); today, however, more particular research is being done into the origin and the working method of the so-called higher psychic functions, such as consciousness, thought, feeling, etc. Knowledge of these matters has been greatly stimulated by modern physics and mechanics, and especially by what is now known as cybernetics, a term which must be coupled with the name of Norbert Wiener (1949, 1954). I will discuss this presently, but first I would like to point out that, notwithstanding this imposing increase of knowledge, one constantly encounters among leading neurophysiologists and neuroanatomists the view that what actually takes place in the brain during the exercise of the higher functions is not known. Adrian, for instance, says: "The real trouble comes from the feeling that there may be an important part of the picture which can never be fitted in, however long we may work at it." Also: "It is a far cry from the nerve cell or even the cerebral hemispheres to the thoughts and desires of mankind." Sherrington says: "Aristotle, 2000 years ago, was asking how the mind

287

is attached to the body; we are asking that question still." Le Gros Clark affirms that he has a "hunch" and wants to introduce time—"the time involved in the transmission of the impulses (travelling along nerve fibres), from one relay centre to another"—as a very important factor. But he continues: "The difficulty, however, is that the time intervals are so short—a matter of a thousandth of a second." He is more optimistic as regards the results of future research into the anatomical basis of the mind, but remarks all the same: "No more than the physiologist is he able to suggest *how* the physico-chemical phenomena associated with the nervous impulses from one part of the brain to another can be translated into a mental experience." W. Grey Walter, in *The Living Brain* (1953), relinquishes all attempts to localize the higher functions exactly in the brain.

I could quote further and similar pronouncements made by well-known neurophysiologists and neuroanatomists, but instead will concentrate on the significance of modern mechanical physics to brain physiology and therefore to psychology also. Here, as I have just remarked, cybernetics is more particularly important. It is chiefly the so-called feedback mechanism which Wiener and most of the neurologists bring into context with an analogous mechanism in the living organism. Wiener, generally speaking, compares the functioning of the modern, complicated automatic machine with that of the central nervous system. As a mathematician, he realized that cooperation between experts on various branches concerned with cybernetics was necessary. He got into touch, or cooperated in teamwork, with physicists, well-known physiologists, engineers, psychologists, and sociologists. To name a few: Rosenblüth, von Neumann, MacCulloch, Pitts, Goldstine, Bigelow, Lee, Cannon, Penfield, and others, both in the United States and in Mexico and Canada. We gain the impression that this teamwork by scientists with varied talents and possibly some degree of genius, which as well as in others may be suspected in Wiener himself, is bound to be very fruitful. It was moreover greatly stimulated by the distress caused by the Second World War. Physicists and mathematicians were compelled to pass on what they knew to engineers and technicians, to those engaged in the construction of automatic arms and weapons. When such weapons were put to use, it was found that man with his cerebral apparatus was an extremely important factor offering further possibilities of, and setting limits to, their use. A typical instance was that of Air Force pilots. Owing to the great plasticity, the result of the marked differentiation of the human organism and more especially of the mind, and by means of technical aids, these limits were considerably extended. We may think for instance of the special clothing which combats the effects of the cold at high altitudes: of the oxygen apparatus, which decreases or does away with the rarefied air; the training in resistance to irritation, shock, and fear. But notwithstanding these aids, there are limits to the pilot's powers of performance. This was doubtless one of the reasons for the construction of the so-called automatic pilot. Machines took on the tasks originally performed by the thinking and active human being, so that we have now begun to speak of the "thinking machine" and even of the "artificial brain."

Attempts were made on the other hand to explain the function of the human brain by means of physicomechanical terminology. Several authorities consider that these attempts have been but partially successful, as may be gathered from the excerpts quoted, and this gives us courage to continue the attempts by arguments of our own. To begin with I will try to give some description of the analogies between the working of the brain and that of the machine, following Wiener in doing so.

Simple calculating machines (digital machines) receive their information through human agency; by means of certain manipulations they can add up figures, and this they do more rapidly than the human brain. But the machine, too, is vulnerable. When, for instance, one particular part of one manipulation is wrong or faulty, the result goes wrong and the machine stops. Therefore, as a rule, rather more complicated machines are constructed; in these, one given element corresponds not only with one particular stage in the operation, but with several. Thus a selection process is taking place at every moment. As Wiener puts it, a "majority report" and a "minority report" result. That is to say all the (intact) parts of the machine (i.e., in a well-constructed machine the majority), are supreme and the machine can continue to function. The faulty (very small) part that gave the minority report had no influence on the current event, but warns, by means of the minority report, that there is a defect. The faulty part can then be replaced without interrupting the work. The automatic telephone, for instance, functions on this principle. There is, however, as Wiener remarks, a "critical level of failure." If an apparatus such as the automatic telephone is kept below this level, the machine will be found to function very efficiently, but as soon as this level is reached, the machine ceases to function. A "catastrophic traffic jam" may result.

I will now mention some of the coincidences between the events that take place in the machine and the processes involved in the functioning of the brain of a living organism. Again I follow Norbert Wiener. The machine obtains its information externally through the instructor or the person using it. This person can be replaced by an automatic instructor, as, for instance, in the case of a photoelectrical apparatus coupled to the machine. But the photoelectrical apparatus has previously received its information from its constructor. The central nervous system, too, receives information from without through the sense organs from the environment and through the afferent nerve fibers from the rest of the body by means of sensory irritation and through the blood by a physicochemical process. In the machine, electric wires and switches take care of communications, the relaying of the message. In the living organism communication is achieved by means of nerve fibers and the highways and circuits in the central nervous system. We have just described the control system contained in the machine: this is based on what is called a "feedback mechanism." A simple example of the feedback is the thermostat. When a heating mechanism has reached a certain temperature, a signal reaches the source of heat, and the supply is discontinued. There is, therefore, control and regulation of its activities. A similar thing occurs in the organism. Constant signaling from the periphery to the central nervous system attends each movement, each activity. Thus the action is regulated and normally leads to the result intended. By way of the electrical potentials in the nerve circuits and neurones, the various stimuli reach their appointed goal, as, for instance, the stimuli awakened by light, which arrive at the center of vision and so on. They are then conducted further until they reach the cortex, where they may lead to various psychic processes, motor action, behavior, etc. Connection is brought about in the synapses, and as neurones are in correspondence with a great many synapses, extensive areas of the central nervous system may become involved in the action. Very complicated psychic processes thus result.

The analogy between the complicated (thinking) machines and the brain is therefore that both are capable of receiving communications from the outside and that both have the means of transmitting this communication. According to the scientists, however, there are further analogies. One of the fundamental properties of the brain is memory. The machine, too, is capable of storing incoming information as a memory, for instance by means of photography, magnetic wires or tapes, etc. These fixed recollections are able in their turn to influence further actions, in the machine as well as in the human brain. Control in both systems is applied by means of the feedback system already mentioned.

But there are further analogies between the performances of the modern machine and of the human brain. The machine is capable of prediction and also of learning. The former characteristic, "prediction," was until recently thought to be solely a human characteristic, the second, learning, was attributed only to living beings, i.e. animals and man. But cybernetics and modern mechanics have conferred these capabilities on the machine as well. In many cases and under certain conditions prediction is achieved much more easily and rapidly by a machine than by man. Machines have been constructed which can calculate the future position of an airplane, flying on a given track at a given speed, far more quickly than a man could. Such machines can also compute the relative possibilities of eventual deviations and changes. The learning mechanism too can be constructed automatically. Wiener even indicates that it will in the future be possible to construct an automatic chess player. He adds, however, that such a machine would at best be able to cope with a mediocre human chess player, and considers the construction of an automatic chess expert as a further possibility. This is not the time to become involved any further in Wiener's extremely fascinating train of thought on this topic, or to discuss the remarkable opinions of Père Dubarle, who, in a review of Wiener's *Cybernetics*, proposes the question whether or not a "governing machine" could be constructed. This would have to be a machine by whose means peoples, states, or even mankind as a whole could be ruled in a direct and logical manner more so than actual governments and politicians manage to do it today.

All this sounds extremely fantastic, and to many people rather frightening. The fear of new technical inventions is not an unusual one. In former times people were equally frightened by the gun, the first steam engine, the electrical machine, the airplane, etc. The daily press presents us with terrifying stories about robots, machines which might come to rule over humanity. Luckily we also hear, even from the side of the scientists, pronouncements which put one's mind at rest. Even Wiener himself, in connection with Père Dubarle's ideas, has said that the "thinking machine" of today is unable to cope with more than one-thousandth part of direct independent human behavior. There is therefore no danger that a machine could ever assume autonomous control over humanity. A Dutch physicist, Schouten, has presented the Dutch people with a reassuring picture: he suggests that if it were possible to build into the Amsterdam athletic stadium all the accessories, such as vacuum tubes, wires, switch elements, etc., appertaining to the modern machine, such a machine would possess the intelligence of a field mouse. But, he adds, this is not possible, for such a machine would explode, burn out, in fact, destroy itself. Apparently it is out of the question to construct a machine, even one the size of a room or a house, capable of completely imitating all possible actions of the ten billion neurones, with their synapses and nerve fiber connections, which exist together in the small human skull.

Not only the cyberneticists but also the brain anatomists and neurologists reassure us on this subject. And with a little consideration on our own part we, technical laymen, can reassure ourselves. After all, the modern thinking machine, the "artificial brain," has been invented by the "living brain," the brain of man. Without the latter, no machine can come into existence, let alone obtain power over mankind. The British anatomist Zuckerman has said: "The pattern of stimuli to which an artificial brain will respond is built into the machine by an external agency during construction. The patterns to which a real brain responds are, on the other hand, established through past experience. A living brain is thus self-organizing, establishing its own connections, its own pattern of memory, and the feedbacks necessary for the maintenance of equilibrium." And later, when discussing the machine which predicts the future position of a plane with high speeds, he adds: "It can do this only for one major task or run at the time. The run of a human brain lasts an entire lifetime."

The human brain is not only an extremely complicated switchboard, like the machine; it also embraces the switchboard operator, and this latter cannot, at any rate as yet, be defined and localized by anatomy or neurology. We might call this operator the creative mind, and that is something the machine lacks.

Why then, is mankind anxious as a result of undreamed-of technical progress, and why has it taken fright at modern machinery? Wiener explains this as follows: "Its real danger is that such machines, though helpless by themselves, may be used by a human being or by a block of human beings to increase their control over the rest of the race, or that political leaders may attempt to control their populations by means not of machines themselves, but through political techniques as narrow and indifferent to human possibility as if they had, in fact, been conceived mechanically." The fear is, therefore, of the manner in which man may make use of his own inventions: fear that their use will not serve to increase the well-being of mankind, but lead to destructive activity which will bring discomfort, sorrow, or even annihilation.

Man's propensity to make his inventions serve widely contrasting ends can no longer be explained mechanistically. The physicochemical basis of processes such as memory, thought, reason, and so on, must be imagined as being localized in the extremely complicated network of our brain cells and circuits. We might possibly also imagine that the fact of certain circuits being open or closed forms the organic basis of a given psychic quality, as, for instance, conscious or unconscious. For the time being, at any rate, we are unable to comprehend how judgments, intentions, thoughts, resolutions, etc., could be arrived at by the location of circuits or neurones. Apparently there are forces or tendencies active in the life process which we cannot localize anatomically, even when we are aware that their source of energy resides in the physical processes of the living organism.

Generally speaking, life has a strange place in the scheme of things.

We do not know whether it is confined to our earthly sphere or whether other planets have produced events analogous with life as we know it. In any case, life shows a tendency to differentiate, which is peculiar to only a given number of systems in the universe. Modern physics recognizes as the first law of thermodynamics that the total energy remains constant in a closed system, even when this energy is capable of changing its form. The second law lays down that in an open system there may be a general tendency toward increase of entropy, i.e., spontaneous gradual discharge of energy. In the universe there is a general tendency to the increase of entropy, in other words, to dedifferentiation, disorganization, chaos. But there are systems which show a tendency to decrease of entropy, and therefore an urge toward higher differentiation and organization. One of these systems is "life." To quote Wiener once again, "Organism is opposed to chaos, to disintegration, to death." And later: "Organisms (men) tend to maintain the level of their organization as a local enclave in the general stream of increasing entropy, of increasing chaos and dedifferentiation. Life is an island here and now in a dying world." "The process by which we living beings respect the general stream of corruption and decay is known as homeostasis." According to Ludwig von Bertalanffy (1950), life is an open system. To perform work it must be, not in complete equilibrium, but tending to attain a steady state. It exchanges materials with the environment and, getting energy from importation of material from the outside world, it can avoid the increase of entropy. I cannot go further into these important theories here.

The tendency to higher organization and differentiation which is characteristic of life is met with in the evolution of lower organisms toward highly complicated beings. Among the higher mammals man is obviously the most differentiated, even when we consider that, in comparison with analogous ones found in anthropoid apes, some organs are declining; for example, the teeth (Bolk and others). In any case, the human brain is the highest organized central nervous system known to us. It has even been able to invent mechanized systems—the above-mentioned thinking machines—which have defied the law of increase of entropy, at any rate for a series of actions. No other type of animal has ever achieved anything of the kind.

But mankind is part of the universe, and as such is subjected to the law of entropy. This is made plain by the fact that the single individual does become disorganized and dies. The power to live, and therefore to achieve higher organization, is transferred to the next generation through propagation.

Physics teaches us that highly differentiated systems are more vulnerable than simple ones, as with Schouten's machine on the Amsterdam stadium. There is a limit to the power of functioning. As we said above, every machine has its "critical point." When too great an influx threatens, the catastrophic traffic jam occurs and the machine no longer functions because vacuum tubes, switch elements, etc., have been eliminated. Wiener assumes there is also a limit to the human brain's capacity of functioning. A too severe psychophysical taxing would lead to defects of neurones, synapses, fibers, and circuits, and so induce psychopathological symptoms, such as insanity.

Here let us pause for a moment. We know of a number of mental disturbances founded on anatomical defects of the brain. But a study of our neurotic patients has revealed a number of psychic disturbances which prove to be reversible. It would be possible to imagine that, in such cases, the circuits have temporarily ceased to be thoroughfares, but such an event cannot be compared with the defect in vacuum tubes and switchboards. I imagine that we have now arrived at the point of which Adrian remarks that the brain physiologist and anatomist begin to flounder, and where, according to him, the psychologist can and must take over. Adrian here expects the aid especially of extended psychoanalytic psychology. He calls psychoanalysis "a new science which has gradually become an established part of our outlook on human behaviour."

I quote Adrian not only in order to justify my intention of co-opting psychoanalysis, but also because he defines analytic science as an "outlook on human behaviour." The opinion that psychoanalysis occupies itself solely or principally with subjective experiences happens to be widespread. But this is by no means the case. Even during the practical application of psychoanalysis, i.e. in therapy, the analyst does not confine his attention solely to the subjective experiences of the patient. A study of his behavior within and apart from the analytic situation has an important place in the therapy. A great many defense mechanisms which, for instance, have hardened into qualities of character and attitudes, can only be approached in this manner. Analytic science has always striven to study human behavior as a whole. The difference between it and the other branches of psychology is that it does not function only phenomenologically, i.e. observe phenomena in order to describe them. Analysis endeavors to trace the process of development of what it has observed; in other words, it has a genetic nature. Moreover, analysis studies the play of forces which takes place in the psychic process; it attempts to explain the psychic happenings genetodynamically. As a matter of course, analysis must continue to seek cooperation and augmentation by means of the other branches of psychological science and natural science of which I have spoken.

To sum up once again: brain physiologists and anatomists have partially discovered the physical basis of the mind. Modern physics and mechanics have enabled man to design machinery which copies certain functions and mechanisms of the brain. When and where we are as yet unable to explain certain manifestations of the mind by means of these disciplines, psychology must lend its help. An example is found in a phenomenon on which I have already remarked: the fear of its own creations which sometimes assails mankind. I repeat: why should man be afraid of the modern machine, the "robot" he has himself contrived? Apparently the living organism contains a number of principles of an active nature apart from the tendency to decrease entropy, to urge still greater differentiation and increased organization. This possibly is a point Wiener overlooked, or at least failed to describe sufficiently. He does draw attention to the principle of homeostasis, the search for a state of balance, inherent in the living organism. But the additional implications which this homeostatic principle brings in its train he does not mention. Homeostasis is the modern word used by Cannon, and is related to the constancy principle of Fechner. This principle, as we know, was applied by Freud to the psychic processes also. The homeostatic principle is founded physiologically in metabolism. The living cell and the organism strive for a certain constancy in the internal environment, i.e. the temperature of the body, the chemical composition of the blood, the pressure in the tissues, the acid-base ratio, the oxygen supply through breathing, etc. In psychic processes, physiological homeostasis is reflected by the tendency to retain certain tensions at their proper level. And this is the point where the experience factor counts. Freud described the pleasure-unpleasure principle as the psychic representative of the constancy principle. Tensions of a given intensity or a given rhythm may be experienced with pleasure; if the intensity increases or the rhythm is varied, they are experienced with pain. The mind urges toward the unloading, the discharge of the tensions. We assume that the pleasure-unpleasure principle is present in the higher types of animals as a regulating mechanism for the tensions. In the human being we encounter it in a far more differentiated form. Moreover we must not forget that the process of maturation is a much slower one in man than in animals (see also Hartmann). The patterns of behavior which are developed to obtain pleasure and avoid unpleasure we term instinctive behavior. In most animals these are coupled with the functions of seeking food, self-preservation, and propagation. Observations and experiments made by animal psychologists and ethologists such as Baerends, Lorenz, Tinbergen, and Kortlandt have proved that birds, for instance, develop extremely complicated patterns of behavior during the courting and mating period.

I should like to point out at this juncture that the instinctive patterns of behavior, which may be observed in the lower forms of animal life, such as insects (ants and bees), as well as in the higher animal types, are already highly complicated processes. In my opinion we should distinguish very sharply between the principles "instinctive behavior" and "drive." By "drives" Freud seems to mean, at any rate in his later theories of drives, the forces or tendencies active in the mind. Personally I feel that a better description or perhaps a reformulation of the psychoanalytic drive theory is required. This might make it possible to disentangle the disastrous confusion occasioned by the English use of "instinct" as the equivalent of the German *Trieb*. I will not say any more on this point at present. The instinctive patterns of behavior in animals, directed toward the search for food, the construction of the nest, courtship before mating, etc., result, as is generally accepted nowadays, from built-in mechanisms (innate release mechanisms), which, after birth and by means of the "learning mechanism," attain their final shape. The reflexes are also considered as built-in mechanisms. These also can be changed or conditioned, as Pavlov's experiments show. Zuckerman, too, remarks that "learning can occur in probably all organisms." When, for instance, a worm is put into a forked tube and given an electric shock every time it creeps into the left-hand fork, it will be observed after some time always to creep into the right-hand one. This, then, is conditioning, sometimes equated with learning. Ashby (1952) distinguishes between conditioning and learning. Both forms of adaptive behavior are based on "ultrastability of the organism" but in "learning" the feedback mechanism is activated, and this is wanting in "conditioning." Higher types of animals, such as monkeys, can be taught a great deal (Yerkes, Zuckerman, et al.). Monkeys can be taught to distinguish between quantities, one or more, and this not only when dealing with concrete objects. When monkeys are shown drawings, circles or squares, they will in the long run come to know the difference between a sheet of paper containing one and a sheet containing more figures. The thing we *cannot* teach these highly developed animals is to count, to abstract, to think abstractly, in short, to use symbols and signs which we humans use in our speech. The capacity of learning by insight is limited to man alone, whereas animals can only learn by "trial and error." Speech is a specifically human quality. Wiener says: "Speech is the greatest interest and most distinctive achievement of man." When discussing the remarkable fact that chimpanzees, who can learn a great deal, are never capable of learning to speak, he assumes that the human brain must possess a built-in power which enables man to "learn to speak." In the monkey this power is lacking. "The chimpanzee has no built-in mechanism which leads to speech." Later on Wiener remarks: "Speech seems to be an innate interest in coding and decoding, and this seems to be as nearly specifically human as any interest can be."

Now learning to speak, the use of language, and thinking are functions which the human young does not develop until quite some time after birth. The newborn child has very few reflex mechanisms at his disposal. The young bird is able to use instinctive patterns of behavior very soon after birth; these serve feeding purposes. The newborn human infant only disposes of a sucking mechanism where feeding is concerned. Ethology teaches us that geese, for instance, continue to follow the object that first brings them food. In the natural course of things, this object is the mother goose, but it can be replaced by another, a human object also. The innate release mechanism at this critical stage of the impression process is fixed by the learning mechanism, usually for life (Heinroth, Lorenz, et al.). The higher types of mammals, immediately after birth, are also dependent on the mother animal for food and for adapting themselves to the world around them for a while, but no newborn creature is so helpless and dependent for so long as the human child. Some children, just before birth, are apparently capable of sucking *in utero*, but on the other hand there are also newborn infants who do not suck when first applied to the breast: they have to "learn" even this. As we know, Freud considered that the child's helplessness and his long dependence were responsible for the intensity and complexity of the attachment of the human child to his mother (as well as the later attachment to other human beings). The adaptation by means of conditioning or learning during the human child's first few years may be compared to the analogous processes of learning in animals, as for example rats, cats, dogs, and monkeys. These animals are able to learn a variety of complicated reactions and mannerisms. Several reactions, such as fear raised by frustration, have been observed in animals. Szekely (1954), for example, writes in a very interesting article that fear in the infant is in origin very likely an inherited reaction to certain configurations (shapes) which can be replaced by dummies. These might then correspond to the "enemy scheme" in animals, the scheme which leads them to recognize dangerous enemies, such as beasts of prey. In the human being this danger might not be so much fear of a strange type of animal as a threat from a fellow man. The terrifying configuration was to consist of a movable two-eyes-and-forehead pattern (Kaila, 1932). This has also been determined by René Spitz, who studied the reactions of babies to a dummy consisting of two eyes and a forehead (1950). Here we have to remind ourselves of the interesting branch of psychology named the Gestalt (configuration) psychology (Koffka and Köhler).

We are prepared to accept that the earliest reactions and adaptation to the world outside are "learned" by man and animals (acquired through training) in an analogous manner, though by man at a slower speed because of his slow maturation, as already mentioned. However, from the moment that the specifically human capacity for learning to speak and think begins to develop an entirely new form of learning is added. Talking is gradually learned between the first and fourth year, though it passes through a great many stages. Developmental psychologists such as Bühler, Piaget, Rapaport (1951), and others have demonstrated that logical and abstract thought, which in the mature person is the basis for scientific practices and the enormous inventions which modern technical knowledge has produced, is developed over the course of many years and is capable of further development long after maturity has been reached. It seems as if the high organization and the subtle differentiation of the human brain take place at the cost of the instinctive behavior so highly developed in the higher animal species.

Neurophysiologists, cyberneticists, and possibly many other scientists in general recognize the specifically human in the flight of logical and creative thinking. The psychologists, and especially the psychoanalysts, know that there is another part of the spiritual life in man which has developed itself in a specific manner. This is the emotional life. From the first strong bond of love between the child and the mother an extremely rich and varied emotional contact is developed. Animals are able to become attached to others of their species; some birds for instance live in conjugal fidelity. But the subtly differentiated forms of affection, the feelings of sympathy, tenderness, respect, appreciation, admiration, and adoration, which develop from the original sexual love and erotism are not found among animals. It is the same with the feelings of hatred, envy, jealousy, contempt, etc., which we count among the aggressive tendencies.

While scientists therefore usually consider human intelligence and intellect as the qualities deserving most appreciation, others, artists for instance, set a still higher value on the subtler emotional expressions. Whatever our opinion on this score, we cannot deny that the strongly differentiated emotional life of man must be considered as typically human as his remarkable capacity for speech and thought.

Even less is known about the physicoanatomical basis of the human affective life than about the localization and the manner of functioning of the thought processes. That there actually is an innate somatic basis is made evident by the study of identical twins. Recognition of human thought and emotion, of human spiritual life, does not, to my way of thinking, imply that, because of our ignorance with regard to the physical basis of such processes, we must cling to supernatural, religious, or transcendental explanations. A psychology founded on the natural sciences should be able to accept the limits of its knowledge just as well as any other natural science. The frank recognition of its limits should become a stimulus to further research.

Neither do I consider it proper to use the fact of this higher differentiation and organization to feel excessive pride in man's performances and to feel ourselves elevated above our nearest companions in life: the animals. We are aware that man, living for so long in helpless dependence, has a strong urge to seek support from stronger and greater powers, such as he creates in the world of fantasy, the imagination. Religious and philosophic systems are our witnesses. The uncertain child who lives on in every adult is always attempting to hide his impotence beneath dreams of grandeur and power. Our spiritual life may indeed appear to us incomprehensible and miraculous, but is not life itself equally incomprehensible? Biochemistry teaches us the constitution of albumen, of the giant molecules which build up the living protoplasm of the unicellular organisms, but how and why and by what means living protoplasm can come into existence out of inorganic material is as great a mystery to us as is the manner in which the human mind develops. When we regard the mother of our life, the earth, and see it for what it is, one small planet in the solar system, and then remember that that solar system is one among billions of others, it is but fitting that, notwithstanding our great knowledge of astronomy and physics, we should feel just as astounded. The actual secret of the world's order cannot be approached by even our boldest fantasy. We simply must have the courage to say: I do not know.

To return to our human world. We also know the reverse of our high differentiation. I have already remarked that a highly differentiated mechanical system is far more vulnerable than a simple construction. The complicated structure of our brain and the exceptional differentiation of our mental and emotional life make us human beings very unstable, spiritually and emotionally. It is very difficult, especially for man today, living in the extremely complicated and highly structured society of our time, to achieve and to retain inner harmony. Doctors and analysts are particularly impressed in this regard. In the course of their day's work they constantly meet people who are neurotic, psychotic, and psychosomatic patients who live at variance with themselves.

Here I would dwell for a moment on the problem of neurosis. In order to describe the analogies as well as the differences between human and animal development, I must return to the development of the child. In order to make a clearer picture of how such disharmony and inner conflict have arisen and how they act, psychoanalytic science uses certain dynamic and structural hypotheses. The structural theory presents the human mind as consisting of various systems, of several provinces, so to speak. Freud called these id, ego, and superego. These cannot as yet be localized anatomically, though Kubie and others have begun to attempt this.

I think that, following Freud's initiative, we must, when dealing with animals, at least with the higher types of animal, speak of a differentiation between id and ego too (of a primitive superego perhaps only in the case of domestic animals). The id of animals, as in human beings, embraces the drive needs. This does not mean that the contents of the animal id and the human id are the same. I agree with Hartmann's opinion that the id contents in the human being differ from those in animals, though the underlying biological forces may be identical. The animal ego, again as in the case of man, concerns itself with self-defense, self-preservation, and adaptation to the surroundings. It has, or develops in very little time, the necessary instinctive patterns of behavior. These deal with the food supply, warn against dangers, etc. After a short period of maturation the animal also uses instinctive reactions to achieve mating and the consequent external changes such as nesting, making a lair, etc. The young animal's ego is, as said above, relatively much more mature than that of the human infant. Relatively, too, it is soon at the end of its possibilities of development. Normally the pattern of behavior of the young animal is fixed after a short spell of learning and as a rule it will remain in this stark form of fixation for the rest of its life.

The newborn human infant is relatively speaking much more of a "drive" creature than his animal counterpart. His ego needs much more time to develop the various functions and patterns of behavior; moreover, he cannot dispense with the relation to his mother and other external objects for a considerable time during the developmental process. We have said that the learning of language, in speech as well as in understanding, is out of the question without emotional contact with other people. But a number of other functions belonging to the ego, such as adaptation to the outside world, social demands (as, for example, bowel training), are also developed through object relations. The relative supremacy of the id (the vital urges) over the as yet primitive ego organization of the human young sets this ego an exceptionally heavy task during the complicated adapting and learning process. For, only too soon, education appears on the scene with demands no less exacting. It requires that the drive needs and impulses of the child must not be satisfied or indulged with unchecked immediacy. Practice has shown that the restraining of the id impulses is a wearing business. The as yet untamed drives form a menace to the primitive ego organization. The ego is forced to repress and to produce other defense mechanisms. The normal reaction and adaptive patterns may be used as defense forms against the id impulses. The defense process cannot, at any rate in our so-called cultural society, be called an abnormal process. For the development and maturation of the individual in his environment it is indispensable. It also permits the process of desexualization and neutralization of drive energy to take place. Thus the ego receives the necessary indifferent energy to achieve its performances (Hartmann et al.). The maturing processes of id and ego in their parallel courses take place amid constant interplay and mutual influencing. Environment at the same time applies unabated pressure through education, but also provides sources of satisfaction. During every stage and at any moment the harmonious unfolding may be disturbed. Too much repression of drive or too much indulgence may lead to mutilation of the ego functions, to a disordered adjustment to the environment. And a further complication arises when the superego is established as the third psychic agency, making fresh demands on the ego. The psychic growth of the child becomes yet more laborious owing to the specifically human events which accompany the late appearance of sexual maturity. Only in the human being do we encounter a recurring flowering of the drives. The latency period and puberty make their own demands on the maturing child. It is tempting but not possible here to go into some of the details of this growing process. But we understand that faulty developments of this complicated entity would lead to neurotic and other psychic disorders.

I feel, however, that I still owe an answer to the question: Why is humanity afraid of the self-constructed robots? The vulnerability of the highly differentiated ego organization quickly leads the ego into dangerous situations, menacing it from the outside as well as from the inside (i.e. from the id and the superego). Among the drive impulses the aggressive are especially important in this connection. The aggressive drives which cannot be used constructively in a sublimated form threaten to take the ego by surprise. Subsequent actions are then no longer determined rationally, but are directed against the individual and the outside world in a destructive manner.

Our previous arguments have brought us to the question: What are mental health and illness respectively? I feel that this question is exclusively a *practical* one. Scientific theory cannot determine just what is neurotic and what is healthy. Several psychoanalysts, such as Hartmann (1939b), and recently Kubie (1954), have explained that the terms sickness and health are to a great extent dependent on the current opinion of a particular group of people at a given time. The meaning is variable, subject to changes under the influence of social, economic, and cultural factors. Although Kubie calls sufficient attention to these factors, he finally arrives at a very simplistic definition of the essence of neurosis. He feels, apparently, that unconscious, constrained action is neurotic, and conscious, flexible, free action is healthy. I cannot agree with these conclusions, which are too limited. They neglect our knowledge of the structured nature of the mind, the dynamic processes of defense and repression, and the genetic factors. They are descriptive, and may easily be proved wrong by means of examples. One might agree with Freud's definition: "Neuroses (and other psychic disturbances) are disharmonies of the ego." But the curious researcher will immediately ask: How, why, and when have these discords arisen? Personally I feel that we cannot do better than admit that we can only enumerate a number of factors which may direct the development in a healthy or disordered direction.

In summing up, I would return to Freud's conception of the complementary series I mentioned at the beginning of this chapter; every development, healthy as well as unhealthy, is ultimately the result of the interplay and mutual influencing of the built-in factors, experiences, and influence of environment. The built-in factors may be traced:

(1) In the disposition of the drives, i.e. the id in the narrow sense, in the relative relation of power between the drives, perhaps peculiarities in the rhythm and timing of the underlying forces. In view of this it is a matter of course that these factors are linked with and inseparable from somatic organic processes (metabolism, internal secretion, etc.)

(2) In the ego disposition (the ego nuclei) which indicate the possibilities and the limits of the ego functions, instinctive behavior, intelligence, thought, adjustment functions, reaction mechanisms, etc. Somatically these are linked with the central nervous system. At this point, therefore, we are assisted on our way by neurophysiology and anatomy. It is conceivable that the quantity or nature of the neurones, circuits, synapses, etc., will prove to be determining factors also. For the present, according to the neurologists and anatomists, we know too little of this subject.

Here peculiar innate organic qualities may be of great importance.

But even if future research should teach us more about the physical basis of the ego functions, our knowledge would be increased with regard to only a few factors out of very many.

As the third group of dispositional factors I would mention:

(3) The mutual relative relation between built-in id potentialities and ego capabilities, possibly complicated by potentialities which color and direct the subsequent superego development. These relations, however, cannot at present be measured; they can only be deduced from a study of human behavior. The study of many life histories gives promise of fruitful help here.

305

With the other pole of the complementary series, the influence of the environment, I can deal briefly. I need not explain in detail here that, during the first months and years of life, it is mainly the behavior of the mother which determines whether the child will develop healthily or inharmoniously, while later on the previously mentioned influences of wider environmental and social conditions in their various ramifications will be of particular significance.

I turn now to the question whether the abnormal behavior displayed by animals during laboratory experiments, when through frustrations etc. they are conditioned to given factors or taught to perform various unusual actions, may be compared with the human neurosis. Masserman (1953) draws a far-reaching comparison here. He speaks of neurotic animals and even mentions a therapy for their neurosis. For myself (in agreement with a number of other research scientists) I shall answer this question in the negative. Animals when experimented upon are able to demonstrate reactions such as fear, excitement, rage, etc., but the neurosis in the human being is something different. It comes into existence owing to a complicated defensive process which appears as a result of the interaction of external factors and internally active conflicts. The inner conflicts can only arise owing to the higher differentiation of the human psyche, which in animals is lacking. There is, possibly, a group of disorders of which a given number of built-in factors may be discussed a little more fully. These are the so-called psychosomatic disorders. We know that psychosomatic patients usually exhibit neurotic symptoms as well. Moreover, neurotic and psychosomatic symptoms often interchange and relieve each other. We note that patients suffering from psychosomatoses and neuroses usually have similar character structures and experienced similar environmental influences. Several researchers treating psychosomatic patients, such as Alexander, Groen, and others, have published schematic outlines of personality structures and behavior, coupled with certain family influences and stress situations which they considered to be typical for a certain type of psychosomatosis. But usually these schematic outlines can also be applied to psychoneuroses. It appears, however, to be definitely established that psychosomatic patients have certain built-in factors which can be isolated in the somatic situation; I refer to an ailment such as eczema of the skin. Here we must consider certain predispositional peculiarities of the skin. Diseases such as, for instance, ulcus ventriculi and duodeni, asthma, bronchitis, etc., show that the mucous membranes harbor factors which predispose the subject to these diseases. We are reminded of Freud's conception when he spoke of a somatic compliance when dealing with hysterical conversion symptoms. In the case of babies, where we cannot speak of hysteria, such a somatic, predisposed center may lead to the recognized eczema, bronchitis, pylorospastic syndromes, etc. It is more than possible that the very first experiences of the newborn infant, whose needs are somatically determined, play an important part in infectious diseases, alimentary disorders, etc. (see also Grinker). The attitude of the mother is bound to have an important influence on this somatic reacting of the infant.

Summing up, I would say that recent research in the fields of neurophysiology and anatomy together with cybernetics and ethology have greatly increased the scope of our knowledge of the physical basis of the mind and its earliest developments. In order to widen our outlook on the higher psychic functions and their unfolding in mankind we cannot, for the time being, do without psychoanalysis. The further development of this branch of science and its continued cooperation with the first-named sciences must not only be our constant hope, but, to my mind, is a definite necessity.

CHAPTER 23

On Adolescence

(1960)

Adolescence is often regarded as a "stepchild" in psychoanalysis, in a theoretical as well as in a practical sense. A number of analysts consider the treatment of adolescent boys and girls to be very difficult, sometimes even impossible, though in some cases good results have been achieved, especially with inhibited, depressive, and compulsive-neurotic patients.

Many authors stress that our theoretical knowledge of adolescence is incomplete. I shall not review the literature in detail, but refer to the surveys of this subject by Leo Spiegel (1951) and by Anna Freud (1958).

Out of the many problems of adolescence, my paper will focus on two points: (1) a practical experience; and (2) some theoretical considerations, especially in connection with the formation of superego and ego ideal.

I

Anna Freud (1958) has reminded us of the fact that "our knowledge of the mental processes of infancy has been derived from reconstructions in the analyses of adults and was merely confirmed and enlarged later on by analyses or observations carried out in childhood." It is Anna Freud's opinion that in the treatment of adult cases one seldom succeeds in reviving their adolescent experiences in full force.

I think most authors will agree with this statement, and I have done so myself. However, a number of years ago two adult patients came to

308

me for analytic treatment, a man and a woman, both in their early thirties, in whose analyses a wealth of adolescent experiences, real events as well as fantasies and impulses, came to the fore with remarkable liveliness and were accompanied by strong emotions and impulses. I hasten to add that this re-experiencing only emerged in the later phases of the analyses. In the beginning of treatment the adolescent material was brought forward merely as an account of the patient's life history in the way described by Anna Freud. The most interesting point was that the reliving of affects connected with this material did not become possible until the patient's childhood had been uncovered and reconstructed. Confronted with these observations, I recalled a statement which Freud made to me some thirty years ago. Freud told me about a young woman who had cooperated well in her analysis and whose childhood development had been fairly well reconstructed—but without a therapeutic result. Most of the patient's symptoms had persisted until she suddenly and vividly recollected a traumatic experience that had occurred in her fifteenth year of life. After this traumatic situation and all the emotions involved had been worked through, the patient was cured.

My own observations led me to review a number of other cases, and I gained the impression that in some of them the failure or incompleteness of success might have been due to the lack of revival of the adolescent experiences. Of course I now had to ask myself what causes might have been responsible for the fact that in these cases childhood development could be reconstructed without difficulty and re-experienced with full emotional force, whereas the adolescent period remained deprived of a full affective conviction.

From the direct study of adolescent cases we are all familiar with the charged atmosphere in which the adolescent lives, with the intensity and depth of his feelings, the sudden and unexpected mood swings, the strength of his impulses, and the force of anxiety and despair. However, are we really entitled to assume that in small children feelings, impulses, demands, unforeseen swings from complete happiness toward deepest sorrow and desperation are less intense than similar phenomena in adolescence?

There is indeed a difference in the demands of the instinctual drives

309

in childhood and in adolescence, because infantile sexuality is different from genitality, which has to become the leading factor in the adolescent and adult love life.

I have the impression, however, that it is not merely the intensity of feelings, impulses, and mood swings, but that there are other factors which are more responsible for the difficulties of reviving the adolescent mental processes. These factors seem to lie in ego and superego development.

The little child's ego, undeveloped as it is, has to rely upon the auxiliary ego borrowed from the mother in order to master outer and inner conflicts. The superego is not yet established as an independent mental agency in infancy. Norms and restrictions are imposed upon the child by the parents. Not until the oedipal phase does a structuration of the personality take place. In latency the child develops into a more or less individual personality, though he is still dependent upon the parents. Numerous ego capacities are established and mature during this period. In the sphere which is relatively free from conflict, intelligence, knowledge, special talents, and abilities are developed, whereas in the conflictual sphere, adaptations, reaction formations, and defense mechanisms gradually become character traits. The superego as an inner institution supervises the latency child's behavior to a large extent.

This brief outline of a child's development is very sketchy and incomplete, but it may suffice as a prelude to our considerations about adolescence.

When in puberty the instinctual drives make their new and intensified demands upon the youngster, they encounter a personality different from the one they encountered in childhood. The adolescent ego has many more ways and means of coping with the drives; in a certain sense, we could call this ego stronger. However, on the other hand, it lacks the support of the parents' auxiliary ego because the adolescent turns away from the parents. The loosening of the ties with the parents is a difficult and protracted process, often accompanied by genuine mourning, as Root (1957) and Anna Freud (1958) have pointed out. In this respect the adolescent ego presents itself as much weaker than the child's ego. A similar process is going on in the superego. On the

310

one hand the adolescent superego is now established as an inner conscience; on the other hand its foundation is shaken by the very process of turning away from the parents and the parental norms and morals. The adolescent has to rely upon his own superego. The adult, looking back upon his life history, feels more responsible for his adolescent than for his infantile behavior; he feels more guilty and more ashamed about his adolescent conflicts, disharmonies, and oddities. As he usually remembers the factual events of adolescence, he tries to escape the revival of the accompanying guilt- and shame-burdened emotions, either by suppressing and denying every emotion of that period or by retreating to infantile experiences.

This is precisely what we often observe in analytic treatment. The patient brings us a wealth of infantile material, more and more, in different forms and associations, even when the childhood history has already been fairly well reconstructed and re-experienced. He clings tenaciously to infantile material; yet when we look at this material closely we realize that adolescent features have entered into the picture. The patient has used the infantile material in order to ward off adolescent experiences. The analyst must then analyze the defensive character of, and the underlying anxiety in regard to this material and confront the patient with his adolescent feelings of shame, guilt, hurt pride, etc. In a number of cases the result will be a real revival of the patient's adolescence in full force.

In trying to accomplish this task we encounter difficulties not exclusively due to the patient's reluctance to face his own adolescent problems, his unbalanced behavior, his extreme feelings, his extravagant emotions, and his oddities. We also have to cope with the analyst's reactions. The analyst is prepared to encounter the patient's acting out in the transference. When the patient transfers impulses upon the analyst from his childhood period and in an infantile form, it is much easier for the analyst to keep to his attitude of friendly understanding and neutrality. The adolescent has made use of all of his intelligence, capacities, and special gifts to ward off his forbidden impulses, his disappointments, and his conflicts. This is especially true in connection with his hostility toward parents and toward adults in general. Hence, in encouraging an adult patient to relive his adolescent experiences

311

the analyst must cope with a refined form of the patient's aggression.

One can smile at a little child's direct form of aggressive behavior, but an adolescent's aggression is clothed in a much more irritating, tormenting, and sometimes nearly intolerable shape. It may happen that the analyst, being a human creature himself, is (unconsciously) inclined to follow the patient in his flight toward infancy in order to escape the patient's refined criticisms, reproaches, and hostile demands. In every adult, traits not only from the little child but also from the adolescent persist. This is especially true for our patients. They tend to excuse themselves for their accusations and tormenting attacks in taking for granted that the analyst is an omnipotent and therefore invulnerable person. The interplay between the patient's desire to relive his adolescent emotions and conflicts and the analyst's unconscious reluctance to bear the adolescent forms of aggression might be one of the causes of the difficulties we encounter in analyzing and working through an adult patient's adolescence.

II

I now come to my second point: some theoretical considerations, which, I hope, will contribute to our understanding of the practical difficulties just mentioned as well as of adolescent psychic life in general. In the scope of this presentation I can throw light upon only a few points. My assumptions are based partly on material gained in the treatment of adolescents, but mainly on reconstruction of adolescent experiences in adult cases.

A youngster's ego can react in an infinite variety of ways to the newly flourishing demands of his instinctual drives and to the newly arising social demands which are so different from those made upon the little child. The adolescent has on the one hand the ardent wish to be grown up because he usually imagines that adults are free, independent, and self-supporting, and he tries to use all his faculties in order to equal or even to better them. On the other hand, however, he wants to remain a little child in order not to have to relinquish his infantile ties with the parental objects. It is very well known how difficult a task this is. Having lost a beloved person or even having renounced the love of a still existing object is followed by a certain amount of "work of mourning" (see Anna Freud, 1958). Whether the outcome of the mourning process will be a relatively normal or a pathological one depends upon many factors, among them upon the amount of aggression originally directed toward the parents. We know that the little child holds his parents responsible for his distress and losses, and he responds to all sorts of pain with hatred and death wishes toward them. When in puberty the infantile object relationships are revived, the adolescent begins to react in a similar way. The more intense his archaic hostility, the more difficulties he will have in dealing with his death wishes. The mourning processes are colored by the aggression turned inward. The result may be a depressive neurotic disorder, psychotic reactions, acting out or antisocial behavior, or a combination of these various disturbances. Many authors have described several outcomes in clinical and theoretical papers.

I shall now turn to another problem of adolescence which is very different from childhood processes and nevertheless very closely dependent upon them. I mean the superego problems. I have already mentioned that in adolescence the superego has become an inner agency, whereas in early childhood behavior was directed by the parents' demands, prohibitions, and morals. The little child cooperates with them mainly in order to avoid loss of love or punishment. Only gradually does he internalize the parental norms, which subsequently become the content of the superego. Now in adolescence he must give up his old incestuous ties to the parents—a process partly equivalent to losing the love object. But in addition he must also give up a fundamental part of his superego content—those parts of the restrictions, norms, and ideals which, though internalized, are still closely linked to the incestuous object representations. The very fact that these superego contents are internalized implies that the adolescent must give up something that has become an essential part of his self. To turn away from a love object is a hard and painful process; to disengage oneself from a part of one's own personality is still more difficult to achieve.

In order to examine these events more closely I propose once more to distinguish between the superego in a narrower sense as the restricting and prohibiting agency and the ego ideal as comprising ethics and ideals. I have made this distinction in previous papers and it has, in my opinion, some advantages. The compliance with parental restrictions

313

and prohibitions requires renunciation of direct pleasure, but this compliance is rewarded with love and approval from the parents. The formation of ideals, however, has an additional function and has already been on the way long before parental restrictions have become internal demands. The little child idealizes the parents and conceives of them as perfect, omnipotent creatures. He clings tenaciously to these ideas because he feels himself so extremely powerless. The introjection of the almighty and faultless parental images is a compensation for the feeling of helplessness; it begins in very early childhood and is a narcissistic satisfaction *par excellence.*These introjected images give rise to fantasies of grandeur and omnipotence, which in the magic phase of development are among the fundamentals of the child's self-esteem and self-maintenance. It is well known that part of the feelings of grandeur continue to exist, though unconsciously, throughout life.

The adolescent must bear not only the pain of losing love objects, of coping with the attending mourning, and of revising old patterns of restriction and prohibition. In addition to all these hard tasks, he must endure the narcissistic injuries caused by the experience that his self-esteem is being shaken in its fundamentals and therefore more or less lost. We know too well that a certain amount of narcissistic cathexis of the personality is indispensable for healthy development. When the basis of the ideal formation has gone to pieces, the youngster is utterly helpless. I hasten to add that the loss of love is of course partly felt as a narcissistic injury as well. The finding of a new love object raises the person's self-esteem, too. However, it seems to make a considerable difference when an essential part of the ego (ego ideal) is damaged or lost and has to be newly built up. New love objects are relatively easily found in adolescence in teachers, leaders, companions, etc. New ideals that compensate for the essential helplessness of human beings are more difficult to acquire (at least in our civilization). The youngster very well knows, and feels, that adults are not omnipotent but vulnerable creatures. With this acknowledgment, his ideals of perfect and omnipotent parents must collapse, and consequently his ego ideal is impaired. We find a confirmation of this assumption in studying those adolescents who do not respond to offers of love and guidance from a new object (relative, teacher, therapist, companion, etc.). These youngsters could not overcome the depth of their inner narcissistic injuries as a consequence of the disturbance of their ideal formation. They then are indifferent to supplies of love from the outer world. It is possible that a number of strange reactions, unexpected attitudes, and unpredictable mood swings are due to this basic disturbance in the economy of narcissistic libido and the ego's failure to restore it with another acquisition of ideals. Moreover, it is just the narcissistic injuries that are pre-eminently likely to give rise to aggression, and this hostility in turn diminishes a person's susceptibility to another person's loving assistance and to the offer of new ideals and norms.

In the transference during treatment we can observe that a patient's deep and refined hostility, severe criticisms of the analyst, reproaches that the analyst is impotent and worthless go side by side with an unconscious, archaic conviction of the analyst's omnipotence. The ideal image of almighty parents and analysts is not only indispensable for the youngster's maintenance of narcissistic cathexis, but is secondarily used to diminish the guilt feelings aroused by precisely this same hostile and aggressive behavior. It is as if the youngster says to himself: "Parents and analyst are omnipotent, consequently they are invulnerable; so I can scold, torment, and act out every aggression without having to feel guilty or reproach myself."

It would be tempting to illustrate these assumptions with detailed analytic material. However, in this paper, I merely wanted to emphasize the importance of the problems around the ego ideal in adolescence. The adolescent's clinging to the very archaic, idealized parental images makes it very difficult for him to cope with the narcissistic injuries occasioned by the disappointment of losing his infantile idealized images and by the necessity of having to give them up and finding new ideals in a more reality-adapted form. Furthermore, they need to hold on to this idealized picture because it also serves as a defense against guilt and shame engendered by the intense hostility.

Since many analysts agree that adolescent patients are often not suitable for analytic treatment, we must, in our attempts to understand adolescent psychology, rely mainly on observations and reconstructions of adolescence in adult cases. But even these reconstructions, as has been pointed out, are extremely difficult to achieve. This paper has endeavored to investigate some of the obstacles in the way of such reconstruction and to indicate means of overcoming them.

I believe that we might be successful in reviving adolescence in a number of cases if we made an effort to overcome our own resistances against the patient's adolescent forms of aggression, if we focused our and the patient's attention upon his hidden ideals and fantasies of omnipotence attributed to his parents and later on internalized, and if we supported the patient in enduring his narcissistic hurts and in giving up the defensive character of his archaic ideal. I believe that this effort is worth while.

CHAPTER 24

Ego Ideal and Superego

(1962)

Originally the terms "ego ideal" and "superego" were used by Freud interchangeably. This fact can be explained historically. From the study of psychopathology, especially of melancholic disorders, Freud concluded that a part of the ego (a province within the ego) could oppose itself to the ego proper, making demands upon it and punishing it as formerly the parents had done. This means that through the process of identification the superego is formed as a substructure of the ego. In the course of development this process occurs at the end of the phallic phase (at the onset of latency) as a result of the solution of the oedipal object relationships. The superego is, according to Freud's formulation, the heir of the oedipus complex, and comprises the child's wish to be like the parents (ideal formation) and to comply with the parental restrictions and demands (superego in a narrower sense). These conceptualizations could account for and explain a variety of pathological phenomena in individuals (Freud, 1914, 1917, 1923b, 1924a, 1924b, 1925, 1931b) as well as in mankind (Freud, 1921, 1927b, 1930, 1937-39). In addition, they also explained normal psychological processes, e.g., humor (1927a).

Notwithstanding the gains in insight, there continued to exist a number of problems and inconsistencies which, according to Freud, were in need of further study and explanation. In recent years several authors have made contributions to the superego problems. For a more detailed review of the literature, I refer the reader to Sandler (1960).

From a structural point of view, I think we must adhere to Freud's conception of the superego as a special substructure in the human mind established at the onset of latency. Yet how are we to explain the difficulties and confusions around this concept which many authors have mentioned? Structuralization of the mind is a maturational and developmental process. The genetic point of view has brought about many clarifications of mental processes. I therefore propose to turn to the genesis of mental substructures of the ego in approximately normal development and to examine separately the ideal formation and the self-criticizing punishing agency.

THE GENESIS OF EGO SUBSTRUCTURES

The Genesis of the Ego Ideal

The child is born with an unstructured mind. The inborn potentialities out of which a structured mind is developed during growth are called by Freud the id in a wider sense; Hartmann (1939a, 1950) speaks of the "undifferentiated phase." The newborn has vital needs which have to be satisfied sufficiently to guarantee survival and to ensure the reign of the pleasure principle. As long as the infant-mother unity is need-satisfying there is no stimulation for accelerating the maturational process. However, birth itself causes unpleasurable sensations and soon afterward the satisfaction of needs does not occur immediately and completely enough to avoid unpleasure. The experiences of alternate pleasure and pain stimulate development, and gradually a primitive structuralization of the mind comes about. A number of functions begin to develop: sensual stimuli are laid down in memory traces (structuralization of the brain), outside and inside are distinguished (object and self), testing of reality begins, etc. I do not need to mention all of them; they are well known as functions which later on will be organized. In the structured mind they build up the ego organization which must attempt to allow sufficient satisfaction of needs and wishes and at the same time to adjust to the necessities of life and to the demands of the environment.[1]

I will now turn to a special function of the very primitive ego, al-

[1] Modern ego psychology is so far advanced as to give us a fairly good insight into the development of a number of functions of the ego organization (Hartmann, 1939a, 1950; and many other authors).

ready manifesting itself in the first months of life, because I think it has a bearing on our topic, the genesis of the later-established ego ideal.

When the little baby becomes aware of unpleasurable stimuli and tensions he is bodily still too immature to take appropriate action. He cannot produce food or warmth or comfort when he is hungry or cold or nearly overwhelmed by inner tensions. When the mother is not instantly available the infant takes refuge in "hallucinatory wish fulfillment," as Freud called it in earlier times.

I think these hallucinations already occur at a time when the function of distinguishing between self and outside world is not yet established. They appear during the narcissistic stage, when the mother (or the breast) is still part of the internal narcissistic milieu and not yet an object (Hoffer, 1950). However, as "hallucinating" does not abolish unpleasure in the long run, whereas the mother does, we may consider these processes as the starting point for the development of the distinction between inner and outer worlds.

As long as no object outside the self is recognized, these hallucinations are not yet fantasies centering around an object that provides pleasure or abolition of unpleasure. They are self-centered and, as far as they can temporarily alleviate discomfort, the gain is narcissistic satisfaction.

The reason why I dwell so long on this early and primitive ego function is that, in my opinion, we encounter here the basis of the ego ideal. In terms of structuralization we could speak of a forerunner of the ego ideal. According to this assumption, the genesis of the ego ideal is to be found in an ego function, which serves to provide pleasure and to undo pain, caused by frustrations. This latter function has already been described by me in Chapter 10. The ego ideal is an *agency of wish fulfillment*. If we pursue the further development of these primitive hallucinatory wish fulfillments, I think we find confirmation of this assumption.

When the infant has learned to distinguish between self and outer world he makes an object attachment to the breast and the mother, and he expects the mother to provide satisfaction. This object attachment is still a narcissistic one; the mother is loved not for her own sake, but merely as a need-satisfying object.

During this period of differentiation between self and object new sources of unpleasure arise for the infant when the mother does not provide satisfaction and love as completely and as instantly as he wants them. Even the most loving and devoted mother is unable to fulfill every wish, to abolish every pain or discomfort in her child. There are always situations when the child feels disappointed, frustrated, and above all *powerless* because he is unable to bring about a change in this painful state of unpleasure. To deal with this condition, so dangerous for his self-esteem (his narcissistic equilibrium), the child develops alongside the primitive hallucinatory wish fulfillments his comforting fantasies of grandeur and omnipotence. Together with the formation of object relations (first need-satisfying attachments, and later on relations of object constancy), the fantasies of omnipotence and idealization of his self continue to exist. They can easily be observed in toddlers in the preoedipal phase.

I mention two examples, among many: little John, aged two years, ten months, told his mother his penis would grow to be as big as the garden hose; he would fill the ocean and a big steamer would take him overseas.

Little Ann (three years) said: "When my penis is as big as Dick's [her elder brother]. . . ." When her mother remarked: "But you are a little girl, only boys have a penis, why do you think you will get one?" Ann replied: "When I want it, I'll get it!"

The fantasies of grandeur are a narcissistic gratification and they heighten self-esteem. But gradually they begin to fail to do so because the child has the painful experience that they have no influence upon the actual events, and he feels his total powerlessness vis-à-vis reality. He then takes refuge in a second edition of fantasies which provide narcissistic gratification. He idealizes his parents and attributes to them omnipotence, in which he himself partakes. These images of ideal and almighty parents persist much longer, because the parents are, in comparison with the child, really much stronger and more powerful. These fantasies flourish especially during the oedipal phase in which the child identifies himself with the parent of the same sex in order to replace him (or her) with the other parent. In normal development the child at the end of the oedipal phase accepts reality more or less through recognizing his powerlessness and the impossibility of being the mother's (or the father's) lover. His attachment to the parents is desexualized and a more reality-oriented change takes place in his ego ideal. The contents of the ego ideal are no longer exclusively "I am as potent in sexual life and in other achievements as the parents." The ideals are partly transferred to attainable goals: learning, development of bodily and mental skills, understanding of reality and life in general. We know that even so-called "normal" adults sometimes take refuge in former fantasies of omnipotence in narcissistically frustrating situations. However, when they are able to live up to their own mature ideals and ethics, they experience a more lasting and much greater satisfaction. *The ego ideal*, even when developed into ethics and social ideals, *remains essentially an agency of wish fulfillment*, and it supports the ego in dealing with the inevitable disappointments and frustrations inherent in human life. In a way, it is still an ego function. However, just because it has its own contents and because it sometimes puts a distance between itself and the other organized ego functions, we can speak of an established substructure (or province) within the ego.

I shall next discuss the self-criticizing, prohibiting, and punishing agency which we could term "superego in a narrower sense" or "conscience."

The Genesis of the Superego

Before the infant distinguishes between self and outside world there is no question of "prohibitions, demands, or punishment." The infant merely experiences sensations of unpleasure. When the distinction between self and environment has been established the infant may experience restrictions of his needs and wishes from outside as prohibitions or demands. It seems plausible to assume that the earlier unpleasurable sensations form the basis of his experience of these restrictions. When he protests against complying with them, anxiety may arise. In order to avoid anxiety and to preserve the object (later on the love of the object), he will begin to try to live up to the demands.

The toddler may, to a certain extent, internalize the parental demands and even their punishments. The acceptance of the inevitable environmental claims leads to the establishment of an ego function

321

which can be considered to be a forerunner of conscience and which thus is an *agency of restriction* imposed upon the little child from outside. The conflict is between child and environment and is likely to arouse anxiety but not yet guilt. Only at the end of the oedipal phase, when the child must give up his sexual wishes, do the environmental demands and restrictions become an inner property. The ego functions of renouncing certain wish fulfillments and of complying with parental demands can now be structuralized into the judging superego or conscience.

In normal development the superego and the ego ideal guide the ego in its double task, on the one hand of allowing the person to have sufficient satisfaction of drives, needs, impulses, etc., and on the other hand of modifying and sublimating parts of them in order to live up to the demands of the outside world and to cope with the inevitable restrictions.

Summary

The genesis of the ego ideal is different from that of the restricting superego or conscience. The ego ideal is originally and essentially a *need-satisfying agency*, whereas the superego (or conscience) is originally and essentially *a restricting and prohibiting agency*.

In the development of the ego ideal four phases can be distinguished:
(1) "Hallucinatory" wish fulfillment in the narcissistic phase (in which self and outer world are not yet distinguished).
(2) Fantasies of grandeur and omnipotence of the self after the infant has become aware of a distinction between inside and outside.
(3) Fantasies of the parents being omnipotent, and the child's sharing their omnipotence after experiencing his own powerlessness.
(4) Formation of ethics and ideals as attainable goals after disillusionment by the idealized parents.

In the development of the restricting superego, four phases can be distinguished:
(1) Experience of sensations of unpleasure.
(2) Renunciation of wish fulfillment and compliance with parental demands in order to preserve the parents' love.

322

(3) Internalization of single demands through identification with some parental demands during the preoedipal phase.

(4) Inner conscience and internal acceptance of restrictions and punishments imposed by the parents and the wider environment in order to guarantee a social relationship within a certain class or group or milieu.

Now the question arises, how was it that originally both ego ideal and restricting superego were seen as one single agency and one substructure within the ego? I believe it is because at the onset of latency their establishment is centered around the same object representations, the parental images, the purely narcissistic prestages having been abandoned. The content of the ego ideal, once the third phase of its development has been reached, could be expressed as follows: "I am like my parents (that is, in fantasy: omnipotent)." The content of the superego from an early stage of its development onward could be described in the following way: "I will live up to my parents' demands, and punish myself the way they punished me when I fail to do so (that is, in fantasy: I have to be obedient to avoid the loss of parental love)."

The ego ideal's content, "I am like my parents," implies taking over parental ideals and ethics. The superego's content, "I have to do what my parents require of me," implies taking over parental restrictions and prohibitions. Both institutions are marked by identification with the parents and the parental images. From the structural point of view, we can describe them as substructures within the ego, as a change of part of the ego through these identifications.

If we examine their functions, however, they serve opposite ends. The ego ideal serves wish fulfillment and is a gratifying agency. The conscience (superego in the narrower sense) is a restricting and prohibiting agency. However, in this strictly schematic sense, this statement is true in childhood, but later on only in a very harmonious development. Because both agencies unite into one substructure after the passing of the oedipus complex, they may considerably influence each other's functions. The ego ideal's content, "I am like my parents," can acquire an imperative compulsive character: "I must be like my parents." Later on high ideals in general may be experienced as demands.

Even within the range of so-called "normality" there are many individual differences which can be explained in two ways: (1) we may assume a definite and rigid change of function after the establishment of the substructure superego in the wider sense; and (2) we may see them as individual variations which already show a tendency toward inharmonious development. I myself am inclined toward the second explanation, because in a number of cases we clearly observe that living up to ethics, ideals, and norms is and remains a source of pleasure. It may provide real satisfaction through heightening self-esteem and self-assurance and so promote a number of gratifying ego activities. A strong compulsion to normative and ethical behavior (Kant's categorical imperative) points to an oversevere, judging superego, as is, for example, often found in persons with obsessional-neurotic characters. As in many other instances, the transitions between "normality" and "pathology" are fluid.

Be this as it may, the origins of both agencies can be traced back to infancy. In certain circumstances (most clearly in pathology), a disintegration of the one or the other, sometimes of both at the same time, takes place and regression to primitive, infantile stages occurs. Identifications with the mother and with the father naturally differ from one another. These as well as identifications made on different levels of development may again come to the fore and may cause splits in the entity of both agencies.

THE VISIBILITY OF STRUCTURE IN THE MIND

I now want to take up a problem which Freud mentioned on several occasions but to which other psychoanalysts have not paid sufficient attention. In the behavior of a "normal," well-integrated, harmoniously developed adult, we cannot always directly distinguish the different structures and substructures of the mind, because in this case the mind acts as a whole. When a person's ego has secured sufficient satisfaction of needs and impulses and when the ego is able to master the id strivings which cannot be satisfied, using their (neutralized) energy for constructive purposes, it is no longer possible to distinguish clearly what share the ego and id have in a number of activities. The same applies to a distinction between shares of the (judging) superego and the ego ideal in these activities. A person capable of living up to his inner ethics and ideals *and* capable of sound self-criticism, who can provide himself with sufficient gratifications in accordance with his own environment, acts as a whole, as an entity. The fact that the provinces of the mind were originally separate functional entities becomes apparent only in special circumstances. In "normal" persons this occurs in specific life situations which require a reorientation, e.g., in adolescence when the former balance between id and ego, ego ideal and superego has to be revised owing to the maturing sexuality, love life, and object choices. I described some of the problems involved in Chapter 23. In the menopause and in old age other problems arise. In these phases of relative unbalance the different structures of the mind and the various identifications may become much more visible until a new harmony is again achieved. It then becomes very clear that a variety of new contents has been added to the original ones.

In disturbed, inharmonious development which leads to neuroses, ego distortions, delinquency, psychoses, etc., the structuralization of the mind becomes much more observable. Partial and unequal regressions to earlier developmental stages of id, ego, ego ideal, and superego provide a clearer picture of how the mind is structuralized in the course of maturation and development.

For practical purposes we try to assess the nature and gravity of given disturbances and their accessibility to psychoanalytic (or other psychotherapeutic) treatment. Treatment aims at tracing back the disturbances to their origins in order to enable the mature ego to employ the mental energies in a different (and healthier) way. In this context it is necessary to look for criteria enabling us to assess the extent to which different parts of the structured mind have contributed to the disturbance. In its final outcome, the differences in the development of the superego and ego ideal may play an important role.

Some Practical Considerations in Regard to Psychopathology

The Classical Psychoneuroses

In hysteria, phobia, and obsessional neurosis a regression of libido and aggression to earlier developmental stages takes place in consequence of severe guilt feelings and strong castration anxiety. This early statement of Freud's can still be confirmed in our daily analytic work. The primary regression of the drives is sometimes followed by a secondary regression of a number of ego functions in connection with defensive processes, and of some rigid defense mechanisms.[2] We then speak of ego distortions. The functions of ego ideal and restricting superego may participate in these events. This is clearly observable in obsessional neurotics. Here the drives regress to the anal-sadistic phase and this regression is followed by a restriction of ego activities, e.g., of sublimated actions, and by a regression of the restricting superego, which becomes a very sadistic agency through sexualization and turning of aggression toward the self. The ego ideal secondarily regresses to the phase of fantasies of grandeur and omnipotence, and of magical thinking. These processes cause distortion of reality testing. Usually a part of the ego is still very well able to judge reality, while another part follows the regressed ego-ideal functions and adheres to a belief in the possibility of magically influencing the environment. Thus, splits in the ego and ego ideal have come about, and the patient feels torn apart.

In hysterical patients, the ego disturbance observable as a consequence of the regression of libido to the phallic phase seems to be less severe. It limits itself to an inhibition of some functions, e.g., of memory. The function of memory is more or less impaired through the defense mechanism of repression, which causes gaps in the patient's life history and may have a bearing on his judgment of reality factors.

Narcissistic Neuroses, Borderline Cases, and Psychoses

A different process seems to have occurred in these disorders. Here we may assume a regression of ego functions together with the libidinal regression. Both could be called primary regression. An alternative could be a disturbance of ego activities in the prephallic stage, an arrest of ego maturation, or a severe retardation in development already originating in the preoedipal phase. In narcissistic neuroses, it is sometimes difficult to decide whether we are dealing with an early ar-

[2] The distinction between primary and secondary ego regression is used by Anna Freud in the assessment of childhood development.

rest or with regression. In psychoses and borderline cases, there seems to be a closer tie to an early level of ego development. Concerning large areas of the restricting superego and of the ego ideal we clearly observe a position of an infantile nature. In these patients we see that the restricting superego has only partly reached the state of an inner voice, of a real conscience. These patients can submit only to the actual restrictions coming from outside, and then under the pressure of severe anxiety and primitive fears. The internalized part is limited mostly to self-punishment of a very sadistic, cruel, archaic nature. The contents of the ego ideal of borderline patients are still the primitive ideals of the little child, the fantasies of grandeur and omnipotence. A development toward adult morals and ethics is lacking or defective. Naturally, the interplay between the id and the defective ego and superego functions may cause further distortions of the ego ideal, and thus interfere with its normal functioning.

Delinquents

A special discordance of the superego and ego-ideal development is found in delinquents. In Chapter 10 I described some vicissitudes of the defective development of ideals and conscience. It is well known that delinquents often suffer from a severe, punishing superego, and that they often commit antisocial acts in order to satisfy their need for punishment. In many of these offenders we find a poorly developed ego ideal clinging to very primitive fantasies of grandeur. These pleasurable fantasies are retained in order to compensate for the pain experienced in the clash with the environment. The ego ideal has in principle preserved its original character as a wish-fulfilling agency. The superego in turn holds to its restricting and punishing function, though both are distorted and fail to function in an adequate way. The ego ideal's failure to provide real and adequate wish fulfillments creates new frustrations, which in their turn cause further regression to primitive fantasies of omnipotence.

These sketchy remarks on different developments, normal and abnormal, are necessarily oversimplified. We must never forget that the different stages of preoedipal development contribute to the genesis of the ego, the restricting superego, and the ego ideal. The archaic state of mind scarcely ever disappears completely. Even with minor disturbances an inharmonious growth of these agencies can come about. I have already mentioned that in approximately "normal" adolescence, disharmonies between the different parts and functions of the mind can be observed (Chapter 10). Within the ego-ideal functions proper, there may be unbalance as well. A person can have highly developed ideals and ethics in one area along with defective ones in other areas. One example out of many can be found in delinquency. A group of delinquents can adjust to a severe code of ideals within their own group while offending the ideals of the larger community and society. The same is valid for the restricting superego. Very severe demands and self-punishment in one area can exist side by side with refusal to accept inevitable restrictions in other fields, e.g., where property and interests of other people are concerned.

SUMMARY

The ego ideal and the restricting superego originate alongside each other in primitive forerunners in infancy. They may be considered as special ego areas with their own functions. At the onset of the latency period they are centered around the parental images.

In harmonious development, they act together as a substructure within the ego organization, guiding the ego in its achievements. Throughout life the ego ideal remains essentially an agency of wish fulfillment. The superego is a restricting agency, necessary for living in a given community.

In abnormal development, traces of the origins of both ego ideal and superego can be observed as a consequence of fixations on and regressions to primitive developmental stages. The different identifications may be used as defense mechanisms in a pathological way and so add to the disharmony of the person.

CHAPTER 25

Symptom Formation and Character Formation

(1963)

To deal with this very broad topic in a single presentation seems impossible. It is not my intention to focus on one clinical constellation. Apart from theoretical reflection, there is a practical consideration, namely the fact that we hardly ever meet with a "simple" neurosis in our patients. I will therefore try to present a few aspects of the general theme. I do not intend to give a systematic presentation, and in order to make my points I shall elaborate upon themes not strictly falling under the title of this symposium.

It is true that Freud started his psychological investigations with hysterical patients. However, it soon became clear that most patients reveal a mixture of symptoms belonging to different neurotic pictures, for instance a combination of hysterical and obsessional-neurotic, of phobic and depressive constellations.

Freud discovered that the foundation of obsessional neurosis was a childhood neurosis of the hysterical type, and established a close relationship between the symptoms of conversion hysteria and anxiety hysteria or phobia, as well as between those of phobias and obsessional neurosis. Moreover, in a number of cases that could be labeled as mainly hysterical neuroses we encounter character traits of a definite obsessional neurotic origin, and the reverse is encountered as well.

Other observations teach us that many patients cannot be classed in a special neurotic category. They show various disturbances: symptoms

329

as well as inhibitions, depressive states, etc., which we usually term "neurotic disorders," not to mention those with more severe disturbances, such as borderline cases, psychotics, and delinquents. In the analysis of neurotic patients we often meet with psychotic mechanisms which manifest themselves, for instance, in a kernel of delusions. In addition, a mixture of symptoms and character distortions reveals itself in many cases.

In view of these various considerations, I intend to try to highlight some aspects of the processes involved in the genesis of symptoms and character traits, especially from the more recently developed structural-dynamic viewpoint. Before embarking on this endeavor, I want to point out a peculiarity of our topic. Symptom formation is a psychopathological phenomenon, whereas character formation is in itself a "normal" developmental process. However, as psychoanalysis has shown that there is an easy transition from "normality" to pathology, and that mental processes are more easily studied in the context of pathological phenomena, I will stick to the traditional line of using the manifestations of abnormal development in trying to describe some aspects of what may be termed a "normal" character formation and personality development.

SYMPTOM FORMATION

During the development of psychoanalysis, Freud used different terms for the description of symptom formation. I will cite a definition given in *Inhibitions, Symptoms and Anxiety* (1926, p. 91):

> The main characteristics of the formation of symptoms have long since been studied and, I hope, established beyond dispute. A symptom is a sign of, and a substitute for, an instinctual satisfaction which has remained in abeyance; it is a consequence of the process of repression. Repression proceeds from the ego when the latter—it may be at the behest of the super-ego—refuses to associate itself with an instinctual cathexis which has been aroused in the id.

Freud elaborates upon the subject in many very important directions. I mention only two of them.

(a) He points out that repression is only one of a variety of defense mechanisms, though it has a special place among them and a special relation to hysterical neuroses, without being the *only* mode of defense in this disease.

(b) He reconsiders the problem of anxiety, conceiving of it as an ego activity signaling a danger situation, from without as well as from within.

The first statement is an enlargement, the second a modification of former theories. Both have been of great significance for the stimulation of the development of ego psychology in more recent times.

When we now consider the coming into being of a symptom, we encounter Freud's early discovery of a conflict between the ego and an instinctual id impulse that cannot be satisfied. At that time the ego was conceived of as an entity opposing itself to the id because it had to mediate between the person's needs and the demands of the environment. In later periods Freud described the ego as an organization of different functions, and drew attention to the influence of the conflict on the ego organization. He spoke of an impoverishment, an impairment, a distortion, of the ego.

We often encounter the view that a conflict is a *pathological* phenomenon. I want to stress explicitly that conflict is a normal event in the dynamics of living beings. It is inherent in the life process. Every creature experiences clashes with its environment which it has to cope with in order to preserve its own existence. In the highly differentiated and complicated structure of the human mind conflicts not only originate from an encounter with the environment, but to a great extent they take place between internal subareas. The process of development is centered around and stimulated by inner and outer conflicts. The decision whether a "normal" solution of a conflict is achieved or whether a symptom or some other pathological outcome finally emerges, depends upon the intactness of an ego capacity, the integrative or harmonizing ability. In Chapter 24 I called the original and basic function of the superego an agency of restriction, that of the ego ideal an agency of wish fulfillment. I now want to add that I consider the basic function of the ego to be the synthetic or integrative one. The ability to achieve harmony is the outcome of a complicated process in ego development. A number of achievements are necessary in order to enable the ego to use the basic function in a satisfactory way. If the ego is capable of solving the conflicts, in synthesizing the different demands made upon the personality (the "self") from the inner as well as from the outer world, we speak of a "normal" psychic process. This means that the ego is able to allow the personality a sufficient satisfaction of instinctual and affective needs without disturbing the relation with the environment in agreement with superego and ego ideal demands and without impairing its (the ego's) own capacities. This is in accordance with the pleasure principle or its modified version, the reality principle. It does not mean that conflicts are eliminated forever from the mind. New conflicts continually arise, so that the integrative capacity has to come into action repeatedly. It is not a static but a dynamic process. Whether in a given situation harmony can be achieved through conflict-solving depends upon a number of factors, which can be brought under two headings: (a) the relative strength of the synthetic capacity (the economic aspect); (b) the mobility and the reversibility of the harmonizing process. The factors involved emerge from the different areas of the personality.

When we examine our patient's neurotic symptoms in the making, we observe an impairment of his synthesizing faculties. The patient starts by complaining of his symptoms, which he feels as alien intruders in his "self." He suffers from anxiety states, from obsessions, from depressive and other painful moods, and so on, which he is quite aware that he cannot escape. His incapacity to feel in harmony with his self is apparently a very painful experience. This state of mind does not imply that the capacity for integration is totally and forever eliminated; on the contrary, its working is apparent from the fact that in the long run the ego tries to integrate the symptoms into its organization. But it has failed to operate in a conflict-solving way. The conflict-causing id impulses had to be warded off (or repressed); they are now inaccessible to the ego, which is unable to influence them in any way. As the drive impulses constantly put pressure upon the ego demanding discharge, the latter agency must strengthen its anticathexis by using new defense mechanisms. The defensive procedures require energy that is withdrawn from other activities, including autonomous, ego-syntonic performances. The result is an inhibition, an impoverishment of the ego.

332

A further consequence is a reduction of pleasure gain. A substitutive masochistic satisfaction from suffering and a secondary gain from illness are now the only modes of gratification available, so far as the diseased part of the personality is concerned.

Before turning to the examination of the defensive processes, the origin of the mechanisms of defense and their influence upon ego development, I want to indicate briefly the factors Freud made responsible for the failure to solve conflicts and to prevent neurotic conditions.

In analysis neurotic symptoms can invariably be traced back to an infantile neurosis. As the little child's ego organization is still in a state of immaturity, it is a "loose" and "feeble" agency which cannot deal appropriately with the demands of the drives. Drives and impulses are perceived as dangerous and have to be warded off. Anxiety is raised by the ego as a signal, indicating that a danger is present and that the ego has to take countermeasures. Though in principle a person can take refuge in "flight" before external dangers, such as oversevere demands and punishments, the child is too dependent upon his environment to do this. Therefore he has to undertake similar defensive action against both environmental and inner demands. When the parents' prohibitions have become internalized and laid down in the superego, the ego is still more intimately influenced by them and can take refuge exclusively in warding-off mechanisms. In connection with these facts Freud (1926) names three prominent factors that play a part in the causation of neuroses:

(a) A biological factor, the long period of helplessness and dependence during childhood.

(b) A phylogenetic factor, namely, the flourishing of the instinctual life in early childhood, followed by the interruption in the development of the drives during latency ("the biphasic onset of sexuality") which leads to a genuine incapacity for satisfaction of the needs and impulses in the first years of life.

(c) A psychological factor, the differentiation of the mental apparatus into id and ego (and superego), due to the necessity for dealing with the influence of the external world.

Here I would add that the third point (c) was later revised to show that the differentiation of id and ego is an inborn maturational factor affected and influenced by environmental stimuli.

I think we all adhere to Freud's statements when we examine the material presented to us by our patients. The three factors mentioned can help us to understand a good deal about the causation of symptoms, in so far as they explain the vulnerability of the child's mind. There are many children, however, who do not show neurotic symptoms in their first years of life or who "outgrow" their slight infantile neurosis and do not become neurotics in later life. We must therefore look for special factors which make for neurotic development or for "health." One important question is: What factors cause a lasting impairment of the ego's integrating capacity?

It is self-evident that we have to look for these factors among the three agencies of the structured mind and their dynamic interplay under the influence of the environment. Dynamics can only be understood when we consider genesis, course of development, and economic (quantitative) proportions. The magnitude of all these different relations is so confusing that we shall have to simplify by merely sketching some facets of the various processes.

Our knowledge is most advanced as regards the maturational process of the drives (the id). A smooth course for this process is certainly dependent on inborn peculiarities of the drives, for example their relative strength, which may lead to acting out and antisocial behavior, on the quantitative relationship between sexual and aggressive drives, their fusion and defusion, important in depressive and paranoid states, and perhaps on other factors, such as flexibility, rhythm, etc. However, the course of development is also strongly influenced by the attitude of the environment, by the way the mother responds to the infant's needs. The extent to which she is able to guide the development into favorable paths can be decisive.

The same is true with regard to the development of the ego functions and their organization into a structured part of the mind. Though psychoanalytic ego psychology has made great advances during recent decades (Hartmann, 1939a, 1950; Rapaport, 1958, and many others), it is still not far enough advanced to enable us to give an exact survey of the development of the different functions in chronological order. I will therefore limit myself to the description of some well-known facts and a few tentative suggestions.

Let us start by examining the "autonomous" ego functions (Hartmann, (1939a, 1950). Ego development is a maturational process dependent upon bodily growth as well as upon innate Anlage factors. At the same time it is a learning process influenced by the environment. The mother may stimulate the development of certain ego functions, as she stimulates drive development. On the other hand, she may hamper the developmental processes, in connection with peculiarities of her own personality and character, and her affective relationship with the child (see, e.g. Provence and Ritvo, 1961). The outcome can be a fortunate, smooth, as well as an uneven, disturbed growing up of the child.

We assume the mental ego to emerge from the "body schema" (or body ego) (Greenacre, 1960; Winnicott, 1960, et al.). According to Winnicott, the infant perceives his own body as a whole in the second half of the first year. So the basic function of synthesis is already present in the body ego at an early date, perhaps consequent on the binding, integrative tendency inherent in the life process. The differentiation between the self and the outer world probably begins in the first six months, though in a very incomplete way. Even when the child perceives his body as a whole, he still at times experiences a oneness with the mother. The newborn perceives stimuli from within as well as from without. So perception also is one of the first ego functions to develop. At what exact time memory traces begin to be laid down we do not yet know; probably as early as the first months.

Bodily sensations gradually give rise to motor activities, which develop into purposeful actions, e.g. crying, grasping, crawling, walking, etc. Memory traces, which in the beginning are laid down as images, begin to be connected with words after the child has learned to understand speech and gradually to use words himself, at the end of the first year and during the second. Learning starts with imitation. This is especially observable in the development of speech. Vocal communication without word symbols is present in the human infant as it is in the higher animals. But words can be learned only by *imitation*. In addition, connected with the *emotional* ties to the mother, the mechanism

335

of identification begins to be used in the (normal) process of adaptation, precipitating the learning of speech as well as of other functions. Here we encounter an example of the mutual influence of emotional with autonomous ego development. During the first years of life a number of other adaptational mechanisms and processes come into existence. The complexity of the different interrelationships makes the child's ego a vulnerable organization and often interferes with the process of integration. In addition, a complication arises when as an outcome of the oedipal situation the forerunners of superego and ego ideal are internalized into one substructure of the ego. In a "normal" case, however, we have to assume the existence of a basically integrated organization of the ego functions at the end of the oedipal phase. This does not, of course, mean that the learning (and developmental) processes have come to a standstill. Learning continues throughout life, and influences the dynamics of all vital processes. I now come back to the role of the ego in the various symptom formations.

During the preoedipal phase the growing, still "vulnerable" ego encounters a number of danger situations in which anxiety is experienced. "Dangers" come from the outer world in the shape of limitations of need satisfaction and of demands from the environment. They come from the internal world inasmuch as the child feels powerless to provide himself with sufficient satisfaction of needs. From the mother he fears punishment and loss of love; from the inner world it is the narcissistic injury of feeling powerless and threatened by id impulses that is experienced as an unbearable and inescapable danger. Now when the ego is not able to solve the conflict in a harmonious way, it has to take refuge in defensive measures, using several defense mechanisms.

We must, however, distinguish sharply between pathological neurotic defensive processes that lead to an inhibition and impairment of ego activities, and a sound conflict solution that may leave its imprint upon the ego, but without impairing the ego's autonomous functions (in the "conflict-free ego sphere," Hartmann). I suggest, therefore, the following formulation: If the capacity for integration *fails* to solve conflicts without damaging the ego, the impaired ego becomes unable to prevent several adaptation mechanisms from being drawn into neurotic defensive processes, and thus being employed as pathological defense

336

mechanisms. The latter, then, may in their turn cause damage to the ego organization.

The following question here arises: What events are responsible for turning normal adaptation mechanisms into defense mechanisms, made use of in pathological processes? It may sometimes be difficult to decide whether we are dealing with a "normal" or a "pathological" process, because in a number of cases easy transition from a "healthy" to a "pathological" use of mental mechanisms is apparent. With hysterical symptoms, especially in conversion hysteria, a special defense mechanism, namely repression, is predominantly used. Is repression exclusively a pathological defense mechanism? We cannot confirm this. It is well known that (at least in our civilization) large parts of childhood experiences have become unconscious in persons whom we consider to be quite "normal." Memories are repressed. In hysterical neuroses, however, a number of autonomous ego functions have become involved and damaged; e.g., in hysterical conversion symptoms the employment of the motor apparatus may be paralyzed, or the sensorial functions are disconnected, in some instances perception is eliminated, etc. Furthermore, the symptoms cannot be removed without special measures in a treatment situation. Apparently the ego is using the mechanism of repression, which includes an anticathexis against the repressed impulses. It has not succeeded in mastering anxiety and danger situations sufficiently.

In phobias we encounter, among others, one special defense mechanism: avoidance. Do examples exist where we can consider avoidance of danger situations, signaled by anxiety, as a "sound" reaction? Apart from realistic dangers in the outer world which every "healthy" person will try to avoid, we encounter for example, persons living in special circumstances with whom certain id impulses, usually satisfied, have to be held in abeyance in consequence of these unusual circumstances. We do not call it pathological when the person in question avoids situations where these impulses are specially stimulated and apt to raise anxiety. All of us could give examples of such events, e.g. during wartime. In these cases, however, the avoidance remains restricted to the special situation, and as soon as the abnormal circumstances have ceased to exist, the avoidance will be removed also. Here too the mechanism served an adaptational process; it proved to be reversible, and did not involve other ego functions in a permanently damaging way. The phobic patient cannot give up the avoidance; in trying to do so, he is overwhelmed by anxiety and unable to have any kind of sound ego activity. Here, too, we have to assume an additional countermeasure against the id impulses from the side of the ego, that fixates the avoidance and makes it irreversible. The anti-cathecting activity of the ego is most clearly observable in obsessional neurotic symptoms (Freud, 1926). The immediate cause of this disease is the same as in hysteria, and exists in impulses of the oedipal situation which cannot be mastered by the ego. As repression does not succeed in keeping the drive impulses unconscious, according to Freud either because the genital drive organization was too feeble or because the ego began the struggle against the drives prematurely, namely during the anal-sadistic phase, the ego takes refuge in a number of other methods of warding off. First regression takes place, and impulses and fantasies now reveal themselves in an anal-sadistic shape. The ego defends itself against them with an anticathexis, e.g. in the form of reaction formations. Under continual pressure of the id the ego has to produce ever more defensive actions, using such mechanisms as turning against the self, isolation, undoing, denial, etc. Many of the defensive actions are initiated by a severe superego and serve self-punishment. In serious compulsion neuroses more and more ego functions become gradually involved and damaged. The impoverishment of the ego is partly a secondary result of the struggle with the id. But the ego not only *opposes* the id, it also *participates* in the regressive process, and thus falls back upon earlier, more primitive modes of action. This is clearly observable in a regression toward magic thinking and magical acting out. Removal of severe obsessional neurotic symptoms belongs to lengthy psychoanalytic work, and in many cases the symptoms prove to resist any recovery, especially when intellectual understanding of mental connections is isolated from emotional experiences and intellectualization is used in the defensive processes. We know that many of the reaction formations represent exaggerations and distortions of character traits. Cleanliness, orderliness, and economy are reaction formations against the pleasurable impulses to smear, to mess, and to waste. They are considered "normal" and valuable qualities. As we have already described character formation as a "normal" process, we have to look for the boundaries between "normal" and pathological reaction formations. I will come back to this point when embarking upon the study of character formation. Before doing so, I want to examine some more defense mechanisms. Apart from regression and reaction formation, we encounter, in obsessional neurotics, *isolation* and *undoing*.

Isolation is a mental mechanism that finds its place in normality, e.g. in thought processes. Logical and scientific thinking has to isolate thought and to eliminate affect-laden representations ("wishful thinking") from abstract ideas. For abstract thinking neutralized energy is necessary; in wishful thinking drive-cathected energy is employed. Thus the two modes of thinking have to be separated, isolated from each other. Here too, however, the process (of isolation) can be abandoned at will, whereas in neurosis it has become rigid and unalterable. The same is valid for "undoing." "Healthy" people often consider an action, as well as a thought which is a trial action, as unjust, whereupon they will try to undo it by a counteractivity. In our neurotic patients the process of undoing has acquired a compulsive character, and is maintained in situations where it is no longer realistic and appropriate. With paranoid symptoms we encounter identification and projection as defense mechanisms. Both are "normal" adaptive methods in their origin. We have already mentioned the important role of identification in learning processes, as well as in mastering emotional situations. Projection is a "normal" way of dealing with unpleasurable sensations in the infant, and it promotes the distinction between self and outer world. In delusions, however, both mechanisms have become fixated, unchangeable modes of reaction.

In defensive actions the ego may also make use of certain vicissitudes of the instinctual drives which come into existence in the course of development. The "turning inward" of drive impulses is a natural occurrence in the formation of the superego, when aggression is internalized. The process promotes adjustment to the environment. In pathological cases, however, the result is not a better adaptation but a masochistic mode of behavior in consequence of a strong need for self-punishment. Here quantitative factors are decisive. Reversal of drive impulses, e.g., from activity to passivity and vice versa, is continually occurring. The ego makes use of it in a number of adaptational processes. In learning, for example, a passive surrender to the objects and to verbal or written instruction is necessary. The constructive assimilation of what is learned needs a good deal of activity. Fixation of the one or the other tendency leads to pathology. Sublimation or neutralization of drives providing energy for a number of ego achievements is of special importance in many respects. I will return to this point later.

In summary, we may say: Adaptation mechanisms can be employed in neurotic symptoms as (pathological) defense mechanisms. We have to consider the outcome of the process as "health" if the mechanisms are made use of by ego activities in a flexible and changeable way. They belong to pathological phenomena if the process has become fixed and irreversible.

So far we have described merely neurotic disorders (the so-called transference neuroses). We assume that in these neuroses ego development has advanced more or less "normally" until the time of solution of the oedipal complex. In connection with traumatic events (e.g. an overwhelming castration anxiety) a danger situation emerges, resulting in a neurotic defensive attitude on the part of the ego. The formation of symptoms is the outcome of this struggle, together with an inhibition of ego functions. A *secondary* consequence may be regression of ego functions to points of arrest in earlier developmental stages. Symptoms are signs of and substitutes for instinctual satisfaction. This is above all apparent in compulsive actions which can, for example, be substituted for masturbatory acts. Furthermore, the pleasure principle reveals itself in a secondary gain of illness, in a narcissistic satisfaction by rationalization, magical thinking, and in fantasies of omnipotence, etc. The curtailed synthetic capacity comes to the fore in the attempt to incorporate the symptoms secondarily into the ego organization. But often the reverse takes place. Then the ego is secondarily drawn into the sphere of conflicts, sometimes under the impact of a severe superego, and it is invested with drive energy. The result is a paralysis of many of the ego functions including the harmonizing capacity, so that the ego can no longer mediate between the different demands from id, superego, and environment.

CHARACTER FORMATION

In the introduction I recalled the fact that psychoanalytic theory has developed out of the study of ailments in our neurotic patients. Though character formation is a "normal" process in itself, I will keep to the line of including the influence of psychic disorders in our study of the development of character. I have already mentioned the reaction formations leading to a compulsive character that shows distortions of "normal" character traits. This is obvious in the case of exaggerated cleanliness, orderliness, and economy (the so-called "triad of compulsion neurosis"). Earlier, Freud described these qualities as reactions against anal drives which in "normal" development are methods of adaptation to the educational demands of the environment. They are called anal character traits. Similar processes find a place in connection with oral and urethral impulses. Outcomes of them are seen in certain qualities of well-adjusted persons, e.g. in eloquence, based upon oral tendencies, in productive ambition, developing out of urethral strivings, etc. In neurotic patients in whom the ego has failed to solve the anxiety-provoking conflicts in a harmonious way, the qualities become over-emphasized and rigid with more or less damage to other ego functions, including autonomous ones. There are, however, other factors to be examined. Since we see "character" as the usual (habitual) way in which a person deals with the inner and the outer world" (Fenichel, 1945) it is clear that it comprises more than the ego's reactions to id impulses alone; we have to consider the vicissitudes of the development of the ego organization as well. In the "conflict-free sphere" the ego's autonomous functions come into existence. To begin with, the *inborn* potentialities out of which the ego will develop determine to a great extent the outcome of the process of growth. The amount of intelligence, of capacities of perception, reality testing, thought processes, etc., and last but not least the power of neutralization and sublimation, are decisive factors. If one or more of these natural abilities is lacking (or too feeble), the evenness of ego growth will be disturbed and the integrative process is likely to be interfered with, though the synthetic function itself may be normal. But even with a favorable innate disposition opportunities may arise for a maldevelopmen of the ego from the very beginning of life. The disturbances may come from within as well as from without. I have mentioned the influ-

341

ence of an unfavorable drive disposition upon the coming into existence of mental disturbances. Especially is a disproportion between sexual and aggressive drives likely to disturb the course of maturation of the id as well as of ego functions, even in the first years of life, in the pregenital stages. Furthermore, the environmental influence is very important, because the ego, like the id, develops in the interplay of the mother's mind with the infant's mind.

Again we start by looking at pathological phenomena. The "simple" (transference) neuroses originate mainly in the oedipal phase in connection with uncontrollable castration anxiety. The origins of the more severe disturbances, such as borderline cases, psychoses, delinquency, and even so-called character distortions, are to be found in the pre-oedipal phase, and particularly in an early arrest of ego development. When a motherly object is not available, or when the mother herself is very disturbed, the conditions for a healthy development of ego functions in the infant are lacking. The autonomous functions and the learning processes through imitation and identification are in need of an example as well as of stimulation by love, support, and understanding. The mother's love is equally (or even more) indispensable for the infant's learning to cope with id impulses. Too much frustration hampers the ego's growth, resulting in an arrest on primitive levels and an inadequate manipulation of the requirements of the drives. In entering upon the oedipal situation the ego functions are poorly organized, with the consequence that the strong demand for a solution of the oedipus complex and for mastering anxiety leads to an incomplete solution and sometimes to a total disintegration. When, for example, an arrest took place in the phase where the body schema began to be developed (that is, in the phase where the infant perceives his own body as a whole, as different from external entities), the function of distinguishing between self and outer world cannot be formed adequately. In schizophrenic patients we often observe representations of parts of their own bodies as being separate from other parts, as well as a fusion of the boundaries between the self and the object world. In other words, there is a kernel of confusion between self-representations and object representations, and the need to be "one" with the mother cannot be adequately dealt with. A mother who, clinging to the child, is unable to let him develop his own personality, will promote the arrest of the child's ego development at this point (Sandler, 1962). A very disturbed mother, confused, egocentric, distracted, or rapidly changing from love to hate, does not provide the child with a stable image for identification. Consequently, the development of delineated object representations will be defective. The confusion between self and object influences the function of reality testing. A number of other ego functions may be drawn into this pathological process as well. The development of motor actions is dependent upon bodily sensations, including passively experienced movements. A disturbed, unloving mother is unable to hold and to carry around her baby with loving attention (see Winnicott's "holding position" [1960]). This can lead to a lack of satisfaction in the motor sphere, resulting in a poor development of motility in the child.

The lack of a suitable object with which to identify impairs the development of ego activities that have to be learned, such as speech, grasping, walking. In the emotional sphere the child is in need of a loving mother in order to advance from a need-satisfying object relationship toward object constancy. In order to deal adequately with id impulses the ego has to be equipped with a sound self-esteem which can only develop normally if there is a firm object tie.

The lack of a satisfactory love relationship may lead to an arrest of ego ideal development in the magical sphere, where the fantasies of grandeur and omnipotence have to compensate for the various frustrations. In some cases the advance from magical wishful thinking toward realistic logical thinking is never adequately made. When a child with a similar early disturbance of development enters the phallic phase, his ego will certainly be unable to find a more or less harmonious way of solving the many problems involved in the various vicissitudes of the oedipus complex. The defective ego organization is not able to master castration anxiety, and alongside the regression of the drives to pregenital stages the arrested ego functions will overaccentuate the archaic, untimely modes of behavior.

I have already pointed to the differences in the genesis of the classical (transference) neuroses on the one hand and the manifestations of borderline and psychotic disorders on the other (see Chapter 24). In the first ailments the process of organization of ego functions has pro-

343

ceeded in an approximately "normal" way until the oedipal situation. The regressive ego phenomena emerged as a *consequence* of the regression of drives and in connection with the defensive processes provoked by this instinctual regression. In the second conditions, the process of organization of ego functions never reached the level normally belonging to the phallic phase. The ego defects are therefore of a primary nature.

What, now, is the impact of early arrests in ego development upon the formation of a person's character? Our former definition of character as the habitual way of dealing with the inside and the outside worlds can be reformulated in view of recent ego psychology as follows: Character is the habitual way in which integration is achieved, that is, in which a person's ego solves conflicts with the internal world (id and superego), conflicts with the environment, and conflicts within its own organization (between its various functions and capacities).

It is clear that an unevenness in the development of the organizational process, an arrest of some functions and a "normal" course for others, must give rise to conflicts within the ego organization which cannot be solved in a harmonious way. In addition, therefore, to the pathological reaction to needs and instinctual tendencies, to superego and environmental demands, borderline and psychotic patients will show an ever-growing inconsistency in their ego organization, leading to irreversible splits within their egos. The result may be a chaotic ego in which no synthesis is achieved. As a consequence the development of a "habitual way of reacting" is impeded, and stable character traits cannot come into existence. If we still wish to speak of the "character" of these patients, we can designate it only as an unpredictable mode of behavior. A further complication is due to the poor, unequal development of the ego ideal which stops, at least partly, at the stage of unrealistic omnipotent fantasies, provoking magical behavior. In connection with the unstable object relations, the internalization of parental demands gives rise to precarious contents in the superego. But as the "free-floating" aggression that the immature ego was unable to master is incorporated into the superego, the superego can become very sadistic toward the self, with the remarkable outcome that one of the very few habitual reaction patterns in these patients is a rigid masochistic behavior. Processes that will normally be accomplished by ego functions with the use of neutralized energy are in the patients "sexualized" and "aggressivized," that is, invested with deneutralized drive energy. In summary, pathological character formation could be classified under two main headings:

(1) Neurotically diseased persons show distorted character traits in consequence of defensive processes in which anticathexis and reaction formations have produced rigid and irreversible behavior patterns owing to a secondary regression toward stages in ego development of a primitive nature.

(2) Psychotic and borderline patients present a failure of character formation as a consequence of early arrests in ego maturation which could never be passed over and a primary defect in the organization of ego functions, ego ideal, and superego contents.

I want to stress once more that this grouping under two headings is made for the purpose of presentation. In practice we meet with transitions between the various phenomena. Neurotics, for example, may show psychotic mechanisms; obsessional neurotic patients may reveal paranoid traits, delusional and projective processes, etc.; psychotics may start with neurotic disturbances, and they may continue to employ neurotic mechanisms alongside psychotic reactions, depending on the different stages of development the various functions may have reached.

Let us now turn to the question of how we are to envisage the course of events that leads to the molding of a "healthy" character. So far I have placed the words "normal" and "healthy" in quotation marks. It is often said that normality and health are arbitrary concepts. This is certainly true in connection with the moral judgment of a person's behavior. In a given society or group of persons a certain line of conduct can be evaluated as "normal" or "healthy," whereas in another community it may be judged very "abnormal" and "sick." But from a scientific point of view we have, I think, to follow a different line. We speak of bodily health when the various organs of the body function in such a way that stimuli from inside as well as from outside can be assimilated and vital processes are not disturbed.

In psychology I think we should consider a person to be in psychic health when the different areas of the mind have reached a cooperation leading to optimum mental functioning. As the ego is the structured part of the mind that has the disposal of the capacities of action upon stimuli (needs) from the inside as well as upon stimuli (demands) from the environment, we have to look at the nature of the ego organization, and especially at the disposition of its synthesizing capacity, in order to decide between mental health or sickness.

"Character," being the habitual way of dealing with inner and outer worlds, is a property of the ego. "Habitual" implies some kind of constancy in a person's reaction patterns. We know, however, that life is not a static condition. Life processes involve change and fluctuations. The maturational processes reach a certain equilibrium (steady state) in adulthood, but they never come to a complete stop. Learning continues throughout life. Conflicts with the environmental demands and between the different substructures within the personality belong to the ordinary life processes. Therefore the ego organization and its synthesizing capacity have to possess some flexible qualities. We have already said that both id and ego develop out of inborn potentialities. The organization of the various ego functions gradually comes into existence in interplay with the drives in their maturational stages and with the simultaneous object relationships. Therefore character traits, though dependent upon innate qualities are largely the outcomes of adaptational processes. They represent the various adaptation mechanisms, among them reaction formations against id impulses. In addition, character formation develops in interaction with the objects, through imitation and identification. (I want to stress the fact that the concept of "adaptation" includes an active change of the environment whenever such an influence is appropriate and within the person's power.)

As the adaptational processes are in need of a certain amount of constancy in order to function well, we again come upon the fact that a harmonious development requires both constancy *and* mobility. In what way is this seemingly contradictory state of affairs to be achieved? We may compare the state of mind with the oscillation of a pendulum. The central point is to be found in the nature of the ego's synthesizing capacity. Its constancy is to be found in the well-known automatisms based upon innate factors, and developed during growth. When conflicts (from within or from without) arise, the ego is alarmed by signal anxiety and an integrating action is initiated. If a harmony or adapta-

346

tion cannot be achieved, some defensive actions are provoked; regression, for example, can take place. But when it remains "regression in the service of the ego" (Kris, 1952) it will be only temporary. If the ego has at its disposal enough knowledge of the factors involved in the conflict (of demands from the id, from the environment, and from the superego as well as from the ego ideal), and if it has the power to master the different demands, the pendulum will swing from the one side (regression) back to the central point. Perhaps it will temporarily swing to the other side (a defensive compensation), but in the course of time the central point will again be reached. This means that a new equilibrium is achieved. Of course this description applies to an "ideal" concept of a "healthy" character. In practice this ideal will seldom be found. But slight deviations do not impair the person's performances and his well-being, and do not seem to be appreciable. However, an arrest in the pendulum on the one side or the other will cause disturbances of the integrative process, the flexibility having been abolished. Instead of describing more reactions and mechanisms subject to oscillations, I will now summarize as follows: it is a question of quantity (intensity) and of reversibility that decides whether a healthy or a pathological character development will take place. In other words, it evidently depends upon the intensity and the nature of the *energy* involved.

As the character develops in connection with the simultaneous interplay of ego and id, and as mental energy stems, at least largely, from the drives, we have to examine once more the conflicts involved in this interplay. Intensity of energy employed in adaptation and defense is correlated with the intensity of the drive demands in their maturational stage. Regarding the nature of the energy employed, it is decisive whether enough neutralized energy is available for the ego to build up its autonomous functions and to adjust to inner and outer worlds. I think the process of neutralization is dependent upon an inborn nature of the drives, but at the same time also upon an ego quality. This is most clearly seen in sublimation, an adaptation mechanism *par excellence*. Sublimated activities are performed with the use of neutralized energy, but they can only come into existence if the ego has specific talents and properties at its disposal. Logical, scientific thinking requires a special ego ability; artistic performances come about only if the ego possesses enough of the necessary talent.

When a person is gifted with a strong capacity to neutralize drive energy and at the same time with great talents and ego abilities, we may expect him to reach a high degree of integration. It often happens, however, that very talented people are subject to a rigid drive constitution which does not allow for much neutralization. In these cases the development of the ego is impaired in spite of its original gifts, with the result that no synthesis is achieved. The talents and abilities originally present shrivel up. A reduced personality emerges with neurotic symptoms and/or neurotic, rigid character traits. This is especially observable in cases with a lack of congruence between sexuality and aggression, that is, with exceptionally strong aggressive drives. In the struggle against aggression, there cannot be enough energy neutralized, and the surplus of free aggression is internalized into the superego. The sadistically deformed superego demands self-punishment and more restriction of pleasurable activities. It counteracts the development of the person's talents and of many other ego capacities. The rigidity of the masochistic character is well known, and does not need further exposition.

On the other hand, we often encounter a relatively poor ego equipment, and here the main cause for a disturbed development lies in the ego's incapacity to deal with the id, even when the distribution of the drives is not an unequal one. A variety of outcomes is possible, and transitions from a slight unevenness in some ego areas to total inhibitions of nearly every ego activity are observed.

I want to point once more to the fact that the concept of "health" does not cover the concept of "valuable performances." "Health" designates a state of mobile equilibrium of the psychic apparatus. It is a scientific concept and not applicable in a system of values. An interesting example is genius. A man of genius is gifted with great talents, with a high ability to neutralize energy, and with a flexibility of mental mechanisms. But he reveals a strong tendency to conflict. Integration can be achieved in the areas of his creative activities. In other areas of the personality, however, the conflict-solving synthesis may have failed. Here highly valued performances may go together with neurotic symptoms and/or character distortions.

348

As I cannot do justice to all the vicissitudes and outcomes of the various processes touched upon in this paper, I will present the following:

CONCLUSIONS

(1) Conflicts are normal manifestations in the processes of life.

(2) Conflicts stimulate development whenever a person is able to solve them without damaging his integrity.

(3) The solution of conflicts is one of the activities of the ego organization.

(4) The outcome of this solution depends upon a number of factors constituting the synthetic or harmonizing ability.

(5) The nature of this integrative capacity is decisive for a "healthy" as well as for a pathological result.

(6) The capacity to synthesize develops out of innate properties in connection with the other ego functions, in interplay with the development of the instinctual drives, and influenced by object relationships, by the environment at large, as well as by the nature of superego and ego ideal. In connection with object relations, identification is of special importance for the development of ego faculties.

(7) The properties of the instinctual drives, the distribution of libido and aggression, and especially the amount of possible neutralization (sublimation), have a strong bearing upon the final outcome of ego and personality development.

(8) Equally important for a harmonious growth is the ego's capacity to make use of neutralized energy in developing qualities in the conflict-free sphere and to undertake sublimated activities.

(9) Pathology emerges when the integrative process fails; neurotic symptoms are formed when the ego, in conflict with the id, cannot synthesize id impulses and the demands of superego and environment without the pathological use of defense.

(10) Character traits are formed as precipitates of mental processes. They originate in innate properties; they come into existence in the mutual interplay of ego, id, superego, and ego ideal, and the influence of object relations and environment.

(11) "Healthy" character traits allow the ego's synthesizing capacity to oscillate around a central point representing the character constancy.

The oscillations express the mobility of the character and permit of change and reversibility.

(12) "Pathological" character traits are exaggerations and distortions of a "normal" character; they are rigid and irreversible, and may lead to a hardening of the impaired ego organization and its various functions.

CHAPTER 26

Superego, Ego Ideal, and Masochistic Fantasies

(1963)

In this presentation I shall try to elaborate and enlarge on a few points made in previous papers. In Chapter 5 I raised the question what factors play a role in the persistence with which many patients cling to masochistic masturbation fantasies and moral masochistic behavior. In this connection I stressed the importance of narcissistic injuries inherent in the castration complex and penis envy. At that time (1937) I was concerned mainly with the drive manifestations. The essence of my point was that the pain of narcissistic injuries was more intolerable than the suffering from masochistic behavior and fantasies. I illuminated this point by citing the little girl's fantasy, originating in the phallic phase in connection with her penis envy: "I was once in possession of a penis; however I was deprived of it as a punishment for having masturbated." Apparently, masochistic satisfaction compensates for the narcissistically painful idea of having been inferior from the very beginning of life. I gave a few examples of male patients with a strong masochistic attitude in whom the idea—sometimes arising in connection with circumcision—of having an inferior genital organ in comparison with adults or older boys had led to a similar narcissistic wound. In addition, I pointed to the fact that after the establishment of the superego agency, guilt feelings and the need for self-punishment came into action, demanding suffering and reinforcing masochistic behavior. However, at that time I did not go into this problem any further, not

351

yet being aware of the subtle differentiations within the ego and super-ego organizations.

At the present time our knowledge of the structuring of the mind has deepened, and I think we can enlarge our understanding of masochistic behavior and fantasies also by studying the phenomena from the viewpoint of ego psychology and the differentiation between ego ideal and superego proper.

In Chapter 24 I described the ego ideal as an agency that originally serves narcissistic wish fulfillment, with ideals developing out of wishful thinking and fantasies of grandeur and omnipotence. The superego was regarded essentially as an agency of restriction, originating from a lack of immediate need satisfaction, followed by the acceptance of environmental demands and curtailments. In addition, I pointed out that the contents of both ego ideal and superego are centered on the parental images during the oedipal phase. In this period ideals may be briefly described as: "I want to be like my parents" (as omnipotent as I imagine them to be). The superego imposes on the child compliance with parental demands: "I *must* behave as my parents want me to." The consequence of this centralizing process is not only that at the end of the oedipal phase both ego ideal and superego grow together into one substructure of the ego organization, but also that the functions of both agencies become strongly influenced by each other. The fantasies of the oedipal phase, latency, and even more those of adolescence bear the imprint of this mutual interplay.

Fantasies are mental products which compensate for unavoidable deprivations in life. Instinctual impulses can be satisfied directly only to a limited degree. Sexual as well as aggressive tendencies can find a certain discharge in masturbation or masturbatory equivalents during childhood and adolescence. However, the accompanying psychic needs have to find an outlet in fantasies as long as an adult love life with a partner is not yet available. This state of affairs is responsible not only for limited instinctual satisfaction, but may also cause narcissistic injuries at the same time. The experience of being powerless to fulfill sexual needs to a full extent hurts the person's self-love and self-esteem and may reinforce inferiority feelings connected with the little girl's wish for a penis and with the boy's idea of having too small a genital.

Simultaneously, oedipal wishes and rivalry have produced conflicts, anxiety, and guilt feelings. Fantasies of grandeur that are to compensate for the feeling of powerlessness and inferiority become intermixed with the need for self-punishment in connection with guilt. Therefore, fantasies in latency and adolescence often reveal drive satisfaction mingled with punishment and pain. They result in sadomasochistic (masturbatory) fantasies, and sometimes in masochistic acts and behavior. In a patient suffering from masochistic perversions it is quite clear that being beaten, humiliated, or tormented provides him with masochistically deformed drive satisfaction. Usually this holds true only as long as the suffering does not go beyond a certain limit, though in very disturbed patients, such as many psychotics, the damage done to their own bodies and the accompanying masochistic excitement can rise to an astonishingly high level. The problem of masochistic pleasure gain is not yet fully understood, as Freud repeatedly stressed. Where no perversion is present and the situation of being beaten or tormented is merely fantasied, the imagined suffering can reach a great height as well. Yet this is less surprising than the actual self-mutilations of some psychotics.

Nevertheless, we feel entitled to wonder whether guilt feelings, the need for punishment on the part of the superego, and the attempt to deny the idea of having an "inferior" genital apparatus can sufficiently explain the origin of and the clinging to masochistic fantasies. We may ask whether other factors and modes of satisfaction may not be involved, especially when we see masochistic fantasies continuing to exist in our patients during analytic treatment even after the oedipal guilt feelings have diminished or been removed. Moreover, while the idea of a person's clinging to masochistic pain-pleasure to avoid the greater evil of a narcissistic hurt is descriptively valid, it still does not afford a satisfactory explanation of the tenacity with which masochism is retained.

It is my belief that the additional factor is to be found in part in the intermingling of the superego's demands for punishment with the ego ideal's fantasies of grandeur and superiority. Even if the latter feelings are not contained in the wording of the fantasy, the person may unconsciously derive a strong narcissistic satisfaction from them.

Here we have one of the causes that make the masochistic fantasy so persistent and sometimes so resistant to therapeutic influence. If we do not take our patient's communication of his masochistic fantasies at face value, but continue the analysis of those fantasies after bringing to consciousness their sexual and self-debasing meanings, we invariably come upon ideas of self-glorification. It is striking to observe how strongly many patients struggle against the unveiling of their fantasies of grandeur. It often happens that a patient renounces his resistance to oedipal strivings and the connected anxiety and guilt feelings, only to retire behind a nearly unconquerable stronghold of defense, so as to cling to his fantasies of self-aggrandizement. The patient feels himself to be a *unique, exalted person, an exception, superior to his fellow men, a martyr*. These ideas supply him with narcissistic gratification. *The tendency to experience punishment and suffering has become one of the patient's ideals,* his original ideals of being powerful and grand having been deformed into those of being pitiful and grand—*grand in martyrdom*. The severe superego has by now influenced the ego ideal and caused a distortion of its contents.

The first impression on examining masochistic patients might lead to the view that the ego ideal had completely given up its function of wish fulfillment because of the patient's loud and alarming complaints. However, as we have already seen, the idealization of his sufferings is a *hidden* but sometimes *strong source* of gratification. We might say that ideals that normally procure positive, constructive achievements, when guiding the ego in its actions, lead in these patients to negative, unproductive activities. In German we would say that he has become a *Tiefstapler* rather than a *Hochstapler* (a negative rather than a positive swaggerer).

Nevertheless, both forms provide satisfaction, although in the masochist the satisfaction is mixed with distress and pain.

A second mode of influence which a severe, punishing superego may exert on the ego ideal is to impart a compulsive quality to the ideals, which then become imperative demands. In such a case, the idea "I *want* to be as good and powerful as my parents" is replaced by "I *must* be as grand and almighty as my parents." The narcissistic pleasure gain of the fantasy of grandeur is now mixed with the unpleasurable feeling of having to yield to force, of being "unfree." The compulsive quality may now override the pleasurable experience of having a free choice of ideals.

Here I wish to make a point: the question whether a human being is a "free creature," whether a "free will" exists, has occupied the minds of philosophers throughout man's history. I do not intend to go into philosophical questions. It is undeniable that the forces of nature and the necessities of life limit man's freedom to experience pleasure and happiness. What I have in mind here is that the process of mental growth—in this case the development of gratification-providing ideals out of primitive fantasies of grandeur—is inhibited or disturbed by the interaction with a severe, sadistic, compulsive superego which makes for the feeling of inner unfreedom. That this neurotic process is either the consequence of or attendant upon a drive regression toward earlier developmental states is a well-known fact.

The mutual influence of superego and ego ideal revealed in masochistic manifestations comes to the fore in latency and still more clearly in adolescent fantasies and behavior, as I have already mentioned (see also Chapter 23). In psychoanalytic literature we find a wealth of descriptions of sadomasochistic fantasies and fantasies of grandeur and omnipotence. The most beloved books of many children in latency and prepuberty deal with tortured heroes and martyrs, and we know how strongly their ardent readers identify with these heroes. From both a theoretical and a practical point of view, I think it is important to realize the genesis of the intermingling of those two kinds of fantasies in the mutual influence of primitive ideals and the need for punishment.

When we analyze the fantasies of adolescent patients or adults who are emotionally still in adolescence, we are impressed by the fact that it is just the narcissistic gratification of the distorted ideals that makes the patient cling so tenaciously to his masochism. The erotic pleasure derived from his surrender to the torturers (originally parental figures by whom the child imagines he is loved if he submits to punishment and pain) is generally easier to bring to consciousness and release from its pathological outlet than the narcissistic satisfaction of being a great sufferer and a grand martyr. Whether one can succeed in freeing a patient from these primitive ideals of heroic suffering, allowing them to develop into attainable ideals which may provide realistic gratification, depends upon a number of factors, of which I shall later mention three. First, I wish to present some illustrations of my points from clinical material.

It is remarkable to note that we do not only encounter fantasies of grand martyrdom in severely disturbed patients. We may find them in comparatively "healthy" persons as well. I was much impressed by the highly significant role of these fantasies in the mental make-up of a young man who was very successful in his work. His marriage provided sexual satisfaction. However, he felt unable to love and appreciate his wife as a human being of equal merit, as a real companion for life. The patient was an ambitious, highly trained chemist, suffering from strong rivalry with his colleagues. He developed a state of excitement and anxiety whenever he had to demonstrate his capacities in lectures or chemical experiments, though he was highly appreciated and praised by his superiors. He could not escape a feeling of worthlessness and the conviction of being a failure each time he stood before an audience. However, once he had started his performance, everything would go well and he was very successful.

A number of factors connected with his suffering came to the fore, such as anxiety and guilt feelings related to his exhibitionistic tendencies; a strong need for punishment; a fear of passive wishes to surrender to his employer; guilt resulting from rivalry and death wishes toward his competitors; a wealth of sadomasochistic masturbation fantasies; some anal character traits, etc. The patient had been an only child until his tenth year of life, when a sister was born. He had been strongly attached to both parents. His sister's birth had aroused a considerable amount of rage and fury as a reaction to his jealousy and feeling of being rejected in favor of the baby. At the same time, he was very envious of his mother, who had produced a child, a performance he himself would never be able to achieve. During the analysis of this material, there was an improvement in his relationship to his wife, who had borne him three children, and he could be much more tender to her after he understood how strongly he had unconsciously been competing with her and his colleagues. But the anxiety states connected with his work did not subside. We had touched upon fantasies of omnipotence which had originated in early childhood. The patient remembered a strong desire to be grown up in order to be as omnipotent as he imagined both parents to be. However, he could not re-experience these fantasies emotionally. Only after many years of analysis did we discover the cause of his lack of emotion. Part of his fantasies were deformed in a masochistic way. He was no longer the almighty hero who could perform everything he wanted; instead, he imagined himself to be a poor, inferior, worthless, but suffering little child. However, he was an exception, different from any other child, and a grand martyr. This deformation of his fantasies of grandeur was due in part to an identification with his mother, who suffered from many fears and displayed self-pitying, masochistic behavior; in part it was the outcome of his inner ambivalence, later reinforced by guilt feelings and a need for punishment, and acted out in his relations to colleagues and superiors. Fortunately, the adult patient had been able to prevent a considerable part of his talents and abilities from being drawn into the masochistic behavior. He usually could master the compulsion to act out his martyr fantasies before really embarking upon his pursuits. Apparently, some of his ideals had developed into a mature striving for constructive productivity, others had persisted in (and regressed to) an infantile idealization of martyrdom. It was precisely this primitive area of his personality that was responsible for his inhibitions and anxieties.

The various processes described were vicissitudes of the patient's neurotic development, which I shall not discuss in detail. What is relevant to our theme is the nature of the patient's ego ideal, which to some extent regressed to a point of arrest in his early childhood development. In the preoedipal phase the child produces fantasies of omnipotence as a reaction to the narcissistic injuries caused by feelings of powerlessness and inferiority. In this patient, who had been alone with his parents for so long and who had always competed with them, these fantasies were deformed masochistically. Not being able to be "grown up" and as powerful as his parents, he had tried to protect his self-esteem (narcissism) by imagining himself to be a "grand" martyr. The ideal of martyrdom became part of his ego ideal. The *compulsive* character of this ideal was due to the influence of guilt and a severe superego. The very fact that a number of ego functions and some of his ideals had remained outside the neurotic development proved to be decisive for the patient's relative "health" and the final analytic success in mastering the infantile residues in his personality.

Unfortunately, not all cases follow a similarly favorable course in analytic treatment. I can think of another, equally intelligent and gifted male patient, who suffered from a more severe work inhibition, although in many life situations he apparently acted quite normally. His work disturbance proved to be a result of distorted ideals similar to those cited in the previous example. In addition to numerous guilt feelings and acts of self-punishment analysis revealed fantasies of grandeur deformed into the idea of being a "grand martyr." They were covered up, however, by the notion that all people besides himself were worthless and inferior. These notions had acquired a nearly delusional character. They were used as a defense against the distorted ideals of his being an exceptionally grand martyr, and may be considered another part of a "personal delusion" described by me in Chapter 8. There I drew attention to an observation made about individuals who functioned normally in several areas of life but who harbored deeply hidden ideas of being rejected and hated by their environment. At the present time I consider these imaginings to be only part of the delusional system. They are reversals of fantasies about other people being inferior and worthless, fantasies which in turn are used to hide the deeper layer of megalomanic "grand martyr fantasies." This patient succeeded only incompletely in mastering his delusional ideals. A core of them retained the delusional aspect, coming to the fore time and again, continuing to exist, and resisting every therapeutic influence.

We encounter these phenomena in female patients as well. At first glance we might be tempted to expect them to be of even greater significance because the little girl's feelings of inferiority are based on the anatomical fact that her genital is inside her body and not visible from the outside, as is the boy's organ. Her wish for a penis is the consequence of a biological datum that underlies her psychic reaction of feeling inferior and is "rock-bottom," as Freud pointed out in "Analysis Terminable and Interminable" (1937). However, we must take into account the fact that normal femininity requires surrender to a male partner and that feminine ideals do not necessarily have to cling to fantasies of grandeur and superiority. Only in so far as the active, masculine part of her personality is concerned, does a woman need fantasies of grandeur similar to men's. In female patients with a strong masculinity complex we do, as a matter of fact, come upon omnipotent fantasies comparable to those of men. I can remember a young woman who displayed an abundance of ideas about being inferior, worthless, and incapable of any achievement in spite of her intelligence and her professional standing. It was nearly impossible to convince her that fantasies of grandeur were hidden behind her self-depreciation. In defending herself against these (masochistically distorted) omnipotent ideas, she behaved as if she were feeble-minded. Finally, she could consider the possibility that fantasies of being a "grand martyr" were present in the hidden depths of her personality. However, she never succeeded in mastering them adequately and a core of a distorted ego ideal and some disturbed ego functions continued to exist.

I now want to re-examine a fantasy of one of the two women patients discussed in Chapter 1. At that time (1927) I wished to draw attention to the developmental stages of little girls prior to the establishment of the positive oedipal complex, the feminine attachment to the father. Some years earlier Freud had shown that this father relationship was initiated by the castration complex; that is, the little girl's discontent with her genital apparatus and her desire for a penis made her turn to a passive love for her father, the penis wish being replaced by a longing for a child from him. In my 1927 paper, I was able to demonstrate a still earlier developmental stage in which the little girl loves her mother actively and strives to possess her in a way similar to that of the little boy. This is the period in which the little girl has not yet accepted her own genital and the lack of a penis, and still believes that one will grow. In other words, the female negative oedipus complex precedes the castration complex, which in its turn initiates the positive oedipus situation. The negative form corresponds to the phallic stage of the preoedipal phase of development, the preoedipal mother attachment as it was called by Freud later on.

I return now to the fantasy of the young girl mentioned above. Her life history revealed a number of events, re-experienced in part in the transference situation, which seemed to prove the point in question. It came to the fore with particular clarity in a fantasy (Freud, 1919). Between her eighth and tenth years of life my patient produced what she called her "hospital fantasy." I cite from my previous paper:

> The gist of it [the hospital fantasy] was as follows. A large number of patients went to a hospital to get well, but they had to endure the most frightful pains and tortures. One of the most frequent practices was that they were flayed alive. The patient had a feeling of shuddering pleasure when she imagined their painful, bleeding wounds. Her associations brought recollections of how her younger brother sometimes pushed back the foreskin of his penis, whereupon she saw something red, which she thought of as a wound. The method of cure in her fantasy was therefore obviously a representation of castration. She identified herself on one occasion with the patients, who at the end always got well and left the hospital with great gratitude, but generally she had a different role. *She was the protecting, compassionate Christ, who flew over the beds in the ward in order to bring relief and comfort to the sick people.*

The patient's further associations affirmed that the identification with Christ in the hospital fantasy depicted her possessive love for her mother, Christ having been born "without a father" and therefore being his mother's sole possessor. The idea of being her mother's lover was followed by castration (Christ's crucifixion), that is, by the patient's acceptance of the lack of a penis, leading then to a passive love for and surrender to the (God) father. The detail of flying around the ward is symbolic of masturbation.

In re-examining this fantasy now, we are immediately struck by the form it took. Alongside the sadomasochistic pleasure gain in the sphere of the instinctual drives, it provided the patient with a narcissistic gratification in the glorification of the self. It is a fantasy of grandeur *par excellence*. Apparently, it has to compensate for the narcissistic injury of the girl's conviction that her genital is "inferior." The Christ identification, however, reveals a special feature of the fantasy of grandeur. The omnipotent idea of being a God was cast into the form of being a *suffering* God, a crucified martyr, grand in power as well as

360

in martyrdom. It is a perfect example of the deformed fantasy described above, which shapes and colors the ego ideal. Obviously, in our patient, too, the Christ-hospital fantasy had been absorbed by her ego ideal. However, at the time of her analytic treatment I did not realize this state of affairs. I did recognize the narcissistic satisfaction, but I did not see how strongly the patient's ideals were influenced by her fantasy. I now find proof of its active power in the patient's behavior after the termination of her analysis. In spite of the fact that she was an artist with remarkable talents, she decided to become a nurse, obviously being forced to act out the fantasy in life. Her ideal was now to care for suffering people, to tend and cure them. Of course the omnipotent facet of the fantasy could not be realized and this caused a permanent disappointment. After a year of nursing she came to see her error, gave up the hospital work, and returned to her artistic profession.

It would be interesting to speculate whether the acting out of the fantasy in real life might have been prevented if I had recognized during the analytic treatment the significance of the fantasy in the patient's ideal formation, its place in her ego organization and total mental make-up. Unfortunately, I cannot answer this question, as the relative proportions of the different processes and forces involved are not measurable.

However, in a number of more recently treated cases I have the impression that sometimes a thorough analysis of the deformed ideals may bring great relief and a better adjustment to reality and realistic ideals.

I now return to the earlier question what factors may be responsible for a person's production of primitive "grand martyr" ideals. I promised to mention three of them.

In the first place, the personalities and attitudes of the parents (and other idealized figures) are important. If both parents (or the one with whom the patient is most strongly identified) are themselves sadomasochistic characters, the primitive ideals will from the very beginning bear a masochistic imprint. In Chapter 23 I pointed out how difficult it can be for a young person to give up his ideals formed through identification with parental images. Therefore it is sometimes almost impossible to induce an adolescent patient to exchange his infantile masochistic ideals, acquired from parents who are themselves sadomasochistic, for other, more suitable ideals.

A second factor is to be found in the patient's own personality; on the one hand, there is the nature of his drive equipment; on the other, there are the talents, the abilities, and the ego's capacity for sublimation, which the ego ideal can make use of in building up ideals with positive, constructive goals. Gifted persons, if freed from their inhibitions, masochistic symptoms, and guilt feelings, will have a much better opportunity for finding suitable ideals and realizing them to a certain extent than the majority of limited people. The endeavor to free a patient to such an extent that he can adjust his ideals to his innate and early acquired potentialities is a difficult but valuable enterprise.

To avoid misunderstanding I want to add that I do not have in mind "gifts," "talents," and "ideals" in the framework of a system of values. I mean only a more extended range of possibilities for neutralized activities, regardless of how they are valued by a given society, group or community. The milieu's value system is of importance only in so far as the person in question is dependent upon approval or disapproval from the environment. Complete independence rarely occurs, but degrees of dependency vary considerably.

This leads us to the third factor, which is provided by the person's wider environment in still another connection. The realizing of his ideals is determined not only by his own capacities. The environment must provide satisfactory opportunities for their realization, or it must be possible for the individual to change environmental circumstances according to his ideals. (Here emerges a sociopsychological problem with which I shall not deal.)

In conclusion, I want to make two additional points.

(1) Masochism is a mode of instinctual gratification that in itself need not be pathological. Up to a certain point, it finds a place in normal sexual life. It has a special relation to female sexuality, as Freud and others have pointed out on several occasions. In a sublimated form masochism can be helpful and even necessary for learning to bear the inevitable distress and pain inherent in human life, with its illnesses, natural catastrophes, and unavoidable misery of a

social nature. With these "normal" events masochistic pleasure is not sought exclusively for its own sake. It enables the person to attain a certain resignation alongside productive activities in his personal and social life. In pathology, and especially in moral masochistic behavior, the person is restricted to masochistic pleasure, and his distorted ideals do not allow him to find satisfaction in constructive sublimated pursuits.

(2) My last point concerns an evaluation of recent ego psychology. It is often doubted whether the theory of the structuralization of the mind is of any value for the practical application of psychoanalysis. I have two answers to this question:

(a) A general one, which applies to every science: psychoanalytic theory always was and continues to be the outcome of a wealth of observations made on human beings, first by Freud and then by other psychoanalysts; it is constantly being enlarged and modified by new observations, the understanding of which has been made possible by theoretical knowledge.

(b) A specific one: our refined insight into the different functions of the structured mind, and their mutual interplay, enables us to support our patients in the comprehension and the mastery of their inner conflicts in a much more thorough and differentiated way than formerly.

I have presented this paper as a case in point, and I hope it has demonstrated the value of our theoretical knowledge for practical purposes. It is the suffering of our patients and of mankind in general that stimulates us never to give up our endeavor to deepen our knowledge of the functioning of the human mind.

CHAPTER 27

Remarks on Genesis, Structuralization, and Functioning of the Mind

(1964)

In psychoanalysis the genetic approach to mental phenomena has proved its intrinsic value for the understanding of the human mind. For the explanation of adult behavior, normal as well as pathological, the tracing back to its origins in early childhood is a necessary procedure. However, the genetic approach is only part of the picture. Without taking into account the maturational processes, including the development of the different functions, the structuralization and the differentiation of the mind, the influence of the environment and the inner and outer conflicts which give rise to reactive and defensive processes, the explanation remains one-sided and incomplete.

I am aware of the fact that these statements are self-evident and generally accepted. The reason I mention them here lies in the fact that though they are common knowledge, they nevertheless are often neglected. I am referring to those authors who do not clearly distinguish between genetic determinants (to borrow a term of Hartmann's) and developmental end products of mental processes, especially in connection with the structuralization into id, ego, and superego with their different functions. This lack of distinction may lead to oversimplifications in two opposite directions. On the one hand, functions and activities of an adult's ego organization are sometimes described as if they were merely a defense against "oral," "anal," or "phallic" tendencies, which may be genetic determinants, but certainly do not cover the whole picture. This lack of a clear distinction between function and genesis was repeatedly stressed and criticized by Hartmann (1955), by Hartmann and Loewenstein (1962), etc. On the other hand, processes occurring in infancy are sometimes described in terms of an adult's (pathological) behavior (Melanie Klein, e.g.). Some authors speak, for instance, of an infant's or toddler's "schizophrenic ego split." It is quite clear that an infant's ego organization does not yet exist as a system and therefore cannot yet be "split." This kind of confusion was mentioned by me in connection with the antedating of the system superego in the infant's first months of life (Chapter 6). Thus I am in agreement with Hartmann that it is necessary to distinguish clearly between genesis and function and I think all psychoanalysts should take his warning to heart.

However, a number of questions arise in view of this general statement. I shall try to enter into a few of them. What happens to the different mental functions in the course of the maturation and development into adulthood? For the sake of clarity it seems preferable to examine the substructures of the mind separately, although I am quite aware of the fact that development occurs in a constant mutual interplay.

We begin by examining the id, the area of the instinctual drives. Freud pointed out at an early stage of psychoanalysis that the id functions according to the pleasure principle. The drives strive for instinctual gratification. This basic id function remains in existence during an individual's whole life. However, the shape of the drives changes in the course of the development. In infancy we observe the partial drives, oral, anal, and phallic, which gradually develop into the mature genital drive. I need not go further into this part of psychoanalytic theory which is well known and affirmed by numerous observations.

We next turn to the ego. Nowadays we prefer to speak of the "system" ego as an organization of a number of functions. In the earliest stages of psychoanalytic theory formation Freud used the term "ego" in different, not always clearly defined, ways. However, in *The Ego and the Id* (1923b) he definitely describes the ego as a structured part of the mind, as a "coherent organization of mental processes." It comprises consciousness, it controls partial processes, it is master of motility, and it is the agency which makes use of repression (and defense) in cases where intinctual strivings cannot be discharged or are not allowed to become conscious. The ego is that part of the mind which has direct contact with the outer world and acts according to the reality principle. Its basic functions are mediation between inner and outer world (passive and active), adaptation, and, finally, synthetization (or harmonization) of the various demands from inside and from the environment. The mature ego has developed a large number of singular functions, which may participate in the achievements of the basic functions of adaptation and integration. With Hartmann we distinguish between primary autonomous ego functions, e.g., perception, memory, reality testing, judging, etc., and other ego functions, which develop as reaction to or defense against instinctual tendencies and environmental demands. The latter group of functions may obtain a "secondary" autonomy if they are able to solve the conflicts with the id and the milieu and to enter into the "sphere free of conflict." However, both the primary autonomous and the secondary autonomous functions may be drawn into the sphere of conflict at a later stage and in pathological development the ego may not be able to get back its ability to master the conflicts, at least not without impairment of the ego organization itself.

We now return to our question: what happens to the different functions (and here we speak of ego functions) in the course of life? Ego functions are not yet present in the newborn child, though we assume with Freud and Hartmann that the individual potentialities out of which they are to develop are present in the archaic Anlage; but they come into being only after birth and under the influence of experience and learning processes. The infant is also in need of support of his mother's love and care in order to develop them in a favorable way. An organization of the ego functions into the system ego finds place only in a much later stage. In order to explain the great and obvious differences between the adult's and the little child's ego activities Hartmann has introduced the concept of "change of function," a very valuable concept indeed. However, I think we have to investigate to which ego functions this concept applies. In examining those ego functions which emerge in the conflictual sphere, e.g., in a conflict between instinctual tendencies and the ego, we have to accept that a change of function takes place if the ego succeeds in mastering the id striving that cannot be discharged directly. I shall give two examples out of many that could be described: (1) During the anal phase of instinctual development the little child has to learn to abandon the pleasure of messing and soiling himself, his clothes and his surroundings. The child's ego may reach this achievement by developing reaction formations of cleanliness, orderliness, and economy (the well-known "anal triad"). These reaction formations may gradually become character traits, automatisms. Later on these character traits, though originated as a defense against id strivings, may change their function and, for instance, enter into hygienic or economic activities which serve quite different purposes of a personal as well as of a social kind. They may have their share in processes of adaptation and organization and sublimated activities. (2) Compassion can genetically be traced back to a reaction formation to strong sadistic impulses. As a character trait in later childhood and adulthood it no longer functions as a defense, but it may serve social adaptation, integration, and contact with fellow men. At least, this state of affairs applies to "normal" development, where the ego's original defensive function may gain secondary autonomy. In pathological cases the conflict fails to be solved and the ego has constantly to ward off the pressing instinctual demands. To summarize: change of function in defensive processes can be observed in normal development; in pathology the defensive function persists.

In regard to the primary autonomous ego functions I think we observe the reverse situation. Perception and reality testing, for instance, continue to exist throughout life, though their contents may be enlarged by learning processes. More knowledge about the real facts of life may widen the scope of the fields covered; the functional side of the processes, however, need not be changed in "healthy" development. On the other hand, in pathological cases the autonomous functions may be drawn into the conflictual sphere with the consequence of a change of function, e.g., in being employed for defensive purposes. This is most clearly observed with psychotics. A case in point is a patient suffering from delusional jealousy. During a walk with his wife, he perceives an acquaintance greeting them and for a few seconds looking at his wife. This perception is instantly drawn into the patient's delusional system; it is used for accusing his wife of infidelity and functions as a warding off of his own impulses to commit adultery. The patient's reality testing is distorted in a way similar to his perception and both have changed their original function of learning about the real facts of life into the defensive function of warding off unacceptable instinctual tendencies.

Regarding the "basic" (or general) ego functions of mediating between the inner world and environmental influences, of adaptation and integration, I think we encounter a similar situation. In "normal," harmonious development those basic functions persist essentially unchanged throughout life. They merely become more consolidated and cover a larger field of knowledge through learning. In pathological conditions the functions may be changed, probably mainly to be used in warding-off processes.

If this train of thought should prove to be correct, we may summarize as follows: under "normal" conditions a change of ego functions takes place in the area of secondary autonomy, whereas the general, basic functions and the primary autonomous singular functions keep to their original aims. Under pathological conditions, however, every ego function is exposed to change by being drawn into the pathological process. It is decisive for the form and the severity of the mental illness how many and which functions share this fate. Here emerges the necessity for detailed, clinical research, which I cannot pursue at this time. A single tentative remark suggests that a contribution to the theme of "choice of neurosis" is to be expected from these considerations. In all mental disturbances the basic functions of adaptation and integration are affected, though in psychoses they are much more severely affected and lead to a more or less complete withdrawal from the outer world, whereas in neurotic disorders a certain contact with the object world is maintained.

Could it be that one important factor in these differences is to be found in the fact that in neuroses *secondary autonomous* ego functions lose their autonomy on re-entering the sphere of conflict and are subject to change, whereas in psychotic disorders the *primary autonomous* ego functions are impaired from the very beginning of the illness and therefore lose their orignial function? Several authors have described this process as occurring on the basis of an irregular, faulty, or interrupted development of ego functions in very early childhood and a regression to these points of arrest.

This seems to be the place to recall to mind an early paper of Freud's (1911) in which he describes how the pleasure principle, which originally governs the mental life, is gradually replaced by the reality principle as a reaction to disappointments and frustrations. At that time there did not yet exist a workable psychoanalytic theory of ego development. Now we know that the substitution of the reality principle for the pleasure principle occurs in connection with the growing organization of ego functions, a process which under normal conditions is stimulated by frustrations. We should not forget that in the same paper Freud states that this substitution does not abolish the pleasure principle. In fact, Freud says, the reality principle is its safeguard: an immediate, but in its consequences uncertain pleasure experience is renounced in order to gain a later, but certain one acquired along new paths. We may add: not only along new paths, but also with new means, new contents, and last, but not least, with a new mode of satisfaction. Though ways, means, contents, and modes of satisfaction change during the course of development, the original tendency to gain some kind of gratification is retained. Maybe we could assume that no mental action whatsoever is taken without the (often unconscious) expectation of acquiring some kind of gratification or of avoiding unpleasure. It is hardly necessary to recall that under the pressure of overpowering forces in the outside world it may happen that neither goal is attainable to the slightest degree. On the other hand, even neurotic suffering, which originates in the person's own mental life, contains some mode of satisfaction. In Chapter 26 I give an example of "pleasurable" suffering in the shape of grandeur fantasies of being an exceptional and very great martyr.

This idea brings us to our next point, the examination of the third mental substructure: the superego and ego ideal system. In Chapter 24 I tried to investigate the precursors (or, to use Hartmann's term, the genetic determinants) of both conscience and ideals. I preferred to examine them separately because their original functions are opposite to each other, the conscience (superego in a narrower sense) coming into being as a restricting and prohibiting agency, whereas the ego ideal emerges as an agency providing satisfaction through hallucinating, magical wishful thinking, and fantasies of omnipotence. I also drew attention to the fact that in the course of development, that is, at the time of the passing of the oedipus complex, both agencies merge together in one substructure of the mind, the superego in a wider sense. This close contact necessarily provokes a mutual influence so that ideals may become "oughts" (you "ought" to live up to a certain ideal, instead of you "wish" to live up to it), and prohibitions may become ideals, e.g., complete obedience to the demands of an authority may be idealized. However, they show a compulsive character and are used as a defense against anxiety-provoking impulses. As far as they limit the person's inner freedom to choose his own ideals and restrictions, we are entitled to see them as having entered the realm of pathology.

In connection with the merging into one mental substructure of ideals and prohibitions during the passing of the oedipus complex Hartmann and Loewenstein (1962) prefer to speak of the superego system *tout court* and to distinguish between the idealizing and the self-criticizing functions of the superego. I agree with the authors, that their conceptualization is simpler, more in line with the concept of the ego, being an organization of functions and therefore more appropriate than the one, used by me so far, which conceived of the ego ideal and the restricting superego as two sides of the "superego in a wider sense."

In another context Hartmann and Loewenstein propose to apply the concept of "change of function," used in ego psychology, to the system superego as well. However, the authors do not indicate which functions are subject to such a change and under which conditions the changes take place. I shall try to make some remarks to this point in following a path similar to my previous one regarding ego functions. As a matter of fact it is quite obvious that a number of a "normal" adult's ideals are very different from the little child's grandeur and omnipotence fantasies and the idealization of his parental images, though we should not overlook the fact that much of the original

370

magic and wishful thinking is still present in the conscious or unconscious mind of a "healthy" adult. Hartmann and Loewenstein also mention this fact.

However, I think we are entitled to put the question: *what* has changed in the more mature ideal functioning? Obviously the *contents* have changed, under the influence of the total personality as it increasingly takes reality factors into account. I also suggest that the mode of satisfaction provided by living up to the ideals has changed. Gratification drawn from thinking, from intellectual activities, from scientific and artistic, in short, from sublimated performances, is clearly different from direct instinctual satisfaction as well as from the narcissistic gratification provided by imagining oneself omnipotent.

But has the original *function* of procuring some kind of satisfaction really changed? I do not see that this is the case, at least not in harmonious development. Hartmann and Loewenstein (1962) describe as an example of a "change of function" in the superego system the more mature ego ideal's "striving after perfection," "a direction-giving function, which is relatively independent of the objects and relatively independent also of the instinctual precursors." I quite agree with the authors as to the description of the possible shape of an adult's ego ideal. However, is "striving after perfection" not a search for satisfaction? After all, as long as a person believes more or less that "perfection" can really be achieved by any human being, is it so far away from magic, wishful thinking?

My notion is that the *basic* function of ideal formation—the aiming at narcissistic gratification and the attempt to guide the ego's activities in that direction—has not been changed in principle. The little child also, though not very successfully, tries to realize his wishes of being as powerful and perfect as he imagines his parents to be. What has undergone a transformation are the form and contents of the ideals and the paths along which the person attempts to gain satisfaction. The transformation, I think, has become possible in connection with the development of ego functions through learning and experience in contact with the outside world, in short, under the impact of the reality principle. Among the many special ego qualities which are of importance for this transformation process is the ego's capacity for neutral-

371

izing drive energy, which then may allow the superego system to make use of more or less neutralized energy. This point is more extensively elaborated by Hartmann and Loewenstein.

Under pathological conditions, however, e.g., in the above-described case where ideals have a compulsive character, the function may have changed from a pleasure-providing into a restricting one. In a similar way the "oughts" and "ought-nots" of the restricting superego which have become ideals may give satisfaction, but both processes, in adopting each other's original functions, have caused a distortion of the system superego and cannot be looked at as a harmonious developmental outcome.

Therefore I propose the following summary: if functions of the superego system are drawn into the sphere of conflicts for which the personality is unable to find a "sound" solution, pathological conditions have entered the picture with the consequence that a change of superego functions may take place. In harmonious development the *original* functions persist, though their *contents* and the *modes* of both gratification and unavoidable renunciation may be subject to transformations. This train of thought seems to be in line with Freud's statement that the superego is closer to the id than is the ego. This is valid not only as to the dynamics and economics in mental life, which are clearly described by Hartmann and Loewenstein in connection with aggression; it seems to apply also to the functions of *pleasure-seeking* and *renouncing* under the pressure of object relations. The superego has no direct contact with the real factors in the environment. It is only the ego that through its different functions, i.e., perception, action, reality testing, etc., can react to and act upon the outer world, and learns to store knowledge about all kinds of reality factors. And only through the mediation of the ego organization is the superego indirectly influenced by the environment, as is the id.

We here touch upon a field in need of thorough research, namely, on the influence which the mutual *interplay* between id, ego organization, and superego system exercises upon the various functions of the substructures of the mind as well as upon their contents and the modes of satisfaction. Many investigations in this field have already been carried out by Freud and others in a general way. However, more detailed research is still needed to gain a deeper insight into the manifold conditions which lead to the development of a harmonious personality or to pathological disturbances. I am quite aware of the fact that the propositions brought forward here are of a tentative nature and in need of either confirmation or substitution by more appropriate ones.

Bibliographical Notes

CHAPTER 1 was originally published as "Zur Entwicklung des Oedipuskomplexes der Frau" in the *Internationale Zeitschrift für Psychoanalyse*, 13:269-282, 1927. The English translation appeared in *The International Journal of Psycho-Analysis*, 9:332-345, 1928, and was reprinted in *The Psychoanalytic Reader*, ed. R. Fliess. New York: International Universities Press, 1948, pp. 207-222.

CHAPTER 2 was originally published as "Zu den Problemen der Weiblichkeit" in the *Internationale Zeitschrift für Psychoanalyse*, 19:385-415, 1933. The authorized English translation by Irmarita K. Putnam appeared in *The Psychoanalytic Quarterly*, 2:489-518, 1933.

CHAPTER 3 was originally published as a review of Rado, S.: *Die Kastrationsangst des Weibes* in the *Internationale Zeitschrift für Psychoanalyse*, 21:598-605, 1935. It is here published in English for the first time.

CHAPTER 4 was originally published as "Hemmung und Narzissmus" in the *Internationale Zeitschrift für Psychoanalyse*, 22:198-222, 1936. It is here published in English for the first time.

CHAPTER 5 was read at the Fourteenth Congress of the International Psycho-Analytical Association, Marienbad, 1936. It was originally published as "Masochismus und Narzissmus" in the *Internationale Zeitschrift für Psychoanalyse*, 23:479-489, 1937. It is here published in English for the first time.

CHAPTER 6 was originally published in *The International Journal of Psycho-Analysis*, 20:408-417, 1939.

CHAPTER 7 was originally published in *The Psychoanalytic Study of the Child*, 2:75-83. New York: International Universities Press, 1946.

CHAPTER 8 was originally published in *The International Journal of Psycho-Analysis*, 28:7-11, 1947. It was reprinted in *The Year-book of Psychoanalysis*, 4:50-60. New York: International Universities Press, 1948.

CHAPTER 9 was presented in a slightly different version at a meeting of the Nederlandse Vereniging voor Psychotherapie, October 18, 1947. It is here published in English for the first time.

CHAPTER 10 was originally published in *Searchlights on Delinquency*, ed. K. R. Eissler. New York: International Universities Press, 1949, pp. 246-255.

CHAPTER 11 was read before the annual meeting of the Nederlandse Vereniging voor Psychiatrie en Neurologie, December 11, 1948. It was originally published in *Folia Psychiatrica, Neurologica, et Neurochirurgica Neerlandica*, 53(1):18-31, 1950. It is here published in English for the first time.

CHAPTER 12 was read at the Congrès de Psychiatrie, Paris, 1950. It is here published in English for the first time.

CHAPTER 13 was originally published in *The Psychoanalytic Study of the Child*, 5:153-174. New York: International Universities Press, 1950.

CHAPTER 14 was the opening paper in the Symposium on "Re-evaluation of the Rôle of the Oedipus Complex" at the Seventeenth Congress of the International Psycho-Analytical Association, Amsterdam, August 5-9, 1951. It was originally published in *The International Journal of Psycho-Analysis*, 33:335-342, 1952.

CHAPTER 15 was originally published in *Drives, Affects, Behavior*, ed. R. M. Loewenstein. New York: International Universities Press, 1953, pp. 153-168.

CHAPTER 16 was the introduction to the discussion in the Symposium on "Problems of Psycho-Analytic Training" at the Eighteenth Congress of the International Psycho-Analytical Association, London, July 28, 1953. It was originally published in *The International Journal of Psycho-Analysis*, 35:184-187, 1954.

CHAPTER 17 was originally published as "Groepsbesprekingen met Stiefmoeders" in *Maandblad voor Geestelijke Volksgezondheid*, 9:305-312, 1954. It is here published in English for the first time.

CHAPTER 18 was read at the Nineteenth Congress of the International Psycho-Analytical Association, Geneva, July 24-28, 1955. It was originally published in *The International Journal of Psycho-Analysis*, 37:354-359, 1956. It was also published as "Anmerkungen zur psychoanalytischen Triebtheorie" in *Entfaltung der Psychoanalyse*, ed. A. Mitscherlich. Stuttgart: Klett, 1956, pp. 194-204; and in *Psyche*, Heidelberg, 10:194-204, 1956.

CHAPTER 19 was originally published as "Psychoanalytische Ich-Psychologie und ihre Bedeutung für die Fehlentwicklung bei Kindern" in *Acta Psychotherapeutica, Psychosomatica et Orthopaedagogica*, 4:195-202, 1956. It is here published in English for the first time.

CHAPTER 20 was a contribution to the Symposium on "The Theory of Technique" held at the Centenary Scientific Meetings of the British Psycho-Analytical Society, May 5, 1956. It was originally published in *The International Journal of Psycho-Analysis*, 37:456-459, 1956.

CHAPTER 21 was originally published in *The Psychoanalytic Sudy of the Child*, 12:114-126. New York: International Universities Press, 1957.

CHAPTER 22 was originally published in *The International Journal of Psycho-Analysis*, 40:169-179, 1959.

CHAPTER 23 was read at the Twenty-First Congress of the International Psycho-Analytical Association, Copenhagen, July, 1959. It was originally published in *The Psychoanalytic Study of the Child*, 15:95-103. New York: International Universities Press, 1960.

CHAPTER 24 was read at the Twenty-Second Congress of the International Psycho-Analytical Association, Edinburgh, August, 1961. It was originally published in *The Psychoanalytic Study of the Child*, 17:94-106. New York: International Universities Press, 1962.

CHAPTER 25 was the subject of a discussion at the Twenty-Third Congress of the International Psycho-Analytical Association, Stockholm, July-August, 1963. It was originally published in *The International Journal of Psycho-Analysis*, 44:1-11, 1963.

CHAPTER 26 is here published for the first time.

CHAPTER 27 was originally published in *The Psychoanalytic Study of the Child*, 19:48-57. New York: International Universities Press, 1964.

Bibliography

Abraham, K. (1920), Manifestations of the Female Castration Complex. *Selected Papers*. London: Hogarth Press, 1927.

———(1921), Contributions to the Theory of the Anal Character. *Selected Papers*. London: Hogarth Press, 1927.

———(1924a), A Short Study of the Development of the Libido, Viewed in the Light of Mental Disorders. *Selected Papers*. London: Hogarth Press, 1927.

———(1924b), The Influence of Oral Eroticism on Character Formation. *Selected Papers*. London: Hogarth Press, 1927.

———(1924c), Character Formation on the Genital Level of Libido-Development. *Selected Papers*. London: Hogarth Press, 1927.

Adrian, E. D.(1946), The Mental and the Physical Origins of Behaviour. *Int. J. Psycho-Anal.*, 27.

Aichhorn, A. (1925), *Wayward Youth*. New York: Viking Press, 1944.

Alexander, F. (1923), The Castration Complex in the Formation of Character. *Int. J. Psycho-Anal.*, 4.

Ashby, W. R. (1952), *Design for a Brain*. New York: Wiley.

Balint, M. (1954), Analytic Training and Training Analysis. *Int. J. Psycho-Anal.*, 35.

Bibring, E. (1936), The Development and Problems of the Theory of the Instincts. *Int. J. Psycho-Anal.*, 22, 1941.

Bibring, G. L. (1954), The Training Analysis and Its Place in Psychoanalytic Training. *Int. J. Psycho-Anal.*, 35.

Bolk, L. (1918), *Hersenen en Cultuur*. Amsterdam: Scheltema en Holkema.

———(1926), *Das Problem der Menschwerdung*. Jena: Fischer.

Bonaparte, M. (1949), De la Sexualité de la Femme. *Rev. Franç. Psychanal.*, 13.

Breuer, J. & Freud, S. (1895), Studies on Hysteria. *Standard Edition*, 2. London: Hogarth Press, 1955.

Brierley, M. (1947), Psycho-Analysis and Integrative Living. *Trends in Psycho-Analysis*. London: Hogarth Press, 1951.

377

Brun, R. (1953), Über Freuds Hypothese vom Todestrieb; eine kritische Untersuchung. *Psyche*, 7.

Brunswick, R. M. (1940), The Pre-Oedipal Phase in Libido Development. *Psychoanal. Quart.*, 9.

Deutsch, H. (1925), Zur Psychoanalyse der weiblichen Sexualfunktionen. *Neue Arbeiten zur ärtzlichen Psychoanalyse, 5.* Vienna: Internationaler psychoanalytischer Verlag.

——(1930), The Significance of Masochism in the Mental Life of Women. *Int. J. Psycho-Anal.*, 11.

Eidelberg, L. (1935), Das Problem der Quantität in der Neurosenlehre. *Int. Z. Psychoanal.*, 21.

Eissler, K. R. (1953), The Effect of the Structure of the Ego on Psychoanalytic Technique. *J. Amer. Psychoanal. Assn.*, 1.

——(1955), *The Psychiatrist and the Dying Patient.* New York: International Universities Press.

——(1960), The Efficient Soldier. *The Psychoanalytic Study of Society*, 1. New York: International Universities Press.

Elias, N. (1937), *Über den Prozess der Zivilisation.* Basel: Falken, 1939.

Fenichel, O. (1926), Identification. *Collected Papers*, First Series. New York: Norton, 1953.

——(1945), *The Psychoanalytic Theory of Neurosis.* New York: Norton.

Fliess, R., ed. (1948), *The Pychoanalytic Reader.* New York: International Universities Press.

Flugel, J. C. (1945), *Man, Morals and Society.* New York: International Universities Press, 1947.

——(1953), The Death-Instinct, Homeostasis and Allied Concepts. *Int. J. Psycho-Anal.*, 34 (Suppl).

Freud, A. (1922), The Relation of Beating-Phantasies to a Day-Dream. *Int. J. Psycho-Anal.*, 4, 1923.

——(1936), *The Ego and the Mechanisms of Defence.* New York: International Universities Press, 1946.

——(1945), Indications for Child Analysis. *The Psychoanalytic Study of the Child*, 1.*

——(1949a), Aggression in Relation to Emotional Development: Normal and Pathological. *The Psychoanalytic Study of the Child*, 3/4.

——(1949b), Certain Types and Stages of Social Maladjustment. In *Searchlights on Delinquency*, ed. K. Eissler. New York: International Universities Press.

---

* *The Psychoanalytic Study of the Child*, ed. R. S. Eissler, A. Freud, H. Hartmann, & M. Kris; currently 19 Volumes. New York: International Universities Press, 1945-1964.

———(1951), Observations on Child Development. *The Psychoanalytic Study of the Child*, 6.

———(1958), Adolescence. *The Psychoanalytic Study of the Child*, 13.

——— & Burlingham, D. (1942), *War and Children*. New York: International Universities Press, 1943.

——— ———(1943), *Infants Without Families*. New York: International Universities Press, 1944.

Freud, S. (1894), The Neuro-Psychoses of Defence. *Standard Edition*, 3.†

———(1895), Project for a Scientific Psychology. *The Origins of Psychoanalysis: Letters to Wilhelm Fliess, Drafts and Notes: 1887-1902*. New York: Basic Books, 1954.

———(1896), Further Remarks on the Neuro-Psychoses of Defence. *Standard Edition*, 3.

———(1900), The Interpretation of Dreams. *Standard Edition*, 4 & 5.

———(1905a [1901]), Fragment of an Analysis of a Case of Hysteria. *Standard Edition*, 7.

———(1905b), Jokes and Their Relation to the Unconscious. *Standard Edition*, 8.

———(1905c), Three Essays on the Theory of Sexuality. *Standard Edition*, 7.

———(1911), Formulations on the Two Principles of Mental Functioning. *Standard Edition*, 12.

———(1912), Contributions to a Discussion on Masturbation. *Standard Edition*, 12.

———(1912-13), Totem and Taboo. *Standard Edition*, 13.

———(1914), On Narcissism: An Introduction. *Standard Edition*, 14.

———(1915), Instincts and Their Vicissitudes. *Standard Edition*, 14.

———(1916), Some Character-Types Met with in Psycho-Analytic Work: Criminals from a Sense of Guilt. *Standard Edition*, 14.

———(1917), Mourning and Melancholia. *Standard Edition*, 14.

———(1918 [1914]), From the History of an Infantile Neurosis. *Standard Edition*, 17.

———(1919), A Child Is Being Beaten. *Standard Edition*, 17.

———(1920a), Beyond the Pleasure Principle. *Standard Edition*, 18.

———(1920b), The Psychogenesis of a Case of Homosexuality in a Woman. *Standard Edition*, 18.

———(1921), Group Psychology and the Analysis of the Ego. *Standard Edition*, 18.

---

† *The Standard Edition of the Complete Psychological Works of Sigmund Freud*, 24 Vols., translated and edited by James Strachey. London: Hogarth Press and the Institute of Psycho-Analysis, 1953-   .

———(1923a [1922]), A Seventeenth-Century Demonological Neurosis. *Standard Edition*, 19.

———(1923b), The Ego and the Id. *Standard Edition*, 19.

———(1924a), The Economic Problem of Masochism. *Standard Edition*, 19.

———(1924b), The Dissolution of the Oedipus Complex. *Standard Edition*, 19.

———(1925), Some Psychical Consequences of the Anatomical Distinction between the Sexes. *Standard Edition*, 19.

———(1926), Inhibitions, Symptoms and Anxiety. *Standard Edition*, 20.

———(1927a), Humour. *Standard Edition*, 21.

———(1927b), The Future of an Illusion. *Standard Edition*, 21.

———(1930), Civilization and Its Discontents. *Standard Edition*, 21.

———(1931a), Libidinal Types. *Standard Edition*, 21.

———(1931b), Female Sexuality. *Standard Edition*, 21.

———(1932), New Introductory Lectures on Psycho-Analysis. *Standard Edition*, 22.

———(1937), Analysis Terminable and Interminable. *Collected Papers*, 5. London: Hogarth Press, 1950.

———(1937-1939), *Moses and Monotheism*. New York: Knopf, 1947.

———(1940 [1938]), *An Outline of Psychoanalysis*. New York: Norton, 1949.

Geleerd, E. (1943), The Analysis of a Case of Compulsive Masturbation in a Child. *Psychoanal. Quart.*, 13.

Gitelson, M. (1954), Therapeutic Problems in the Analysis of the "Normal" Candidate. *Int. J. Psycho-Anal.*, 35.

Greenacre, P. (1957), The Childhood of the Artist. *The Psychoanalytic Study of the Child*, 12.

———(1960), Considerations Regarding the Parent-Infant Relationship. *Int. J. Psycho-Anal.*, 41.

Hartmann, H. (1939a), *Ego Psychology and the Problem of Adaptation*. New York: International Universities Press, 1958.

———(1939b), Psychoanalysis and the Concept of Health. *Essays on Ego Psychology*. New York: International Universities Press, 1964.

———(1948), Comments on the Psychoanalytic Theory of Instinctual Drives. *Essays on Ego Psychology*. New York: International Universities Press.

———(1950), Comments on the Psychoanalytic Theory of the Ego. *Essays on Ego Psychology*. New York: International Universities Press, 1964.

———(1952), The Mutual Influences in the Development of Ego and

Id. *Essays in Ego Psychology*. New York: International Universities Press.

———(1955), Notes on the Theory of Sublimation. *The Psychoanalytic Study of the Child*, 10.

———(1960), *Psychoanalysis and Moral Values*. New York: International Universities Press.

——— & Kris, E. (1945), The Genetic Approach in Psychoanalysis. *The Psychoanalytic Study of the Child*, 1.

——— ——— & Loewenstein, R. M. (1946), Comments on the Formation of Psychic Structure. *The Psychoanalytic Study of the Child*, 2.

——— ——— ——— (1949), Notes on the Theory of Aggression. *The Psychoanalytic Study of the Child*, 3/4.

——— & Loewenstein, R. M. (1962), Notes on the Superego. *The Psychoanalytic Study of the Child*, 17.

Heimann, P. (1954), Problems of the Training Analysis. *Int. J. Psycho-Anal.*, 35.

Hoffer, W. (1949), Mouth, Hand and Ego-Integration. *The Psychoanalytic Study of the Child*, 3/4.

———(1950), A Reconsideration of Freud's Concept "Primary Narcissism." Unpublished Ms.

———(1954), Defensive Process and Defensive Organization: Their Place in Psycho-Analytic Technique. *Int. J. Psycho-Anal.*, 35.

Horney, K. (1923), On the Genesis of the Castration Complex in Women. *Int. J. Psycho-Anal.*, 5, 1924.

———(1926), The Flight from Womanhood. *Int. J. Psycho-Anal.*, 7.

———(1932), The Dread of Woman. *Int. J. Psycho-Anal.*, 13.

Jones, E. (1953), *The Life and Work of Sigmund Freud*, Vol. 1. New York: Basic Books.

Kaila, E. (1932), Die Reaktionen das Säuglings auf das menschliche Gesicht. *Annal. Univ. Aboensis*, 17.

Klein, M. (1928), Early Stages of the Oedipus Conflict. In M. Klein (1948).

———(1932), *The Psycho-Analysis of Children*. New York: Norton.

———(1948), *Contributions to Psycho-Analysis, 1921-45*. London: Hogarth Press.

Kris, E. (1951), The Development of Ego Psychology. *Samiksa*, 5.

——— (1952), *Psychoanalytic Explorations in Art*. New York: International Universities Press.

Kubie, L. S. (1948), Instincts and Homeostasis. *Psychosom. Med.*, 10.

———(1954), The Fundamental Nature of the Distinction Between Normality and Neurosis. *Psychoanal. Quart.*, 23.

———— (1958), Some Implications for Psychoanalysis of Modern Concepts of the Organization of the Brain, *Psychoanal. Quart.*, 27.

Lampl-de Groot, J. (1927), The Evolution of the Oedipus Complex in Women. *Int. J. Psycho-Anal.*, 9, 1928.

————(1933), Problems of Femininity. *Psychoanal. Quart.*, 2.

————(1935), Review of Rado, S.: *Die Kastrationsangst des Weibes*. *Int. Z. Psychoanal.*, 21.

————(1936), Hemmung und Narzissmus. *Int. Z. Psychoanal*, 22.

————(1937), Masochismus and Narzissmus. *Int. Z. Psychoanal.*, 23.

————(1939), Considerations of Methodology in Relation to the Psychology of Small Children. *Int. J. Psycho-Anal.*, 20.

————(1946), The Pre-Oedipal Phase in the Development of the Male Child. *The Psychoanalytic Study of the Child*, 2.

————(1947a), On the Development of Ego and Superego. *Int. J. Psycho-Anal.*, 28.

————(1947b), The Origin and Development of Guilt Feelings. Presented at the annual meeting of the Nederlandse Vereniging voor Psychiatrie en Neurologie.

————(1949), Neurotics, Delinquents and Ideal-Formation. In *Searchlights on Delinquency*, ed. K. R. Eissler. New York: International Universities Press.

————(1950a), Some Remarks on the Development of Psychoanalysis During the Last Decades. *Folia Psychiat. Neurol. Neuroch. Neerlandica*, 53(1).

————(1950b), Discussion on Evolution and Present Trends in Psychoanalysis. *Congrès de Psychiatrie*, Paris.

————(1950c), On Masturbation and Its Influence on General Development. *The Psychoanalytic Study of the Child*, 5.

————(1952), Re-evaluation of the Role of the Oedipus Complex. *Int. J. Psycho-Anal.*, 33.

————(1953), Depression and Aggression: A Contribution to the Theory of the Instinctual Drives. In *Drives, Affects, Behavior*, ed. R. M. Loewenstein. New York: International Universities Press.

————(1954a), Problems of Psycho-Analytic Training. *Int. J. Psycho-Anal.*, 35.

————(1954b), Groepsbesprekingen met Stiefmoeders. *Maandbl. Geest. Volksgezondh.*, 9.

————(1956a), The Theory of Instinctual Drives. *Int. J. Psycho-Anal.*, 37.

————(1956b), Psychoanalytische Ich-Psychologie und ihre Bedeutung für die Fehlentwicklung bei Kindern. *Acta Psychother. Psychosom. Orthopaedag.*, 4.

————(1956c), The Role of Identification in Psycho-Analytic Procedure. *Int. J. Psycho-Anal.*, 37.

————(1957), On Defense and Development: Normal and Pathological. *The Psychoanalytic Study of the Child*, 12.

————(1959), Psycho-Analysis and Its Relation to Certain Other Fields of Natural Science. *Int. J. Psycho-Anal.*, 40.

————(1960), On Adolescence. *The Psychoanalytic Study of the Child*, 15.

————(1962), Ego Ideal and Superego. *The Psychoanalytic Study of the Child*, 17.

————(1963), Symptom Formation and Character Formation. *Int. J. Psycho-Anal.*, 44.

Laslett, P. (1950), *The Physical Basis of Mind*. Oxford: Blackwell.

Loewenstein, R. M. (1957), A Contribution to the Psychoanalytic Theory of Masochism. *J. Amer. Psychoanal. Assn.*, 5.

Lorenz, K. (1950), The Comparative Method in Studying Innate Behaviour Patterns. *Symp. Soc. Exp. Biol.*, 4.

Masserman, J. H. (1953), Psycho-Analysis and Biodynamics: An Integration. *Int. J. Psycho-Anal.*, 34 (Suppl.).

Menninger, K. A. (1954), Regulatory Devices of the Ego Under Major Stress. *Int. J. Psycho-Anal.*, 35.

Nunberg, H. (1932), *Principles of Psychoanalysis*. New York: International Universities Press, 1955.

Ostow, M. (1954), A Psychoanalytic Contribution to the Study of Brain Function. *Psychoanal. Quart.*, 23.

Penfield, W. & Rasmussen, T. (1950), *The Cerebral Cortex of Man*. New York: Macmillan.

Piaget, J. (1936), *The Origins of Intelligence in Children*. New York: International Universities Press, 1952.

————(1937), *The Construction of Reality in the Child*. New York: Basic Books, 1954.

Provence, S. & Ritvo, S. (1961), Effects of Deprivation on Institutionalized Infants. *The Psychoanalytic Study of the Child*, 16.

Rado, S. (1926), The Psychic Effects of Intoxication: Attempt at a Psycho-analytic Theory of Drug Addiction. *Int. J. Psycho-Anal.*, 7.

————(1933), Fear of Castration in Women. *Psychoanal. Quart.*, 2.

Rapaport, D., ed. (1951), *Organization and Pathology of Thought*. New York: Columbia University Press.

————(1958), A Historical Survey of Psychoanalytic Ego Psychology. In: *Psychological Issues*, #1. New York: International Universities Press, 1959.

Reich, A. (1951), On Countertransference. *Int. J. Psycho-Anal.*, 32.

Root, N. N. (1957), A Neurosis in Adolescence. *The Psychoanalytic Study of the Child*, 12.

Rümke, H. C. & Carp, E. A. D. E. (1947), article in *Psychiat. Neurol. Bladen, #5.*

Ruyer, R. (1954), *La Cybernétique et l'Origine de l'Information.* Paris: Flammerion.

Sandler, J. (1960), On the Concept of Superego. *The Psychoanalytic Study of the Child*, 15.

———(1962), Psychology and Psycho-Analysis. *Brit. J. Med. Psychol.*, 35.

Simmel, E. (1930), Zum Problem von Zwang und Sucht. *Bericht V. allgem, ärzt. Kongress Psychotherapie*, Baden-Baden.

Spiegel, L. A. (1951), A Review of Contributions to a Psychoanalytic Theory of Adolescence: Individual Aspects. *The Psychoanalytic Study of the Child*, 6.

Spitz, R. A. (1949), Autoerotism. Some Empirical Findings and Hypotheses on Three of Its Manifestations in the First Year of Life. *The Psychoanalytic Study of the Child*, 3/4.

———(1950), Anxiety in Infancy, a Study of its Manifestations in the First Year of Life. *Int. J. Psycho-Anal.*, 31.

Szekely, L. (1954), Biological Remarks on Fears Originating in Early Childhood. *Int. J. Psycho-Anal.*, 35.

Tinbergen, N. (1951), *The Study of Instincts.* Oxford: Clarendon Press.

Van der Waals, H. G. (1943), Aanleg en Ontwikkeling. *Mensch en Maatschappij*, 19(4).

———(1946), [On the Rorschach Test]. *Psychiat. Neurol. Bladen*, 49.

Van Ophuijsen, J. H. W. (1918), Contributions to the Masculinity Complex in Women. *Int. J. Psycho-Anal.*, 5, 1924.

von Bertalanffy, L. (1950), The Theory of Open Systems in Physics and Biology. *Science*, 111.

Waelder, R. (1936), The Problem of the Genesis of Psychical Conflict in Earliest Infancy. *Int. J. Psycho-Anal.*, 18, 1937.

Walter, W. G. (1953), *The Living Brain.* London: Duckworth.

Weiss, E. (1932), Bodily Pain and Mental Pain. *Int. J. Psycho-Anal.*, 15.

Wiener, N. (1949), *Cybernetics.* New York: Wiley.

———(1954), *The Human Use of Human Beings.* New York: Doubleday.

Winnicott, D. W. (1960), The Theory of the Parent-Infant Relationship. *Int. J. Psycho-Anal.*, 41.

Index